THE

HISTORY OF HUNGARY

AND

THE MAGYARS:

FROM THE EARLIEST PERIOD TO THE CLOSE OF THE LATE WAR.

BY

EDWIN LAWRENCE GODKIN.

WITH ILLUSTRATIONS.

NEW YORK:
ALEXANDER MONTGOMERY, 17, SPRUCE STREET.

1853.

LIBRARY
JUL 11 1967
UNIVERSITY OF TORONTO

PREFACE.

Many of the facts detailed in this work will possess no novelty for students of history. The writer does not profess to have derived his materials from any extraordinary sources. With most, if not all, of the books he has consulted, the literary world is, more or less, familiar.

His object has been simply to present, in a popular form, the history of a great people, concerning whom the mass of English readers have no information except what can be gleaned from the stray and scanty allusions contained in the various accounts of the wars and revolutions of the German empire. He has dwelt at considerable length upon the relations existing between Hungary and the House of Hapsburg, because it is mainly upon the peculiar nature of these that her claims to the sympathy of Europe are founded. He has endeavoured throughout to make the narrative as plain and succinct as possible; and for the attainment of this object has, in many places, sacrificed a great number of collateral details. Foreign wars, as the least interesting episodes in a nation's life, when they leave behind no marked results, he has in many instances passed over with a mere mention. His great aim has been to convey a clear idea of the nature and the origin of the late revolution to the minds of those who have hitherto given but little attention to European politics. For information regarding the war of independence he has consulted most of the works which have since appeared on the subject. To that of General Klapka, as the most trustworthy, perhaps, he is under greater obligations than any. The interest which the Magyars excited in 1849 is kept alive by the certainty, which every one who pays any attention to the state of affairs on the continent must feel, that, in the next great European convulsion, they will play, if possible, a still more important part than in the last.

A history of Hungary, which will satisfy all the requirements of criticism, can never be written until her archives are in the hands of the rightful owners, and until the restoration of her liberties shall have enabled foreigners to study her institutions with the attention they merit. To such a character, therefore, this one lays no claim.

London, *September, 15th*, 1853.

CONTENTS.

HISTORY OF HUNGARY.

CHAPTER I.

ROMAN PERIOD.

If the reader will look at a map of the Roman Empire, as it was in the third and fourth centuries of the Christian era, he will find that large tract of country now surrounded by the modern empires of Austria, Turkey, and Russia, set down as Pannonia and Dacia. This formed the north-western frontier, and was the scene of the fiercest struggles recorded in history. As it lay right in the course of all the hordes of various races who poured from the forests of the north and the plains of the east, during the earlier part of the Christian era, hurried on, as if by an irresistible impulse, to precipitate themselves upon the declining empire, it was seized and ravaged now by one and now by another —belonging to all of them by turns, but to none of them long.

The Romans were the first to lift up the veil which shrouded all that region in ancient times. The Greeks, who knew more of everything than they did of geography, had a vague notion that it was peopled by a simple pastoral race whom they called Peones. The face of the country was covered by vast forests, with here and there a swampy meadow, intersected by great rivers rolling on darkly to the ocean, with no sound on their banks but the howl of the wolf or the cry of the heron. The Gauls, it is said, invaded this district about the year 587 B.C., one detachment settling in the part now known as Western Hungary, and the other pushing on into Greece, where, amongst other outrages, they pillaged the temple at Delphi. The Romans themselves for a long time peopled northern and western Europe with ogres, until Cæsar's victories in Gaul helped to dissipate their delusions. The legions under Drusus, Germanicus, and Tiberius, were engaged in the subjugation of Dalmatia, when they were suddenly assailed by wild hordes from the banks of the Danube and the Teyss, whom it required all the strength of the empire to beat back. But Tiberius did not rest satisfied with repulsing them; he followed them to their fastnesses, and, after a tremendous struggle, Pannonia and Dacia became provinces of the empire.

It was part of the wise policy of the Romans never to rest content with subduing; they always endeavoured to assimilate as well. No sooner was resistance at an end, than the work of civilization commenced. Scholars, lawyers, artists, merchants, artizans, nobles, even, settled in the newly-conquered territory, and soon made it reflect back the image of the mother country. In this way, Pannonia and Dacia were soon numbered amongst the most flourishing and civilized of the provinces. The frequent visits of the lieutenants of the emperors, or of the emperors themselves, for the purpose of repelling the incursions of the barbarians who hung about the north-west boundary of their dominions, brought, every year, fresh bands of colonists, who mixed freely with the natives, and soon inspired them with the tastes as well as the wants of civilized life, taught them their language, the rich and sonorous Latin, made them sensible of the advantages of a well-administered system of law.

The face of the country soon became changed. Cultivated fields and smiling meadows took the place of the waving sedge of the marshes and the half-scorched reeds of the steppe. The axe of the Roman backwoodsman soon opened fields and roads in the heart of the thick oak forests, wherein the wolves had howled, and the Druids sacrificed for centuries before; and the ploughman, with his goad and his rudely-yoked oxen, following in the track of the pioneer, soon presented to the astonished gaze of the natives a smiling garden, on the ground where previously stood the thick fastnesses through which their forefathers had hunted the wild boar. The labours of the legionaries soon covered the province with a net-work of great roads, built as if to last for ever, and private enterprise lined them all along with inns, and post-houses, and farms, and gorgeous villas; and on all the sunny slopes, the vine, the present of the Emperor Probus, flourished under the watchful eye of the husbandman. Wherever a military fort had been built, splendid mansions of the rich provincials sprang up around it, furnished with all the luxury that distinguished the voluptuous retreats at Tiburnum or Tusculam. Cities soon rose, which received their priests and magistrates from Rome, and were decorated with magnificent temples, and statues of Greek workmanship instead of the rude images of the Celtic divinities. The Roman polytheism supplanted the Gallic pantheism; and the transition was the easier, as many of the divinities differed only in name. Phoran was another Jupiter, Hesus another Mars, and Baal an Apollo.

But this period of glory and prosperity did not last long. Even when Dacia and Pannonia were conquered Rome was in her decline. While her hands were stretched forth to grasp the uttermost ends of the earth, a cancer—the cancer of corruption and vice—was preying at her vitals. Slowly, and not without many a struggle, did she succumb to the assaults of her enemies. But the crisis, so long averted, came at last; the legions slowly retired, and the barbarians of the north swept like an avalanche across these scenes of luxury, art, and wealth, leaving naught behind but a howling waste, in which children, amidst blackened ruins, sought nourishment from the slaughtered bodies of their mothers.

Of all the great works executed during the period of Roman domination, a few remains only are to be seen at the present day, and these can give but a faint idea of the splendour they have outlived. Below Columbacz the Danube rushes rapidly between high walls of rock, which give an air of grandeur to its course. In this neighbourhood traces of the Roman occupation become more numerous, and at last the most remarkable of any is seen after having passed Rogács. This is known as Trajan's Tablet, and is an elegant piece of sculpture graven in the solid rock, and containing the inscription

IMP. CÆSAR DIVI. NERVAE F. TRAJANUS. AUG. GERM. PONTIFEX MAXIMUS. TRIB. P. O. XXX.

The tablet is supported by two wings, and is surmounted by a Roman eagle. It is supposed that this was intended to commemorate the piercing of the rocks by the legions when making the great road called after the emperor *Via Trajana*. Another of his mighty works is seen in the remains of the bridge which he threw across the Danube, near the modern town of Orsova, in his expedition against the King of Dacia. It was erected over a formidable rapid that no boat could pass without imminent danger. Upon each side of the river there still stand two enormous piles of masonry, about twenty feet in height, which were no doubt used as supports for the two arches at the extremities, spanning the bed of the river; the piles upon which the others rested still remain, until the debris has formed a small island around them. Dion Cassius, who was governor of part of Pannonia in the reign of Adrian, Trajan's successor, has left some few details of the construction of this gigantic work. According to him, every buttress was sixty feet in circumference, and the distance from one to another 170 feet. The passage was defended by two towers of solid marble, one at each end. The erection of the whole was superintended by Apollodorus, the architect of the Forum, and of Trajan's Column at Rome. The bridge was destroyed seventeen years after its erection, by Adrian, in the year 120, upon pretence of securing the frontiers against the incursions of the barbarians, or, as some say, through mere jealousy.

The last relic of this period which we shall notice is one in some respects more interesting than any.

About two leagues from Karansebes, upon a hill in the midst of a charming landscape, stands a small square tower of great antiquity. This is known as *Ovid's Tower*, and popular tradition asserts that in it the poet was confined, when he was banished by Augustus, professedly because of the immorality of his treatise "De Arte Amandi," but in reality for some crime which history has not recorded. Classical scholars and commentators assert that his real place of

OVID'S TOWER.

TRAJAN'S TABLET ON THE DANUBE.

banishment was Tomi, in Thrace; but the popular tradition which transfers it to this romantic spot will, without doubt, in the case of most people, outweigh the soberer testimony of history. An English tourist,* who has given a good deal of attention to the subject, sides with the Transylvanians, and in support of his arguments, asks, and not without plausibility, where could Ovid with more of truth than in this country have exclaimed,

> "Lassus in extremis, jacio, populisque locisque
> Heu quam vicina est ultima terra mihi!"

It scarcely falls within our province to balance the arguments on either side.

RUINS OF THE GOTHIC CHURCH OF ZAMBEK.

It is at least certain that the memory of Trajan and Ovid still lives amongst the Wallacks; and the peasant of the valley of Temes still tells, with an air of authority, that when the Roman army passed that way, the soldiers crowded eagerly to visit the prison in which their great countryman had been confined.

* Paget's "Hungary and Transylvania," London, 1839.

After the Roman power had been overthrown, and the crowd of unknown races rushed across the Danube and laid waste Pannonia, Dacia, and Dalmatia, no people, of all those who from time to time occupied Hungary, left any permanent records of their stay except the Goths. These were converted to Christianity, at a very early period of their occupation, by a bishop named Ulphus, and in the ruins of their religious edifices which still remain, we have ample testimony to the ardour of their faith, and the rapid progress in the arts which they had made through contact with the people whom they had vanquished in arms.

One of the most beautiful of these relics is the ruins of the Gothic church of Zambek. It is supposed to have been built by the Visigoths, who, when dominant in Hungary, sent forth armies to the conquest of Italy, Sicily, Gaul, and Spain. It is a splendid specimen of the first attempt at a style of architecture which has since covered Europe with some of the grandest monuments which have ever been raised in honour of religion.

CHAPTER II.

THE HUNS—ATTILA.—A.D. 337-453.

The vast plains to the north of China, from time immemorial, were peopled, or rather possessed, by a number of hardy nomade tribes, who were known to the Greeks and Romans under the general appellation of Scythians, and who bid defiance to the mightiest conquerors of the ancient world. The skill and discipline of the armies of Cyrus and Alexander were useless against a foe whose valour exhausted itself in a single onset, or in distant discharges of arrows, and whose retreats were so rapid that pursuit was out of the question. Their whole wealth lay in their horses, flocks, and herds. They were bound by no tie to any one spot on the vast expanse of their native steppes more than to another. Removal caused them no regret, for they left behind neither houses nor the fruits of labour. The worst that an invader could do was to drive them prematurely from a luxuriant pasturage, but without reaping any reward for his pains. Wherever he turned he found himself assailed in flank and rear by an active and vigilant enemy, who continually attacked, but never gave battle. Discomfiture and disaster were the unvarying result of all the attempts we read of that were made to subjugate them. But in those early times in no instance were they the offenders. If unmolested, they were content to roam peaceably from one grassy plateau to another; and they were known to the western nations only as a distant and barbarous people, of exceeding fierceness, who skirmished on horseback, and whose subjugation was the topmost point in the ambition of their great military leaders.

But to the old and civilised empire of China they proved troublesome neighbours. When chance brought them to the borders of the celestial dominions, they could not help looking with greedy eyes upon the wealth and magnificence which the skill and industry of the inhabitants had created, and the Great Wall remains to our day a gigantic testimony to the fierceness of their marauding attacks and the terror with which they inspired the Chinese. The latter, with rare condescension, ascribe to these Tartars an origin as remote as their own. Their historians relate that previous to the year 200 B.C., many dynasties had reigned over them, and that they had had chiefs and legislators, renowned for their valour and wisdom, who ruled an extent of territory wider than that of the Roman empire in its palmiest days. The same authority informs us that under the reign of an emperor rejoicing in the euphonic appellation of Pou-nou-Tanjou, a great nation amongst these Tartars or Scythians,—the Huns became greatly enfeebled by a devastating famine, and that their old enemies, taking advantage of their forlorn condition, proceeded to wreak vengeance upon them for all their former outrages. So heavily did the weight of their misfortunes press upon them, that they determined to separate into two tribes or divisions, one of which was subjugated, and remained in bondage on their native soil for a long period. The other, called the northern tribe, set off in search of a new country and better fortune. This was about the year 87 of the Christian era.

After having wandered about Asia for more than two centuries, this tribe had the hardihood once more to attack the Chinese, who, however, inflicted upon them so signal a defeat, that they turned their faces towards Europe, and bid adieu to Asia for ever. This was the commencement of that series of inroads upon the Roman empire which ended in its fall. The southern Huns, some centuries afterwards, followed the example of their brethren, and appeared in Europe under the name of Turks, and established their head-quarters in Constantinople. It is from the former, however, that the modern Hungarians claim descent, and to them, therefore, our attention must be confined.

But if we omitted to mention that a great deal of what we have been here stating rests upon no better foundation than vague tradition, which national, and certainly pardonable, vanity puts forward as history, we should be concealing a part of the truth. Very little of what the Chinese tell us of their own origin is credible, and the temptation to give exaggerated accounts of the power and numbers of the Huns was increased by the fact, that the greater their strength could be made to appear, the greater would be the glory of having defeated and expelled them from their territory. Gibbon is of opinion that the connexion between the modern Hungarians and the ancient Huns, in point of descent, is feeble and remote in the extreme, but he acknowledges the identity in origin of the Turks and Magyars. Recent philological researches have, however, gone far to show that the Fins, the Turks, Magyars, as well as the Mogols, and the less civilised Tartars of central Asia, all belong to the same stock, just as the different nations of modern Germany; but in the vast political changes which they have undergone, have lost their similitude of language. This question of origin, however, is one which, with regard to nations as with regard to great men, it is almost always difficult to settle satisfactorily. It is, therefore, gratifying to know, that in neither case is it of much moment, and in ceasing to trouble its head about it the world shows that it is making some advance in good sense.

When the Huns precipitated themselves upon Europe, they found that the Goths and Vandals had preceded them, had done their share in the work of devastation, and were already enfeebled by luxury and success. They drove them before them triumphantly, and abandoned themselves without restraint to plunder and rapine. But they, too, soon exhausted their strength in intestine quarrels and petty predatory excursions, so that their power seemed on the point of dissolition, when a leader arose in the person of Attila, whose valour, ferocity, and ability restored to their name its ancient terror.

His uncle and predecessor, Rugilas, was a man of great power and ability, and was distinguished by his warlike exploits. In his time, beyond all doubt, the Huns did encamp in the country now called Hungary, and thus placed, as it were, midway between the eastern and the western empires, were enabled to keep both in a continual state of alarm. At the solicitation of the celebrated consul Aetius, on behalf of the usurper John, Rugilas, upon one occasion, marched 60,000 men

ATTILA.

to the very borders of Italy; but nothing short of the total cession of the province of Pannonia was sufficient to induce them to return. He also threatened Constantinople itself, and with such appearance of sincerity, that Theodosius, the Greek emperor, was obliged to ward off his displeasure by the payment of an annual tribute of 300lbs. of gold. So open an acknowledgment of the greatness of their power was not the way, however, to pacify the rude barbarians, whose impatience occasionally broke through all bounds; and war was impending, and only prevented by tedious negotiations, when Rugilas died. (A.D. 434). His nephews, Attila and Bleda, succeeded him, and by them a treaty was concluded, by which the unfortunate Greeks underwent still greater humiliation. Bleda was soon deposed and executed, and Attila became the sole sovereign of the Hunnic nation. This extraordinary man is claimed by the Magyar historians as one of their kings, and this, independently of the wonderful part he played in the history of his time, entitles him to a full share of our attention. The modern Hungarians trace his descent till, in the thirty-fifth degree, it reaches Ham, the son of Noah; but, unfortunately, they are not acquainted with the real name of his father. He himself, with less ambition, was content to deduce it from a noble or royal house amongst the old Huns who had battled with the Chinese along the Great Wall. The only descriptions of him that have come down to us have been traced by the hands of enemies, who had every reason for hating him, and very little scruple about doing him injustice. His portrait, however, presents all the features which characterise a Calmuck Tartar at the present day—a large head, swarthy complexion, deep-seated eyes, a flat nose, a few hairs in place of a beard, and a short square body possessing great muscular strength. But whatever might be the disadvantages of his personal appearance, he had the soul of a hero. In his walk, in his look, almost in every act of his life, he gave evidence of conscious superiority to the rest of mankind. He had a custom of rolling his eyes in a peculiarly fierce fashion, and seemed highly to enjoy the terror which his very looks inspired. He was fond of war, and was undoubtedly in possession of great personal courage; but it was not his mere valour which gained him sway over his countrymen, so much as his skill in working upon their passions and credulity. The latter is a prominent characteristic in all barbarous nations. The more wonderful an affair is, and the less support it receives in the shape of evidence derived from experience, the greater is their disposition to believe it. Craft, therefore, is the quality which amongst them is the surest guarantee of power and influence. In Attila this was united with great military talent, an iron will, and a commanding presence. By making a good use of the national superstition, he gained an ascendancy over his countrymen which no amount of warlike success could ever have bestowed upon him. The Huns, like all other nations of antiquity, worshipped the god of war with more than ordinary devotion; but too rude to mould a statue, they adored him under the form of an iron scimitar. One of their shepherds having perceived a wound in the foot of a heifer, followed the track of the blood, till it led to an old sword sticking up out of the ground. He dug it up and presented it to Attila, who received it with a devout air, declared that it was the sword of Mars, and that he, as its possessor, had a divine right to the dominion of the earth. He henceforth assumed, in the eyes of his subjects, the character of a deity, in whose service it was as honourable to fight as it was glorious and fortunate to die.

He may be said from this time to have divided the empire of the world with the Romans. They possessed the civilised portion of it—he the barbarian. Not only did he hold undisputed sway over the Scythian tribes, but over the German also.

The Franks and Burgundians trembled at his nod; he received a tribute of furs from the cold regions of northern Europe, which more civilised potentates had assailed in vain; his power was felt on the banks of the Volga; the Geugens thought him a magician, who, by means of the enchanted stone *gezi*, could excite storms of wind and rain. He made an alliance upon equal terms with the Emperor of China, and the great and powerful tribe of the Ostrogoths were amongst the most submissive of his supporters. All the kings and chiefs—and their name was legion—who acknowledged his supremacy, took it in turn to attend on his person as guards and domestics; and when he took the field, he could muster an army of five, or as some say seven, hundred thousand men.

When Attila ascended the throne, he was by no means disposed to continue the negotiations which his uncle had been carrying on with the Greek emperor Theodosius, and only wanted a pretext for commencing hostilities. This was a thing which no barbarian ever wanted long, and particularly a Hun in the fifth century. A free market was at that time held on the northern, or Hunnic, side of the Danube, under the protection of a Roman fort called Constantia. The Huns one day made a foray into the market-place, killed the traders, and levelled the fortress with the ground, and justified the outrage by asserting that it was committed by way of reprisal for the trespass of the Bishop of Margus, who entered their territory with the design of discovering and concealing a secret treasure belonging to their king, and they demanded the extradition of the prelate, and of those who aided and abetted him. But the Byzantine court had not yet reached so low a pitch of degradation as to surrender a Christian into the hands of pagans, and refused to comply. The people of Margus were amongst the first to applaud the emperor's firmness. When the Huns, however, crossed the frontier with fire and sword, and destroyed two towns in their immediate vicinity, the citizens changed their minds, and began to think of surrendering the bishop themselves. But that worthy individual, however, was not of opinion that a bishop should be sacrificed to save a town, but, on the contrary, that a town ought to be, by all means, sacrificed to save a bishop. He, therefore, sent a secret message to Attila, secured his pardon by a solemn oath of allegiance, and testified the sincerity of his submission by opening with his own hand, at an appointed hour, the gates of the city to a chosen band of the barbarian army.

The career of the invader was after this but a series of successes. Town after town fell before him, and the whole extent of Europe, from the Euxine to the Adriatic, was laid waste and desolate. The Roman armies, hastily collected from various quarters of the empire, wanted both the courage and the skill to make an effectual resistance. They were defeated in three successive battles, and the ravages of Attila were extended to the very walls of Constantinople itself. Seventy cities of the eastern empire, rich in all that the art, industry, and commerce of the time could achieve or collect, and crowded by a busy, civilised, and luxurious population, were totally destroyed and up-rooted, so that nothing save charred and blackened ruins marked their sites. From this one fact alone some idea may be formed of the ferocity of the invader, and the terrible calamities the unfortunate inhabitants had to undergo. Gibbon * endeavours, in the absence of all positive testimony upon the subject, to form some idea of the treatment of the vanquished by the Huns, by supposing an analogy between their practice and that of the Moguls, men of the same race and same manners. The mode of procedure followed by the latter upon the capture of a town has been accurately recorded. The inhabitants, if they had surrendered at discretion, were assembled in some open space near the city, and divided into three classes. The first, consisting of the young men able to bear arms, were either enlisted in the ranks of their conquerors, or slaughtered on the spot. The second, consisting of young and beautiful women, artificers, professional men, or merchants, from whom a ransom might be expected, were distributed in equal shares. The remainder, consisting of the old, and decrepid, and poor, were dismissed, with contemptuous pity, and obliged to pay a tax for being permitted to live amidst the ruins of their homes.

But all this took place only when the conquerors had been received with abject submission. The smallest amount of resistance, a smile, a look, which could be construed into a token of defiance, were sufficient to cause the massacre of the population of a whole province. Acts like these caused a hermit in some cave in Gaul to apply to Attila the epithet of *The Scourge of God*, and the tradition runs, that on its reaching his ears it so pleased the haughty conqueror, that he adopted and inserted it amongst the titles of royal dignity; and so great was the terror that his very name inspired, that in the far-off provinces of the empire, it was commonly believed by the people that the grass never grew on the spot where his horse had once trod.

In this war great numbers of the Romans were carried off captive to the Huns, and employed as domestic slaves. Those who could exercise some useful handicraft, such as masons, smiths, armourers, were highly valued and well treated. The clergy were respected; lawyers were despised or abhorred; physicians, naturally enough, held the highest rank in their estimation; but the lowest of all in the scale were the Greek sophists or philosophers. All these, however, notwithstanding their servile condition, must have been the means of diffusing amongst their masters a taste for the arts, and love for the luxuries of civilised life.

The conditions of peace which Attila imposed upon the Greek emperor were humiliating enough. Theodosius was compelled to surrender a fertile tract of country lying along the southern bank of the Danube, fifteen days' journey in breadth, or according to others only five; † to promise an annual subsidy of

* Vol. III. p. 233. Milman's Edition.

† Niebuhr's Byz. Hist., p. 147.

2,100lbs. of gold, and to pay without delay 6,000lbs. of gold to defray the expenses of the war. The treasury was exhausted at this period by the cost of military preparation and the shameless extravagance of the court, so that the latter demand had to be met by a personal contribution imposed upon the members of the senatorial order, and rigorously exacted. Attila was so impatient, or the nobles were so poor, that they had to raise the amount by the public sale of their wives' jewels and the heir-looms of their palaces. Among the latter, according to Chrysostom, every wealthy house possessed a semicircular table of massive silver, such as two men could scarcely lift; a vase of solid gold weighing forty pounds, and cups and dishes of the same metal.

FLASK, CUP, AND CAMEO BEARING A MINIATURE OF ATTILA.

The third and last condition was more humiliating than all; it stipulated that all Huns, who had been taken prisoners in war, should be restored without ransom; that all Roman prisoners, who had effected their escape, should pay twelve ounces of gold each, and that all barbarian deserters from the standard of the conqueror should be delivered up without promise or condition. The performance of this part of the agreement occupied a considerable length of time. It was an easy matter to restore the captured Huns, but it was by no means easy to oblige the Romans, who had made their escape from captivity, to pay a ransom, or to oblige the deserters, who had fought under the imperial standard, to return to a certain and cruel death.

Almost every week embassies arrived from Attila to reproach the Roman emperor in haughty terms with the delay in carrying out the treaty, and to declare that he could with difficulty restrain the impatience of his followers. Theodosius did the best he could to appease the anger of the barbarian, by making rich presents to the envoys; and the private secretary of the king of the Huns having demanded a wealthy and noble Roman wife, his master supported his request with such zeal as to make it an affair of state. After a good deal of hesitation, a rich widow, a woman of great beauty, and renowned amongst the aristocratic matrons of the day for her virtues, was selected as the victim, for so her friends considered her. When this had been resolved upon, Attila demanded that the Romans should send an embassy to him in return for the many that he had sent to them. His request was complied with it, and it is to this that we owe most of our knowledge of the manners and customs of the Huns, and of the usages in force at the court of their king. The chief of the embassy was a certain Maximin, a courtier of considerable talents, both civil and military, and he invited his friend, Priscus, the historian, to accompany him. The latter has recorded every circumstance of their journey and reception, as Lord Macartney his progress to the court of the celestial empire; and his relation gives us a curious insight into the manners of the time, as well as places in ominous contrast, along every step of the way, the haughty insolence of the Huns and the fallen pride of the Romans, courtly and magnificent even in their degradation.

They made their first halt at Sardica, where the Romans gave a banquet to the barbarian envoys, who were returning with them from Constantinople; and Priscus, with quaint minuteness, tells us what one said to another at the table, of the quarrel which arose between the representatives of the two nations, and of the presents that were made to heal the breach. Proceeding thence upon their way, the Romans soon saw enough to make them tremble for the fall of the empire and the imperial city, and convince them that the existence both of one and the other depended on the nod of Attila. They found Naissus—which had been a mighty city in its time, and had given birth to the great Constantine, whose name, in his day, had made barbarians tremble—a heap of blackened ruins, amongst which a few sick and cripples, whom the conquerors thought beneath their vengeance, found a precarious shelter; and all along, for many a mile beyond, the bones of the slain lay thick on the ground, like the track of a plague-stricken caravan in the Arabian deserts. Upon entering Hungary, they passed rapidly through the forests and over the rivers in small canoes, until they arrived in the neighbourhood of the royal camp. Attila haughtily forbad them to pitch their tents upon an eminence, because his were below upon the plain; and sent messengers to them, to whose keeping they were requested to commit their business and instructions. Upon their making the well-founded objection, that this would not only be disrespectful to their own sovereign but in direct contravention of the established law of nations, they received no decisive answer, but were compelled to undertake a long and toilsome journey to the north, so that Attila might have the satisfaction of receiving, at one and the same time in his camp, envoys from both the eastern and western empires. During this long circuit they were supplied plentifully with provisions from the neighbouring villages; mead indeed instead of wine, millet in place of bread, and a certain liquor, called *camus*, distilled from barley—rough fare certainly when compared with the dainties of Constantinople, but under the circumstances very acceptable. Upon one occasion they were overtaken, when encamped upon the edge of a morass, by a violent storm, which overturned their tents, drenched themselves and their baggage, and sent them wandering in the darkness along unknown roads. They at last reached a village, the property of the widow of Bleda, Attila's murdered brother. The good lady roused her people, prepared a blazing fire of reeds, before which the travellers dried their garments; and she appears to have embarassed them by her singular politeness, in placing at their disposal a number of beautiful and obliging maidens. In return for all these kindnesses, they presented her with silver cups, red fleeces, dried fruits, and Indian pepper. After this they fell in with Attila's march, and at last reached his capital.

About its precise situation there has been an immense deal of disputation. Gibbon only guesses at it; the description of Priscus is too vague to enable us to come to any positive conclusion; so that we are at last compelled to fall back upon the popular tradition, which, in the matter of places, is seldom far from the truth. According to this, it was on the spot where the modern village of Jasbereny now stands, in the midst of the district inhabited by the Jasyges, between the Danube, the Teyss, and the Carpathian Hills, in the plains of Upper Hungary. These Jasyges, though now mingled with the Magyar population, had inhabited the country from a very early period; and it is even said, that when the Emperor Trajan marched against the Dacians, they followed his standard as auxiliaries. They were distinguished by the rapidity of their evolutions, by their courage, and by their armour. Both horse and man were clothed in mail of very stout texture, which rendered them almost invulnerable. They were extremely dexterous in the use of the bow and arrows, and were able to launch javelins both in front and towards the rear at the same moment. Their descendants may still be distinguished by the pure orientalism of their accent and intonation, and by their daring feats of horsemanship, which caused them, during the last war, to be numbered amongst the ablest defenders of the national liberty.

In the midst of these, according to the most probable accounts, Attila fixed his camp. It was at best but a huge village, composed of rows of tents, which the king's long residence here had rendered permanent; it afforded ample accommodation, however, for the host of servants, retainers, and tributaries, who followed the march of the barbarian conqueror. The habitations of the common soldiers were merely huts of mud and straw, but those of higher rank dwelt in wooden houses, in which there was some attempt at a display of rude magnificence, and the nearer the palace of the king the more honourable the position. The palace itself was built entirely of wood, and covered an immense space of ground; it was surrounded by a lofty wall, also of wood, flanked by high towers. Inside this enclosure lay the houses of all who were attached to the royal person. Each of the king's wives had separate apartments. The mansion of Cerca, the queen, was supported on lofty round columns, and the wood was curiously carved and turned. When the ambassadors paid her a visit, not only were they graciously received, but, such was the charming simplicity of her manners, were all permitted to kiss her. When they first saw her, she was reclining on a carpet, and her maids around her engaged in some sort of embroidery, just as we may suppose any of the ladies in the days of chivalry, or even in later times, passed the long hours in their husbands' gloomy castles. The interior of the houses of the nobles was profusely decorated with gold and silver plate and ornaments; their swords, and shoes, and bucklers, were set with jewels; and they dined off plates and vases of the precious metals which the Greek captives had made. But in the palaces of the monarch the severe simplicity of the ancient Scythians still reigned. He and his household eat off wooden platters; flesh was their only food, for bread was a luxury that the great chief never tasted. Other curious details of Attila's domestic life have been handed down to us, and they all display the same mixture of severe simplicity and barbaric pomp.

Amongst those who accompanied the Romans from Constantinople was an ambassador of the Huns named Edecon, who, during his stay at the imperial court, had been induced by a large reward to enter into an engagement to murder his master upon reaching home. This had been effected through the instrumentality of a eunuch named Chrystaphius, and with the full cognizance and approbation of Theodosius. At the eleventh hour Edecon repented, and revealed the plot to Attila. The latter, with a high-minded heroism which in a Pagan contrasted favourably with the baseness of the Christian emperor, sent a message full of stern rebuke to Constantinople, and contemptuously pardoned the delinquents. Theodosius did not long survive this humiliation: his horse fell when out hunting, and, by breaking his rider's neck, ridded the world of a base and effeminate tyrant.

His sister Pulcheria succeeded to the imperial throne, and soon after married a senator of high standing named Marcia. This man had ideas of Roman dignity which would have been better suited to the days of Julius Cæsar than his own, and upon Attila pressing for the payment of the tribute, he returned a haughty and disdainful answer. The barbarian king instantly prepared to invade the empire. But he affected to despise the eastern empire, and determined to postpone the conquest of it until he had overthrown the western. This was not, however, so easy a matter as he imagined. The leader of the Roman armies at this time, a lieutenant of the emperor Valentinian, was Aetius, "the thrice-appointed consul," to whom "the wretched Britons" vainly sent "their groans and tears," when fiercely attacked by the wild hordes of the northern highlands—

a man of great military talents, who for twenty years was the stay and support of the declining majesty of Rome. Through his tact and dexterity, an alliance was entered into with the powerful nation of the Visigoths, the ancestors of the modern Spaniards, who at that time possessed the southern part of the province of Gaul, and he was thus enabled to present a formidable front to the invader. But Attila was not easily daunted, and with such a host as he could muster he should have been a mighty warrior who could have stayed his progress.

But even in that rude age the still small voice of right and justice was heard, though in faint accents, above the din of arms, and the loud clamour of the camp; and it reached even the ears of Attila, fierce fighting-man though he was, who had marched to power and fame across hundreds of thousands of corpses. He had the men, the horses, the armour, the courage, the skill, and prestige, necessary to assure him of success in his enterprise. There was but one thing wanting,—a reasonable excuse that would satisfy his own conscience, and do homage to the public opinion of the world. The emperor of the east had refused to pay him the tribute his predecessor had agreed upon, and had accompanied his refusal with insult. But from Valentinian he had received no wrong. The pretext came at last in a way that he little expected, by an affair which might well be considered a piece of incredible romance, if it were not verified by the unanimous testimony of contemporary historians. Valentinian, the Roman emperor of the west, had a sister named Honoria, to whose beauty not written descriptions merely, but medals still extant, testify. Her brother feared that if married, her husband might prove a dangerous rival, and in order to elevate her above the hopes of any of his subjects, he bestowed upon her the title of *Augusta*. Honoria felt but little pride in her new greatness, and never ceased to deplore the unhappy fate which had placed a bar between her and the gratification of the fondest wish of a woman's heart. At the age of sixteen, in a moment of weakness or folly, she so far forgot herself as to favour the advances of her chamberlain Eugenius. Her shame soon became apparent, and was made more widely known by her banishment from the imperial court, after a long term of imprisonment. The unhappy princess fixed her residence at Constantinople, and passed her time in retirement, brooding over her sorrows and misfortunes. While here, she daily heard the name of Attila on every lip. His ambassadors passed frequently in barbaric pomp before her window, and many were the wild stories that were told of their master's power, and valour, and ferocity. Whether it was that she wished to revenge her disgrace upon her relatives at Ravenna, or that her imagination, nursed and strengthened by suffering and solitude, was dazzled by the splendour of success—always so powerful in its influence on weak minds—and pictured the barbarian conqueror as the ideal of her dreams, the soul of poetry and love, will never be known; but, at all events, she cast aside not only the prejudices by which Roman women had been bound for more than a thousand years, and which in their eyes rendered the daughter of the humblest citizen too good for a foreign king, but all the restraints which nature, as well as custom, has in every age imposed upon her sex, and wrote to Attila, offering him her hand, and sending him a ring as the gage of her love. Her proposal was at first received with cold and silent contempt; but when he came to perceive the vantage ground upon which it would place him in a quarrel with Valentinian, it was eagerly accepted, and her hand formally demanded of her brother. In all his weakness and danger, the emperor still retained some spark of the family pride of the old Roman patrician, and the demand was peremptorily refused, and Honoria shut up in a prison, from which she never issued in life.

Attila instantly invaded Gaul at the head of a numerous host. All the nations of Germany and Scythia, from the Danube to the Volga, thronged to his standard; and when he poured his myriads across the frontier, city after city fell before him, notwithstanding the performance of divers miracles by the patron saints of the various localities, which our space will not permit us to record—an omission the less to be regretted, however, as they do not seem to have had the smallest influence upon the general results of the invasion.

At last the Huns laid siege to Orleans, but all their attacks were baffled by the courage of the inhabitants, until the arrival of the combined army of the Visigoths and Romans compelled them to raise the siege. Attila then retreated into the great plain around Châlons, then known as the "Catalonian Fields," and there offered battle (A.D. 451). For the first time in his life he seems to have been doubtful of the issue, and sought to animate the courage of his followers by a martial address, when on all other occasions his presence alone had been considered sufficient to ensure a triumph.

The conflict which followed was one of the bloodiest on record. The magnitude of the interests at stake, the skill and fame of the opposing leaders, the difference of race, language, and religion, the hopelessness of safety or escape in case of defeat—all combined to add fresh fuel to the ardour and animosity of the combatants. There was but little attempt at manœuvring. The total want of discipline, the wide dissimilarity in the arms, mode of fighting, manners, and language of the barbarians, precluded the possibility of any display of tactics on the part of the leaders, so that the result was left entirely to the isolated efforts of individual valour. The battle began by a discharge of arrows and javelins, in which the superior dexterity of the Huns gave them the advantage, but these weapons were soon cast aside, and the cavalry and infantry, on both sides, closed in a frightful *melée*. Theodoric, the king of the Visigoths, was knocked off his horse by the stroke of a spear, and was trampled to death under the feet of the combatants; and Attila, who exposed his person in the thick of the carnage, was exulting in the confidence of victory, when the rashness of the Huns gave an unexpected turn to the fortune of the day. They had broken through the Roman centre, but rushing forward with too great impetuosity, they were surrounded, attacked in the flank, and the darkness alone saved them from total destruction. They passed the night behind entrenchments formed of their waggons, in disheartened mood enough, and Attila himself, with a ferocious desperation worthy of his past career and exploits, ordered the rich furniture of the cavalry to be collected into a funeral pile, ready to be fired, and on which, in case the enemy forced his position, he was prepared to end his life, rather than fall into their hands.

But the Romans and Visigoths had purchased their victory too dearly to think of following it up by any such attempt. Between 160,000 and 200,000 men lay dead upon the field, nearly one-half of whom had belonged to the allied forces, and in those that remained were placed the hopes of the Western Empire. Aetius and Torismond, the son and successor of Theodoric, assembled their scattered forces and retreated, leaving Attila at liberty to pursue his march. The latter, after remaining for several days in his entrenchments, through fear of some trap or ambuscade, at last sallied forth and directed his course once more to Hungary, the Franks all the way hanging on his rear. His course was marked by the horrid cruelties perpetrated upon the inhabitants of the adjacent districts by the Thuringians, one of the tributary nations who served under his standard. They massacred hostages as well as captives; and one is led to excuse the ferocity of the North-American Indians in the early border wars, when we read, that on one occasion during this retreat two hundred young maidens were first tortured with exquisitely ingenious cruelty, were then torn asunder by wild horses, or crushed piecemeal beneath the wheels of baggage-waggons, and their remains abandoned to the dogs and the wolves.

In the following spring (A.D. 452) Attila collected his forces afresh, and set out with the intention of invading Italy, and on reaching Aquileia laid siege to it as well as he was able. A siege in that age was a slow process, and the barbarians had neither the skill nor the patience which Roman armies would have brought to the work. But the town was at last carried by storm, after a breach had been effected by the aid of battering-rams, and though Aquileia was one of the most populous and wealthiest cities of the western world, after this the site was scarce marked even by ruins. All modern Lombardy fell before the resistless arms of the conqueror. Vicenza, Verona, Milan, and Pavia were, sooner or later, obliged to open their gates and admit him, and the treatment received by the inhabitants was good or bad in exact proportion to the amount of resistance they had offered. In Milan, Attila saw in the royal palace a picture which represented the Roman emperor seated in awful state upon a throne, and some Scythian princes prostrated in submission at his feet. He called for an artist, and with a ferocious smile ordered him to reverse the figures and attitudes—place the Scythians on the throne, and the Cæsars as suppliants.

The King of the Huns was in the habit of boasting, that the grass never grew where his horse had once trod; but it must for ever remain a striking monument of the vanity of earthly wisdom, and the weakness of human valour, that the ferocious conqueror of the western empire should have laid the foundation of one of the mightiest states of modern Europe; and that the fierce bands, who gave form and consistency to feudalism, should also have provided a nursing mother for commerce and art.

The province of Venetia, or Henetia, included, in ancient times, a large fertile tract of Italy, and was the seat of many flourishing and populous towns. Two of them, Aquileia and Padua, were the chosen residence of opulent knights and senators, and were renowned for the vast extent of their agricultural and manufacturing industry. But when the barbarians for the first time entered Italy, and effaced whatever traces yet remained of the prestige of ancient power, this fertile garden was turned into a howling wilderness. Those of the population who, bereft of property and liberty, were still left in the enjoyment of a precarious and degraded existence, looked around for some refuge in which they might dwell, it might be in hardship, or perhaps in want, but at least in security. Within half an hour's sail of their coast, a hundred muddy islands rose feebly from the sluggish waters of the Adriatic. These sand-banks—for they were little else—were the deposits carried down, during the course of many centuries, by the thirty rivers which discharge their waters into this part of the gulf. The narrow channels which separated them could only be navigated by skilful and experienced pilots, and were a sure defence against the approach of a foreign invader. To these the terrified Venetians fled in crowds from the mainland; and here, for many a year, noble families, who had been accustomed to revel in luxury, were content to earn a scanty subsistence by fishing, and the extraction of salt from the waters of the sea. Cassiodorus compares them to water-fowl which had fixed their nests on the bosom of the waves, and expresses his earnest sympathy with their poverty and misfortune. Nothing tends so much to the growth and formation of energy and determination of character as a struggle against adverse circumstances and unpropitious fortune. Devotion and heroism, which slumber in the lap of prosperity, spring into life and action when prosperity has deserted us and fled. The first efforts of the Venetians were directed towards the supply of the necessaries of a coarse and hard existence; but when the continued exercise of self-reliance had proved more than sufficient to satisfy these demands, the desire for wealth and its concomitant power rapidly succeeded. The far-famed Rialto—a sort of port to Padua—was already in existence, and other buildings began to spring up. Ships were built, an commerce and navigation extended. The foundation of some of the principal buildings was laid on the 25th of March, early in the fifth century; "the day," says the old historian, "on which Christ was conceived in the womb of the Virgin, and Adam, the parent of mankind, was formed by God." The neighbouring sands were soon peopled by other fugitives, and, with a feeling of devout thankfulness for the refuge they had found, the townsmen of Altino gave to their adopted asylum the name of the "Port of the Deserted City."

The barbarian conqueror was now encamped amidst the scenes which the

BATTLE OF CHALONS.

genius and glory of the Augustan age had consecrated; and groves and valleys, in which poets had mused and senators sauntered in luxurious indolence, rang with the loud laughter and coarse revelry of the northern soldiers; and Attila at last declared his intention of marching upon the imperial city itself. The emperor and the nobles sent him a deputation, headed by the wealthiest and proudest of the senators, humbly imploring him to spare the last relics of imperial greatness. Their request was granted upon condition that they paid him over Honoria's dowry as a ransom. This was done, and the army of the Huns once more turned homewards, as much surprised as the Romans at their master's moderation. But tradition says that it was not due altogether to a feeling of pity for the misfortunes of the vanquished, but to a superstitious fear of the consequences of laying sacrilegious hands upon the majesty of the eternal city. The old men of the camp whispered to him mysteriously that Alaric had not long survived his assault upon Rome; and his imagination was still further impressed by the venerable aspect of Leo, the aged Christian bishop, who was one of the ambassadors sent to solicit his clemency. We suppose it was with the view of rendering the whole story more effective that the monks have related, that the blessed Apostles Peter and Paul appeared to Attila in the dead of the night, and threatened him with death if he did not desist from his enterprise. Whatever merit the legend may possess, it has been immortalised by Raphael, whose picture of the apparition still hangs in the Vatican.

The conqueror, at all events (A.D. 453), turned his face once more towards home, threatening, however, to return in the following year, more wrathful than ever if Honoria were not in the meantime delivered up to him. To solace himself in the interval, he added to the number of his wives a beautiful girl named Ildico, and the wedding was celebrated with great pomp in one of his wooden palaces, close to the Danube. He and his bride retired to bed early, and at a late hour in the morning they had not re-appeared. The attendants at last became alarmed, and entered the chamber. Ildico was weeping by the bedside, and on it Attila, the terror of the world, lay dead. A blood-vessel had burst in the night, and he was suffocated by internal hemorrhage. It was reported by the Romans that his wife had slain him; but, we believe, without any good foundation. His funeral rites were celebrated with great pomp. His body, covered by a silken pavilion, was placed in the midst of a plain, and the Huns rode round it in squadrons, singing his glory and exploits in measured strains, and lamenting him as a hero "glorious in his life, invincible in his death, the father of his people, the scourge of his enemies, and the terror of a world." To show their grief, they cut short their flowing hair, and, as so great a chieftain should be mourned, not with women's tears, but the blood of warriors, they gashed their faces with frightful wounds. The body was then enclosed in three coffins—the first of gold, the second of silver, and the third of iron; and thus he was buried, silently and in the dead of night; and, that the prisoners who dug his grave might never insult the hero's memory by engaging in any less sacred employment, they were all slaughtered on the spot.

He was no sooner dead than the Hunnic empire went to pieces. It was built up by conquest, and it existed only as long as the conqueror was living to give it support and glory. The nations who had been bound together by admiration of his military genius or the terror of his arms, were once more left free to follow the dictates of their avarice or love of adventure. The Huns themselves dispersed or fell back upon Asia; and from this time their primitive name no longer appears in history. Other tribes of the same family succeeded them upon the political arena, and the history of Pannonia for a long period presents only the spectacle of incessant struggles. Before the entrance of the Huns into Europe, the country which is denominated Hungary at the present day, and which was the centre of their empire, had been peopled from remote ages by the Pannonians and Illyrians, races of Greek origin, with some mixture of Celtic blood. In the northern part, on the borders of the Danube, dwelt the Quadi and Marcomanni, two tribes often mentioned by Cæsar in his Commentaries, who were Germanic in their origin. To the east, in modern Transylvania, Moldavia, and Wallachia, the great nation of the Dacians, belonging to the Thraco-Greek family, had established itself. Last of all, in a corner at the foot of the Carpathian Mountains, between the Quadi and the Dacians, were the Jazyges, a people belonging to the Sclavonic stock. The Huns found all these people in subjection to the Romans, or Goths. Their invasion had set in motion many other tribes of the same race as themselves, who were then encamped near the shores of the Black Sea, in the way of the Asiatic races in their march towards Europe. The Avars, a branch of the Huns of the south, arrived upon the confines of Europe about the year 558. They resembled the Magyars of the present day, in their physiognomy and general appearance. The lightness of their complexion, and the regularity of their features, attracted the attention of the Greeks and Romans. They wore their hair in flowing tresses, tied with gaily-coloured ribbons, a custom which still prevails among the Magyar peasantry, but in other respects they were dressed as the Huns.

This people precipitated themselves upon the Roman empire with the same violence as their predecessors, and established themselves in Pannonia. Their sway extended in 582, under their Khan Bayan, from Thuringia to Italy. In 646, having lost Dalmatia, and some other provinces in succession, they retained possession of Pannonia alone, and the countries bordering on the east. Charlemagne, who had extended his empire as far as the Ebro in Spain, resolved to drive them beyond the eastern frontiers of Europe. It took four campaigns, however, when he was in the zenith of his power, to accomplish this. Having obtained possession of Upper Pannonia, he formed it into a margravate. One division of the Avars then returned to Asia, and the remainder became blended with the rest of the population, so that their famous name entirely disappeared from history. Their ruin was achieved by the same people who had overthrown the Hunnic empire. The Franks and Germans put an end to their domination after it had lasted for three centuries.

Then came the Croats, from the foot of the Carpathian Mountains, to occupy the countries now known as Croatia and Dalmatia. Swatopluk founded in the north-west the kingdom of Great Moravia; and the Bulgarians, who were another branch of the Hunnic race, established themselves in the countries lying to the east. It was about this time, also, that some other tribes of the Sclavonic family commenced to settle in some parts of those districts, now known as Hungary and Transylvania.

CHAPTER III.

A.D. 884—954.

THE MAGYARS—ORIGIN—MANNERS—FIRST APPEARANCE IN EUROPE—THEIR RAVAGES IN GERMANY AND ITALY—FINAL OVERTHROW BY OTHO THE GREAT.

The Magyar historians, anxious as they are to trace the descent of their countrymen from so renowned a race as the soldiers of Attila, are still compelled to acknowledge that the connexion between them is so faint as to admit of no better proof or support than conjecture. That there was an affinity of origin and a striking resemblance of manners and customs between the Huns and the immediate ancestors of the modern Hungarians is a fact that hardly admits of dispute, but all evidence of any nearer relation was lost in the whirlwind of war, change and devastation, which for three centuries after the death of Attila swept the plains of Pannonia.

The Hungarians first made their appearance in Europe about the year 884 of the Christrian era. Their national and oriental appellation was *Magyar*, but they were known to the Greeks as a tribe of Scythians, called Turks, from the same region as that from which the Huns had issued. They were undoubtedly the brothers of the fierce Mahometan hordes who afterwards overthrew the imperial city; and it is said that they for a long time kept up a correspondence with their countrymen on the confines of Persia, and that when some of their missionaries, after their conversion to Christianity, visited the ancient seats of their ancestors, they were welcomed as kinsmen by the rude tribes which still lingered there, spoke the old language and bore the name of Hungarians.

The Magyars were first looked upon by the inhabitants of the western world as the Gog and Magog of the Scriptures,* and their appearance as a warning that the end of all things was at hand. The clergy took the matter into their most serious consideration, but, unfortunately, could not come to any decision that would either allay or confirm the fears of their flocks, until their response, whatever it might have been, would have assumed the form of a prophecy after the event. And in truth there was good reason for alarm, and excuse enough for those freaks of imagination in which superstition and fanaticism are ever prone

* Milman's Gibbon, vol. v. p. 294.

to indulge. The new comers fell by no means below the standard of the Huns in ugliness or ferocity. Men usually disfigure what they fear and hate, but after making all due allowance for the exaggerations of terror, we may presume there was enough in the manners and appearance of the invaders and in the wide-spread devastation which they committed, to enable the inhabitants of western Europe, whose condition already presented some resemblance to the peace and luxury of the empire, to connect them without difficulty with the bloodshed and ruin which the prediction had taught them should precede the second coming of the Lord.

The Magyars were a people of Fennic origin, as is clearly proved by the affinity between the idioms of their language and those of the language of the Fennic race, a barbarous people who once occupied the northern parts of Europe and Asia. The name *Ugri* or *Igours* is still found in the countries bordering on the west of China, and a similar one has been discovered in the southern quarters of Siberia. The remains of these Finnish tribes are now scattered thinly through northern Russia and Lapland. But how great the difference between Laplanders and Hungarians of the present day!—the one a hardy, athletic, warlike, and intellectual race, jealous of their independence and fond of oriental pomp, not in language only, but costume and style of living, the very types of life in its highest material development; the other grovelling savages, wresting a scanty subsistence from an inhospitable climate and a barren soil, small in stature, animal in their appetites, and possessing few marks of intelligence which can be classed much higher than instinct. In comparing the two peoples, we are presented with an impressive lesson of the folly of associating peculiar traits of character with particular races, without reference to the circumstances by which they have been surrounded through a long course of years. Oppression would make slaves and liars of Spartans just as a polar climate has made Laplanders of Magyars.

The tents of the Hungarians were of leather, and their garments of fur. They shaved their hair and scarified their faces. They were slow in speech and prompt in action. They possessed most of the vices as well as most of the virtues of barbarous nomade tribes. Pardonable national vanity has induced some Magyar historians to describe the social life of their forefathers as one of charming simplicity, in which the crimes, follies, and meannesses of civilisation were unknown. In this they are not alone. Shepherd hordes, from whatever cause, have in all ages been objects of admiration to those whom a more advanced stage of culture has fixed to one spot, and employed in the soberer pursuits of commerce or the tillage of the soil. Arcadia has always been the chosen seat of simplicity and contentment. But in reality there is no counexion between herding flocks and roaming from place to place, and the practice of virtue, save in the imagination of poets and enthusiasts. The Magyars, like other nations in a state of barbarism, were content with what they had, only because they saw nothing better; when they saw it, they coveted it, and used force to gain possession of it. Rude warriors, whose proudest boast was their valour, and to whom fighting was an exciting pleasure, they seldom lied, because lying is a sign of fear and weakness; but where force could not avail them, they had no hesitation in calling in the aid of fraud. Engagements and treaties, however solemn, were readily broken, when they could be broken with impunity.

They supported themselves partly by fishing and hunting, and partly by keeping immense herds of sheep and oxen. Accompanied by the latter, they moved from place to place, abandoning each as soon as the pasturage became scanty. At the close of a day's march their tents were pitched, without order, and without defensive precaution, save what was afforded by their troops of light cavalry, which scoured the country for miles round, and soon detected the approach of an enemy. When they first entered Europe, their only arms were the bow and arrow, in the use of which they possessed wonderful dexterity. From his earliest boyhood every warrior was practised in horsemanship and archery. To ride boldly and aim surely were the two great accomplishments, to the acquisition of which his life was devoted. In the most rapid charge or most hasty retreat, he could discharge his arrows in any direction with equal force and precision, before, behind, or into the air. Onsets were made with disordered ranks, loosened reins, and wild cries, and the army fled without hesitation, if it were not at the first moment successful, but woe to the enemy that ventured too far in pursuit. He was soon taught that when the Magyars turned their backs it was no sign of fear, but part of a system of tactics. When successful, they made a terrible use of the victory. As they never asked for mercy, so they never gave any. Their dreadful ferocity astonished and horrified those who remembered the attacks of the Saracen and the Dane, and whose grandfathers had handed down to them traditions of the devastating vengeance of Attila. They not only sacked and pillaged the towns, but slaughtered the inhabitants of every age and sex. This barbarian cruelty was relieved by one trait of honour and humanity. In their wildest ravages they never inflicted upon women any worse injury than death—and this shows the existence, even then, of a spark of nobility, which has since kindled into the chivalrous gallantry by which modern Hungarians are distinguished. In the laws they enacted for their own internal government, they evinced good sense and discernment, and a strong spirit of justice. Theft, as the commonest and most disgraceful offence in a camp, where all property was exposed, was punished with death, and all other crimes with less, but proportionate severity.

Their manners in domestic life were simple as possible. The ceremony of marriage was unknown. A man lived with one, or two, or three women, as inclination prompted or his means allowed, and some traces of this easy arrangement are to be found in some of the Magyar idioms at the present day. A man is not said to marry, but "make a house or a household."* A Magyar virgin still calls

* *Házasság, házasodás.*

herself *hajadon*, or "girl with uncovered hair;" the married women wear bonnets. There is still another phrase, meaning "a girl for sale!" which, perhaps, implies the existence of a custom in those primitive times, on the part of the bold warriors, of purchasing with money or cattle the partners of their domestic joys and sorrows. Some of their proverbs give evidence of a knowledge of higher and better principles than their manners indicated: "The three things most conducive to happiness are, labour, sobriety, and moderation in pleasure." "Man's life is but a

THE PANNONIAN MOUNT.

migration," &c. They measured time by the changes of the moon. Sunday received the name of *vas*, or *vasarnap*, from the circumstance that on that day was held a great iron-market, when they were settled in the vicinity of Mount Altai, in Asia.*

Of their religious belief previous to their conversion to Christianity little is known. That they were monotheists is certain, for the word *Isten*, God, is the only word in the language, even to the present day, which expresses the idea of a supreme being; but they sacrificed white horses, on some occasions, to demons of subordinate position, but whether good or evil cannot be ascertained.

Their first conquests and final settlement in Europe extended beyond the Roman province of Pannonia, or the modern kingdom of Hungary. Up to that period it had been thinly occupied by the Moravians, a tribe of Sclavonian origin,

* La Hongrie Historique.

which Charlemagne had partially subdued. Their dukes, however, refused to obey his successors, and Arnulph invoked the aid of the Magyars to subdue them. The latter joyously answered to the call; but, having once entered the confines of the civilised world, they made up their minds never to return. During Arnulph's lifetime they remained peaceable; but, during the minority of his son Lewis, they made such good use of their opportunities, that, in a single day, in the year 900, they laid waste a tract of country fifty miles in circumference. At the battle of

ANCIENT MAGYARS.

Augsburg, the Christian army was totally routed, and the Hungarians carried fire and sword through Bavaria, Swabia, and Franconia. To the terror they inspired the feudal castles and walled towns owe their origin;* for both barons and burghers had to take precautions against the attacks of a foe who swept over the country with the rapidity and destructiveness of a simoom of the desert. The German empire was for thirty years compelled to pay tribute, through the fear of seeing put

* Milman's Gibbon, vol. v. p. 300.

into execution a threat to carry all the women and children into captivity, and slaughter all the males above the age of ten years. At last they approached the confines of Italy, and pitched their camp on the Brenta. But they were surprised and alarmed at beholding the apparent strength and populousness of the country which lay beyond, and asked leave to retire. The Italian king, in the first flush of exultation, rashly refused it. In the battle which followed, 20,000 of his soldiers were slain, and his army totally defeated. The invaders now poured over the country like an avalanche. Pavia, the first city of the west in wealth and splendour, was burnt and plundered, forty-three churches being consumed in one day, and of the population only two hundred were spared, who bought their lives by a quantity of gold and silver collected from amongst the smoking ruins. The churches that escaped during the inroads of which this was but the commencement, embodied in their litany the fearful prayer, "Oh, save and deliver us, thine unworthy servants, we beseech Thee, from the arrows of the Hungarians!"

"Nunc te rogamus, licet servi pessimi,
Ab Ungerorum, nos defendas jaculis!"

The sum of ten bushels of silver was paid as a ransom for Italian subjects who had fallen into the invaders' hands, and were threatened with death; but it is said the latter were cheated in the settling of the account. The Hungarians next turned their attention to the eastern empire, routed the Bulgarians, and presented themselves before Constantinople. The Greeks were protected by their walls; but one of the Magyar warriors, in a spirit of haughty defiance, rode up, and struck his battle-axe into the Golden Gate. They were at last, by the united influence of tribute, expostulation, and entreaty, induced to retrace their steps, and leave the imperial city to be sacked two or three centuries later by another horde of the same race.

At last, in the year 934, the power of the Hungarians was broken, and a stop put to their ravages by Henry the Fowler, and his son Otho the Great, two Saxon princes. The former rose from a sick bed to take the command of his army when he heard of their approach. He advised his countrymen to receive the first discharge of the Magyar arrows upon their bucklers, and prevent a second by closing with their lances. They obeyed his injunctions and won a complete victory, which Henry commemorated by having it painted upon the walls of the great hall in his castle of Merseburgh.

Twenty years afterwards (954), when Henry was dead, they again invaded the dominions of his son Otho the Great, with 100,000 horse, and passing the Rhine and the Meuse, penetrated to the heart of Flanders. The vigour and energy of Otho stayed the torrent. The German princes united against the common foe, and passed their combined forces in solemn review upon the plains of Augsburg. They consisted of eight legions, composed of various tribes from the different provinces. All the aid which religious devotion in a superstitious age could give to support the courage of the troops, was called into requisition. They were purified by a fast, and the camp was blessed by the relics of the saints and martyrs. Otho girded on the sword of Constantine, the first that had ever conquered under the banner of the cross, grasped the spear of Charlemagne, and waved the banner of St. Maurice. He carried with him likewise, as his surest ground of hope, the holy lance, the point of which was made from the nails of the true cross, and which had been purchased from the Duke of Burgundy by the gift of a province. Thus fortified, the Christian warriors awaited the pagan onslaught. The Hungarians crossed the Lech secretly, and followed on the rear of the German army, plundered the baggage, and carried confusion into the ranks of the Swabian and Bohemian legions. The Franconians came to the rescue, and restored the fortune of the day, and the Saxons, incited by the example, and inspired by the voice of their leader, performed prodigies of valour, and achieved a victory surpassing in magnitude and importance any that had been won for three centuries before. The Hungarians were totally routed, and their retreat being cut off by the rivers of Bavaria, they were slaughtered without mercy, their past cruelties having deprived them of all claim on the pity of their conquerors. Three of their princes were hanged at Ratisbon, and the fugitives who escaped were but too glad to settle down in weakness and disgrace upon the plains from which they had so often issued to spread terror and dismay throughout Europe. There the Magyars mingled with the Jazyges, the Moravians, and the Szeklers, and derived fresh energy from intermarriage with the thousands of robust captives whom they had carried from all parts of Europe in their forrays. They now began to adopt the customs of civilised life, and established a regular form of government, under the most famous of their chiefs or *dukes*, Arpad. The country was divided into a number of districts or counties, each governed by an electoral chief. Cities somewhat resembling those of the Romans, but ruder and less solid, began to spring up. All great state affairs were decided by a mounted assemblage of the warriors in the plains bordering on the river Teyss. The colonies of foreign races and the western captives were suffered to pursue their occupations in peace, and enjoyed the protection of the law; but the men of pure Magyar blood retained a supremacy, which in later days ripened into the modern Hungarian nobility.

CHAPTER IV.

A.D. 894—1095.

THE DYNASTY OF ARPAD.

ARPAD reigned, in 894, over a million of Magyars, over whom 215,000 composed the armed force of the nation, and with wisdom in advance of his age, he devoted his attention to the consolidation of his power, as the surest means of securing it; and for this purpose he convoked an assemblage in a large plain, under the open sky, to consult upon the measures to be adopted. In this we find the origin of the Hungarian Diet, and of the privileges which the Magyars reserved to themselves alone, to the exclusion of the conquered tribes, and which at that time were necessary for the preservation of their conquests. The Magyars were all equal, and those of them who have not preserved their nobility down to the present day, have lost it in consequence of their long refusal to become converts to Christianity. Arpad's memory is still held in veneration amongst the Hungarians, as he is considered the real founder of the nation.

Of his immediate successors little is known. The Magyars were separated from the rest of Europe as well by language and religion as by the memory of their past cruelties and the dread of future inroads. The last instance upon record in which they revived the ancient terror of their name, was an attack upon Venice in the reign of Duke Zoltan, Arpad's successor. Under him the Magyar hordes once more abandoned the plains on which they had settled, and, forcing the passes of the Alps, penetrated to the shore of the Adriatic (A.D. 900). Excited by rumours of the wealth and magnificence of Venice, which even at that early period was renowned for the enterprise of her merchants and the extent of her commerce, they determined to cross over and attack her. They hastily embarked in the first boats that came in their way, and Citta Nuovo, Equilo, Capo-d'Argere, and Chiozza speedily fell victims to their fury. The chain of islands forming a sort of pier or jetty, the two extremities of which touch the mainland, was now invaded, and they had but to cross the narrow arm of the sea which separates Venice from Malamocco. Terror and disorder reigned in the capital. The Doge, Pietro Tribuno, hastily equipped the fleet, and rousing the courage of the Venetians by reminding them of their victory over Pepin in the same place and in as great an extremity, led them against the enemy. We can hardly suppose that the Magyars, unacquainted as they must have been with the art of navigation, and provided only with such vessels as they happened to find in the ports on their route, were in a position to offer a vigorous resistance to the hardy and experienced sailors of the "city of the sea." There was little to sustain their courage save the thirst for plunder, and fury at being opposed when they had all but grasped it. The doge, profiting by his knowledge of the locality, and the dexterity and skill of his crews, speedily routed them. The majority made a hasty escape to the mainland, but the sea

ARPAD.

remained covered with the arms, clothing, and dead bodies of a great multitude of the slain.*

The successor of the three terrible dukes, Arpad, Zoltan, and Zoxis, Geysa, married a Bavarian princess, and caused himself to be baptised into the Christian faith. During the reign of Charlemagne in Germany, missionaries had, under his auspices, made strenuous efforts to introduce the Christian religion into Hungary, and had been partially successful; but no sooner was he dead than most of the

* Daru's *Histoire de la République de Venise.*

converts relapsed into paganism, and the few who remained faithful to their principles were compelled to worship in secret, in order to escape the violence and persecution of their countrymen, who looked upon them as innovators and impious contemners of the religion of their forefathers. The Christians met by night, as the Roman churches had done eight centuries before, to celebrate the rites of baptism and the Lord's supper, and sought to keep alive the fire of faith by frequent intercourse with the people and clergy of the neighbouring nations.

After Geysa had ascended the throne, his inclination towards the new faith was soon made manifest. Making due allowance for exaggeration in the eulogies which the church and the national historians have heaped upon him, he appears to have been a man superior in intellect, and perhaps in cultivation, to the mass of the people whom he was called upon to govern, and to have seen with regret that robbery and murder were looked upon by them as the only occupation worthy of Magyars. He perceived also the vast superiority possessed by the neighbouring nations in the arts and sciences and the comforts of life, and ascribed the whole, or at least the greater part of it to the religion they professed. He resolved to act the part of Numa, and become the reformer of the creed as well as of the manners of his countrymen. He therefore collected great numbers of Christian missionaries from various parts of Europe to instruct them in the rudiments of the true faith. All the national prejudices were at once roused against him. The old Magyars, who recounted with pride the exploits of Zoltan and Zoxis, the dangers and glory of which they themselves had shared, and told how Italian mothers soothed their perverse children by the mere mention of the terrible warriors of Pannonia, were enraged at his departure from the faith in which their fathers and brothers had conquered and died; and the young men, and even the women, mocked at the effeminacy of a chief who was more intent upon empty ceremonial and the idle jargon of foreign priests than the exercises of the camp and preparation for war. The duke was, however, supported by the adjacent nations, particularly the Saxons, who were not a little pleased to see their troublesome neighbours about to undergo the softening influences of the Christian faith, and was thus enabled to bring his reign to a peaceful close without any open demonstration of discontent on the part of his subjects. He founded a considerable number of schools and colleges for the education of the clergy, and made some attempts to put down robbery and murder—then but trifling offences in the eyes of the people, to whom it seemed almost natural that the warriors, who had inflicted so many evils upon foreigners, should now and then, by way of relaxation, turn their arms against their own countrymen. He died without seeing the darling object of his life—the conversion of the nation—in reality much nearer its accomplishment than when he commenced his reign; but he had at least sown the seeds of Christianity.

Upon his death, his son Stephen ascended the throne, of whose birth a curious story is told as to the means taken by the saints to announce to his parents the great destinies that were in store for their offspring. Its truth to us seems more than doubtful; but as at the present day there are almost as many degrees in faith as varieties in physiognomy, we leave our readers to judge.

The name of Geysa's wife was Saroltha, to whom, while pregnant, the protomartyr Stephen appeared in a dream, and thus addressed her:—"Woman, be of good courage, and put thy faith in Christ; know that thou shalt bring forth a fortunate son, unto whom this kingdom shall be given. Such a wonderful man as he shall be Pannonia has never seen, nor after his death shall ever see again; and after his departure he shall be numbered amongst the saints. I am Stephen, the protomartyr; give him my name."

Upon awakening, Saroltha returned thanks to God, and ordered masses to be said in honour of the saint upon all the christian altars in the kingdom; and after her son's birth, he received in baptism the name of Stephen. The boy was carefully educated, and his father, shortly before his death, presented him to the people in a solemn assemblage, expressing his belief that it was reserved for him to win them to civilisation and Christianity, as the Lord had appeared to him in a dream, and informed him that the part he had taken in war and rapine in his youth had unfitted him for succeeding in so holy a work. Stephen was immediately saluted duke by the assembled warriors, and after his father's decease entered upon the government under the most favourable auspices. Geysa's work of evangelisation was steadily carried out; and though the earlier part of his reign was disturbed by conspiracy and rebellion, his efforts were completely successful. Churches were built in all parts of the country, parishes marked out, and priests appointed to their cure, and the ancient Scythian rites finally abandoned. The altars were decorated with sumptuous magnificence, and everything that ecclesiastical ingenuity could devise was displayed in profusion to impress the untutored imaginations of the people. Having accomplished to his satisfaction this change in the religion of the country, Stephen turned his attention to the chastisement and subjugation of the various tribes surrounding his dominions, who under his father's peaceful rule had grown insolent with impunity. His arms were in every case successful, and, with a propagandist zeal quite in keeping with the character of the man and the spirit of the times, the adoption of Christianity was made an essential condition in every treaty made with the vanquished.* For all these pious labours he received from Pope Sylvester II. a royal crown, and the title of "Apostolic King," which the emperors of Austria bear at the present day.

His political reforms were scarcely less important than his religious ones. The influence of the Catholic clergy, and daily contact with the neighbouring states, whose government was rather feudal than democratic, induced Stephen to substitute a constitutional monarchy for the rude and loosely organised military republic,

* Bonfinius Rer. Hung. Dec. ii. p. 215.

of which his ancestors had simply been the chieftains. He established three different orders in the state—prelates, magnates (*seniores domini*), and the inferior nobility (*nobiles servientes regales*). Each of these orders had an actual share in the administration of the government, but in the diets they could come to no decision unless they were unanimous.* The palatine (*Nagy-ur*) was, next the king, the most important personage, and filled the monarch's place during his absence or illness. Stephen afterwards appointed a supreme judge (*országbiró*), a treasurer, and other superior officers and magnates, who constituted the order of barons of the empire. Under this head were included the chiefs of the ancient Magyar class or tribe. It will be seen that the republican government was thus entirely destroyed. In the new order of things the church, as usual, came in for the lion's share of power and profit. The clergy, by working on the religious disposition of the king, managed to secure a high political position and the first rank in the three orders. Stephen, also, was the first to establish the districts called counties, which exist down to the present day; and each of these retained the right of administering its internal affairs independent of all others. The members of the nobility generally occupied seats in the council, and the king himself was frequently present at the meetings. The counties were, in almost every respect, minor republics, and, besides, had the right of convoking periodically assemblies which exercised a direct influence upon the general administration of the central government. This whole arrangement has always been so highly prized by the Magyars, that tradition says that Stephen made it under the inspiration of the Deity.

The military organisation differed in some respects from the civil, but was found to be extremely well adapted for the defence of the country. The military division consisted of sixty-two or seventy-two *citadel counties*, the commanders of which resided in the fortresses—hence their title of *Comites Castri*. For purposes of defence simply there was a sort of militia upon a scale suited to the habits and traditions of the people. The magnates formed the "king's army" (*Király Sereg*), and the nobles in general—the national army at present called the *insurrection*, and it was obliged to be always in readiness to repel any attempt at foreign invasion. As a natural consequence of this, the possession of land in Hungary was even more intimately connected with the rights of the nobles than elsewhere. Two general principles regulated the privileges of the nobles, or, in other words, of the conquerors. First, that ever after Stephen's reign, the crown was the proprietor of all the land in the kingdom. In strict law, the nobles were only the possessors or occupiers of their estates; what we call the right of property being known amongst the Magyars as the right of possession (*jus possessionarum*). Secondly, all persons not noble could not possess land, and were, consequently, not called

* This is the statement of the national historian Michael Horváth. Other writers assert that at this period there existed merely a senate with a consultative voice.

upon to defend the kingdom. The entire soil was thus divided amongst the warriors, the companions of the first dukes or chieftains, just as in England after the Norman conquest. The original inhabitants met with the same fate as the Saxons, but, unhappily, the same good fortune was not in store for them.

The usual condition attaching to a gift of land in Hungary was the ordinary feudal one of a military service. In every case the sovereign stipulated that in

ST. STEPHEN.

case of failure of heirs male of the grantee, who alone could fulfil the duties attaching to the tenure, the estate should revert to the grantor, or his heirs, or successors.

Stephen wishing, a short time previous to his death, to appoint a successor to his kingdom in some way related to himself, now that his son Emerik was dead, sent hastily for Vazul, the son of his cousin, a young man who, for his licentiousness, had been shut up in prison, and ordered him to be liberated and brought to him forthwith. But upon Gysla, the queen, hearing of this, she entered into a conspiracy with Buda, the messenger, to frustrate the king's intentions, in order that a favourite of her own might succeed to the throne. She, therefore, gave orders to Sebus, Buda's son, to precede his father to Vazul's prison, and there put out the eyes of the latter, and fill up his ears with molten lead. Sebus literally carried out his instructions, and then fled into Bohemia. On the following day Buda arrived and led the unfortunate Vazul, thus mutilated, into the presence of the old king, who, on seeing him, gave way to the loudest demonstrations of grief and indignation. But his advanced age, and increasing infirmities, had so far detracted from the vigour of his earlier years, that he was unable to take any steps either for the discovery or the punishment of the perpetrators of this foul crime, and after a feeble attempt to secure the safety of the sons of his cousin Ladislaus, by advising them to fly into Poland, he resigned himself to die, about the year 1034, after a long and glorious reign of nearly forty years.

The changes he had wrought in the religion, manners, and government of the kingdom, having won a barbarous and cruel people from habits of rapine and violence, and having taught them to cultivate the arts of civilised life, and dwell in peace with their neighbours, would have been sufficient, in the infancy of the world, to procure his translation to Olympus, without the pain or humiliation of death, and would have caused ten thousand altars to smoke with incense for ages afterwards in honour of his memory. In the eleventh century they were quite sufficient to admit him to the goodly company of the saints and martyrs. For forty years his body lay unnoticed in the tomb, until, in the reign of Ladislaus, a missive was received from the Pope, according the honours of canonization to those who converted Hungary to Christianity. Chief among these was the deceased king. Upon the receipt of the authorisation, Ladislaus ordained a fast of three days' duration, and directed all persons of every class to implore, by prayers and supplication, the Divine blessing upon the ceremonial they were about to perform. A solemn procession marched to the tomb, but, on reaching it, it was found that no efforts could remove the stone from the entrance. After several attempts had failed, the popular voice began to ascribe the difficulty to a miraculous manifestation of Divine displeasure, and the king looked around in sore perplexity for the explanation of the mystery. A certain virgin named Charis came to the rescue, by informing Ladislaus that the reluctance of the stone to quit its position was due to his having imprisoned his brother Soloman a short time previously, in consequence of a quarrel; and prophesied that until he had been released all efforts to remove it would prove futile. Her advice and rebuke were attended to: Soloman was released, the stone thrown aside, the body carried forth, and a volume would not suffice to enumerate all the blind who on that day received their sight, all the deaf who heard, the lame who walked, the lepers who were cleansed, and all the doubting who were confirmed, or blasphemers who were confounded. So runs the chronicle or tradition.

Peter, the grandnephew of Stephen, having obtained the crown through the machinations of Gysla, the old king's wife, had no sooner ascended the throne than he disgusted all parties by his tyranny. Not only did he refuse to tread in the footsteps of his uncle, whom the Magyars loved to call the Charlemagne and Clovis of Hungary, but he did not even fill the kingly office with ordinary show of outward dignity and decorum. From the very first he insulted and professed to despise the nobility; evinced marked partiality for the Germans and other foreigners, invited them to his court, and acted in everything in accordance with their advice. German garrisons, contrary to the express laws of the kingdom, were placed in the towns and fortresses, and Germans were appointed to fill some of the highest offices in the state. The courtiers affected to contemn the natives of the country as untutored barbarians, and were encouraged in their insolence by Peter himself. In addition to this, he outraged the feelings of the people by an open licentiousness foreign to the national manners, and hitherto unknown in Hungary. The wives and daughters of some of the first families in the kingdom were subjected to the most cruel insults from himself and his satellites.

The magnates at last sent a deputation to lay before him in detail the various grievances of which they complained, and to implore him to restore the high offices of the state to men of his own nation, to drive the foreign favourites from his court, and last of all to reform his own manners. Their prayers were listened to in contemptuous silence, and rejected with insult. Peter declared that not only would he not expel the Germans, but that he would load them with still greater honours; that these complaints were dictated by the native turbulence of the Magyars, and that he would show them right speedily that he was sole ruler in his own dominions.

The result was such as might have been expected. The deputation retired in indignation, and the nobles instantly met in council, and solemnly entered into a league to dethrone the tyrant, and fixed upon Aba, a man of royal blood, as his successor. Aba was forthwith led before a public assemblage of the armed warriors of the nation, and by them unanimously saluted king with loud acclamations, and instant preparations were made to march against Peter. When the latter heard of what had occurred he was seized with consternation, and finding himself deserted by all those who in the days of his prosperity had been loudest in their protestations of fidelity, he fled precipitately into Bavaria.

Aba then called together a grand council of the nobles, explained the cause of the rebellion, defended the part he had himself taken in it, and after enumerating Peter's crimes and outrages, solemnly declared his intention of restoring and upholding the ancient order of things, and of governing in accordance with the laws and constitution of the kingdom as established by Stephen of blessed memory. All the illegal decrees of the late king were forthwith revoked, the civil and military officials who had been dismissed to make way for the foreigners were restored, and all Germans expelled from the country. Aba had scarce reigned for three years, when (1042) Peter suddenly prepared to invade the kingdom at the head of a large German army, sent to his aid by the emperor, Henry III., who himself accompanied the expedition. Ambassadors were forthwith despatched to learn from Henry the cause of this sudden attack. The reply which that monarch gave proves that even at that early period, and amongst a people whose history and manners were a standing protest against irresponsible power, the doctrine of divine right, in these latter days productive of so much evil to mankind, was beginning to gain ground. He declared that he could never lightly pass over injuries done to his friends, and in particular the outrage upon Peter, as kings should, from the very nature of their office, be held sacred amongst all nations. Aba replied, that amongst them, the persons of their kings were held sacred, but to tyrants they could never submit. Henry was, however, inexorable, and Aba resolved to anticipate him by suddenly raising an army, and, entering Austria and Bavaria, laid waste the country on both banks of the Danube, and slaughtered the inhabitants, and re-entered Hungary with a vast amount of plunder and a great number of captives. Henry was celebrating the feast of Easter when he heard of the occurrence, and instantly enumerated, in a full assemblage of the German princes, all the atrocities that had been committed by the Magyars, and announced his intention of marching instantly to inflict summary vengeance upon the perpetrators. Scarcely had he finished, when ambassadors from Hungary presented themselves, who, on learning the intention of the Germans, declared that Aba was quite ready to return the captives and the booty, but as to the restoration of Peter, it was a thing not to be thought of, and which they would rather die than submit to. But Henry had already pledged himself to Albert, Duke of Austria, whose sister Peter had married, that the restoration of the exiled king should be accomplished at all hazards, and therefore dismissed the ambassadors without any answer. Internal troubles in his own dominions, however, caused the postponement of the intended expedition, and Aba, in the meantime, endeavoured to amuse him by fair words and fine promises which he neither intended nor had the ability to fulfil.

In the interval dissensions and discontents arose in the kingdom, the exact origin of which we have now no means of ascertaining. By his attempt to improve the condition of the peasants, or serfs, Aba appears to have excited the hostility of the nobles, but what measures he adopted for that purpose, or in what manner he attempted to carry them out, we know not. The descendants of the ancient Dacians, and the debris of all the tribes who from time to time had settled in Pannonia in the earlier centuries of Christianity, and been obliged to submit to more powerful invaders, had, as we have already said, under the Magyar domination sunk into the abject condition of tillers of the soil for their conquerors' benefit, and came at last to be numbered amongst the chattels on the farm. The condition of these people, as in all other countries of Europe where a conquest had taken place, was deplorable. They were not allowed to change their place of residence, except by consent of their owners; were incapable of acquiring property; and were daily subject to all the outrages which unbridled power in a rude and barbarous age could inflict.

It is more than probable that Aba was a man of philosophic mind, and humane disposition, that he pitied these unfortunate men, and risked his crown in the attempt to liberate or elevate them: but as all the accounts of his quarrel with the nobles and its consequences which have come down to us are not only meagre in the extreme, but are from the pen of chroniclers whose prejudices were in favour of the conquering party, they must be received with great suspicion.

His attempts at innovation and intrenchment on their rights and privileges excited the ire of the nobility to such a degree, that they considered the offences of Peter small in comparison,* and forthwith began to conspire to bring about his restoration. The plot was discovered before it was ripe: some of the conspirators were arrested, tried, and put to death; some fled to Henry's camp; and others, being induced to appear at court for the purpose of discussing their grievances openly with the king, were secretly despatched by his guards. The fugitives implored the German emperor to rid the kingdom of this cruel monster, who would never fulfil his engagements, who had insulted the nobility, and degraded the kingly office by frequent and familiar intercourse with serfs and ploughmen, and whose crimes called loudly for vengeance. Henry listened to their supplications with a willing ear, and began his march, under the guidance of the refugees, and coming up with the Hungarian army, instantly offered battle. The contest was long and bloody; but while the issue was still doubtful, the defection of a large body of his forces threw Aba's army into confusion, and led to his total defeat. The Germans ascribed their victory partly, of course, to their own valour, and partly to the timely appearance of a sign in the heavens, upon which a great wind arose, and blew into the faces of their antagonists a thick cloud of dust which blinded and disheartened them. Whatever we may think of the miracle, there is no doubt about the result of the engagement. Aba fled precipitately across the Danube, until, on arriving at a village on the Teyss, he was slain by some of his own followers, and buried in a neighbouring church (1044).

Peter was now restored to the throne which he had lost by his folly, but he appeared to have learnt nothing and forgotten nothing in adversity. He again surrounded himself by foreigners, repaid the services of the nobles who had joined Henry's army by insult and neglect, and soon convinced them that the exchange they had made was by no means for the better. A spirit of discontent spread through the whole nation, and when the three princes, Andrew, Bela, and Leventa, whom Stephen had sent into Poland for safety after the mutilation of Vazul, appeared once

* "Usque adeo insolens effectus est, ut competitore perniciosior esse videretur, quippe qui et fovere humiles agrestesque, et in nobiles immaniter saevire, coeperat."—*Bonfin.* Dec. ii. lib. ii. p. 219.

more on the scene, their advent was hailed with acclamation. They had been received by Misco, the king of Poland, with great kindness and cordiality, and one of them, Bela, had distinguished himself during his stay in his dominions by an act of romantic valour, which in that age powerfully impressed the imaginations of the people. A dispute had arisen between the Poles and the Pomeranians as to the payment of tribute, which the former claimed from the latter. The contending parties were about to decide it by an appeal to arms, when it was proposed that, instead of a general engagement of the two armies, a champion should be chosen on each side, to whose strength and valour should be confided the assertion of the rights of his countrymen. If the Pole proved victorious, the Pomeranians should pay the tribute; if not, not. Bela came forward, and volunteered his services as the champion of Poland. They were accepted, and in the first onset he unhorsed his antagonist, and then despatched him with a single blow of his sword; for which exploit Misco loaded him with favours, bestowed on him large estates in Pomerania, and gave him his daughter Gysla in marriage, by whom he had two sons, Geysa and Ladislaus. The other two brothers, Andrew and Leventa, after various wanderings amongst the Cumans and the Russians, returned at last to Hungary, upon hearing of the feeling of discontent which pervaded the minds of the people. Here they were presented to large assemblages of the Magyars, who unanimously saluted them kings, and called loudly for the destruction of all foreigners and priests, the overthrow of the Christian religion and the churches built for its worship, and the restoration of the ancient Scythian rites—a striking proof of the superficial nature of the conversions effected at that period amongst the barbarians of northern Europe. Putting themselves at the head of the multitude, the two princes marched rapidly towards Buda, the chief city of the kingdom. Some priests, and most of the bishops, were slaughtered on the way. Peter attempted once more to find safety in flight, but found himself encompassed on every side by enemies, and was at last captured in the village of Zamur; and his eyes having been put out, he died of grief and vexation three days afterwards, in the third year from his restoration to the throne.

The foreigners having been everywhere expelled, Andrew and Leventa marched to Alba Regia, the royal residence, where the former was solemnly crowned king, with the consent and approbation of the magnates, but only three bishops could be found to assist at the coronation, the others having been slain or having taken flight (1047).

Andrew had no sooner ascended the throne, than he issued an ordinance, commanding all Hungarians, upon pain of death, to abandon all pagan rites and ceremonies, and return to the worship of the true God, and of his son Jesus Christ; and ordering all towns and villages in which any church or chapel had been destroyed, to repair or rebuild it forthwith. As far as we can learn, these injunctions were obeyed without a murmur, the more readily, as Leventa, who was a firm adherent of the pagan faith, died a few days after his brother's coronation. It seems as if the people disliked Christianity simply because, during Peter's reign, it had come to be associated in their minds with foreign influence and domination, and they returned to paganism because it was the religion of nationality. Our own history contains a similar instance of the antipathy of a people to a creed, because it was the creed of alien oppressors. If England had not been Protestant, in all likelihood Ireland would not now have been Catholic.

Andrew's attention for the next few years was occupied with the settlement of differences, either by the sword or negotiation, with the surrounding nations. To enter into the details of these squabbles would be tedious and uninteresting, even if it were instructive. Amongst the semi-civilised people of northern Europe, at that time, they were perpetually arising, and exhibit the same monotonous features of treachery, violence, and rapine, redeemed by no better trait than physical courage.

When Andrew found himself childless, and in the decline of life, he sent a message to Bela, his brother, who, as we have said, was settled in Poland, requesting him to come into Hungary with his wife and children, that he might assist in calming the contentions and disorders by which the nation was agitated, and that they might divide the kingdom between them (1051). Bela, immediately upon the receipt of this, laid aside the dukedom with which Misco had invested him, and started for his brother's dominions. He was received with the utmost joy, not only by Andrew, but by the whole population; and an assembly having been held, the kingdom was divided into three parts, two-thirds being reserved for the king, and the remainder being assigned to Bela. The two monarchs ruled over their respective dominions for some years in perfect harmony, but the calm was rudely broken by another vigorous attack from Henry III., of Germany, who had collected a large force with the avowed intention of avenging the injuries sustained by Peter, and the perfidy and inconstancy of the Hungarians. He entered Hungary at the head of a powerful army, and laid vigorous siege to Presburg, a town on the Danube. He launched floating towers upon the river, and attacked the walls by the aid of every machine in use at that period, at the same time maintaining a strict blockade on every side, so as to starve the garrison into submission. Upon the latter the attack had come unexpectedly, and being totally unprepared for a lengthened defence, they were obliged to resort to stratagem to open up the passage of the river. A skilful swimmer, named Zothmund, dropped silently from the walls into the water in the dead of the night, and swimming round the enemy's vessels, bored holes in their sides below the water-mark, and before morning the majority were sunk, in spite of all the efforts of the crews; and the emperor was compelled to raise the siege in haste. The news having animated the courage of the Hungarians, the Germans were attacked upon every side, and compelled to retreat precipitately into their own country.

In the following year, Henry, chagrined by his failure, fitted out another expedition, and again invaded Hungary. Andrew and Bela hastily collected their forces, laid waste the frontier districts, so as to deprive the enemy of all supplies on his march, and then awaited the issue. The Germans, after enduring terrible sufferings, were impatiently expecting their fleet by the Danube, when a letter from the admiral to the emperor having fallen into Andrew's hands, a forged answer was returned, commanding him to sink his vessels and join the army at Ratisbon, as the expedition was abandoned. The order was obeyed, and Henry was still in uncertainty, when his camp was suddenly attacked in the night by a large force of Hungarian archers and slingers, who, in the darkness and confusion, slaughtered a vast number of the Germans. He was now fain to solicit peace. Some years previous to this, Andrew, haunted by the fear of dying childless, had married Agmunda, the daughter of the Duke of the Muscovites, and by her had two sons, Soloman and David. To the elder of these, Soloman, the emperor offered to betroth his daughter Sophia, as a pledge of the peace and amity which he wished henceforth to maintain with the king of Hungary. His offers were accepted; a treaty was made, provisions were sent in abundance to the German camp, and a short time afterwards the nuptial rites were celebrated with great pomp. The former had not yet emerged from boyhood, and was thus but too soon made acquainted with the cares and anxieties of the world. Andrew was now seized with paralysis, and believing his end to be approaching, declared Soloman his heir, before an assembly of the prelates and magnates, by whom he was solemnly crowned. At the ceremony, according to custom, the words of Isaac to Jacob were chanted or recited: "Let the people serve thee, and nations bow down to thee. Be lord over thy brethren, and let thy mother's sons bow down to thee;"* and although this was interpreted to Bela as signifying Andrew's intention that he and his two sons, Geysa and Ladislaus, should be subject to the sway of Soloman, it does not appear that he made an objection to the claims of the young prince to what was certainly his lawful inheritance.

But in a very short time some of the nobles, who bore no good will to Bela, made it appear to Andrew, that as long as his brother lived, his son would never enjoy the kingdom in peace, and they advised him to employ stratagem to learn Bela's intentions. The latter was accordingly invited to court, and Andrew received him reclining on a couch in the open air, having a sword and a crown placed on the ground at his side. The former symbolized the dukedom, the latter the kingdom. Bela was to be offered his choice of the two as a present; if he chose the crown, it was to be taken as a proof that his intentions were sinister, and he was to be slain on the spot, if he chose the sword, that he was content with his position, and would never attempt aught against his nephew's supremacy. The plot was revealed to Bela by the treachery of a servant, and he prudently chose the sword.

* Gen. xxvii. 29.

Transported with delight, the old king sent him away laden with presents, and being convinced of the sincerity of his attachment, solemnly committed the interests of his son to his keeping. But Bela was so alarmed by the dangerous position in which his brother's suspicions had placed him, that in three months afterwards he fled with all his family to the court of Misco, his father-in-law, told him of all the injuries and insults he had received from Andrew, and besought him to aid him in taking possession of the Hungarian crown, supporting his prayer by drawing a glowing picture of the advantages that would result from the close alliance of the two kingdoms. Misco complied with his request, and placed a strong force at his disposal, with which he invaded his brother's dominions.

Andrew, on his side, was not idle; he sent an embassy to Henry representing the dangers of his situation, and asking for an auxiliary force. The emperor instantly sent him 12,000 men, and a similar contingent was furnished by Bratislaus, King of Bohemia. The two armies met on the banks of the Teyss; the German troops crossed the river, and fiercely attacked the combined Polish and Hungarian forces of Bela. The battle which ensued was long and bloody, and ended in the total defeat of Andrew, who was taken prisoner, and died on the following day, leaving Bela in undisturbed possession of the kingdom (1062). Bela, immediately after his coronation, turned his whole attention to internal reforms. He established a regular system of coinage, appointed places and times for the holding of markets, and even took upon himself to fix the prices of commodities, and admitted the use of Byzantine coins. He secured to all Soloman's family and relatives the full and undisturbed enjoyment of their property. The exercise of pagan worship throughout the whole of his dominions was strictly forbidden upon pain of death. To him also belongs the honour of organising the two legislative chambers. His energy, impartiality, and pure administration of justice, tended greatly to the development of the national resources, and it was not without unfeigned sorrow that his subjects received the news of his death, which was caused by the falling of a ruined wall, which broke his limbs in such a manner as to baffle the skill of the physicians of the time (1065). Soloman, Andrew's son, immediately called upon Henry IV. of Germany, the son and successor of the late emperor, to restore him to his father's throne, and by his aid, Geysa and Ladislaus were compelled to fly into Poland, and Soloman was put in undisturbed possession of the kingdom. In a short time the two brothers again made their appearance upon the frontier with a Polish army, and there appeared every probability of another civil war. By the mediation of the clergy, however, a reconciliation was effected, by which the kingdom was ceded to Soloman, and to Geysa was reserved his father's dukedom.

This was a period of new conquests. Between the years 602 and 641 great hordes of Serbs and Croats, quitting the countries in which they dwelt beyond the Carpathian mountains, settled in the northern part of the Greek Illyria, that is to say, in the south of modern Hungary. Those who took up their abode in the extremity of the district adopted the name of the town of Delminium, in order to distinguish themselves from the others, and called themselves Dalmatians; the Croats, at present established in the countries to the south-west of Hungary, preserved their original appellation, as did also the Serbs, who retired further towards the east. The name of Sclaves (Schiavoni) was given by the Venetians to a tribe dwelling between the Croats and the Serbs. Crecimir, the first Croat prince, attained to a very high degree of power, which was the means of securing to his son, Dirsizlaw, the title of King of Croatia, about the year 970. In the time of Soloman, Peter Crecimir, a descendant of the great Crecimir, an able and courageous monarch, occupied the throne, and enlarged his dominions by wresting Dalmatia from the Venetians, and subduing a part of Sclavonia. Having been attacked by Berthold, the Duke of Carinthia, Crecimir invoked the aid of the Magyars, which Soloman cheerfully rendered; by his help, Berthold was totally defeated (1089).

Soloman and his two cousins did not long continue to exhibit an example of fraternal unity and concord. Urged on by evil counsellors, Soloman began to long for the expulsion and destruction of his rivals; and after laying a variety of snares for them, all of which they escaped, he at last openly took up arms against them. After several battles, he was at length totally defeated, and was driven out of the kingdom. In his reign the incursions of the Cumans and Bohemians had been checked by a long series of wars, into the details of which it would be impossible to enter.

When Geysa and Ladislaus found themselves victorious, they marched forthwith to Alba Regia, the state residence of the Hungarian kings, where the former, as the elder brother, was formally crowned and proclaimed king, with the approbation of the majority of the nobles, and Ladislaus was by him appointed duke or palatine of the kingdom.

Soloman immediately sought the aid of his brother-in-law, Henry IV. of Germany, who led a large army, well provided with stores of every description, into Hungary, while a well-equipped fleet followed his march down the Danube. The two brothers were not slow in making defensive preparations, and marched resolutely to meet the invaders. While besieging the town of Nitria, the garrison made a sally, and engaged hand to hand with the Germans; but the conflict was like some of the battles between the rival states in Italy in the fourteenth and fifteenth centuries, in which, after the combat had lasted from early morn until eve, none were slain and but few hurt. One of the Hungarian officers, Opus Bathor, being at last disgusted with what he considered child's play, rode straight into the ranks of the enemy and killed a man before the eyes of the citizens. His horse immediately fell, pierced by a hundred javelins, but Bathor, nothing daunted, valiantly maintained his ground on foot, and fought his way out uninjured. The German emperor beheld the feat with astonishment, and asked Soloman how many soldiers of equal strength Ladislaus and Geysa had in their army. Soloman, more considerate of the fame of his country than of his own success, replied that the Hungarian forces contained not only many that were equal, but thousands that were superior. "Then believe me," was Henry's rejoinder, "you will never recover your kingdom."

It was not the intention of Geysa, however, to decide the quarrel by force of arms, as long as other means remained open to him; and he diligently set about bribing the German nobles and military leaders to dissuade Henry from following up his enterprise, and by the same instrumentality a serious mutiny was excited amongst the soldiery. The emperor was persuaded that he was unwisely risking the safety of his own army in a quarrel in which he had no sort of interest; and, overcome by his fears, he struck his camp, and returned precipitately into his dominions. Soloman, in the meantime, took refuge in Presburg, and, by means of the intrigues which he carried on, gave great uneasiness to the two princes. They then commenced negotiations with him for peace and reconciliation, in the midst of which Geysa died, after a reign of three years.

After the funeral ceremony was over, the question of a successor began to be agitated. Legitimacy was undoubtedly upon the side of Soloman, but the people found it impossible to forget the splendid services which Ladislaus had rendered to the state, and his piety, wisdom, fortitude, and prudence; and he was, in consequence, unanimously elected by the prelates, magnates, and nobles. Shortly after he had ascended the throne, Zelomir, the king of Croatia and Dalmatia, his sister's husband, died childless, leaving his kingdom to his wife. The widow was soon attacked by her enemies abroad, and assailed by sedition at home, and in her perplexity appealed to her brother for protection and assistance. He immediately marched with a powerful army to her aid, and soon restored peace; but as she had no children, and was wearied by the cares of state, she resigned her dominions to Ladislaus, and Croatia and Dalmatia were henceforth subject to the Hungarian crown.

Soloman, in the meantime, did not desist from his intrigues for the recovery of his father's kingdom; but a treaty was at length concluded by which he abandoned his claims, and consented to retire into Germany, upon condition that he received a yearly stipend sufficient to support him in princely style. He soon became tired of his forced exile, and sent to request an interview with Ladislaus, for the purpose, as he pretended, of more cordially confirming their reconciliation, but in reality in order to seize him and carry him off. Ladislaus received timely warning of the snare, and placed a powerful body of troops in ambush in the vicinity of the place of meeting. Everything turned out as he expected. The attendants of Soloman arrested him, but, as they were marching away, the captors were surrounded and led captive, and Ladislaus released. Soloman, chagrined and humiliated by the want of success attendant upon his treachery, was led prisoner to Visegrad, and there kept. In a very short time he managed to enter into a conspiracy with a tribe called the Chuni, and induced them to attack Hungary; but on hearing of their utter defeat by Ladislaus, fearing that proofs of his complicity might have been discovered, he effected his escape, and sought refuge amongst his discomfited allies, whom he once more stirred up to invade Bulgaria, where they laid waste the country and slaughtered many of the inhabitants. Nicephorus, the Greek emperor, forthwith led an army against them, and routed them with great slaughter. Soloman, with a few hundreds of his followers, rode off the field towards the Ister. On the way they stopped in a small deserted town, where, to their surprise, they suddenly found themselves surrounded by a body of Greek troops, who closely invested the place, and seemed determined to starve them into subjection. The unfortunate Soloman, with a courage worthy of a better reward, resolved to die in a manner becoming his descent, and, calling around him the most devoted of his adherents, boldly charged the besiegers, and, to his own surprise, succeeded in cutting his way through them unhurt, and, pursuing his course with such of his companions as had survived the fray, found the Ister frozen over, and crossed it in safety. Upon reaching the other side they took refuge in a wood, in order to rest themselves and their horses. Soloman, after giving them a few directions, laid aside his arms, and, disappearing through the trees, was never afterwards seen. It was long believed that, wearied of the strife and turmoil of the world, and despairing of recovering his inheritance, he had taken up his abode in some remote fastness, and was expiating by a life of prayer and penitence the crimes and follies of his early years.

Not very long after his disappearance from the scene, the Chuni once more, taking advantage of the absence of Ladislaus in his newly acquired dominion of Croatia and Sclavonia, entered Hungary, laid waste the country with fire and sword, and carried great multitudes away captive. Ladislaus, upon hearing of the outrage, returned by forced marches, and coming up with the enemy on the banks of the Temes, roused the fury of his soldiers by pointing out the probability that their own wives and children were amongst the number of the captives whom they saw winding down the side of the hill in a long line, and falling upon the barbarians, who, laden with booty and intoxicated with success, were incapable of making an effectual resistance, he committed so great havoc among them, that in all probability but few of the tribe would have survived to tell of their defeat, had not the king stayed the impetuosity of the Hungarians, by reminding them that the conversion of these pagans to Christianity would cover a multitude of sins.

The Chuni, upon hearing of the loss of their bravest warriors, and of their chief Kopulk, who had been slain in the combat, ordered a general mourning throughout their territory, and seeking the alliance of the various tribes in their neighbourhood, prepared once more to march against Hungary, to avenge their defeat and recover the captives. Previous to setting out, however, they sent ambassadors to Ladislaus to demand satisfaction, with an air of insolent haughtiness that would have comported the victor much better than the vanquished. He sternly refused to comply with their requests, and anticipating their attack, advanced to the frontier to meet them, and fell in with them once more upon the banks of the Ister, upon a Sunday morning. He rode forward in front of his forces and challenged the bravest of the enemy to single combat. All remained silent. He then loudly called their leader by name, who could not, when thus addressed, decline the contest. He came forth, but in a few minutes, Ladislaus ran him through the body and killed him on the spot. Upon seeing their general fall the Chuni fled, and thus ended the last attack they ever made upon Hungary. Invasions made by the Russians and Poles were repulsed with equal vigour, and it is said that for the purpose of chastising the latter he pushed his victorious arms to the very walls of Cracow, which surrendered to him after a vigorous resistance, but that after receiving an humble submission from the inhabitants, he, with rare moderation, restored them their city without condition and without injury. He then turned his arms against the Bohemians, and soon made that turbulent people sensible that they could not offend him with impunity.

With peace abroad and tranquillity at home, he had now an opportunity of gratifying his inclination and soothing his conscience by the performance of works of piety and devotion. Churches and chapels, dedicated to the Virgin and various saints arose at his command in all parts of the kingdom, as tokens of gratitude for the uniform good fortune that had attended all his enterprises, for the victories which had shed lustre on his name, and for the care which had covered his head in the day of battle, and sheltered him from the snares of his enemies. There was still, however, one duty which he longed to fulfil, ere he rested from his labours,—to aid in rescuing the Holy Land from the infidels. Peter the Hermit was at this time horrifying all Europe by his account of the terrible indignities which the Christians who sought to worship at the tomb of Christ were receiving at the hands of the infidels. Ambassadors were sent to Ladislaus from the Crusaders, solemnly invoking his aid in their enterprise, for the defence of the religion of which he had all his life shown himself so devout a professor. He listened to their tale with tears and lamentations, and dismissed them with the promise that during that very year he would set out for Palestine, with as large a force as he could collect. He therefore apprized his nephew, the king of Bohemia, of his intention, and desired him to prepare to join him with all the troops at his command. Conrad had no sooner commenced to carry out his instructions, than he was obliged to defend his crown against a competitor of his own blood, who seized Prague in the night, and with the consent of the archbishop, proclaimed himself king. Ladislaus instantly marched to his assistance, but on the way, sickened and died, bequeathing his kingdom to his nephew Almos. He was buried in the church of Varadin (1095), which he himself had founded, with extraordinary pomp and solemnity, and so great was his reputation for sanctity of life, that for a long period miracles were believed by the common people to have been performed at his tomb, as at the tomb of a saint.

Almos did not retain the crown more than a few days. His elder brother, Coloman, whom Ladislaus had compelled to enter the church, but who had fled into Poland to avoid performing the duties of his office, returned to claim his birthright, and it was surrendered to him without a murmur.

Up to this period Hungary had been almost isolated from the rest of Europe. She was the youngest of the nations which had risen upon the ruins of the Roman Empire, and the difference of language and manners, and the reminiscences which the more civilised states of the south and west retained of the ferocity of the inhabitants, combined to cut off all communication between them and the Magyars. The Crusades were now about to break down this barrier, and, by the diffusion of geographical information, to place her among the great family of Christian nations.

CHAPTER V.

DYNASTY OF ARPAD CONTINUED.

A.D. 1095—1301.

It was in the reign of Coloman that the army of the Crusaders first appeared upon the frontiers of Hungary. The preachings of Peter the Hermit, and of the Pope, had done their work, and throughout the whole of Europe, an eager desire pervaded all classes of men to march against the Saracens, for the rescue of the Holy Sepulchre. The serfs hoped by these means to escape from bondage; the debtor to avoid the claims of his creditor; the superstitious and fanatical (and who was not?) to atone for a multitude of sins; the warrior to crown himself with military glory in a conflict which religion sanctified; and the licentious luxuriated in the marvellous stories which pilgrims had told of the passing splendour of Saracen palaces, the gold, and silver, and silk brocade which adorned them, the flavour of the Greek wines, and the beauty of the eastern women. None was to fear danger, for the might of the foe would be feeble before him who fought for the Lord; none was to fear want, for he who won the Lord was abundantly rich; no one was to be kept at home by the tears of those he was leaving behind, for the grace of the Lord would abundantly protect them. During the whole winter of 1095-6, Europe resounded with the bustle of preparation. The demand for horses, arms, and accoutrements was so great, that the prices of these articles rose enormously, while so numerous were the sales of houses, lands, and goods, that their value was depreciated in an equal degree. Those who were prevented from joining the expedition by age, or infirmity, or any other cause, contributed money towards paying the expenses. The 15th of August, 1096, had been fixed by the Council of Clermont as the day on which the army should commence its march; but so great was the enthusiasm, that when spring arrived, the great bulk of the lower orders could be restrained no longer, but prepared to set out forthwith.

"The husbandman," says the old chronicle, "let the plough stand, the herdsman the cattle, the wife ran with the cradle, the monk out of the cloister, the nuns too were among the rest." The people abandoned their towns and villages, and encamped in tents and booths, awaiting the signal to march. And in these assemblies, vice, disorder and profligacy were mingled with piety and sanctity and military ardour in strange confusion. The runaway debtor was seen side-by-side with the armed gentleman, who had fought in fifty tournays; the chaste and devout virgin, with the unholy prostitute, but both in male attire.

In the month of May, thousands assembled in the province of Lorraine of those who had assumed the cross, for the most part rabble, whom the princes had rejected, or those whose impatient zeal could abide no longer delay. So great was their ignorance, that when they got out of the immediate neighbourhood in which they lived, every castle or town they saw, they cried, "Is that Jerusalem?" Eight knights only appeared amongst them, one of whom, Walter the Penniless, led fifteen thousand footmen from France. At Cologne he and his followers abandoned the Hermit and pushed on for Hungary. Neither Coloman nor his subjects had ever shown any great enthusiasm for the holy war, but nevertheless, when Walter and his horde presented themselves on the frontier, and craved a free passage and market, their requests were readily granted, and they passed on unmolested until they reached Bulgaria, a province at that time in subjection to the Greek emperor. Their misery and distress increasing at every mile of the journey their turbulence and licentiousness increased at the same time, and the governor of Belgrade, having refused to furnish them with a provision market, they spread themselves over the surrounding country, burnt the houses, carried off the sheep and cattle, and slaughtered such of the inhabitants as offered any resistance. The Bulgarian peasantry instantly rose in arms on every side, * and falling upon Walter's soldiery in the midst of their revelry, and when laden with booty, slew great numbers of them. Sixty Crusaders perished in the midst of the flames in a church in which they had sought an asylum, and the others found safety only in flight. Walter made his escape with a chosen few, and pursued his march through trackless forests, suffering incredible hardships, till he arrived at Nissa, the governor of which afforded him and his followers food and clothing, and guides to lead them on to Constantinople, where quarters were given them outside the walls, to await the arrival of Peter the Hermit. †

The latter, having traversed Bavaria and Austria, arrived in safety at the gates of a city called Sempronia by the Romans, and Soprony by the Hungarians, and, at the present day, Oedenburg. From this he sent ambassadors to Coloman, to ask a free passage through his dominions, which was granted him upon condition that the Crusaders kept to the road, and paid for their provisions. Peter then led his forces towards the western point of the great lake Balaton, descended into the valley of the Drave, and then, marching along the banks of the Danube, arrived without obstacle at Semlin, to which the pilgrims gave the name of Mala Villa, on account of the misfortunes which there befel them.

Coloman appears to have taken some very natural precautions against the excesses of the Crusaders, which Peter, instead of endeavouring to preserve discipline, magnified into a plot against him and against his followers. The report got abroad that the Hungarians had determined to attack them upon one side of the river and the Bulgarians upon the other, and while in a state of alarm, their

* Keightley's "Crusaders," vol. i. p. 41.

† Michaud's "Histoire des Croisades," tom. i. p. 100.

fears were confirmed and their anger roused by the sight of the arms and clothes of sixteen Crusaders, whom they supposed to have been murdered,—suspended outside the walls of Semlin. The trumpets were instantly sounded, the pilgrims seized their arms and flew to the assault; the garrison, taken by surprise, abandoned their post and fled, and the inhabitants, having quitted the town and taken refuge upon a height, defended upon one side by rocks and woods, and on the other by the Danube, were pursued to their retreat, and more than 4,000

COLOMAN.

barbarously slaughtered, and the dead bodies, floating down the river, brought the first news of the massacre to Belgrade.

The victors remained in the town for five days, feasting on the provisions and plundering the houses. At last a monk, settled in Hungary, brought them the alarming tidings that Coloman was approaching, with an army of 100,000 men, to avenge the slaughter of his subjects. The Crusaders, who fought under the influence of blind fury, were totally wanting in real courage, and their leader possessed a far greater amount of enthusiasm than of military skill. They, therefore, immediately collected boats, formed rafts of timber, and reached the other side of the lake, not, however, without loss, as the Bulgarians, moving about in light canoes, shot many of them with their arrows. After suffering great misery and loss, they at last reached Constantinople, where Alexis, the Greek emperor, strongly advised them to await the approach of the arrival of the princes and commanders, who were to lead the most effective and best organized of the soldiers of the cross. This was salutary counsel, and the Hermit afterwards had reason to regret that he did not take it; but the great chiefs were not yet ready to set out, and other bands were still to precede them on their march, with the same want of discipline, and the same blind zeal.

A priest, named Gotschalk, had preached the crusade in many of the German provinces. Incited by his harangues, about 20,000 men assembled in arms and took an oath to fight against the infidels. Gotschalk, who, like Peter the Hermit, was looked upon as a man inspired by God, was chosen to lead them. Towards the end of the summer they reached Hungary, and as the vintage had been plentiful, they found abundant temptation to excess. In the midst of their debauchery, they forgot alike the cause to which they were engaged, the motives that had induced them to leave their homes, and the object they had in view; and plunder, rape, and murder marked every step of their march. Coloman, in whom a courageous spirit was concealed beneath a feeble and deformed body, assembled a large body of troops to restrain their violence and outrages. But the soldiers of Gotschalk were not wanting in valour, and defended themselves so vigorously that the Hungarians began to fear that, if driven to desperation, they might prove more than a match for them, and therefore resolved to have recourse to stratagem to subdue them. Coloman's general therefore pretended to desire a cessation of hostilities, and the Hungarian chiefs entered the camp of the Crusaders as friends. The Germans laid aside their arms in perfect confidence, but no sooner had they done so, than, on a signal being given, the Hungarians fell upon them and slaughtered them without mercy.

We should feel some surprise in reading of these excesses of the first Crusaders, if we failed to remember that they belonged to the lowest and most degraded class of the people. The civil wars, which at that time were of daily occurrence in every country on the continent, had created great numbers of vagabonds and adventurers, who wandered from place to place, subsisting upon whatever chance or robbery threw in their way. Germany was the scene of more troubles than any part of western Europe, and was consequently full of men brought up in brigandage —the very scum of society—and almost all these enrolled themselves under the banner of the cross, and carried with them into the holy war the licentious and mutinous spirit which had animated them in their native land.*

The notion which at first possessed the Crusaders was that they were bound only to war against the Saracens, for the delivery of the Holy Sepulchre; but they

* Keightley's "Crusaders," vol. i, p. 54.

soon began to believe, that, as soldiers of Christ, it was their duty to commence hostilities against His enemies wherever they met with them. "What!" they cried, "what! are we going to seek the enemies of God beyond the seas, when the Jews, His most cruel enemies, are close at hand?" And upon the poor Jews fell all the weight of their fanaticism. In many of the chief towns of Germany—Worms, Treves, Mentz, and Spires—they were massacred *en masse;* from the child unborn to the toothless old man—none were spared. When this pious duty had been performed, the scattered bands who had been engaged in it united under the command of a certain Count Emico, and a man named William the Carpenter, so called from the weight of his blows, and some other knights of evil fame, noted for deeds of violence and cruelty. At their head were carried a goose and a he-goat, which they believed to be filled with the Holy Ghost, and on whose aid they relied for safety and success. On they went, burning, plundering, robbing, massacring, until they arrived at Mersehurgh, a town on the confines of Hungary. They threw a bridge across the Danube, and attacked the town. Coloman was within, and, hearing that the Crusaders had mounted the walls, he was preparing for flight, when a panic seized them, and they fled precipitately, leaving their baggage behind. The Hungarians pursued them, and slaughtered great numbers; those who escaped returned home, or joined other armies of pilgrims in Germany or Apulia. Count Emico died in Germany; and the old traditions of the country related that long afterwards the ghosts of himself and many of his companions might be seen at night in the neighbourhood of Worms, cased in red-hot armour, uttering the most fearful groans, and imploring the prayers and alms of the faithful to deliver them from their torments.

The main body of the Crusaders at last prepared to march. The misfortunes which had befallen the forces which had preceded them furnished a useful warning of the dangers of neglect of discipline. Consequently, when Godfrey of Bouillon and the other distinguished leaders began their journey, they maintained the strictest order, and inflicted instant punishment upon all who were found guilty of any misdemeanour in the countries through which they passed. When they arrived upon the confines of Hungary, Godfrey sent forward to Coloman twelve knights, who were instructed to say that they had heard that several pilgrims had lost their lives in his dominions; and that they were come to avenge them, if they had perished unjustly, but if otherwise they would exercise no hostilities. Coloman, in reply, gave a faithful account of the atrocities which the pilgrims had committed, and in the following letter expressed his desire for an interview with the duke:—* "King Coloman sends greeting to the Duke of Bouillon and to all the Christians. Thy reputation, my dear duke, hath assured me that thou art a powerful and just man in thine own country, and pious and honourable wherever thou goest, esteemed and praised by all who know thee. I, also, have always

* Michaud's "Hist. des Croisades," vol. i. p. 109.

loved thee, and my chief desire at present is to see thee, and to know thee."* Godfrey consented to the interview, and on the appointed day repaired to the Castle of Leperon with three hundred nobles, where the king advanced to meet him. All difficulties were speedily arranged; Coloman granted a free passage and a market, but required that Godfrey's brother, Baldwin, and his wife and attendants, should be given as hostages for the fulfilment of their agreement. Baldwin, either suspicious of danger, or scorning to become a pledge, positively refused to consent. "Then," said the duke, "I will be the hostage myself, in reliance upon the honour of the king and the good conduct of the pilgrims." Baldwin was thus shamed into compliance. The Hungarians were commanded to furnish a market, and to sell the provisions with good weight and measure, and the pilgrims were strictly enjoined by their chiefs to abstain from plunder on pain of death. The stipulations were strictly observed upon both sides. The Crusaders pursued their march in peace to the frontier, where the Hungarian king took an affectionate leave of the duke, and offered up prayers for the success of his enterprise.

Coloman, who, from his love of learning, was surnamed Bibliophilus, or the *book-lover*, had his attention speedily called away from the Crusaders to affairs of no less importance in Croatia. That kingdom, it may be remembered, had been secured to Helena, the widow of Peter Crecimir, a daughter of Bela, king of Hungary, by the arms of Ladislaus. When she found herself firmly established upon the throne, she chose, as her principal adviser, Almos, the nephew of Ladislaus. On the death of the queen, Ladislaus took possession of her dominions by the right of succession and of conquest; but, in place of incorporating them with Hungary, bestowed them upon Almos, as a kingdom dependent upon the Hungarian crown.

In Coloman's reign, a noble named Peter laid claim to the supreme power, and the former took up arms for his subjugation. In a battle lost by the Croats, Peter was slain, and the Hungarian king finally abolished royalty in that country, and annexed it to his own dominions. Dalmatia, which had been bought back by Alexis, the Grecian emperor, and placed under the protectorate of the Doge of Venice, Vitale Fallieri, had been invaded by the Normans. The Venetians, whose land forces were but feeble, sought aid from Coloman, who after having expelled the Normans, carried his arms as far as Apulia, where Duke Roger was forced to agree to a treaty, the terms of which were dictated by his enemies. From that time (1096), Dalmatia became a part of Hungary, and Coloman, having been crowned king of Croatia and Dalmatia, re-organised the ancient rights of the Dalmatian people. Quarrels with the Venetians and Russians, which, neither in their details nor in their results, possess much historical interest, save that in one of the battles with the Venetians, touching the territory of Dalmatia, the Doge Ordalafa Fallieri

* "La Hongrie Historique," p. 28.

was slain—occupied the remainder of Coloman's life. After long wars and intrigues with Almos, his youngest brother, the latter fell into his hands, and with barbarous cruelty he deprived both him and his son Bela of sight. The king died soon after, in 1114, in the twenty-fifth year of his reign, which, by his warlike exploits abroad and diligent and wise attention to the arts of peace at home, would have been dignified and glorified, if it had not been stained by this domestic tragedy. He left his crown to his son Stephen II

When Stephen ascended the throne he was but a beardless boy,and a council of magnates was appointed to advise him, and under their auspices the affairs of government were administered for nearly eight years with great wisdom and discretion. No sooner had the king attained his majority, however, than he asserted all his prerogative with an impetuosity that alarmed and astonished his subjects, and procured for him, the surname of *the Lightning*. In pride, caprice, and cruelty, he was fully equal to his father, and in promptness for war he was in nowise his inferior. The Venetians had began to ravage Dalmatia, and he instantly resolved to chastise them for their insolence, and in the ninth year of his reign marched an army into that province, where he was received by the inhabitants with joyful acclamations, and having sent reinforcements to the garrisons of all the towns, he assured the people of his watchful care and protection, and returned into Hungary. He then turned his arms against the Poles, whom he accused of offering many insults to his father in times of difficulty and danger, and of having encroached upon the frontier, wreaked vengeance upon them by laying waste the country for many miles with fire and sword, and carried off a great number of captives.

Disputes next arose with the king or duke of Bohemia, whom Stephen invited to an interview, at which their mutual differences might, if possible, be amicably settled. A Hungarian refugee in Bohemia, wishing, if possible, to prolong the discord between the two courts, wrote to each of the monarchs, informing him that the other had formed a plot to carry him off by force from the place of meeting, and warned him against coming without a guard. The consequence was, that each appeared attended by a large armed force, and incensed by the other's treachery, their followers were not long in coming to blows. The Hungarians, seized with a panic, speedily took to flight, and rode furiously into the camp. The king and his officers, taken by surprise, mounted their horses and galloped off the field in dismay. The palatine at this moment came up with a reserve, and staying the fugitives, restored the fortune of the day. After a sharp and murderous encounter the Bohemians gave way and fled, and the palatine and his companions had the satisfaction of hearing from the lips of Stephen a warm eulogium upon their valour and watchfulness. The mistake was afterwards discovered, but too late to inflict upon Soltha, the cause of all the disturbance and loss of life, the punishment which his deceit merited, as he had secured his safety by timely flight.

The king, by this time as impetuous in his passions as in his policy, was exciting great and general indignation by the notorious licentiousness of his manners, by which the ladies of some of the highest families in the land were daily subjected to insult and outrage. The magnates urged him strongly to marry, and to their great surprise, he, without much hesitation, signified his intention of complying with their request, and shortly after espoused the daughter of Robert of Guiscard, the Norman duke of Sicily and Apulia, a woman famous for her beauty and virtue. The nuptials were celebrated with great pomp; but scarcely had they been concluded, when he prepared to interfere in a quarrel between two rival claimants of the ducal throne in Russia, one of whom claimed his aid. But so opposed were the magnates to any intervention in a dispute which in nowise concerned Hungary, and which, however it might be decided, could bring her no advantage, that he was compelled to abandon the enterprise, even after he had entered the Russian territory.

He next turned his army against the Greek empire, his indignation being roused by a domestic broil, which, if had not given rise to a bloody war, history might well have passed over in silence. Ladislaus had given his daughter Prisca in marriage to Kalo (John), the son and colleague of the Greek emperor Alexis Comnenus. This monarch thought fit upon one occasion to apply to Stephen the epithets "inhuman" and "cruel," which his wife, jealous of her kinsman's honour, instantly repelled and retorted, whereupon her lord, forgetful of his dignity, inflicted upon her a severe beating. She appears to have taken the chastisement greatly to heart, as she immediately laid her grievance before the Hungarian king, who resolved to avenge the insult by force of arms, and invaded the emperor's dominions, laying them waste with fire and sword. The Hungarians, after sustaining several severe reverses from the disciplined phalanxes of the Greek infantry, were fain to sue for peace, which was at last made, when each party had done the other vast injury without obtaining any real advantage for itself. During the campaign, Stephen distinguished himself by his merciless cruelty to the captives, upon whom he heaped every indignity that ingenuity could devise or hatred prompt. His blind old uncle, Almos, he banished into Macedonia, where he was cordially received by the Greeks, and lived many years in dignified retirement, affording shelter and hospitality to all those of his countrymen, whom the intrigues of faction or the displeasure of the monarch had driven from their native land.

When Stephen found his end approaching, and that he would, in all probability, die childless, he sent for his cousin Bela, whom his father had cruelly blinded, adopted him as his son, and named him his heir. This was his last public act of importance. He died in the eighteenth year of his reign, in 1131.

Bela II., though blind, proved himself a man of signal ability. He incorporated Bosnia with Hungary, and expelled the Venetians from many seaports on the

Adriatic, of which, during the closing years of the late king's reign, they had taken possession. He also successfully suppressed a combination formed against him by the Poles and Russians by the machinations of Borick, an illegitimate son of the late king. He left four sons, Geysa, Ladislaus, Stephen, and Almos, the eldest of whom, Geysa II., succeeded him, in 1141.

Geysa had not attained the age of manhood when he ascended the throne, but he already gave evidences of great ability, combined with great gentleness and humanity. He was crowned with great pomp at Alba, on St. Cecilia's day, and immediately chose for his ministers some of the ablest men in the kingdom. In the very first year of his reign, a war broke out with Germany, of which Austria, then as now, restless and grasping, was said to be the cause. Henry, duke of Austria, learning that a mere boy had succeeded to the crown of Hungary, thought this would be a favourable opportunity for making a descent upon his territory and appropriating to himself whatever fortune might throw in his way. He was at that period enabled to bring a large auxiliary force into the field, as he was guardian of Henry the Lion, a minor, who ruled over Saxony and Bavaria, and whose troops he could employ in the furtherance of his designs. His first step was to surprise and capture Presburg, a town on the frontier, which was considered the key of Hungary. When the news reached the court, the consternation was great. The diet was instantly summoned, and by their advice the king ordered a general levy of all the forces of the country for its defence against the invaders. The insurrection and the Király Sereg instantly rose in arms in answer to the appeal, and called upon the young king with the utmost enthusiasm to lead them against the enemy. Upon reaching the frontier, they found the Germans drawn up in order of battle to receive them. Geysa instantly gave the signal for action, though his own army was inferior in number. The engagement was long and bloody, and for a great length of time it seemed doubtful to which side fortune would assign the victory. The Germans fought under the eye of their leader, who was himself present in the heat of the encounter, encouraging them by his voice and example; and their heavy cavalry seemed several times on the point of overwhelming the light squadrons of the Magyars. But the fate of Hungary depended on the issue; and the hussars, returning again and again to the charge, flung themselves on the enemy with a reckless hardihood which at last began to take effect, and Henry's veteran legions—many of them grown grey in the western wars—turned and fled, and a general route followed, in which the duke had great difficulty in escaping. Seven thousand Germans were left dead upon the field, and of the Hungarians not more than three thousand. The spoils of the vanquished were appropriated by Geysa to the endowment of churches, and the offering of masses for the repose of the souls of the slain.

A short time after this battle, the preaching of St. Bernard aroused in the minds of the people of France and Germany the desire for another crusade. It was represented to them that Godfrey and Tancred, and their small bands of followers, who held the holy places in Palestine against hosts of infidels, were in danger of being overwhelmed by their adversaries, if they did not receive speedy succour. Great excitement was soon raised, and the scenes which occurred in 1096 were now enacted over again. The principal leaders of the second expedition were Louis VII. of France, and Conrad, emperor of Germany. The latter led his forces through Hungary; and notwithstanding the sacred character of the mission upon which he was engaged, he could ill conceal his lurking enmity to the Magyars. Although Geysa had cheerfully granted him a free passage, the German troops extorted money from the monasteries and churches upon their way, and committed various outrages upon the peasantry.

Louis of France soon after passed along the same route, but he carefully restrained the pilgrims from outraging the hospitality which had been granted them. The fate that awaited them was terrible: wasted by pestilence, famine, thirst, and the arrows of the enemy, they led back their shattered forces in 1152, without having attained one object for which they had set out.

The Crusaders had hardly passed on their way, when more troubles arose on the side of the Russians, who ever seemed weary of their frozen wastes, and longing to precipitate themselves upon their neighbours. They were, as usual, defeated.

Under the reign of Geysa II., emigrants from Germany and Flanders settled in Sepucza in the north of Hungary, where they formed a distinct people, and were governed by their own counts. This was another addition to the evils of divided races, so detrimental to Hungarian nationality. When Stephen III. ascended the throne, his younger brother, Bela, was named by the emperor of the East heir presumptive to the Byzantine empire, and received in possession the duchies of Sirmia, Sclavonia, and Croatia. But afterwards, in consequence of the empress giving birth to a son, his claim was destroyed, and he became simply king of Hungary. Some time afterwards, troubles began to break out in Gallicia, now known as Poland; and the country was put under the protection of the king of Hungary. In 1188, Bela III. asserted this claim against Casmir, the old duke of Gallicia, and for some time the Hungarian king bore also the title of king of Poland. It was in virtue of this right (if right it may be called) that Austria took part in the dismemberment of that unfortunate country. Bela III. married, as his second wife, Margaret, daughter of Louis VII., king of France. This lady was the means of introducing into Hungary a great deal of the refinement and elegance which, even at that early period, distinguished the French court. The Magyar youth began to repair to Paris to complete their education and study foreign manners; and a university, upon the model of that of Paris, was established in Vesprim, a central town of Hungary. After the death of Bela, Henry VI., emperor of Germany, determined upon sending an army to aid the Crusaders in Palestine. At the head of the quota furnished by Hungary, Margaret, the youthful widow, set out in person. What was her motive for this strange under-

MARGARET, QUEEN OF HUNGARY, SETTING OUT FOR PALESTINE.

taking we know not, unless it were that weary longing for rest and consolation in another world, which finely-wrought natures then thought purchaseable only by privation and toil in this. But this picture of female youth and beauty setting out upon a distant and perilous expedition, surrounded by the fierce warriors of the cross, is one of those pleasing gleams of light which now and then shoot across the heavy darkness of the middle ages. Margaret died in Palestine.

Emeric, who succeeded Bela III., followed up the conquests of his predecessor, and subdued Bulgaria and Servia. Andrew, a brother of the king, governed Croatia, as a vassal of the Hungarian crown.

We have now arrived at one of the most memorable periods in the history of Hungary, that which witnessed the reform of the constitution. The close resemblance existing between this important event and the grant of our own Magna Charta by King John, must possess the deepest interest for every English reader. Notwithstanding the foreign wars and intestine broils to which Hungary had for centuries been a prey, the real power of the government rested entirely in the hands of the king. The great dignitaries of the state did not hold their offices in hereditary succession, or even for life. They could be at any moment deprived of them for no better reason than the sovereign's pleasure; but the very fact of their meeting together in the diet, or great council of the nation, secured to them influence, which was becoming every day more and more powerful, and promised at no distant day the right, and perhaps the power, of taking exception to the arbitary acts of the monarch. On the other hand the organisation of the counties was going to decay, though it formed the best bulwark against domestic tyranny or foreign invasion. Things were in this position, when Andrew II., surnamed Hierosolymitanus, a feeble and vain prince, ascended the throne. He carried on war for a considerable length of time against the Russians and the Saracens in the Holy Land, without reflecting upon the evils caused by his absence from his dominions, and the lavish expenditure of blood and treasure which his long contests entailed upon the kingdom. Upon his return he found the affections of the people entirely alienated, and was astonished by the loud and general outcry raised on every side against his extravagance. His quarrels with his son Bela still further increased the number of his enemies. His queen, Gertrude, a woman of very masculine disposition, but who had acquired this manly vigour at the expense of her woman's tenderness and truth, sought to allay the storm by seizing upon the reins of government in her own name. Her unfaithfulness to the instincts of her sex, and to the commonest dictates of honour and religion, wrought her own and her husband's ruin. She encouraged and aided her brother in an attempt to seduce the wife of a proud and haughty noble, Benedict Bor (the famous Bank Ban) the palatine of the kingdom. Enraged at the insult and dishonour, Benedict rushed into the palace, followed by some friends, and struck the queen dead on the spot. The assassins were executed, but this only irritated the malcontents still more. Andrew lost all authority, and with characteristic imbecility, applied to the Pope to re-establish tranquillity. After a long struggle, the prince Bela undertook to act as mediator between the contending parties; and through his instrumentality, important concessions were obtained from the king, and ratified by him at a diet held in 1231. He acknowledged the legislative assemblies to have the same rights as himself, and he confessed that those privileges of the nobility, which Saint Stephen had established upon a firm basis, but which his successors had failed to recognise fully, had been violated by him also. He solemnly confirmed in their fullest extent all the political privileges claimed by the nobles and the free inhabitants of the country, with the addition of the following clause:—"That every time that the king or his descendants should violate the privileges of the Magyar nation, the nobles should be at liberty to rise up, sword in hand, to oppose this breach of the law, without being liable to the charge of high treason." This was a concession at the same time just and dangerous. The right of resistance should be ever present to the eyes of the government; but the people should never look upon it, save as the closing scene in a long vista of unavailing remonstrance and entreaty. In addition to the confirmation of their old privileges, the Magyar aristocracy obtained some new ones. They were declared free of taxes, and none of its members could be placed under arrest except for clearly proved violations of law. They were obliged to arm at their own expense, and attend the king in warlike array as far as the frontiers of their own country; but, if farther, the sovereign should bear the cost. The latter was forbidden to make any office or employment hereditary, or to commit the administration of the finances to Jews or Mahometans; and it was strictly stipulated that a diet should every year be convoked upon St. Stephen's day. All these articles, thirty-one in number, were united in a code, and became the basis of the aristo-democratic constitution, which prevailed in Hungary, with slight modifications, up to the close of the late war, commonly called *Bulla Aurea*, or the "Golden Bull." Andrew was the first Magyar king who was obliged to take an oath, at his coronation, to be faithful to the constitution. Hungary was thus one of the first countries in Europe to obtain effectual guarantees for her liberty; and although her Bulla Aurea, like our Magna Charta, bears unmistakable marks of its feudal origin, it has, nevertheless, every claim to be considered a reform of true and lasting value. It must not be forgotten that the term "Magyar nobles," or "free men," at that time included the whole of the conquering nation.

Bela IV. succeeded to his father, Andrew II. After he had ascended the throne, he showed great force of character, but, at the same time, a great leaning to arbitrary measures. A calamity fell upon Hungary during his reign, from the effects of which she did not recover for many generations. A tribe of the Hunnic race arose about this time, and rendered itself powerful by its conquests under the leadership of its chief, Mogol, or Mogul, whose name it assumed. Under one of his successors, Zengis Khan, it spread terror through the whole of Asia; but that quarter of the world not proving enough to satisfy its ambition, it precipitated itself upon Europe. Poland and Russia bore the first shock of the invasion, but it soon spread to the plains of Hungary, and left them waste and silent as a

HUNGARIAN DIET ON THE PLAIN OF RAKOS.

pathless desert. After having massacred great numbers of the population, the Moguls retreated, carrying with them thousands of captives.

Under this terrible calamity, Bela sought in vain for assistance from the duke of Austria. Hungary was covered with dead bodies and ruined houses, but the king was not discouraged. He introduced a number of German colonists for the cultivation of the soil, and appealed to the people to support him in the execution of the measures designed to ensure their own safety.

Amongst a number of other useful measures, he provided for the regular meeting of the county assemblies. These assemblies were one of the most important of the privileges of the Hungarian people. Their rights, their duties, and their connexion with the supreme power of the state, bore, as we have already said, a close resemblance to those of the states of the American Union. The sovereign authority was vested in the king and the diet with regard to questions of general interest only. If the student, reading of the thousand perils and disasters through which the Magyar nation has passed, unparalleled for their number and magnitude in the history of the world, should ask what was the safeguard of Hungarian liberty while undergoing an ordeal so trying, we can give him no other answer than refer him to the county assemblies. The sittings were all in public, and the eyes of the country were upon all the proceedings. There was the highest of all motives for a man's doing his duty fearlessly. The king or the minister might sway or corrupt the diet, but his labour was in vain whilst the freely elected representatives of the people were meeting in every county to watch over the public liberty, and whose interests and sympathies coinciding with those of their constituencies, in the midst of whom they lived and deliberated, were the most effectual guarantees against any betrayal of the confidence reposed in them. Individuals may be traitors, but no treacherous representative body, save the Irish parliament, has ever been heard of in history. It was in these assemblies that the Hungarians received that political education which has rendered them so much superior to all the nations of eastern Europe. The happy distinction between the legislative and executive powers, the best safeguard of freedom, was recognised by them before any other people in the world.

Bela, when he had in some measure repaired the disasters inflicted by the famine and the invasion, proceeded to chastise Austria for her refusal to assist him in his time of need. Frederic, the archduke, was killed in the campaign, and by a treaty entered into at its close, Hungary obtained the whole of Styria, and an extension of the frontiers of Dalmatia. Bulgaria was also incorporated with the Magyar kingdom as a dependent province. A short time afterwards the Moguls again appeared, but were this time defeated with tremendous slaughter, 30,000 men being killed in one battle.

It is at this epoch that the house of Hapsburgh, which was destined to exercise so baneful an influence upon the future of the Hungarian nation, first appears upon the scene. There was an implacable rivalry going on between Rodolph of Hapsburgh and Ottochar, the rightful king of Bohemia, and the duke of Austria. The former sought the aid of the Magyar king, and by means of it expelled his antagonist from his dominions, and laid the foundation of his own dynasty. It was the eagle lending his plume to wing the arrow that was to drink his own life-blood. The history of the relations of the Hapsburgh family with the Magyars, Kossuth has well designated, "a continued perjury."

All the national writers agree in their opinion of the great merits of Bela IV. During his long reign he surrounded himself and his kingdom with glory. No other prince has ever encountered greater difficulties, and none ever surmounted them with so much courage and ability. Before his death he gave his grand-daughter, Mary, in marriage to Charles Martel, prince of Salerno, a scion of the house of Austria—an alliance which paved the way for the accession of a branch of this French family to the Hungarian throne.

There is nothing worthy of remark in the reigns of his successors, until we come to Andrew III., the last of the dynasty of Arpad. The Pope, who considered Hungary a fief of the Holy See, opposed his election, and claimed the crown for Charles Martel, to whom we have just been referring. Rodolph of Hapsburgh, on the other hand, wished to place his son Albert upon the throne. Andrew III. espoused Agnes of Austria, and it is upon this marriage that Austria afterwards based her pretensions to the Magyar crown.

With a view of bringing about a reconciliation between the contending parties in these disputes, the king convened a grand diet of the nation upon the plain of Rakos. This was the first time the great assembly of the Magyars was held in the open air. It is curious to find this singular custom equally prevalent amongst the Poles and Hungarians. The nobles of both countries met on horseback, to elect a king, upon a vast meadow, clothed in their most splendid garments, a single gentleman often carrying his whole fortune in his own accoutrements, and the rich housings of his steed. There are a number of interesting circumstances, however, in connexion with the Polish Diet, into which at present it is not our province to enter.

Andrew III. died in 1301 without any heir, and with him ended the dynasty of Arpad.

At this period the Hungarian people had made no inconsiderable amount of progress, not in political knowledge only, but in science and the industrial arts. St. Stephen had declared the inviolability of private property, and decreed its transmission from one generation to another by hereditary descent. The Magyars did not reserve to themselves alone the enjoyment of these political rights and liberties. Amongst the free inhabitants of their country were comprised all those stranger populations who had voluntarily submitted to their rule, and even the immigrants who had more recently entered their territory, and claimed to be considered as their guests. Those only who were taken with arms in their hands, and those of the Hungarians who were convicted of theft or adultery, who sought to escape from military service, or who remained obstinately attached to paganism, after the rest of the nation had embraced Christianity, were condemned to a state of slavery or serfdom. The laws against stealing, and against the illicit intercourse of the sexes, were more than ordinarily severe; and any freeman who was detected in an amorous intrigue with the domestic of another was sentenced to have his head shaved. Although the sale of women was strictly forbidden after the introduction of Christianity, these rigorous measures were indispensably necessary to root out the old custom of polygamy. The military superintendents (*ewreok*) formed a police service, and travellers were obliged to be provided with a passport or safe conduct. Royal messengers kept up postal communication between all parts of the kingdom, and each county was obliged to furnish them with relays of horses. This was the origin of those post-houses (*vorspann*) which are seen in every part of the country and of which the tourist is obliged to avail himself at the present day. The expenses of the government were defrayed by the revenues of the royal domains, that is, by the cultivation of the crown lands, and the produce of the salt and gold mines, and by the imposition of a small duty upon certain articles sold in the markets. The administration of the finances was conducted with great prudence and ability. As in western Europe, the towns arose, in nearly every case, in the neighbourhood of the great fortresses or castles, and became enlarged and enriched by the extension of industrial employment, and the influx of foreign colonists; the Hungarians, in general, preferring living in the open country. Many of these towns became in process of time independent of the chatelain, or lord of the castle, and were then called *free* or *royal*. All strangers paid a tax, by way of compensation for the protection afforded them, and their share in the political privileges, and thus greatly augmented the revenue. The consequence of this fixed internal organisation, and the security afforded to labour and property, was a rapid increase in the commerce and manufactures of the kingdom. The agricultural produce was every year more than sufficient for home consumption, and the utmost attention was given by the government to the promotion of industrial employment. St. Stephen sent shoemakers, carpenters, wheelwrights, &c., at his own expense, through most of the towns in his dominions, for the purpose of imparting a knowledge of the manual arts to those desirous of acquiring them. The Magyars were celebrated at an early period for their skill in tanning, and Hungarian leather was in great demand all over Europe; they excelled also in dressing the furs, which formed part of their rich national costume. Their foreign commerce was also extensive. Their merchants had large counting and warehouses at Constantinople for carrying on their trade with the East. They supplied the northern countries with linen, woollen cloth, and arms, and the Germans with corn, cattle, and ale. They received their spices and other foreign products from Venice and Dalmatia, and supported a powerful and well-manned navy for the protection of their commerce.

The foregoing chapters have shown us a barbarous, nomadic people, from the central plains of Asia, possessing all the coarseness and unbridled passion of the savage state, but full of courage, energy, and self-confidence, precipitating itself upon the worn-out civilisation of the Roman empire, and conquering new seats in the heart of another hemisphere. From the chaos which succeeded the breaking up of the old order of things, it arose a young and hardy nation, girding its loins to run the race of civilisation and progress with the other races of modern Europe. We have seen its conversion to the mild doctrines of Christianity; and have watched with interest its growth and improvement in the arts of peace, and its close adherence to the older and sterner virtues of the warrior. We have seen it every day coming out stronger and more self-reliant from the rude shocks and rough turmoils of the middle ages, and gradually building up a constitutional monarchy like our own,—an undertaking the more difficult, because there was then no model to guide in the formation of free institutions. The progress has been hitherto slow, and it may be, at times painful, but always successful. We have now arrived at the era of power, influence, and glory, in which Hungary was the bulwark of Europe against the terrible assaults of the Turks, and its leader in arts, and law, and commerce.

When the Magyars placed Almos, the son of Arpad, upon the throne, it was not so much a recognition of his hereditary right to the succession, as an acknowledgment of the great services of his father, and an expression of their veneration for his talents and virtue. From the same motives they gave up entirely their undoubted right to elect their monarchs, as long as there remained a scion of the house of Arpad to wear the crown; but when, at the death of Andrew III., the dynasty became extinct, they resumed the exercise of their prerogative, and four candidates immediately appeared to claim their suffrages. Two of them, Venceslas and Otho, obtained it one after the other, not so much from their intrinsic merits, as because the remaining candidate, Charles Robert of Anjou, was the favourite of the Pope, who endeavoured to procure his election by lavish threats of excommunication and anathema. The two former, however, having been successively driven from the kingdom, the Magyars succeeded in overcoming their repugnance towards Charles as the nominee of the Holy See, and chose him as their king. Their dislike to him arose from the obnoxious interference with their constitutional privileges made on his behalf by the Pope, whose sympathies and interests have in all ages so often run counter to those of the people.

CHAPTER VI.

ACCESSION OF THE HOUSE OF ANJOU.—CHARLES ROBERT.

Charles was the son of Charles Martel, and nephew of Charles II. of Naples, who was nephew of the celebrated St. Louis, king of France; and, notwithstanding the inauspicious circumstances under which he ascended the throne, the Hungarians had afterwards reason to remember him with pleasure, as one of the wisest and ablest of their monarchs. Notwithstanding his legitimate election, some of the great nobles refused to acknowledge him, and one of their number, Mathew Csak, perhaps better known as Count Trencin, who possessed immense estates at the foot of the Carpathian Mountains, refused to do him homage, and shutting himself up in his castle, bid him defiance. The king immediately put himself at the head of an armed force, and proceeded to enforce submission to the national will; but so powerful was the rebel lord, that it was only after a tedious war, and great loss, that he was compelled to surrender. At the siege of the fortress of Saros, which was commanded by Demetrius on behalf of Count Trencin, and was carried by storm after a gallant defence, the sons of Elias Goergey, the count of the German colony of Sepucza, fought with unshaken courage at the side of the king in defence of the law and the constitution. Little did they think that a man of their race would afterwards make their very name a synonyme through all Europe for whatever is traitorous and base. Arthur Goergey, the recreant of 1848, is the lineal descendant of one of them. As soon as peace was restored, Charles, who was now for the second time a widower, married the Polish princess Elizabeth, and fixed his residence in the fortress of Visegrad, upon the Danube. Crowning the summit of a lofty hill, it delighted the eye by its picturesque situation, and astonished the visitor upon a nearer approach by its grandeur and extent. In the hands of Charles, it became one of the most magnificent royal residences in Europe. He carried to its embellishment all the French taste for what is showy and imposing, chastened and refined by a diligent study and high appreciation of the classic models of antiquity. Nor was his attention diverted from the work by the premature and lamented death of his two sons, or the constant anxiety caused by the ambitious designs of Paul Subies, who claimed the title of Ban of Croatia and Bosnia.

An outrage, disgusting for its coarseness, and rendered terrible by its sanguinary results, at length disturbed the course of this prosperous and happy reign. Casimir of Poland, afterwards surnamed the Great, the brother of the queen, a man of dissolute habits and violent temper, paid a visit to the Hungarian court, for the purpose of regulating the affairs of the Order of Teutonic knights under the immediate superintendence of Charles Robert. Falling violently in love with one of the queen's maids of honour, Casimir brought to bear all the tactics acquired in a long course of dissipation, declarations of the warmest love, prayers, entreaties, and splendid offers, without making any impression upon the cold virtue of the Magyar lady. This unsuccessful wooing inflamed his passion still more, and, seizing a favourable opportunity, he obtained by brutal force what purity and innocence had steadily denied him.

The unfortunate girl, overwhelmed with grief and shame, fled from the palace, and sought relief in pouring out her sorrows to her father, Felix Zacs, a Hungarian noble. Roused to fury by the injury and insult, Zacs rushed to the apartments of Casimir, swearing to wash out the disgrace in the heart's blood of the offender. But the ravisher had fled immediately upon the perpetration of his crime, and the disappointment of not finding him still further increased the rage of the unhappy father. Losing all command over himself, he entered the room at which the royal family were seated at dinner, and struck the queen with his sabre, cutting off the four fingers from her right hand. In vain the king attempted to defend his wife. Zacs wounded him also, and was about to attack his two sons, when three noblemen, with their attendants, entering the apartment; they all fell upon him at once, and cut him to pieces.

The royal vengeance did not rest satisfied with the summary punishment thus inflicted upon Zacs. The gentlemen of the court went armed to his house, and seizing his son, dragged him through the town tied to the tail of a horse, until he died from sheer exhaustion. We may excuse this outrage, committed in the first moments of rage; but nothing can palliate the after cruelties ordered by the king in a calmer mood. Clara Zacs, the unfortunate lady whose injuries had been the cause of all, was compelled to walk through the town, having her nose, lips, and fingers cut off; while the crier proclaimed, "This is the punishment of traitors!" The king's vengeance extended itself to the second generation, and even further. The grandson of Felix Zacs was banished, and the collateral members of his family were obliged to save themselves by flight from torture or mutilation.

This terrible event occurred in 1336.

Charles Robert's attention was soon turned from this dreadful tragedy to other and more honourable employments. In the year 1285, the Tartar Noguis, the inhabitants of Moldavia, united with the Wallacks, the remains of the Daco-Roman colonies, and commenced to devastate Hungary. Having been defeated in some sanguinary engagements, they at length settled peaceably between the Danube and the right bank of the Aluta. The two tribes into which they were divided, uniting under one chieftain, they began to cross the river, and whether it was that Charles Robert was alarmed at their progress, or wished to reduce them to a state of complete subjection, he declared war against them, although Bessarab, the waywode, paid him homage as his suzerain. Despairing of being able to contend against the king in the open field, Bessarab resorted to stratagem. Decoying the Magyar army into a mountain pass by feigning a retreat, he suddenly surrounded them on every side, so that, to avoid the destruction of his forces, Charles was compelled to sue for peace. The wily waywode feigned the most friendly disposition, and protracting the negotiations to as great a length as possible, he in the meantime fortified the entrances to the defile, and crowned the heights with men-at-arms and archers, ready to pour down showers of arrows, and roll heavy rocks upon the Hungarian army at the word of their leader. When the Magyars became aware of the full danger of their position, their consternation was great. They saw every odds that can encourage a soldier, on the side of their enemies—numbers, position, and the certainty of a safe retreat. Their only hope lay in forcing the entrance of the gorge without delay; but long ere they reached it, three-fourths of their number were buried beneath the missiles of their assailants, and the king only, and a few nobles, succeeded, after a desperate combat, in fighting their way out, sword in hand.

Charles Robert had naturally but little taste for war, and this catastrophe completely convinced him that he would meet with greater success in the smoother field of diplomacy.

Upon the death of his grandfather, as the heir of Charles Martel, he preferred his claim to the Neapolitan crown before the papal court at Avignon. Clement V., the Pope, pronounced, however, in favour of Robert, the uncle of the Hungarian king, a brave and experienced warrior, who was very popular amongst the Italians. At the death of the latter, so disgusted was he at the corrupting influence exercised over his own heirs by the French ladies of his court, that he determined to leave the crown to one of his nephew's children. He therefore sent an embassy to Hungary, inviting Charles Robert to Naples, and requesting him to bring with him his second son Andrew. No sooner had the message arrived, than the king set out, accompanied by a numerous and brilliant suite. Upon their arrival at Naples, Robert betrothed his daughter Giovanna, aged only six years, to Andrew, the son of Charles Robert, and declared them his heirs. Andrew henceforth remained in Italy with his tutors, and a suite of Magyar gentlemen.

When Charles Robert regained his kingdom, he found a splendid field for the exercise of his diplomatic talents suddenly opened up to him. Vladislas Loketek, the king of Poland, had died during his absence, and his son Casimir, who committed the outrage already mentioned at Visegrad, had succeeded to the throne. The latter was undoubtedly a man of great personal bravery, and possessed some celebrity as a warrior and patron of the fine arts; but he was given to indulgence in sensual pleasures, indolent, and averse to the transaction of serious business. Charles rightly judged that such a monarch would be continually placed in difficulties, from which the resources of his own uncultivated intellect would be entirely insufficient to extricate him; and that he would naturally look to him as a man of ability, and a near relative, for advice and assistance.

The event answered his expectations. He was constantly referred to as an arbitrator in the troubles which at that time distracted Poland, and his great tact, the gentle and winning courtesy of his manners, and his great superiority when thus placed in comparison with their own monarch, gradually won for him the esteem of the Polish nobles, and caused them to listen with a ready ear to representations which the Magyar king caused to be made to them, of the importance of a change in the order of the succession.

FORTRESS OF VISEGRAD.

At a meeting held at Visegrad, in 1335, Charles, in the character of a mediator, finally succeeded in smoothing away the differences which existed between Casimir and the order of Teutonic knights. In many similar cases he rendered like services, always acting the part of a disinterested arbitrator, but at the same time, gaining over the noblesse by his smooth flattery and the splendour of his presents. He had, nevertheless, a dangerous rival in John, king of Bohemia. Having rendered him important services, however, so dexterously did Charles Robert manage, that the margrave of Moravia, who was the rightful heir of the Bohemian crown, promised his daughter Margaret in marriage to Louis, eldest son of the Magyar king, at the same time engaging to guarantee to him the succession, in case Casimir died without issue. The wife of the latter died childless in May, 1339, and the Diet of Cracow proclaimed Louis of Hungary heir presumptive. Casimir himself came to Visegrad, with a magnificent retinue, to announce the good tidings. He was received with the splendour in which Charles delighted, and never was the exquisite taste and lofty dignity of the Magyar king displayed to better advantage than in this celebration of this consummation of his hopes and labours.

His days were now in the "sere and yellow leaf," and in 1342 he died, after a long and brilliant reign of thirty-two years, in which he had done more for the promotion of the arts, commerce, and manufactures of his kingdom, and the extension of its influence, than any monarch who had gone before him. The Hungarians before his death had learned to love him with an ardour which more than atoned for their former dislike. In the greatness of his talents, and the splendour of his services, they forgot that he owed his elevation, in some measure at least, to the support of a bigoted foreign priest, and remembered only his devotion to the Magyar nation, and the proud position to which his exertions had raised it. This forms a splendid trait in their character. This willingness to abandon prejudices, this homage to talent, to magnanimity, to personal worth, without reference to their antecedents, are the surest evidences of a high and generous spirit.

Vast crowds, amongst whom were Casimir of Poland and the margrave of Moravia, followed the remains of Charles Robert to the tomb; and by their sorrowing aspect, and lowly-muttered lamentations, furnished the last testimony to his valour and wisdom.

CHAPTER VII.

LOUIS THE GREAT.

But the public grief was hushed or forgotten when Louis I. ascended the throne, amidst universal acclamations; in possession of a genius and aptness for affairs which gave early promise that his career would, by its greater brightness, obscure his father's glory. In the commencement of his reign he showed more than usual activity, and in an expedition which he directed against the Saxons, his arms achieved the most splendid triumphs. This people inhabited many towns of Transylvania, to which some of them had come at an early period to submit themselves to the dominion of Charlemagne; others had been settled in different parts of the country at various times as colonists, after the devastations which had been committed by the Asiatic barbarians. Presuming upon the youth and gentleness of Louis, immediately after the death of his father, they refused to pay the public taxes, and the customary tribute exacted from all foreigners. The king, however, entered their territory at the head of a large army, and quickly reduced them to submission. The Wallacks, also, who had so successfully resisted his father, acknowledged his sway, and ever after remained firmly attached to him.

An event occurred in Naples about this time which occupied the attention not of Hungary only, but of all Europe, and which, from its interest and importance, demands as large a share of ours as we can well bestow. Our readers may remember the almost premature engagement which was concluded by Charles Robert between his son Andrew and Giovanna, the heiress of Robert, king of Naples. The young prince, as we have already mentioned, was left at the Neapolitan court at the age of six years, to be brought up under the eye of his intended father-in-law, who, in order to remove all cause of dispute or division, promised that his daughter should succeed him in the kingdom in case she married Andrew. The latter, as he grew in years, prepossessed every one in his favour save his future bride. It is rarely that the human heart will bend its likings or dislikings to accord with the dictates of policy or ambition, and the hatred of Giovanna towards the youth whom she was expected to love and honour, but had not been permitted to choose, grew every day more violent. She and her younger sister Mary were endowed with all the charms of figure and face which poets love to paint as the birthright of the women of the south; but they had also the hot temperament, and longing after forbidden pleasure, which destroys domestic peace in the lands of sunny skies and starry nights, though comparatively unknown amongst the denizens of less favoured climes. Giovanna's beauty won the attachment of the bishop of Cavaillon, a jolly priest and gallant gentleman; called forth the melodious praises of Petrarch, the ardent, but dreaming and sentimental scholar, and secured for her the flattering notice of Pope Clement VI., who plumed himself almost as much upon being an excellent connoisseur in female beauty, as upon wearing the triple crown. All this might flatter the vanity of the young princesses, but the bad example of their mother, Margaret of Valois, corrupted their morals; and Filippa, a depraved woman, who, by her influence over Yoland, a half-brother of Giovanna, obtained the situation of governess in the royal family, finished the work of evil which Margaret had begun. Giovanna's dislike to Andrew manifested itself clearly upon the death of the king, her father. Acting upon evil counsel, she declared, that though her marriage gave him a right to share her bed, she certainly would not permit him to share her throne, and therefore would not concede to him the title of king or allow his coronation. The Pope was the universal referee at that time in all disputes relating to crowns and sceptres, and Clement VI., who was residing at Avignon, was called upon to decide between the husband and wife. In this instance, at least, the successor of St. Peter would ten thousand times rather have waived the exercise of his prerogative. On the one side he feared the great power of Louis, the king of Hungary; on the other, the loss of Giovanna's favour, to whose beauty his vows and her marriage did not by any means prevent his paying court.

In this dilemma he resolved upon sending Petrarch to Naples, to make diligent inquiry into the cause of the quarrel. A worse emissary he could not have selected. Petrarch's disposition was amorous in the extreme, and he was consequently prepared to pardon all faults committed under the influence of the tender passion, and besides all this, was naturally prejudiced in favour of his old benefactor Robert, her father. Louis, hoping to save his brother's rights and Giovanna's reputation before matters came to an extremity, sent on his side his mother, Elizabeth, a high-minded and amiable woman. She therefore set out for Naples, attended by a brilliant escort, but had no sooner arrived than she found it would be impossible that she could exercise any influence at such a court, where all the worst vices were covered over with a show of refinement which increased their allurements at the same time that it deepened their depravity, and where the frank and open manners of the Magyars were stigmatised as gross and barbarous. Nevertheless she endeavoured to bring about a reconciliation, which would in all probability have been lasting, if her efforts had not been frustrated by the harsh sternness of a Franciscan monk, Robert, Andrew's tutor, who placed himself in opposition to the sentimentalism of Petrarch. Robert governed the kingdom in Andrew's name with great vigour and inflexibility, but having no taste for poetry himself, looked upon all poets with profound contempt. He therefore received Petrarch with studied indifference, and paid no attention to the Pope's instructions. The former, though he generally employed his pen in pouring out mournful complaints of the coldness of his mistress, flew to arms, and revenged himself by writing a satirical poem, in which he heaped bitter reproaches upon Robert; a work which he had already amply performed in a letter to Cardinal Colonna, giving an account of his journey to Naples. "Religion, justice, and truth," said he, "are banished. I think I am at Memphis, or Babylon, or Mecca. Instead of a king so just, and so pious (Robert), a little monk, fat, rosy, barefooted, with a shorn head, and half covered with a dirty mantle, bent by hypocrisy more than by age, lost in debauchery while proud of his affected poverty, and still more of the real wealth he has amassed; this man holds the reins of the staggering empire. In vice and cruelty he rivals a Dionysius, or an Agathocles, or a Phalaris!"* Elizabeth was still at Naples, when the titular empress of Constantinople, Catharine of Valois, provided a lover for Giovanna in the person of her son Louis of Tarento, who, in anticipating her husband in the enjoyment of the conjugal rights, rendered him still more odious in the eyes of his wife.

The maternal affection of the Hungarian queen now made her alive to the dangers which threatened Andrew, and she wished to take him back with her from an atmosphere so tainted with treachery and corruption. The Greek empress, however, entreated her to change her determination; the chancellor of the kingdom, Count of Monte Scaglioso, an honest and powerful man, and devoted to the Hungarian cause, expressed his conviction, that if Andrew remained, matters might still be arranged; and Giovanna herself besought her, with tears in her eyes, not to deprive her of her husband. She therefore yielded to their solicitations, and took her departure.

At last the Magyar ambassadors purchased from Clement VI., with a sum of 44,000 marks of silver, some concessions in favour of Andrew. The amount was not sufficient to obtain all. The Pope consented to confer upon him the title of king, and crown him as such, but without any stipulation as to the succession after his death.

The Hungarians rested satisfied with this, but did not perceive, till too late, that all their efforts would be rendered unavailing by the intrigues of the ladies of the Neapolitan court. Agnes de Perigord, duchess of Durazzo, another member of the royal family, jealous of the success of the Empress Catharine on behalf of Louis of Tarento, determined to counterbalance the influence thus obtained. Supported by the Cardinal de Talleyrand, she obtained from the Pope permission for her son, Charles of Durazzo, to marry Mary, the younger sister of the queen. Prompted by Catharine, however, Giovanna refused her consent, and they therefore determined upon carrying off the princess in the night. In this there was a fresh insult offered to Andrew, as Mary had been previously affianced

* Campbell's "Life of Petrarch," vol. i. p. 248. The tone of this description is no more exaggerated than that of Campbell's own account of the whole transaction, which betrays a manifest prejudice against the Hungarians.

to his brother Stephen; and in case Giovanna died without issue, the succession remained to her sister. In this instance he again gave proof of his gentleness and humanity, or, as some may think, his feebleness and incapacity, by pardoning the ravisher. At last a new scandal precipitated the closing scene of this hideous drama. The queen's figure began to afford evidence, every day more unmistakeable, of her infidelity to her husband, and the insult and dishonour were rendered deeper by her own indifference to her disgrace. Some mentioned Bertrand

LOUIS I.

d'Artus, the son of the grand chamberlain, and the sworn enemy of Andrew, others Louis, duke of Tarento, as the cause of it; but Andrew was too proud to exhibit any outward signs of the mortification he felt. Soon after, some courtiers made a banner, with the figures of a block and an axe displayed upon it, and paraded it at a tournament in Andrew's presence, to signify the determination of the court to get rid of him, since they could no longer delay his coronation. On the 18th of September, 1344, he accompanied the queen to a party of pleasure at a country house, near Aversa, and riding out in the country, they stopped to dine at the convent of St. Peter of Morono, some distance from the town. In the evening a messenger came to the royal apartment to summon Andrew, as if for the purpose of delivering to him some important despatches. He had no sooner left the room than the door was closed behind him, and a hand placed on his mouth to stifle his cries. Andrew shook himself loose by a tremendous effort, and ran toward the hall for his arms; but he found all the doors shut, and Giovanna lay quietly in her bed, paralysed by fear or anxiety. At length the noise aroused his attendant, who cried for help; but Bertrand d'Artus, the favourite of the queen, again seized his victim, and urged the assassins to attack him. After a fierce struggle, they hung him from the balcony of the great hall, with a rope which the queen herself was said to have provided. The disfigured and bleeding body was thrown into the garden, and the monks, when aroused, had to search for it during the greater part of the bright summer night before they found it.

When the news reached the town of Aversa, the tumult was great. The women rushed into the streets bewailing the murdered king, and the men went in arms to the convent, and forcing the gates, in blind fury slaughtered every one whom they met, without inquiring as to his innocence or guilt. All, in the bitterness of their grief, thought only of avenging the murder, and forgot to bury the body, which lay for many days before it obtained the rites of sepulture.

The queen, after the first flood of hypocritical tears, set out for Naples, and immediately abandoned herself to indulgence in every sort of licentious pleasure. The birth of an infant son awakened the memory of her past delinquencies, and filled the minds of the people with horror and disgust. Louis of Hungary instantly demanded an inquiry of the Pope, with a view to the discovery and punishment of the authors of this lamentable outrage. It accorded neither with the interests nor the inclination, however, of the papal court to throw any light upon the matter, as the chief offender was the near relative of his holiness. Cutting short the negotiations, Louis required the Cardinal de Talleyrand, and his nephew, the queen herself, Catharine of Valois and her two sons, to be delivered up to him, that they might suffer capital punishment. Being anxious, however, to save his brother's honour, he consented that Charles Martel, Giovanna's illegitimate son, should be educated by Elizabeth at the Hungarian court, and that during his minority, his brother Stephen, duke of Sclavonia, should govern the kingdom of Naples. But he was resolved in any case to punish the queen, and deprive her of the crown, and for that purpose levied an army and marched upon Italy.

This dispute has been rendered one of the most famous in modern history, by the means which were now taken to decide between the contending parties. A man at this time sat at Rome in the chair of the ancient tribunes, who united the austerity and the severe and inflexible justice of the ancient Brutus with the fire of the Gracchi, and the brilliant eloquence of Cicero. Raised from the body of the people, he was their idol; and when he banished from the gates of his native city the lawless nobles, the descendants of their barbarian conquerors, and re-established the reign of pure justice and equal rights, his fellows hailed him as their deliverer. He had humbled the power of the great—and they looked upon him with a jealous eye; but the multitude clung to him as a father. He had become renowned for the largeness of his intellect, and the far-sighted justice of his decisions; and more fortunate than Mazzini, he had gained the confidence of most of the princes of Europe. This plebeian saw crowned heads submit their disputes to his arbitration, and upon him Louis and Giovanna called to decide between them. Giovanna tried him with gold, but found him incorruptible, and then addressed herself to work upon his affections, flattering the vanity of his wife by rich presents, whilst she assured the tribune that she sought only an impartial sentence.

At last the day came on which this great trial, wonderful for the demonstration which it affords of the might of moral power and the force of great traditions, was to take place. Taking his seat upon a throne beneath the mighty dome of the Capitol, with the tribunitial crown upon his head, and the silver ball, the ensign of power, in his hand, he summoned before him the advocates of the rival monarchs, and bid them plead their clients' cause.

The Tribune heard but did not decide.

He feared on the one hand the consequences that might result to himself, in case he declared innocent a woman whom the populace generally believed to be guilty of her husband's murder; and on the other, the enmity of a powerful neighbour in case he condemned her. He had, however, more elevated views, which he kept strictly secret. He postponed his judgment, on the ground that the affair was of too important a nature to be decided hastily; asked for time to deliberate with the principal citizens, and in the meanwhile ordered the various documents and memoranda connected with the case, to be deposited in his chancery. He knew well what a noise the affair would make abroad, and he feared the jealousy of the papal court at Avignon. He resolved, therefore, to write to the Pope, and therein represent himself as a mediator between the contending parties. "I have received," said he, "the ambassadors sent by Giovanna, and the envoys of the king of Hungary, and I have sent back a solemn embassy to endeavour to restore peace between them." In reality, however, the project he had at heart was the dethronement of the queen of Naples, and the formation of a league between Louis of Bavaria, Louis of Hungary, and the Roman people, for the purpose of wresting from the Holy See the disposal of the crown of the Two Sicilies, and vesting it in the Roman Chamber of Representatives, which he had established.*

Louis could not brook the delay, and he consequently refused any longer to leave the matter in Rienzi's hands, but determined forthwith to right himself by force. Sending forward the main body of his army, under the command of Nicolas Henrici,

* "Histoire de Rienzi," par M. de Boispreux, pp. 165 et seq.

a pious bishop (according to the notions of the times) and a brave soldier, he followed himself at the head of one thousand men, as an avenging corps, in the midst of which floated a black banner, carrying a portrait of his murdered brother. Town after town fell before him; the petty princes of the peninsula sent embassies to seek his alliance, and the Pope alone attempted to arrest his triumphant progress. A legate met him, and threatened him with the anathemas of the church, unless he consented to desist from hostilities, and make peace with the queen. Louis' reply was characteristic of the man and of the nation to which he belonged. "The Pope," said he, "has no right to place bounds to my vengeance. He promised to punish the murderers of my brother, and his blood still cries against them from the ground. The criminals still survive, and are sheltered and protected by the Holy See, while I, who have taken arms only for their chastisement, am threatened with excommunication. The holy father reserves his curses for innocence and his favours for crime. Let him excommunicate me. I make no objection. I fear not his empty thunders. There is a higher judge than he, who knows the justice of my cause, and will one day review the decisions of Popes."

He continued his course, and the Neapolitans began speedily to flock to him. The queen was deserted on every side, even by her husband, Andrew's murderer, whom she married in less than a month after his death. She escaped in the night, and landed safely on the coast of Provence.

Upon taking possession of Naples, Louis guaranteed to all the free enjoyment of their liberty and property, except those who had taken part in the assassination of his brother. This promise seems to have re-assured Charles de Durazzo, who rested under the gravest suspicions. The Magyar head-quarters were then at Aversa, and thither the Neapolitan nobles flocked to pay homage to their new sovereign. Durazzo followed their example. This man was a strange compound of bravery and ambition, carelessness of his own interests, and great perseverance. He was constantly mixed up in low and vile intrigues, and was consequently looked upon with great suspicion by the nobles, although his conduct appeared less equivocal in the eyes of the people. He had drawn upon himself the hatred of the archbishop of Naples, who appeared before the Hungarian king as his principal accuser.

A grand council of the Magyar barons was summoned by Louis to deliberate upon the guilt of the culprit and the punishment of his crime. The sentence of death was unanimously pronounced. According to the custom of the time, the king was seated at a solemn banquet in the midst of his lords, when the unfortunate Charles was called before him.

"Duke," said the king, regarding him with a stern aspect, "your lot is cast—you die within an hour. But you must first listen to the recital of your crimes. You hindered the coronation of my brother by your machinations; you ravished Mary, the sister of the queen, who was promised in marriage by her father, first to me and then to my brother Stephen. You have, it is true, pursued the assassins of Andrew, but only that you might further your own ambitious projects. You were the first to invite me to this country, and the first to desert my standard when I had arrived. You shall now expiate your guilt by an ignominous death." It was in vain that Charles begged and prayed for life on any terms; the king spurned him from his feet in disgust. He was beheaded on the same balcony from which the unfortunate Andrew had been hanged.

It would seem as if a curse has for centuries hung over the kingdom of Naples. When Louis conquered it, it was as corrupt, as degraded, as void of honour, humanity, and good faith, as now, when the finest intellects in the kingdom are buried in dungeons thirty feet below the level of the Adriatic. He set to work immediately to introduce some sort of order into the hideous chaos, and afford security to the unfortunate people who had been so long plundered by the nobles and the court. The task was difficult—but it was one worthy the ambition of a great man. He protected personal liberty, private property, and the fruits of honest labour against the open violence of the robber, and the more silent, but no less dangerous attacks of fraud and chicane. "Activity, honour, justice, replaced sloth, jobbing, and corruption, assassination, and dissoluteness of manners, and the people began to revive."*

Louis entertained a feeling of deep disgust at the low state of morality which he found prevailing amongst the mass of the people, and the total want of principle of the nobility. When, upon making his triumphant entry into the capital, the great lords presented him with a magnificent throne, he declined it with evident marks of contempt; and when the orators appeared with their panegyrics, and the poets came to recite their complimentary odes, he refused to hear them.

He had to steer clear of two evils. He had on one hand to avoid offending the pride of the nobles by too great severity, and, on the other hand, to see that the authors of a great crime should not escape with impunity. Under the stern severity of the Magyar rule, however, the Neapolitan barons soon began to regret the gay licentiousness of the old regime, and to long for its return.

A deplorable calamity soon occurred, which hastened the outbreak of their discontents, and enabled them to give form and consistency to their hatred of Hungarian domination. A terrible earthquake shook the whole of Italy, burying towns and villages by the shock, and close upon it followed a pestilence which spread, with greater or less degree of virulence, over the whole of Europe. Hungary escaped with little injury, but Naples was the very centre of the widespread desolation. Louis travelled through the whole kingdom, exposing himself to imminent personal danger, in the attempt to alleviate the sufferings of the wretched inhabitants. His labour was, however, in vain; and, after fortifying the garrisons and distributing troops through the country, at the earnest solicitation of his ministers, he returned to Hungary. No sooner had he disappeared than the

* Mathaeus Villani, l. i, c. 16.

nobles threw off the mask, and sent deputies to Avignon, where Giovanna had taken refuge, beseeching her to return with her husband, and resume possession of her throne. But she had no money; and, in order to raise supplies, she sold the town of Avignon, and the territory attached to it, to the Pope for a sum of 80,000 florins, and even pledged her jewels to fit out an expedition. She arrived at Naples, and was received into the town, although the Hungarian garrison occupied the castle, and Louis of Tarento, her husband, put himself at the head of the army. Charles Martel, Giovanna's son, being at this time dead, Louis wished to marry his brother Stephen to Mary, the widow of Charles de Durazzo, and place them on the throne; but the Pope steadfastly refused his consent, and succeeded in inducing the German levies to desert the Hungarian standard. This defection obliged Louis to suspend his operations for some time; but in the spring of 1350 he again appeared with large reinforcements, and carried everything before him. He was twice wounded at the sieges of two towns, but still persisted in exposing himself in the thick of every fray. At the siege of Melfi, he received a challenge to mortal combat from Louis of Tarento, to which he sarcastically replied, telling him that if they met face to face in a general engagement he should not decline the conflict.

Marching upon Naples, it surrendered to him without striking a blow. Upon taking possession of the town, he informed the inhabitants that he would levy a contribution on their goods as a punishment for their treason. This was the signal of a general outbreak, and, after a murderous conflict in the street, the Magyars, harassed and worn out by the overwhelming numbers of their assailants, were compelled to retreat to the citadel. The Pope seized this opportunity of renewing his offers of peace on behalf of the queen, at the same time declaring his intention of delivering judgment upon the differences existing between the two parties. It was impossible to exculpate Giovanna from the charges alleged against her; but at the same time Clement was by no means willing to have a powerful king as his neighbour, instead of a beautiful woman. To end the matter, he forthwith formed a tribunal of his own creatures, before whom Giovanna was arraigned with a mockery of legal procedure: and, in accordance with the advice of her ecclesiastical counsellors, she declared that, instigated by diabolical witchcraft, by an excess of folly, of which she could not divine the cause, she had, against her will, ordered the murder of her husband, whereupon the Pope declared her innocent of the "witchcraft and its consequences!" The moment the judgment was pronounced, a letter signed "Lucifer, Prince of Darkness," and addressed to "His Holiness the Pope, his representative upon Earth," fell in the midst of the astonished consistory. In the epistle, his satanic majesty informed them of the satisfaction with which the accounts of the manifold vices, misdeeds, and injustice of the Pope and his cardinals were received by the damned spirits in the infernal regions.

The absurdity of this judgment was apparent to every one; but Louis, perceiving that the kingdom of Naples was as difficult to keep as it was easy to acquire, and being disgusted with the shameless immorality of the papal court, at once acquiesced in it. The queen sent him 300,000 florins to meet the expenses of the war; but it was returned with the cold reply, that he fought to avenge his brother, not to accumulate wealth. He immediately evacuated Naples, after having occupied it for six years. Such was the negative result of a conquest achieved by the expenditure of so much blood and treasure.

New successes compensated Louis for the loss of Naples. He was shortly afterwards called by Casimir, the king of Poland, to his assistance against the Bohemians and the Russians. He thus became acquainted beforehand with the genius of the people over whom he was one day to be called to reign. Although the two nations had attained almost to the same stage of culture and civilisation, the straightforwardness, frankness, and magnanimity of the Magyars were more in accordance with the king's tastes and disposition, than the uneasy, restless spirit of the Poles. His partiality for the former was still further increased by the efforts made by the Polish nobles to impose new restrictions upon him, in case he came to rule over them. They stipulated that he should be content with the revenues which accrued to the crown in the time of Vladislaus Loketek, and engage never to attempt to found a right upon the voluntary offerings with which any of his subjects might present him; and, lastly, that he should never visit his new kingdom without the permission of the Diet, who would not, at the same time, bear any part of the expenses of his journey. These conditions well exemplify the jealous hauteur of this proud nobility; but, in imposing them, they committed a fatal error. By prohibiting Louis' residence in his newly-acquired dominions, they taught him to look on them as a distant and dependent province, in whose welfare and prosperity he could feel only a secondary interest. He, therefore, yielded with indifference to their demand that, in case he or his son Stephen died without having male issue, they should possess, without interference, the right of choosing their own kings. From that moment Poland occupied but little of Louis' attention.

Passing over a successful war against the Venetians, concerning the possession of Dalmatia, and a partially successful attempt to act as mediator in the contentions of the petty princes of Italy, we arrive at the death of Casimir, the last of the race of the Piasts, which had given so many great men and great kings to Poland. He was, in many respects, an able and efficient monarch; and, though often faulty, he had that desire to act well which so frequently forms a redeeming trait in listless, decisionless characters. He possessed great personal bravery, and, amidst all his indulgence in the grosser vices, a tender and feeling heart. He did not die without leaving behind him some memorials of his zeal for the welfare of the country. Before his time, there were scarcely any fortified towns in Poland; but during his reign, towns, villages, and castles, built with elegance and solidity, arose upon every side. He had great tact in the discovery of merit, and, when found, he never failed to appreciate and reward it. He created a third estate, composed of the bourgeoisie, or middle class; and if his successors had taken care to foster the new element thus introduced into the constitution, Poland would have made far more rapid progress. But even Casimir himself did only half the work, or rather neutralized the good effects of what he did do, by signing the fatal measure, at the Diet of Wiszliza, in 1347, which constituted a powerful and idle oligarchy to crush the middle and lower classes.*

Upon the death of Casimir, a deputation of Polish nobles repaired to Visegrad, to request Louis to take possession of the throne, according to the treaties already entered into. He received them in state, surrounded by the barons of his empire; but heard their offer with seeming doubt and hesitation. "You know not what you ask," said he to them; "and you," turning to his barons, "know not what you advise. It is difficult to watch over two distinct flocks; and, for this reason, no bishop is allowed to preside over two dioceses. When the Roman empire only counted a few huts as its possessions, two kings were too many to govern it; so, I fear, one king would be insufficient to reign over two great empires."

At last, however, he yielded to their solicitations, and consented to go to Poland to be crowned. The ceremony took place at Cracow; and, after it was over, the chancellor presented him the conditions laid down in the treaty, by which the succession was secured to him. He pledged himself to restore, at his own expense, all the countries wrested from Poland; to bestow no dignity or public office upon any foreigner; to make good to knights and men-at-arms all losses sustained by them in carrying on war out of the kingdom; and, lastly, to impose no new tax upon the property of the church, or of the nobility. This sort of constitutional charter was accepted by the king of Hungary, 1355, and is considered the first of the "*Pacta Conventa*," or covenant between the nobles and the candidate they wished to propose; covenants exclusively formed for their own benefit, and to the detriment alike of king and peasantry.

Louis felt, however, that he and the Polish aristocracy could never work together in harmony. They were too restless, proud, and discontented ever to submit quietly to the rule of any one; and they were too powerful to be coerced into subjection. He had scarcely arrived at Cracow, when his unpopularity commenced. One of his first acts was a direct violation of his agreement, namely, the bestowal of two valuable fiefs of the crown upon two strangers, who had no claim upon them, except their relationship with him; and he added fuel to the indignation which was roused on this score, by removing Casimir's two daughters into Hungary, lest they should contract royal alliances. He committed the government to his mother, Elizabeth; but she, though herself a Pole, found herself unable to carry it on. After the occurrence of numerous scenes of violence, turbulence and anarchy, into the particulars of which we cannot here enter, he

* Hist. of Poland. Lardner's Encycl., p. 92.

convened a Polish Diet at Buda, in March, 1381, and invested Zavicza, bishop of Cracow, and two other noblemen, with the government of the kingdom. The Poles were filled with rage and consternation upon hearing of this measure. They now found themselves placed under the domination of a haughty and irascible priest, instead of the gentle rule of Elizabeth, and Vladislaus, the viceroy, who succeeded her. The bishop, however, did not long continue to give them cause for complaint. The hoary debauchee fell from a ladder, and broke his neck, as he was pursuing a young girl, who, to escape from his brutal violence, had taken refuge in a hay-loft.

HUNGARIAN FLEET IN THE FOURTEENTH CENTURY.

Constantly disappointed in his expectations with regard to Poland, the king of Hungary at length determined to abandon her finally, and leave her to her fate. He assembled another Diet at O-Zolyom (Altsohl), in 1382, and presented to it his daughter Mary, the future queen, and her betrothed lover, Sigismond, son of the emperor of Germany, Charles IV. He had given up the hope of any lasting union between the two countries, and he therefore wished to evidence his desire for the welfare of the Polish people, by offering them as their king the man whom, of all the princes of Europe, he deemed worthy of his daughter's hand. But in doing this he severed the bond that seemed so likely to unite Poland and Hungary for ever. Each nation thenceforth pursued its own course, to meet at last as companions in misfortune, crushed under the same iron yoke.

In the following year a great plague of locusts desolated the greater part of Hungary, utterly destroying the crops, and leaving but little sustenance for either man or beast, so that it was in no very satisfied spirit that the Hungarians received the news of the king's intention to commence hostilities with the Venetians, who had made encroachments upon the Hungarian territories on the Adriatic. He marched against them with 40,000 men, in conjunction with Leopold, duke of Austria, and Francesca Carrara, and most of the towns of Dalmatia speedily fell before his arms. Peace was at length restored by a division of the territory, in which Louis had the lion's share.

The Tartar tribes, who had not yet lost their taste for plunder, made new attempts upon the kingdom during this reign, and several times made invasions into Transylvania. Louis, at last, succeeded in overtaking them, and inflicted upon them so signal a defeat, that they fled to the shores of the Euxine. The Lithuanians, also, who were still idolaters, harassed their neighbours by a succession of inroads, and in particular the province of Russia, which at this period was tributary to Hungary, carrying off from time to time great quantities of booty, and multitudes of captives. They were at length completely subdued, either by force or persuasion, for the Hungarian monarch was an adept in the use of both.

During these conflicts the Hungarian fleet increased rapidly, and practice gave the Magyar sailors an amount of self-confidence and dexterity which could then be rarely found except amongst the Venetians. Their navy was at this period one of the finest in Europe.

Louis died, without leaving any male issue, in 1382, after a reign of forty years, universally regretted by his subjects. The magnates and nobles, to show their admiration of his character and sorrow for his loss, wore mourning for three years after his death. His body was interred in the church of St. Stephen, at Alba, with great pomp and magnificence.

The Magyar historians love to dwell upon the glories of his reign, and above all upon the splendour of his palace of Visegrad, in which he fixed his residence during the greater part of his life. They tell, with pardonable pride, of its vast extent, which could afford ample accommodation for two kings and many minor princes, with all their suite; of its 350 chambers, furnished in a style of dazzling splendour; of its gardens stocked with the rarest exotics, and cooled by the rush of flowing water; of the soft and voluptuous music which every evening, from one of the highest towers, soothed or delighted the courtly guests, and, floating on the breeze, cheered the peasant as he "plodded his weary way" homeward; of the neighbouring mountains, crowned with wood, and studded with pleasant villas or rustic churches; of the pleasant and shady valleys that sloped away to the Danube's edge, and afforded calm and retirement to him who chose to escape for a season from the gaieties of the palace.

It is a subject of more importance to us to consider the changes or improvements Louis wrought in the Hungarian constitution. He had more respect for the rights of the people and nobles than his father, Charles Robert, because he was less wily, more straightforward in his dealings, and had a great dislike to the tricks of diplomacy. In a Diet, held at Buda in 1351, he confirmed the Bulla Aurea, and added twenty-five new articles. After the happy issue of his first campaign in Naples, he established perfect equality amongst the nobles, as an acknowledgment of their services. The distinction between the great seigneurs and the simple nobles was thus effaced, and the name *barones*, *proceres*, and *nobiles* were applied equally to all. At the Diet of Rakos, under one of the last kings of the race of Arpad, the peasants and the *jobbagy* (domestic servants) obtained the right of leaving their lords, and taking up their residence on the estates of another. This was one step towards their emancipation, and it possesses greater weight from the circumstance, that, in all other countries of Europe at this date, the serfs were inseparable from the soil on which they were born. Louis gave full force to this law, and those who fought bravely under his banners not only became free, but in every respect equal to the ancient nobles. The authority and duty of the palatine, of the judge of the kingdom, of the treasurer, underwent no alteration of importance. The palatine, Count de Trencin, already claimed the right of governing the kingdom, whenever the throne became vacant—just as the Lord Mayor of London does under similar circumstances in England. Charles Robert struck an injurious blow at the independence of the counties by placing a number of them in groups under one count, instead of each under its own. These supreme counts took rank among the first barons of the empire, and gave place only to the *waywodes* or *bans*. These great nobles received their emoluments, as did all other officials, in kind, and had besides the right of purchasing a certain quantity of salt. Each county, divided into four districts, had a certain number of puisne or deputy judges, presided over by a superior judge (*feobiro*). Their assessors, a sort of jury composed of nobles, took part in the deliberations, and returned their verdict upon the case. These were elected by the nobles of the district, and none were qualified who had not real property within the jurisdiction of the court. The king himself named the superior courts, and sometimes even the viscounts, who opened the assemblies,—under Charles Robert with the royal permission, and under Louis, when the public safety required it. In these were discussed the legislative and legal affairs of the district, matters of police, and other subjects of local interest, not within the province of the general diet.

The military force of Hungary at first consisted, as we have already seen, entirely of the barons and their immediate followers, who ranged themselves under the banner of the king: and afterwards of the sixty-two bands furnished by the same number of counties or military districts, who were compelled by law to defend the country at their own expense. The Magyars, however bravely they might fight at home, were never disposed to carry the war beyond their own frontiers, even when the king bore the cost; and this was doubtless the cause of the many invasions to which Hungary has been exposed. The old military organisation began, however, in course of time, to fall into abeyance, and Charles Robert endeavoured to introduce a number of useful reforms. He ordained that the inhabitants living in the neighbourhood of the citadels, and every landed proprietor who was not a noble, should furnish his contingent to the general armament. This plan did not, however, answer his expectations, and a sort of militia was therefore created, called *banderies* (from the monkish Latin, *banderium*), upon the plan of the Italian bands or mercenary troops. This was maintained at the expense of the prelates and magnates, who, in their fondness for display, often

CASTLE OF OZOLYOM.

appeared in the field at the head of a greater number of levies than they were called upon to furnish. Charles Robert permitted them to keep their respective troops distinct, and to bring them into battle under their own orders and their own banner.

Besides these, there were the Szeklers, who fought as irregular troops, under no orders, where and in what manner pleased them. These were divided into two corps, archers and slingers. The revenues of the crown lands, it may readily be imagined, were by no means equal to the outlay of princes so enterprising as those of the house of Anjou. They were accustomed to a more lavish and less scrupulous system of finance than they found prevailing in Hungary, and in order to meet the expenses of their long wars, they placed heavy imposts upon all persons not ennobled. Thus, for every load of hay or of straw that entered a farmer's gate, he was obliged to pay a tax of eighteen deniers, and hence the name *porta* was given to it. The ninth part of the produce of their labour and industry was a tax which pressed with tremendous weight upon the poorer classes, and acted with a very injurious influence upon the commerce and agriculture of the country. This was not abolished till 1848. The landed property of the nobles could never be sold or aliened in any way, but was strictly entailed upon the male line, upon failure of which it reverted to the crown. It was, therefore, almost

SZEKLERS.

impossible for any one, who had not a claim to nobility, to become possessor of any land, except as a tenant farmer.

The administration of justice was generally pure, and the forms of procedure simple and direct. The ordeal by fire or boiling water fell into disuse under Bela III. and Andrew IV., and was finally abolished by Lucas Banfi. These princes also introduced advocates into the courts, appointed mayors for the villages, and magistrates for the government of the towns. The nobles had tribunals sitting in every county for the trial of those of their own order. The court of the palatine, the tribunal of final resort in all cases, changed the place in which its sittings were held four times in every year, for the convenience of those residing in the more remote parts of the kingdom. All legal proceedings took place publicly in open court.

The labours of the strangers who were introduced to fill the place of those massacred by the Moguls, gave a prodigious impulse to the commerce and industry of the nation. The vines of Tokay, the juice of which the Hungarians assert to have been the nectar of the gods of antiquity, and which not only ministered to the delicate taste of the epicures of the day, but crowned the splendid feasts of the Magyar monarchs, owed their origin to an Italian colony placed at Olaszi. The immense wealth of the great lords, the splendour of their feasts and entertainments, and the gorgeous magnificence of their dress and equipages, were not without their effect upon trade, whatever might be their ultimate influence upon the manners of the people. In the midst of this manufacturing and commercial prosperity, the arts and sciences, and polite literature, were not forgotten. Many of the Hungarians repaired, to complete their education, to the universities of Paris and Bologna, then famed for the learning and ability of their professors. An academy, known as the *Studium Generale*, was founded at Vesprim during the thirteenth century. Ladislaus IV. bestowed upon it an extensive library, and distinguished professors gave instruction in theology, jurisprudence, and belles lettres. But as literature was at that time peculiarly the province of the clergy, the national language was, for a considerable period unhonoured by the notice of the learned. Though Louis the Great spoke the Magyar with ease and fluency, as his mother tongue, still Latin continued to be the language of the refined and the noble. Amongst the learned men of the earlier part of Hungarian history, the names of Rogerius, archbishop of Spalatro; of Calanus, the historian, bishop of the Five Churches; Simon Keza, the chronicler; and the German astronomer Klingsohr, are mentioned with honour. In 1367, an academy was established in the town of Pecs, and in a short time attained to such a height of celebrity, that 4,000 students are said to have yearly filled its halls. Michas Madius, the Dalmatian chronicler, John Kukeolleo, the secretary of the king, and many others, of equal note, owed the eminence to which they afterwards attained, to the instruction they received here.

Following up the course upon which St. Stephen entered, the dynasty of Arpad, at all times, displayed the utmost zeal for the honour of religion; and as Catholicism was the only form under which it was then known in Europe, the popes soon obtained immense influence in Hungary. They established a crowd of religious orders, and as the clergy entirely monopolised the teaching of the young, they secured an ascendancy and an amount of wealth, which remains almost unimpaired to the present day. After the conversion to Christianity, there was but one archbishop and six bishops in the whole kingdom. When Louis the Great died, there were thirty archbishops and eight hundred bishops.

CHAPTER VIII.

MARIA AND SIGISMOND.—THE TURKS.

1382—1439.

WHILE Louis the Great was in the zenith of his splendour, the storm was brewing which was to put the chivalry of Europe on its mettle, and involve her frontier nations in the most serious and momentous contest of modern times. Amongst the tribes which composed the army of Gellaleddin, the sultan of Persia, in his able defence of his kingdom against the desolating inroads of Zengis Khan, was the small obscure clan which gave origin to the Turks, which had formerly dwelt near the southern banks of the Oxus, in the plains of Mohun and Neza. After the defeat and death of Gellaleddin, they entered the service of Aladin, sultan of Iconium; and in subjection to his sway, and under the rule of one of their own chiefs, Orthogrul, they formed a camp of four hundred families or tents at Surgut, on the banks of the Sangar. Orthogrul was the father of the caliph Othman, under whom the Turks first assumed an independent position, and began to commit ravages upon their own account, by making descents upon the Greek empire, through the passes of Mount Olympus, which the weakness of the emperors had left without protection. The first of these inroads was made on the 27th of July, 1299, and was the commencement of a series of attacks under which the imperial city itself was at last destined to fall. Instead of retreating to the hills, with his booty and captives, whenever he succeeded in taking a town or castle, he held it and fortified it, and endeavoured to wean his followers from the roving, pastoral life which they had hitherto followed, and attach them to the arts and luxuries of civilization.

Under the domination of his son Orchan, the Turks increased in power and ambition, fixed their head-quarters in the the city of Prusa, which they had taken, built in it a mosque and college, struck new coins, and by the fame of the professors whom Orchan endowed, attracted crowds of students from all parts of Asia. The office of vizier was established, and bestowed upon Aladin, Orchan's brother. A regular body of infantry was enrolled and trained, and instead of the mutinous peasants who followed the standard of Othman in loose and undiciplined squadrons, a powerful and well-organized army was formed of the Christian captives, who, taken in their youth, were instructed in the principles of the Moslem faith, and, with the usual zeal of proselytes, proved themselves its most ardent and enthusiastic propagators and defenders. The Turkish power was in this position when its aid was invoked by one of the parties in a civil war which was at that time desolating Greece. The ruin of the empire was from that moment sealed; and soon after we find that their but too efficient allies had wrested from the feeble hands of the emperor, without open violence, but by mere occupation, some of the most valuable portions of his dominions. Amurath, the successor of Orchan, subdued the whole province of Thrace or Romania, from the Hellespont to Mount Haemus, and chose Adrianople for the seat of his government and religion in Europe. The Greeks were in despair, and thought the hour of their downfal had at last come; but it was still delayed by the pride or generosity of the sultan. The emperor John Palæologus and his four sons had, however, to undergo the terrible humiliation of following the march of the conqueror, and witnessing the power of his arms in his expeditions against the Bulgarians, Servians, Bosnians, and Albanians. It was out of the captives that were taken from these hardy and courageous tribes that the formidable corps of janizaries, which long was both the defence and terror of the Turkish empire, was first formed. The youngest and most beautiful of the prisoners were selected, educated in religion and arms, and then consecrated by a celebrated dervish. He stood in front of their ranks, and stretched the sleeve of his gown over the head of the foremost soldier and delivered his blessing in these words: "Let them be called Janizaries (*Yengi Cheri*, or new soldiers); may their countenance be ever bright! their hand ever victorious! their sword keen! May their spear always hang over the heads of their enemies! and wheresoever they go, may they return with a white face!" * When first embodied, the new troops fought against their countrymen with determined valour and fidelity; and, at length, in the bloody battle of Cossova, the Sclavonian tribes were utterly routed, and their league destroyed. Amurath was walking across the field, in company with his vizier, when a Servian soldier, starting up from amongst the crowd of the slain, mortally wounded him in the belly.

He was succeeded in 1389 by Bajazet, surnamed *Ilderim*, or the lightning, who, by his fiery impetuosity, spread the terror of the Turkish arms far and wide through eastern Europe. He reduced the northern provinces of Anatolia to subjection, conquered Iconium, imposed a regular form of servitude upon the Servians and Bulgarians, and then crossed the Danube to seek new enemies in Moldavia.

The Greek emperors, surrounded on every side by this terrible foe, had sought the aid of Louis the Great, who promised to march to his assistance, in case he were joined by the other European sovereigns. But the fervour of Christian hatred for infidels had already cooled. The age of chivalry was gone. The pope refused to preach a crusade in favour of obstinate schismatics, who

* Gibbon, vol xi., p. 482. In latter years the discipline of the Janizaries became relaxed, and their insolence and turbulence made them the terror of their sovereign. They were all massacred in 1826, by the late Sultan Mahmoud.

scouted his pretensions to spiritual supremacy over the Christian church, and the eastern empire was left to its fate. Louis does not appear to have had an adequate idea of the danger to be apprehended from the Ottomans, and at all events his attention was too much engrossed by the affairs of Italy, to allow of his taking proper measures for the defence of his kingdom.

His successor had to bear the brunt of the contest. He left his kingdom to his daughter Mary, to whom the Poles swore allegiance, but speedily threw it off, and elevated Hedwig, a grand daughter of Casimir, to the throne. The Hungarians, though hitherto, owing perhaps to the military character of the people, a female ruler was a thing unknown in their history, saluted Mary queen out of respect for her father; but, as if to mark the exceptional character of the arrangement, they insisted that she should assume the title of king, and affix to all public documents the signature *Maria Rex*.

She had been betrothed by her father to Sigismond, of Brandenburgh, king of Bohemia, who was still very young, and of course incapable of holding the reins of government in conjunction with her. Elizabeth, the young queen's mother, consequently assumed the administration of the affairs of the kingdom, but was wholly under the influence of Gasa, the palatine, a prudent and faithful man, but ambitious and plotting. His advice led to the adoption of several measures militating severely against the nobles, and some portion of the obloquy which this drew down upon him, of course, reached the queen and her mother also. A conspiracy was at last formed for the modification or even total change of the government, which was joined by many persons of high rank, and they decided upon offering the crown to Charles the Little, king of Naples, son of the unfortunate Andrew, and grandson of Louis. This prince, acting without advice upon the dictates of his own ambition, and without heeding the salutary counsels of his wife, agreed to their proposals, and having put the affairs of his own kingdom in order, repaired to Hungary. The conspirators immediately crowned him king, but the coldness of the populace, who beheld the ceremony, was an omen of what was to follow. Mary and her mother were at first seized with despair, on hearing of the success of their rival, but on recovering from their surprise, the first moments of calmness were spent in planning a heinous crime. Amongst the most zealous of their adherents was a brave but unscrupulous noble, named Forgatz, and it was determined in a council, at which the palatine Gasa was present, to commit to him the task of assassinating Charles, as the readiest way of putting a stop to his pretensions. When the necessary arrangements had been made, and the day fixed, Elizabeth and the palatine, accompanied by Forgatz, repaired to the palace, the former under pretence of showing him some letters she had received from Sigismond, the latter of requesting a safe conduct, to enable him to attend at his daughter's marriage, which was to take place at a distance of some leagues. Charles was walking up and down the room, with the conspirators on either side of him, when, at a signal from Gasa, Forgatz drew his sword, and split the king's skull to the very teeth. The doors were at the same time thrown open, and the partisans of Mary rushed in and took possession of the castle, drove out Charles's attendants, who were for the most part Italians, and put a garrison in the place, and then rushing through the streets of Buda in arms, called upon the people to declare for Mary. The populace, instead of manifesting any indignation at the horrid crime which had just been committed, cut the rest of the Italians to pieces, and hailed Mary queen, with loud acclamations.

But the perpetrators of the murder did not long enjoy in quiet the fruits of it. Within a short time after Charles's assassination, they determined to pay a visit to the provinces of Lower Hungary, and for this purpose Mary and her mother, accompanied by Gasa and Forgatz, and attended by a slender escort, set out for Croatia. John Horvat, the ban, a zealous adherent of the late king, no sooner heard of their arrival in his government, than he hastily collected a body of troops, and furiously attacked the royal party. Forgatz and Gasa ably supported their reputation for courage, and defended themselves to the last extremity, till, overpowered by numbers, they were slaughtered before the queen's eyes. Mary and Elizabeth were dragged from their carriage by the hair, and brought before the ban. Elizabeth dropped on her knees at his feet, and implored him, for the sake of her departed husband, from whom he had received so many favours, to spare her life and set her at liberty. But neither her tears nor her prayers had the slightest effect upon Horvat. He ordered her to be drowned in the night, and her daughter to be shut up in a castle.*

Sigismond, upon hearing of the fate of his mother-in-law, and the imprisonment of his bride, marched with a large army into Hungary, and called upon the ban to set the captive at liberty. Horvat, whether moved by fear or pity, did not hesitate to comply with his request; and having exacted from Mary a solemn oath not to take vengeance upon him or his for the injuries she had sustained, sent her with a large escort to Buda, where Sigismond received her in the midst of great rejoicings. Their delight on meeting once more was great in the extreme; but we grieve to add that their nuptials were stained by Mary's perfidy. Notwithstanding her oath, she caused Sigismond to put Horvat to a barbarous and cruel death. He was seized and placed in a cart naked, with his hands tied behind his back, and in this way carried through all the towns and villages in the neighbourhood, the executioners all the while searing his body with red-hot tongs; and at last he was cut into four quarters, one of which was placed over each gate of the city.

Sigismond and Mary now ascended the throne as joint sovereigns (1386). The first year of their reign was disturbed by a revolt of the Wallacks, who, indignant at seeing a woman wearing the crown, rose in insurrection. Sigismond marched against them, and speedily subdued them; but no sooner had he returned to the capital, than they again took up arms, and this time invited the Turks to

* Bonfinius, lib. i., decad. 3, p. 393.

their aid, who eagerly complied with their request. The king again took the field, and coming up with the allied armies, the Hungarian cavalry, in complete armour, charged with such fury, that the Turks, unable to stand the onset, broke and fled, and vast numbers were cut down in the pursuit. Emboldened by his success, Sigismond proceeded to lay siege to Necopolis, a town on the Ister, garrisoned partly by Turks and partly by Hungarians. In the meantime Mary died childless, and her sister, Hedwig, had married Ladislaus, king of Poland, the latter determined to assert his claims to the Hungarian throne, and was proceeding to do so, had not the archbishop of Strigonia set his face against it, and obliged Ladislaus to defer his enterprise to a more favourable season. At home the eagerness of Sigismond to avenge himself upon those who, in Mary's reign, or in his own, had seemed opposed to him, caused new troubles. He caused thirty-two of the principal nobles of the Neapolitan party to be executed, and amongst them was Stephen Conthy, who, as well as the others, disdained to apply for mercy. This outrageous severity produced a strong feeling of hostility in the minds of the magnates, which, however, did not show itself openly until after the disastrous battle of Necopolis.

While he was besieging this town, great numbers of foreign soldiers, attracted by the importance of the struggle, repaired to his standard, French, Germans, and Bohemians. Bajazet advanced at the head of a large army to raise the siege, and offered battle to the Hungarians under the city walls. The French auxiliaries besought Sigismond to yield to them the post of honour, and allow them to combat in the front rank of the Christian forces. Their request was granted, but before the Hungarian army had been drawn up in array, the French, excited by seeing the Turks coolly awaiting the conflict, issued from their quarters, and rode full gallop against the enemy. Upon approaching their ranks, they dismounted and advanced on foot. Their horses being turned loose, galloped wildly back to the camp, where their arrival caused the utmost confusion, from a belief that their riders had fallen, and that the Turks were advancing flushed with victory, and a panic seizing upon the Hungarians, they fled precipitately. The unfortunate French, surrounded on all sides, fought bravely against overwhelming odds for some time, and supported their courage by the hope of succour. But the succour never came, and they were cut off to a man. The Turks then pursued the Hungarians for many miles, slaughtering immense numbers, and returned, laden with booty, and carrying with them a great number of captives. On this disastrous day, twenty thousand Hungarians were left dead on the field, or in the pursuit; and Sigismond escaped with difficulty in a small boat across the Danube to Constantinople, and only reached his kingdom after a long absence and a still longer circuit. The count de Nevers, and seventy-four of the French lords of the highest rank, were reserved for ransom, and the remainder of the prisoners, on refusing to change their creed, were beheaded in the conqueror's presence. The survivors were for a long time carried in triumph from one part of the Turkish territory to the other, and at last were released upon the payment of an enormous ransom.

In the pride of victory, Bajazet threatened to besiege Buda and subdue Germany and Italy, and declared that he would feed his horse with a bushel of oats upon the altar of St. Peter's. His progress was stayed, however, by a severe attack of gout. During Sigismond's absence, the terrible catastrophe which had befallen the kingdom gave the malcontents an opportunity of carrying their designs into execution, by the formation of another plot, the elevation of Ladislaus, king of Naples, and son of the unfortunate Charles the Little, to the Hungarian throne. Charles, however, had too vivid a recollection of his father's fate to be seduced into compliance, and Sigismond was allowed to enter his kingdom in peace. In a very short time a considerable number of the magnates, with the two sons of Gara at their head, went to the palace, as if for the purpose of paying their respects, and seized the king's person, loaded him with chains, and shut him up in the castle of Szicklos. Ladislaus now was once more invited to take possession of the kingdom, but his fears overcame his ambition, and he paused at the frontiers of Dalmatia. In the meantime, the widow of Gara, touched by the king's misfortunes, persuaded her sons, into whose custody he had been committed, to connive at his escape. He instantly betook himself to Bohemia, raised there a large army, at the head of which he re-entered Hungary, took possession of the kingdom, obliged Ladislaus to desist from his pretensions, and, by an unusually judicious mixture of severity and conciliation, restored order and tranquillity.

Having become in succession king of Bohemia and emperor of Germany, his new dignity gave him an opportunity of moving from place to place, gratifying his taste by weaving intricate webs of diplomacy. The rise of the sect known as the Hussites caused great troubles in his Bohemian dominions, and proved the cause of casting a stain upon his memory, and upon the church which he served, which no apology can ever efface. When the celebrated Council of Constance, for the regulation of ecclesiastical affairs, summoned before them John Huss and Jerome of Prague, the two celebrated reformers, whose preaching had inflicted such grievous wounds upon catholicism, they refused to appear, unless they received some guarantee that would insure their personal safety, Sigismond granted them a safe conduct, signed by his own hand; but upon their arrival, joined in sentencing them to be burnt alive. This odious act of perfidy entailed upon Germany many a year of suffering and disaster.

In the meantime, Naples and Venice seized upon various strongholds upon the Adriatic, without any attempt at resistance upon the part of Sigismond; and it was only at the pressing instance of Nicholas Szentpole, that he at length made preparations to avenge the defeat sustained by his army at Necopolis. The war was commenced by the taking of Bosnia by the Hungarian general, Peterfi, who pushed on as far as Nissa, where the grand vizier occupied a strong position, with

JOHN HUNYADI.

an army of 24,000 men. The battle was fought on the fourteenth of October, 1419, and ended in the total defeat of the Turks.

It was in this battle that John Hollos, the adopted son of Butho, a Wallack *boyard*, or nobleman, first made himself conspicuous by his valour. He had served in succession under the banners of Francis Csanadi, and the bishop of Zagrab; and in this battle, where he commanded a troop, his daring attracted the notice of the king, who bestowed upon him the domain of Hunyad, in which he had been brought up. There is a great deal of uncertainty about the origin of this illustrious man; and even in the accounts of those national historians, who ought to have found little difficulty in accuracy, there is a strange mixture of statements that are probably true, with those that are certainly fictitious. We are told that his father was a Wallack, and this we can readily believe; but when it is added that his appellative of Corvinus, derived from the Latinized name of the village in which he was born, joined with the fact that his father was possibly descended from one of the Roman colonists of the province of Dacia, renders it probable that he was a scion of the famous Roman family on whom chance had conferred the same epithet; and that from the mere circumstance of his mother being a Greek, it was likely that the blood of the Cæsars ran in his veins, we cannot help smiling at the absurdities that hero-worship will induce men to believe and to publish. His valour and wisdom made in his day so powerful an impression upon the minds of the Hungarians, that in a country where birth confers so many great advantages, popular tradition could not do less than make him the son of a king. The story of his origin, as the peasantry tell it, is worth notice for its *naiveté*, and in the absence of clear and decided testimony against it, it would hardly become us to impugn its truth.

Sigismond, after the death of his first wife, had married Barbara de Cilly, a perverse and cunning woman, who poisoned her husband's existence, and disgraced her sex by her gross licentiousness. He, therefore, very soon began to abandon her society for that of other females. In 1392, he led his army into Wallachia, and when encamped on the banks of the Sztrigy, he met, in one of his evening walks, a girl named Elizabeth Morsiani, the daughter of a neighbouring boyard, and was captivated by her beauty. The admiration and attention of the king dazzled the simple maiden, and she yielded her honour without even a coy refusal. Sigismond then passed on to the scene of the war, where, also, he was equally successful, and upon his return, the beautiful Morsiani again presented herself at his tent, and asked what reward he would bestow upon her for presenting him with a child. "I will load the child with honours," he replied, delighted with the result of his amour; and handing her a gold ring, told her to come to the palace, and the ring should remind him of his promise. Some months after his departure, Elizabeth married a boyard named Volk Butho, who took her with him into Wallachia, where she soon after gave birth to a son, whom she named John. When Sigismond again arrived in the neighbourhood, and she repaired to the camp, and presented him with the child and the ring. He received her graciously, and renewed his promises of favour and protection, and told her to come to Buda. Shortly afterwards her husband died, and she was making preparations for the journey, when a crow snatched the ring from her son's hand, and flew with it to a neighbouring tree, whereupon her brother, running to her assistance, shot the bird, and restored the bijou. She appeared before the king in his palace at Buda, and he loaded her with favours. When John had grown up, he bestowed upon him the domain of Hunyad, and sixty villages, and gave him as his coat-of-arms, a crow carrying a ring in its bill, and the young man ever after bore the name of his estate, Hunyadi Janos, or John of Hunyad.

At the battle of Sendrecz, Sigismond was again successful, and again Hunyadi made the Turks feel the weight of his prowess. The king was now well stricken in years, and in 1437 he died, and was buried in the cathedral of Great Varadin, leaving the three crowns of which he was in possession at his death to his daughter Elizabeth and her husband, Albert, duke of Austria. He possessed many great virtues, and in reviewing his faults we must take into account the factions, intrigues, and invasions against which he had to contend. He was a man of commanding appearance, profuse in hospitality, and, when not driven into cruelty by real or fancied danger, he was humane and merciful; and, on the whole, was worthy of a happier reign.

He left a daughter, Elizabeth, who had married Albert, archduke of Austria; and by Sigismond's express desire, the latter succeeded him in the dignities he had himself held—as emperor of Germany, king of Bohemia and of Hungary. He ascended the throne of the latter kingdom in 1438, but his reign was short. The Hungarians did not much relish the government of their country by a foreign sovereign, and the mixture which then began to take place between them and the Germans was the cause of continued quarrels and discontent. Albert introduced a practice of appointing a Hungarian or a German, alternately each year, to the governorship of Buda. The Germans, pluming themselves on the fact that the king was a man of their nation, endeavoured, by a series of intrigues, to secure this office entirely to themselves. Amongst the Hungarians none were more opposed to their machinations than a magnate named John Euthues, a man of very high spirit, who had distinguished himself on several occasions by his impetuous resentment of slights thrown upon the Hungarians. The Germans were, therefore, anxious, above all things, to procure his removal. After vainly trying several expedients, they at last entered his house by force, manacled him, and, after immuring him in a dungeon, inflicted upon him excruciating tortures; and, at length, having cut his throat, threw his body into the Danube.

Within a week afterwards, the body rose to the surface, and, drifting ashore, was speedily recognised, though greatly mutilated and pierced with numerous wounds. A great concourse of nobles, from various parts of the country, was at this time assembled in Buda, for the purpose of paying their respects to the new king; and the rumour having gone abroad that Euthues had been murdered by the Germans, the whole Hungarian population of the city sallied out, sword in

CASTLE OF HUNYAD.

hand, and slaughtered, without discrimination of age or sex, not the Germans only, but all foreigners within the walls, and plundered and wrecked their houses.

The Turks, immediately upon hearing of the death of Sigismond, prepared for a new inroad; and George, prince of Servia, believing himself unable to make head against the infidels single-handed, took refuge in Hungary, with the bishops and many of the nobility, leaving his son to hold Sendrecz against the invaders.

TOWN OF PRESBURG.

When the Hungarians learnt that their frontier was thus laid open to the enemy, messengers were sent off in great haste to Albert, who was then in Poland, imploring him to march to the defence of the kingdom. On arriving at Buda, he was informed of the death of George Paloes, one of the highest dignitaries of the state, to whose keeping the regalia had been committed. After taking possession of them, he handed them to his wife Elizabeth, who, in her turn, gave them to an old woman, and then returned to Buda from Strigonia, where the treasure was kept. The king then advanced, without any auxiliaries, against the Turks, and encamped between the Danube and the Teyss. In the meantime, however, while waiting for reinforcements, Sendrecz was taken by assault, and the inhabitants put to the sword. Stephen and Gregory, the prince's sons, were taken prisoners, and some time afterwards, on Amurath's hearing that they kept up a correspondence with their father, they were blinded by being compelled to endure the glare of red-hot plates of brass, although their sister had been for some time his principal wife.* Great consternation prevailed amongst the Hungarians upon the receipt of this intelligence, and it was increased by the breaking out of dysentery in the Christian army, owing to the bad quality of the water they were obliged to drink, the springs having been dried up by the extreme heat of the weather. Large numbers were thus carried off; but the survivors were in some measure relieved from their fears by hearing that the Turks had retreated, leaving merely a garrison in the Sendrecz. Albert was preparing to return to Buda, when he found himself stricken with the prevailing epidemic, and wishing to end his days in his native country, he set out for Vienna, but on arriving at Nesmel he died, in November, 1439.

Whether from a spirit of equity and moderation, or through the need he felt of the Hungarians to defend himself against the Turks, Albert spent nearly the whole of his reign in soothing and conciliating them. When the electors of the German empire offered him the imperial crown, he refused to accept of it, until he had obtained the consent of his Hungarian subjects, and the question underwent a long discussion in the diet. It was represented, and with some foundation, that the number of crowns which Sigismond wore simultaneously distracted his attention and prevented his uniting his forces for the defence of Hungary against the Ottomans; but they nevertheless declared that they had no wish to deprive Albert of the honour which the Germans had offered him. He, in return, gave them a proof of his regard by issuing a decree confirming the oath he had taken at his coronation. In it he declared, among other things, "that there was nothing he had more at heart than the preservation of their rights and privileges; that he would never bestow upon any foreigner any benefice, government, commission, land, or lordship; that he would never intrust them with the keeping of any fortress, and that he would never alien or pledge the revenues of the crown."† His reign only lasted three years, and, although just and moderate, he was the cause of many calamities and divisions, as we shall see hereafter.

* Bonfin. Decad. iii. lib. iii. p. 439.

† "The Decree of King Albert," of the year 1436, in the Prol. Art. v., xvi., &c.

CHAPTER X.

LADISLAUS II.

A.D. 1439—1444.

WHEN Albert died, he left his wife pregnant, and the Hungarians appeared, out of respect for her father's memory, to be very well-disposed to live under her government, and that of Ladislaus, her son. But the power of the Turks had now reached such a pitch of magnitude, and they were making such formidable preparations for the subjugation of western Europe, that it was feared by John Hunyadi that it would be in the highest degree imprudent to leave a woman and child at the head of affairs at such a critical period; and in accordance with the established rights of the diet in such cases, the crown was offered to Ladislaus, king of Poland, a young prince of great valour and ability, upon condition that he should marry Albert's widow, and that Austria and Bohemia should be the inheritance of Albert's son, and Hungary and Poland, of those children whom she might bear to her second husband. The latter was, therefore, formally declared king, and ambassadors were despatched to fetch him. After much discussion and hesitation, he accepted the proffered kingdom, and set out for Hungary.

The queen, upon hearing what had occurred, was loud in her complaints and lamentations, accusing herself of folly in suffering her son to be thus defrauded of his inheritance, and the nobles of treachery and ingratitude. Many, whom other weapons could not pierce, were moved by her prayers and tears, and determined to stand by her at all hazards; and one of the archbishops, the Cardinal Zechi, placed himself at the head of her party. Acting under his advice, the royal infant was carried in his cradle to Alba Regia, and placed on a sort of throne or raised dais, where the cardinal crowned him, but without calling the diet together, or going through any of the other formalities which the laws of the kingdom prescribed. The child's cries and his mother's tears which fell fast throughout the ceremony, filled the spectators with evil foreboding, which subsequent events too fully justified. The queen, immediately after the coronation, fled into Austria, carrying with her the crown, which had been confided to her husband Albert's care.

Ladislaus soon after arrived in Buda, and was met by the palatine, who conducted him to the citadel, and there crowned and proclaimed him king, with all the ordinary solemnities; for want of the royal diadem, making use of wooden crown, taken off a statue of St. Stephen which stood in the hall. During the ceremony, a conspiracy to poison the new monarch was discovered just as the emissary was on the point of executing his detestable commission. He was instantly tried, and condemned to be drawn asunder by four horses, and the sentence was rigidly executed.

The kingdom was now divided into two great parties, that of the queen and her son, and that of Ladislaus. They soon came to an open rupture, which was of course attended with the violence and calamities which civil war usually produces. The conflict was carried on with varied fortune, but without any intermission of suffering on the part of the unfortunate peasantry, who saw their villages burnt, their property carried off, and their farms laid waste, in a quarrel in which they had no interest whatever. The success, however, was generally on the side of the king, who had strengthened his party, both in the field and in the diet, by attaching to his interests John Hunyadi, whom he created waywode of Transylvania. The queen struggled gallantly to the last, but finding she was playing a losing game, she at last gave in, and committing her son and the crown to the care of Frederick III., emperor of Germany, she desisted from open hostilities, but never ceased to cause Ladislaus all the trouble and uneasiness in her power, by continually stirring up intrigues against him, both at home and abroad.

The sultan, Amurath, thought that these internal dissensions would afford him a fair opportunity of attempting another invasion of Hungary, and assembling a large army, he marched along the Danube, till he reached Belgrade, a strongly fortified city, washed on both sides by the Save and the Danube, and considered by the Hungarians the key of their kingdom. On arriving before it, the Turks attempted to carry it by assault, but were vigorously repulsed. They then raised wooden towers and battering rams, to annoy the besieged by missiles, and, if possible, effect a breach in the walls; and at the same time, launched vessels on the Danube, to cut off all succours from Hungary. But owing to the valiant defence of the governor, a Florentine, of distinguished military abilities, all his efforts were defeated. He, nevertheless, continued the siege, in the hope that the garrison would capitulate, before Ladislaus could bring his undivided forces to their aid. The latter, as soon as he had subdued the queen's party, sent an embassy to Amurath, offering to enter into a treaty with him, in case he abandoned hostilities and withdrew his forces. The sultan craved time to consider his proposal, but employed the interval in making preparations for another vigorous assault. A breach had been made in the walls on the previous evening, and in the morning the soldiers, headed by the janissaries, advanced to the assault with great ardour, and succeeded in entering the breach. But no sooner had they done so, than the garrison, aided by the inhabitants, attacked them with such fury, that they were driven back with terrible slaughter. Great numbers were killed in the streets, and Christians having thrown Greek fire into the ditch, by which the faggots and stakes with which it was filled were set in a blaze, many more were burnt or smothered by the smoke when taking to flight. The forces embarked on the Danube fared no better; and it was with no small discouragement and chagrin that Amurath recalled his troops, after having lost, in this single onset, nearly 15,000 of his best men; and being greatly pressed for want of provisions, he at last determined to break up his camp and return home. At his departure, however, he left behind him his nephew, Isa-beg, with a large body of cavalry, who, fixing his head-quarters in Rascia, began to make frequent inroads into Transylvania, burning the houses and carrying away the men and cattle. Hunyadi raised a strong body of horse and foot to defend his viceroyalty, and combining his forces with those of Nicholas Vilach, his most intimate friend and companion, he awaited the Turks at a place about midway between Belgrade and Sendrecz. Isa-beg immediately prepared to attack him. In the first onset the Turks compelled the Hungarian light-horse, which composed the wings of Hunyadi's army, to give way, and then turning, fell upon his centre with great fury. But there meeting with the men at arms, whose cuirasses gave them the advantage, the Ottomans were overthrown after a fierce struggle, and fled precipitately, leaving the flower of their troops dead upon the field. The Hungarians, headed by Hunyadi himself, pursued the fugitives for ten miles, and cut them down without mercy, and returned to Belgrade with a large number of prisoners, and laden with booty. When the news of this victory reached Buda, the joy of the court and of the people was great. Public thanksgivings were offered up in all the churches, and Ladislaus wrote a congratulatory letter to Hunyadi, thanking him for the great service he had rendered to Hungary and to Christendom, and encouraging him to follow up his successes, not only that he might secure fame and wealth in this world, but in the world to come life everlasting.

But Amurath was not yet disheartened. He collected his broken forces, and putting them under the command of one of his pachas, Mezet Bey, a soldier of great valour and experience, he gave him instructions to invade Transylvania, and avenge the losses which the Turkish armies had sustained. He carried out his orders to the letter. He suddenly entered Hunyadi's province, leaving not a soul alive in the track of his soldiers, and turning the entire country into a wilderness. Hunyadi was taken by surprise, and having no force prepared to oppose the Turks, was compelled to take to flight. But he did not neglect his duty: he rode about through all the border towns and villages, particularly those inhabited by the Szeklers, calling on the men to take up arms in defence of their wives and children, and soon found himself at the head of a large force of irregular troops, with whom he pursued the invader by forced marches, and offered him battle.

The engagement which followed was one of the most bloody of the campaign. Information was brought early in the day to Hunyadi that the Turkish general had given strict orders that every effort should be made to capture him or kill him, as the main support of the war. Upon hearing this, a Magyar gentleman,

Simon Kemene, exchanged armour with Hunyadi, and rode into action with a strong body of cavalry. The battle began by slight skirmishes; but at length the Turks perceiving Kemene, and taking him for the Christian general, directed the whole force of their onslaught against the troops which he commanded. The Hungarian soldiers defended their leader to the last, but at length, having fallen one by one, Kemene himself was at last overpowered and slain. The Turks now thought the victory achieved, as their loss had been prodigious; but to their astonishment they now perceived a second Hunyadi advancing against them with fresh troops, and to add to their confusion, the Transylvanian prisoners broke loose in the camp, and snatching up the first weapons they could meet with, fell upon the rear of the Ottomans, who were now utterly routed, and fled in terrible confusion, leaving four or five thousand men, and their general, Mezet Bey, dead upon the field. Their tents and baggage, and all the prisoners they had taken during the invasion, fell into the hands of the victors. The women and children crowded around Hunyadi, and fell weeping at his feet, calling him their saviour and deliverer, and invoking blessings on his head. A waggon-load of the spoil, drawn by ten horses, was sent to Ladislaus and the prince of Servia, who was then with him, containing, amongst other things, a goodly pile of Turks' heads, surmounted by that of the general.

Amurath, enraged beyond measure at hearing of the overthrow of his army and the death of his general, raised a still greater force of 80,000 men in the spring of the following year, and sent it into Wallachia under the command of Sciabedin Bey. This army followed the example of its predecessors, slaughtering the inhabitants and laying waste the country through which it passed.

Hunyadi awaited their approach in an entrenched camp in Transylvania with 15,000 men. The Turkish general was astonished when he heard of the smallness of the Christian army, and determined to surround it on all sides, and overwhelm it by numbers. Hunyadi drew out his forces in the form of a wedge, and kept his flanks protected by the waggons, and after a long and fierce conflict, the Turks once more took to flight, leaving great numbers dead upon the field, and 5,000 prisoners, and 100 ensigns in the hands of the enemy. This was the famous battle of Vascape the greatest that Hunyadi ever gained. He returned to Buda in triumph, and presented the captured standards to the king. After this victory, Ladislaus fearing that the whole power of the Turkish empire might now be turned against him, and that his own forces, however favoured by fortune hitherto, might be unequal to the contest, called together a council of the two legislative assemblies, at which the pope's legate also attended, and consulted them as to the best course to be pursued in future. The legate gave his voice for war, and he was supported by George, the despot of Servia, who recounted to the assembly, with tears in his eyes, the terrible ravages which the Turks had committed in his dominions, declaring that he had been driven into exile by them, and his children separated from him; and imploring them not to abandon him without aid or protection to the wrath of a cruel and relentless enemy, and that enemy an infidel. His prayers seemed to have more effect than the legate's harangue; for the diet, as soon as he had concluded, passed the resolutions necessary for carrying on the war. Ambassadors were despatched to the emperor of Germany, and other European sovereigns, seeking aid against the common enemy. Most of them, however, excused themselves upon one pretence or another; but great numbers of private individuals, both in France and Germany, being prompted by religious motives, took up arms and repaired to Hungary as volunteers.

When the spring arrived, prayers having been offered up in all the churches for the success of the enterprise, Ladislaus started from Buda on the 1st of May, and marching along the Danube, crossed the frontiers of Bulgaria, and laid seige to the city of Sophia, which, being badly fortified, surrendered after a slight resistance, and was burned to the ground, as well as all the villages in the neighbourhood. After leaving this, he arrived on the banks of the Moravia, where his scouts fell in, towards evening, with the advanced guard of the Turks. A council of war was then held in the king's tent, at which it was resolved that Hunyadi, with ten thousand horse, should attack the Ottomans by surprise in the night. The latter, accordingly, set forward, and, shortly before midnight, found himself close upon the enemy's camp; and the moon just then breaking out so as to show him the nature of the ground in the vicinity, the Hungarians charged with loud cries. The Turks, in the first moments of surprise, scarce knew whether to fly or to remain; but true, even in darkness and confusion, to the valorous instincts of the nation, they soon rallied, and stood on the defensive. Hunyadi, in the meantime, urged on his soldiers by the promise of a glorious victory and a heap of plunder; and the report of his presence having gone abroad among the enemy, so great was the terror inspired by his name, that they instantly turned and fled, they knew not whither. The Hungarian cavalry pursued them in the moonlight, cutting them down for miles, without mercy; and the Turks themselves, confused, panic-stricken, and seeing a foe in every one who approached them, in many instances turned their swords against one another, and completed whatever, in the work of destruction, the weakness or fatigue of the Christian army compelled them to leave unfinished. Thirty thousand of the Turks are said to have been slain, and their camp and baggage fell into the hands of the victors.*

It was now determined, by the advice of the legate Julian, to follow up this success, to overrun Bulgaria, and, if possible, to force the passes of Mount Haemus, and attack Adrianople itself. The army, therefore, pushed forward without delay, taking possession of all the towns which lay in the line of their march; a task which, in the majority of instances, was easily accomplished, as the inhabitants were generally Christians, or at least of Sclavonic origin, and bore but a very unwilling allegiance to the sultan. When they approached the mountains, however, they, for the first time, began to perceive the difficulties of the enter-

* Knolles's History of the Turks, p. 278. The number seems to be greatly exaggerated.

prise in which they had engaged. It was now midwinter, and, in addition to the piercing cold of the weather and the hardships and discomfort of a march across a rugged country, through snow and ice, they underwent dreadful sufferings from the great scarcity of food. There were but two passes on the hills, both of which the Turks had strongly fortified; and they had rendered the heights in the vicinity inaccessible to the surest foot and steadiest eye, by pouring down great quantities of water, which the frost soon converted into a sheet of ice.* After several ineffectual attempts, the troops began to lose heart, and it required all the energy and popularity of Hunyadi to prevent their rising into open mutiny. Things were in this position when the leaders were relieved from their perplexity by the news that the Turks had left their strongholds, and were descending into the low ground to offer battle, under the command of Carambey, the pasha of Romania; who, in this, however, was departing from his instructions, as he had received express orders from the sultan to confine himself to the defence of the passes. The Hungarians halted and awaited his approach at the foot of the mountain called Konovics, Nov. 28, 1443. After beating off several irregular onsets of the Turkish cavalry, Hunyadi drew out his forces in battle array, and put himself at their head. "To die once," said he, "is a debt we owe to nature; but to die in battle for faith and fatherland is a favour which the Almighty bestows upon his chosen people only. Follow me! God is with us!" The Hungarians instantly charged, and the Turks meeting them with equal gallantry, a desperate conflict followed. The Christian forces had suffered so much from cold and hunger, that they gladly embraced death in preference to defeat and its attendant miseries in a savage and desolate country at a great distance from home; and the Ottomans were burning with the desire of avenging their recent defeats and retrieving their losses. The Hungarian light horse flung themselves, again and again, upon the enemy with reckless bravery; and though on each onset they left the ground strewed with their dead and dying, they returned, nothing daunted, to the fray. The Turks, at last, began to give ground, when Carambey led down fresh troops from the mountain, and renewed the contest. Hunyadi then sent out some light infantry, armed with pikes and boar spears, who, lying down among the bushes, stabbed the horses of the Turkish cavalry as they rode past, and spread confusion through the whole body. Carambey did everything that valour or skill could suggest, rallying his forces in every quarter of the field, and encouraging them by his voice and example. The fate of the day was thus for a long time kept trembling in the balance, until an unexpected accident, at length, turned the scale. The Turkish general, in riding hurriedly across the field, got entangled in a morass, which the snow, lying thickly on the ground, concealed from his view; and before he could extricate himself, was taken prisoner. The Turks, immediately on seeing their leader in the enemy's hands, fled in confusion.

* Knolles's Hist. of the Turks, p. 279.

After this victory, prince George and Hunyadi were anxious once more to attempt the forcing of the pass, and the king, though at first deterred by the remembrance of their former failure, at length gave a reluctant consent. The expedition was unfortunate from first to last. Encompassed by woods, and bogs, and craggy heights, and exposed to the incessant attacks of the Turks, who sallied from their fortresses, fought while successful, and retreated in safety when worsted, the sufferings of the Hungarian army at last became intolerable, and a retreat was determined upon. After long and toilsome marches they reached Buda, and entered amidst the acclamations of the citizens, who filled the windows and covered the housetops. The procession partook of the character of a Roman triumph in the palmiest days of the republic, but it will for ever remain a stain on Ladislaus and Hunyadi, that, in imitating Roman pomp, they imitated Roman cruelty and pride as well. We should consider it a curious feature in the Christianity of the middle ages, that its charity, and beneficence, and fair dealing were exercised only towards such as embraced and held its tenets, if we did not know that, even in the present day, a still narrower, and in many respects a more hateful intolerance, anathematises men merely for a difference of sect; but it may well excite our surprise that, in an age when chivalry was not yet dead, the champion knight of Christendom should have suffered a brave enemy, whose misfortunes were his only fault, to walk humiliated and degraded through hostile crowds, at his horse's head. Carambey, we are told, walked through the streets of Buda, bound in chains, followed by thirteen bashaws and 4,000 captives of lesser rank, while Hunyadi, clothed in a triumphal robe, rode at the king's right hand.* Ladislaus and all the chiefs of the army repaired on foot to the church of Our Lady, where the captured standards were hung up over the altar, and a solemn *Te Deum* was chanted by the prelates and priests.

Another formidable opponent now rose up against the Turks in an unexpected quarter, in the person of George Castriot, by the Turks called Scanderbeg. His father was hereditary prince of Epirus, or Albania; a small district lying between the mountains and the Adriatic sea. Unable to contend against the sultan's power, Castriot was compelled to accept such conditions as he chose to impose; he agreed to pay an annual tribute, and delivered his four sons as hostages for his fidelity. The youths, after undergoing circumcision, were instructed in the Mahometan religion, and trained in the arms and arts of Turkish policy. The three elder brothers were confounded in the crowd of slaves; and rumour said they were poisoned, but for the truth of this there is no positive evidence. The fourth brother, George, was however treated with favour and attention, and from his youth displayed the spirit and bravery of a soldier. He overthrew successively, in single combat, a Tartar, and two Persians who had carried defiance to the Turkish court, and thus commended himself to the notice of Amurath, and he received the appellation of Scanderbeg (*Iskenderbeg*, the lord Alexander), from the

* Knolles's History of the Turks, p. 382.

Turks. His father's dominions were reduced to a province of the Turkish empire, but to compensate George for the loss of his inheritance, he received the rank and title of Sanjiak, and the command of 5,000 horse, and the prospect was held out to him of still further promotion. He served for a long time with honour in the wars of Europe and Asia; but appears to have had the desire of avenging upon the Turks, whom he secretly hated, his father's wrongs, the fate of his three brothers, and the slavery of his country.* Whether he was ever a sincere Mahometan is hard to determine. The old historians stoutly affirm that he was not; but we find it difficult to believe them, when we know that, from the age of nine, he was instructed in the doctrines of the Koran, and that up to forty, he was a faithful and devoted follower of the sultan. However this may be, we can hardly acquit him of the charge of inexcusable dissimulation protracted through so long a period, and however lightly pious people in that age may have looked on his deceit and treachery, in consideration of the end they served, few at the present day will acquiesce in their apology.

At the battle in which Carambey was taken, in the confusion of the rout, Scanderbeg suddenly rushed up to the reis effendi, or principal secretary, and with a dagger at his breast, extorted a firman, or patent for the government of Albania, and immediately on obtaining it, murdered the writer and his train, to prevent the speedy discovery of the plot. Surrounded by a few bold followers, he escaped in the night from the field of battle, reached his paternal mountains, and on presenting the firman at Croya, the gates were at once opened to him, and he assumed the command of the garrison. He now threw off the mask, abjured the Mahometan religion and his allegiance to the sultan, and declared himself the avenger of his family and country. In an assembly of the states of Epirus, he was unanimously elected general of the Turkish war. He organized an army, adjusted the finances, and without waiting to be attacked, forthwith advanced against the Turkish posts. Petrella, Petra Alba, and Stellusa fell before him, and then passing into the Turkish territories, he laid waste the whole country. Ali Bey was at last sent against him with an army of 40,000 men, but his strength rendering him careless, Scanderbeg attacked and totally defeated him with great slaughter. Amurath was thunderstruck by his losses, and not knowing where the successes of the Hungarians and Albanians might end, he, at last, sent ambassadors to Ladislaus to crave for peace, offering to restore Servia to its prince, to ransom the captives, and to evacuate the Hungarian frontier, making no claim to Moldavia nor to that part of Bulgaria which he had lost during the war.† A diet was summoned at Szeguedin to consider his proposals, which were powerfully supported by George Brankovitz, the despot of Servia, whose interests would have been greatly benefited by the cessation of hostilities. After a long discussion they were agreed to, and a truce of ten years was concluded, Ladislaus swearing

* Milman's Gibbon, vol. xii. p. 163-4.

† Milman's Gibbon, vol. xiii. p. 153. Knolles's History of the Turks, p. 289.

on the holy evangelists, and the Turkish ambassadors upon the Koran, well and faithfully to fulfil and keep it.*

The cardinal Julian Caesarini was present at the discussion and signing of the treaty, but gave no sign of approval. He was secretly opposed to the peace, but being unable to give any valid cause for dissension, he remained silent; before the diet was dissolved, however, he received the welcome news that Anatolia had been invaded by the Caramanian, and Thrace by the Greek emperor, and that the fleets of Genoa, Venice and Burgundy were masters of the Hellespont, and that the allies were impatiently awaiting the return of the victorious army of Ladislaus. Furnished with these materials, the cardinal addressed the diet in a long and artful harangue, reproaching them with deserting their fellow Christians in the hour of need, and when everything promised success; declaring that there existed between them and God prior engagements, which made void the sacrilegious treaty into which they had just entered; that the vicar of Christ on earth was the Roman pontiff, in whose name he absolved them from their oaths and called upon them to renew the war against the infidels. Strange to say, his proposition was adopted on the spot, and preparations were forthwith made for recommencing hostilities. Hunyadi vehemently opposed this gross breach of faith, assuring the king that all the bulls that were ever written could not release him from subjection to the laws of honour; but we regret to add that his scruples were silenced, and his aid secured by the promise of the kingdom of Bulgaria, in case the campaign were brought to a prosperous issue.† Ladislaus could not have been in a much worse position for entering upon the conflict. Upon the proclamation of the peace, the German and French volunteers had departed homeward in disgust; the Poles were exhausted by distant warfare, and perhaps tired of foreign command, and their palatines accepted the first license and hastily retired to their provinces and castles. Even Hungary itself was divided by faction, or restrained by just and laudable scruples. More than one ill omen warned the king against the enterprise upon which he was entering. Drakul, the waywode of Wallachia, whom he called upon to accompany him, with his vassals, on seeing the royal forces, which did not amount to more than 20,000 men, presumed to remark that their numbers did not exceed the hunting retinue that sometimes attended the sultan, and presented Ladislaus with two horses of matchless speed, as if to mark his evil foreboding of the event. But the king felt such implicit confidence in the skill and valour of Hunyadi, and the prayers and protection of the church, that he scarce felt a pang of doubt or of remorse. The Turks on their side literally fulfilled the treaty. They surrendered their strongholds in Servia and Rascia; they restored the captives and hostages

* A recent French writer states that Hunyadi was bribed by Brankovitz to promote the treaty by the gift of a magnificent estate at Vilagosvur, and that at the diet, as if ashamed of his weakness, he preserved an ambiguous silence. As no authority is cited, however, it would be hardly fair to adopt the story.

† Knolles's History of the Turks, p. 292. Bonfin. Dec. iii. lib. vi. p. 485.

BATTLE OF VARNA.

which they held, and ransomed Carambey by a payment 40,000 ducats, and sent home to the despot George his two blind sons.

Ladislaus now sent off notice to the Greek emperor, and Francis the Florentine cardinal, who was then lying in the straits of the Hellespont with a fleet of seventy galleys, that he had resolved upon breaking the treaty, lest they, on hearing of the peace, should desist from hostilities and return home. He also wrote to Scanderbeg, apprising him of his intention, and asking his aid against the infidels. The latter joyfully acceded, and set forward with a considerable force; but on arriving on the frontiers of Servia, the despot, piqued by the retention of some of his fortresses by Ladislaus, refused him a passage.

The Hungarian army in the meantime advanced towards the Turkish frontier, capturing all the towns and castles on their way, until at last, on arriving before Sumium and Pezechium, the Turkish garrisons, trusting to the strength of the fortifications, offered a strenuous resistance. Both places were, however, carried by assault, and above five thousand of the Turks put to the sword.* After the passage of the Danube, two roads might lead to Constantinople and the Hellespont; the one difficult and rugged, but direct; the other more tedious and secure over a level country and along the shores of the Euxine, in which their flanks, according to Scythian discipline, might always be covered by a moveable fortification of waggons. The latter was wisely preferred, and the army marched through the plains of Bulgaria, burning with wanton cruelty the churches and villages of the Christian natives, simply because they happened to be within the Turkish territory, and at last arrived at Varna, a city pleasantly situated upon the sea coast.

In the year 1442, Amurath, tired of the fatigues of government and the toils of war, had abdicated the throne in favour of his son Mahomet, and retired at the early age of forty to a pleasant and secluded residence at Magnesia, where he passed his time in a round of epicurean delights in the society of dancing girls and of terrestrial houris more remarkable for their beauty than their virtue.† He was wakened from his inglorious repose by hasty messages from the bashaws of the European provinces, apprising him of the breach of the truce and the advance of the Hungarian army, and imploring him to take the command of the Ottoman forces, as the extreme youth of the reigning sultan rendered him unequal to so great an emergency. Amurath forthwith left the cloister, and collecting a large army, reached the Hellespont by forced marches, but to his surprize found the passage stopped by the Venetians and the pope's galleys. He was now at his wit's end, but marching along the shore to the straits of the Bosphorus, he there, according to some, awed or seduced the Greek emperor into granting him a passage, and induced the Genoese merchant vessels to transport his soldiers and their baggage to the European shore at the charge of a ducat a head, with the mercenary connivance of the Catholic admiral. He then advanced towards Varna by hasty marches at the head of sixty thousand men. When the Cardinal Julian and

* Knolles's Hist. of the Turks, p. 296.

† Gibbon has here fallen into a curious mistake, which Milman has corrected. He supposes the sultan to have led in his retirement the life of an ascetic, watching, praying, and fasting. See vol. xii. p. 148, note.

Hunyadi obtained accurate intelligence as to the extent of his forces, they proposed the tardy and impracticable measure of a retreat. But the king refused to listen to them. He was resolved to trust to the valour of his army and the fortune of war, and had made up his mind to conquer or die. The arrangement of his forces was committed to the skill and experience of Hunyadi. In order to prevent the Christian army from being surrounded by the mighty hosts of the infidels, their rear was protected by steep hills, one of their flanks by a marsh, and the other by a pile of waggons, and in this position they waited the onslaught of the Turks. The centres were commanded by the two princes, and the beglerbegs or generals of Anatolia and Romania commanded on the right and left against the adverse divisions of Hunyadi and the despot of Servia. The battle began by a series of skirmishes, by which great numbers were slain on both sides, but without any important result. At last Hunyadi charged with the Transylvanian and Wallack cavalry, and overwhelmed the Turkish wing commanded by Karasi Bey, who was slain in the attempt to rally his flying troops. Similar success attended the despot, and confusion speedily spread throughout the whole Turkish army. Amurath, on seeing the flight of his squadrons, despaired of his kingdom and his life, and was turning his horse's head to quit the field, when a veteran janissary seized his bridle rein, and had the courage to reproach him with his cowardice. A copy of the treaty to which the Hungarian king had sworn, had been displayed in the front of the battle, as a monument of Christian perfidy, and the sultan pointing to it in his distress, exclaimed, "Behold, thou crucified Christ, the league which thy followers have made with me, and have, without any cause, violated. Now, if thou be a God, as they say thou art, and as we dream, revenge the wrong now done unto thy name and me, and show thy power upon thy perjured people, who in their deeds deny thee, their God!"

Whether owing to the prayer or not we cannot take upon ourselves to decide, but certain it is, that at this moment the crisis of the day had arrived, and fortune was about to desert the Christian standards. Ladislaus had been placed by Hunyadi in an impregnable position, and the prudent soldier earnestly requested him not to leave it until he received a signal from him which should show him that the proper time for action had arrived. But, unfortunately, the former was surrounded by a knot of soldier bishops, whose martial ardour and hatred of infidels had induced them to abandon the cloister and gird on the sword; and on seeing the Turkish hosts flying before Hunyadi, their zeal began to get the better of their discretion, and they represented to the king that it would be inglorious for him not to share in the honour of the victory which was now all but achieved, and urged him to sally out and take part in the overthrow of the sultan's army, and, it might be, of his empire. The advice but too well accorded with Ladislaus's own desire. He left his position, and charged furiously across the field, and bursting through the disordered ranks of the enemy, speedily found his progress stayed by the impenetrable phalanx of the janissaries, who had not as yet taken part in the engagement. Overwhelmed by a cloud of javelins, he fell at the feet of the infantry, and a Turkish soldier cutting off his head with a scimitar, held it up to the gaze of the Hungarians on the point of a spear. The latter, on seeing their king fall, immediately fled, and all the valour and skill of Hunyadi were not sufficient to restore the fortune of the day. He made several desperate efforts to rescue the body of Ladislaus, but, overwhelmed by numbers, he escaped with difficulty from the melée, and rode off the field at the head of the remnant of the Wallack cavalry. Ten thousand Christians fell on this disastrous day; and though the loss of the Turks did not by any means bear so large a proportion to their total strength, the sultan was not ashamed to confess that another such victory would be as bad as a defeat. By his command, a column was erected upon the spot where Ladislaus fell, bearing an inscription which paid a well-merited tribute to his valour and bewailed his misfortune.

The cardinal Julian Caesarini, a man of noble Roman family, learned and accomplished, a good soldier and a bad priest, who had distinguished himself in the wars of his age, and had attempted to extinguish Bohemian heresy in the blood of Bohemian heretics, met on the field of Varna the fate he merited by counselling the king and the diet to commit the perjury which had led to the defeat. He fled from the battle mortally wounded, and was a short time after found half-naked and in the agonies of death by the edge of a neighbouring forest. It was said that his avarice was so powerful, even in death, that he retarded his flight by loading himself with booty, which tempted the cupidity of some Christian fugitives, and induced them to strip and abandon him. The great mass of the Hungarian soldiers who escaped the sword of the enemy scarce met with a better fate, but were either lost in the adjoining fens, perished of cold and hunger in the woods, or, after wandering about for some days, fell at length into the hands of the Turkish cavalry, and were sent as slaves to distant provinces of the empire. The battle was fought on the 10th of November, 1444.

CHAPTER XI.

LADISLAUS III.—REGENCY OF HUNYADI.

A.D. 1444—1457.

When the news of the battle of Varna reached Hungary, the lamentation was loud and great, but as soon as the first moments of surprise and grief had passed away, the attention of the diet was turned to the necessity of providing a successor for Ladislaus. Their choice fell upon Ladislaus III., then only nine years old, the posthumous son of Albert, whom his mother had committed to the care of Frederick, emperor of Germany, though more out of respect for his grandfather, Sigismond, than from any bud of promise which could as yet be found in him. But, in any case a regency would be necessary for some years, and as in the present emergency it was desirable that the office should be filled by a man of acknowledged energy and courage, John Hunyadi was unanimously chosen governor of the kingdom during the king's minority.

During the ensuing four years, the attention of the Turks being called off by Scanderbeg, the new governor was enabled to devote his whole attention to the internal administration of the country, the allaying of the feuds and quarrels of the nobility, the reform of the courts of justice, and the adjustment of the finances, which had fallen into disorder during the late troubles. His affability, moderation and prudence secured for him the respect and confidence of all classes of men, and enabled him to place the kingdom in an admirable state of defence against the next storm which might arise in the east. He made strenuous efforts to induce Frederick to surrender the person of the young king and the Hungarian crown, which he had in his keeping; but the latter, hoping, no doubt, that their possession would somehow or other at some period advance his own interests, refused to comply, and he was supported in his refusal by a small section of the Hungarian nobility, headed by Ulric de Cilly, the uncle of Ladislaus, who himself claimed the regency.

In 1448, Hunyadi received intelligence that the Turks were again making preparations for another invasion of Hungary, by raising a large army both in Europe and in Asia. Nothing daunted by the disaster at Varna, he called upon the nobility once more to range themselves under his standard, and having joined his forces with those of the waywode of Wallachia, he began his march against the enemy with an army of 22,000 men. Having passed the Teyss, he crossed the frontiers of Servia, and called upon the despot to contribute his quota of aid to the expedition; but the wily George, being jealous of Hunyadi's elevation to the regency, and too proud to serve under his banner, upon one pretence or another refused to comply. This excited the ire of Hunyadi, who punished his lukewarmness in the Christian cause by laying waste the country on the line of his march; and the despot, on the other hand, to be revenged for his losses, sent accurate information to Amurath of the strength and destination of the Hungarian army. The sultan availing himself of the intelligence, suffered Hunyadi to advance a considerable distance into Bulgaria without offering any opposition, and then by a sudden movement, got between him and the Danube, and having thus cut off his retreat, left him no alternative but to fight or surrender. Both armies found themselves in the great plain of Cossova, three sides of which are bounded by mountains, and the fourth by the river Schichniza. Hunyadi encamped on a small hill in the centre, there to await reinforcements from Scanderbeg, as he feared with his small force to encounter the mighty host of the Turks, who numbered full 80,000 strong. Amurath, however, determined to force him to give battle, and for this purpose took every means to cut off his supplies of forage and provisions. At length, no other resource being left, the Hungarian general drew out his little army, divided it into thirty-two battalions, and having communicated his plans to the leaders, delivered a short and stirring address to the men, telling them that their own safety and the safety of their country now depended on their valour; that the Turks to be sure were numerous, but strength did not lie in numbers, but in courage, discipline, and, above all, in the justice and sacredness of the cause for which they fought; and bade them remember that God and the saints were on their side, and would aid in avenging the death of their king and countrymen at Varna, if they but behaved like men.

The battle soon after commenced by distant skirmishing, but the Turks, confident in their numbers, soon advanced to close quarters, and in a hand-to-hand encounter of three hours duration, the Hungarians again and again repulsed the bravest of the Ottomans. Hunyadi had planted a battery on the hill which committed great havoc in the Turkish ranks, and he himself was constantly moving from one point to the other, animating the soldiers by his presence, and whenever he saw the troops in any part of the field giving way, he hastened to restore their confidence by the example of his own prowess. The conflict continued with varied success till dark, and the armies on both sides lay on the field all night—

"The weary to sleep and the wounded to die."

At sunrise on the morrow the combat was resumed; but the Turks now sent into action forty thousand fresh troops, who had not struck a blow on the previous day; while most of the Hungarians were either wounded or worn out by fatigue and watching. Amurath, chagrined by meeting with such opposition from so weak an enemy, led his troops to the attack in person, with terrible threats of punishment in case of failure, and warned them that throughout the day his eye would be upon them, and woe to the coward and the laggard! Hunyadi implored his followers once more to stand fast for the love of God, and the safety of their wives and children, and was answered by loud shouts of "Death or victory!" The Turkish squadrons now charged with redoubled fury, and on being repulsed, pretended to fly with precipitation, and the Hungarians being drawn out of their entrenchments in pursuit, the enemy turned upon them, and great numbers were in this way slaughtered or captured. This ruse was several times repeated, and on each occasion with more or less success, until night once more brought truce and rest. The morning of the third day dawned upon a fearful sight. The field was strewed thick with the dead and dying, and the ground was slippery with gore. Despair reigned within the Hungarian camp. One-third of the Christian army had fallen, and of the survivors hardly one had escaped unhurt. At day-break Hunyadi charged at the head of the Wallack cavalry, and the rest of the nobles followed with their companies, more in the hope of selling their lives dearly than of gaining a victory. Zechel, the nephew of Hunyadi, fell in the first onset, and almost at the same moment several of the most distinguished of the Hungarian officers met with a similar fate. The soldiers, disheartened by the loss of their leaders, began to waver, and Amurath, seeing his advantage, poured in fresh troops upon the fainting Christians, and speedily decided the fate of the day. The wings of the Magyar army gave way in confusion, and at last fled precipitately, and from noon till night the Turkish squadrons followed hard on the track of the fugitives, cutting them down without mercy. The flower of the Hungarian nobility were left on the field, and their camp, and baggage, and standards fell into the hands of the enemy. Hunyadi fled as soon as he saw that all hope was lost, and rode for three days through the wilds of Wallachia without food or drink. On the fourth his horse broke down, and he pursued his way on foot. He was attacked in a wood by two robbers, who stripped him; but beginning to quarrel about a gold crucifix that he wore round his neck, he snatched up a sword, and having slain one, put the other to flight. He soon after fell in with a shepherd, who hospitably entertained him in his hut with bread and water and onions, and his strength having been thus recruited, he made his way to Sendrecz. Upon hearing of his arrival, the despot of Servia caused him to be arrested, and kept him in close confinement until he had obtained the restoration of all the castles and towns which Ladislaus had unjustly detained, and until Hunyadi promised his younger son Mathias in marriage to his daughter, and to surrender his eldest son Ladislaus as a hostage. Hunyadi had no sooner reached Hungary than he assembled a large army, and entering Servia, laid waste the despot's dominions with fire and sword, until he was glad to sue for peace, and send back Ladislaus.

This had been no sooner granted than the unfortunate George found himself involved in new troubles. Amurath, his son-in-law, hearing that Hunyadi had fallen into his hands, fully expected that he would deliver him up to him, and on learning that he had set him at liberty, loaded him with reproaches and invaded his territory. The despot was now forced to crave assistance from Hunyadi, which the latter, from the desire to be revenged upon the Turks, readily granted, and routed them in a battle fought in Rascia.

On the 9th of February, 1451, Amurath died. "Sultan Murad, or Amurath," says Cantemir, "lived forty-nine, and reigned thirty years, six months, and eight days. He was a just and valiant prince, of a great soul, patient of labours, learned, merciful, religious, and charitable; a lover and encourager of the studious, and of all who excelled in any art or science; a good emperor and a great general. No man obtained more or greater victories than Amurath; Belgrade alone withstood his attacks. Under his reign the soldier was ever victorious, the citizen rich and secure. If he subdued any country, his first care was to build mosques and caravanseras, hospitals and colleges. Every year he gave a thousand pieces of gold to the sons of the prophet, and sent two thousand five hundred to the religious persons of Mecca, Medina, and Jerusalem." The accuracy of this portrait has been doubted by many competent to form an opinion, but there can be little danger in affirming, that in all the leading features of his character there was enough of the good and great, making allowance for his creed, position, and education, and the age in which he lived, to entitle him to a place amongst the best of the Ottoman sovereigns.

He was succeeded by his son, Mahomet II., and two years after his accession to the throne occurred one of the most tremendous calamities that have ever befallen modern Europe. Constantinople and a small territory adjoining it had, like the wing of an ancient and honourable house, survived the fall of the western empire, and still preserved, in her language, refinement, arts, magnificence, and even in her vices and profligacy, some remains of the ancient glory of the mighty people who put their feet on the necks of kings. Rome had long before succumbed to the strokes of the barbarians. The Greeks, farther removed from the reach of the invaders, continued to drag on a precarious existence, supported and protected by the prestige of an ancient fame, rather than by present power. But their hour was now come, and the destroyer was at hand.

Mahomet stormed Constantinople on the 30th of May, 1453. Constantine was the name of the last of its emperors, as well as of its founder, and he proved himself not unworthy of it by fighting on the ramparts and in the breach, from the commencement of the siege until he fell covered with wounds, upon the last fatal day. His kingdom departed with his life. Some few of his subjects rallied round him in defence of their city and their faith, but the great majority were licentious, indolent, and corrupt—more intent upon sensual pleasure and hair-splitting in theology, than on the preservation of their liberty and religion. The Magyar ambassadors, who had been sent to mediate between Mahomet and the Greeks, just arrived in time to see the former seat himself upon the throne of his fallen enemy, and divide among his followers the spoils of the vanquished. "Return to your own country," said he, addressing them, "and tell your master he must speedily make his choice between war and peace, for as there is but one

God in the heavens, so also the earth must henceforth have but one ruler." Every preparation was now made for war. The diet voted money with alacrity, and took all other needful steps, to make them ready for the storm that was now rolling towards the frontiers of Hungary. Hunyadi opened the campaign in spring, and in the first engagement defeated Ferez Bey near Sendrecz, in Servia, and returning in triumph to Belgrade, he knighted his son Mathias, who, though not more than fourteen, had already signalised himself by his bravery in battle. Girding on him the sword of Andrew Laczkofi, the companion-in-arms of Louis the Great, he dubbed him knight, in the name of God, of the holy Virgin, and of all the holy kings of Hungary.

During all this time the efforts of Hunyadi were constantly frustrated by the intrigues of the palatine, Nicholas Gara, a man of no talents, and greatly addicted to tricks of low intrigue, who was entirely devoted to Cilly, the king's uncle. But Ladislaus could not forget that he owed his throne to Hunyadi, and the services which he had rendered to the country were so striking, and so widely acknowledged by the people, that it would have been dangerous to have attempted his removal from the post of lieutenant-governor. Perceiving that nothing could be effected by intrigue, the conspirators had recourse to assassination; but Hunyadi escaped the snare. At length, yielding his personal feelings to the interests of his country, he consented to a reconciliation with his enemies, and even to allow his son, Ladislaus, to marry the daughter of the palatine.

In the meanwhile, the other nations of Christendom, becoming terrified at the progress made by the Turks, seemed at last to be about to afford efficient aid to the Magyars in their arduous and, in many respects, unequal struggle. A crowd of English, French, German, Genoese, and Venetian knights hastened to Hungary to enlist themselves under the banner of the king. Ladislaus himself furnished twenty thousand men, but who amongst so many renowned warriors and heirs of illustrious names was to assume the chief command? Hunyadi offered to bring twenty thousand men into the field at his own expense, in case the allied sovereigns allowed him to lead the united Christian forces, pledging himself, in case they adhered to him faithfully, to fight his way to Jerusalem itself. The unanimous voice of the diet bestowed upon him the wished-for post; and Ladislaus, returning from Vienna, without hesitation ratified their decision. As if, however, this short interval of attention to imperative duties had disabled the king for further effort, he secretly made his escape from the camp, and returned to Austria. His flight spread a panic through the whole army, and thousands of soldiers immediately deserted. But Hunyadi was not discouraged. Supported by the monk John of Capistrano, he set out to the relief of the fortress of Belgrade, which was defended by his brother-in-law, Szilagi, against a large besieging force of the Ottomans. Collecting all the boats from the rivers for miles around, he rapidly descended the Danube, destroyed the Turkish flotilla, and threw himself into Belgrade, where he was received with shouts of rejoicing.

The siege which followed was one of the most remarkable in history, from the unexampled bravery of the defence, and the terrible renown of the assailants. Europe watched the conflict in dread suspense. Hunyadi not only displayed the highest qualities of a general, but fought in the trenches as a common soldier, killing twelve Turks in one day with his own hand. The sultan, enraged at his repulse, swore by the beard of the prophet that he would take the town or die. "It is easy to die," said the chief of the janissaries, "but not to conquer

EXECUTION OF LADISLAUS HUNYADI.

Hunyadi." At last, after repeated failures, having in a single assault lost thirty thousand of his best troops, Mahomet raised the siege in despair.

But the victor did not survive to hear the shouts of joy with which the whole kingdom hailed his triumph. The warworn soldier who had faced death upon fifty battle-fields, to whom the bravest of the brave people had looked to lead them in the deadliest onset, escaped the thousand dangers of hostile swords to die by slow disease upon the bed of sickness. The hardships of the siege brought on fever, and, after lingering for some weeks, his iron constitution gave way, and he sank into the grave.

Hunyadi was essentially a child of the people. Even if the story of his kingly birth be true, he derived nothing from it of those great features of his character which caused his countrymen to look upon him as a strong tower of defence against the face of their enemy. To be a graceful courtier he needed but a fine figure and a drop of royal blood, though it flowed through the vilest intrigue that ever sullied woman's fame, or stained the escutcheon of a noble; but to be a gallant warrior, and a great statesman, he needed a true heart, and an iron intellect—precious gifts that crowns and coronets can never bestow. He possessed them both, and few men have used them better. With manners as simple and heart as tender as a child, he was the delight of his immediate friends, whilst his lofty and commanding stature, and lion-like courage, won the affections of the masses. Christendom did not forget to honour its greatest champion. Pope Callixtus III., the head and representative of the visible church, instituted the feast of the Transfiguration to be a continual memorial of the discomfiture of the Mussulmans, and the glory of the departed hero: but his most splendid epitaph is the regret of the Ottoman prince, who sighed that he could no longer hope for revenge on the single antagonist who had triumphed over his arms.

When Hunyadi was gone, the intrigues which he had kept in check had free course, and the malevolence which Ladislaus had always entertained towards him was now vented upon his family. Its first manifestation was in the appointment of Count Cilly to the government of the kingdom, and Nicholas Ujlaki to the command of the military forces. The garrison of Belgrade, irritated at what they considered to be an insult to the memory of Hunyadi, swore to be revenged both on Cilly and the king. On the other side, the count openly declared his intention of repairing to Belgrade for the purpose of "making an end of the dogs of Wallacks," as he called the sons of Hunyadi. Upon his arrival, however, the commandant of the citadel refused to admit the foreign infantry who accompanied him; and although this disappointment in some measure frustrated his schemes, it did not diminish the overbearing insolence of his manner. In his very first interview with Ladislaus Hunyadi, he loaded him with threats and reproaches, and then, drawing his sword, wounded him severely on the head and hands; when the friends of the young soldier, rushing in, cut Cilly to pieces on the spot.

This murder was disapproved of, as a matter of course, by every one. There was nothing to excuse it but gross provocation, or, perhaps, we should rather say the stern necessity of self-defence. The king swore on the Eucharist that no evil should befal Hunyadi for what he had done; but the palatine, Nicholas Gara, the intimate friend of Count de Cilly, at last succeeded in overcoming his scruples, and the two brothers were arrested and imprisoned in Buda, in March, 1457. Without any investigation, or even the form of a trial, Ladislaus was sentenced to be beheaded in the square of St. George. In the full persuasion that throughout his short life he had in everything acted for the safety and honour of his native country, and in a manner worthy of the great name he bore, the young man walked to the place of execution with the firm and heroic air of a martyr, wearing the purple robe with which the king had presented him when he adopted him as his brother. When the vast crowd which had assembled to witness his execution saw the son of their hero ascending the scaffold, with his hands tied behind his back, they could not refrain from uttering a loud groan of grief and indignation. His hair having been cut off, he uttered a few words in justification of the act for which he had been condemned, and knelt to receive the stroke of the executioner. Four times the latter missed his aim, either through cruelty or nervousness, and Ladislaus, rising up, told him, in a calm voice, that it was against the law to repeat the attempt so often. The king, who was present, threatened the functionary with heavy punishment in case he again failed in the performance of his horrid task, and in another moment the head of his victim rolled towards him along the scaffold, as if reproaching him with this great crime. He could no longer remain in Hungary. Whenever he appeared he was followed by a howl of hatred, and he, therefore, took his departure directly for Austria, followed by the curses of the people.

The whole kingdom was roused into a ferment. Hatred to Ladislaus, contempt for his government, and sorrow for young Hunyadi, combined to give rise to scenes of perfect anarchy all over the country; and it soon became evident that it was no fleeting ebullition of popular indignation, but deep-rooted discontent, which could only be quieted by the death of its author. This took place shortly afterwards. He was poisoned by the Bohemians, when on his way to celebrate his marriage with Margaret of France, daughter of Charles VII. No sooner was the news spread abroad, than the revolutionary movements ceased, and the most earnest desire was manifested by all to repair, as far as lay in their power, the injustice done to the family of Hunyadi.

The great objection to an elective monarchy is found in the turbulent intrigues to which it gives rise upon the close of each reign. The right of the people to elect their ruler, viewed in the abstract, does not admit of a doubt; but it may well be questioned, whether it is at all probable that, in a vast multitude of men, agitated by the passions of avarice, envy, ambition, and selfishness, the might of the strong, and the wealth of the great, will not, in many cases, outweigh the calm reason and unbiassed judgment of the thinking and upright minority. The prize is so splendid, that, in the struggle to obtain it, the voice of honour and patriotism and the precepts of religion are too often unheeded. If ever the truth of an observation was well supported by examples drawn from history, this is, above all. An elective monarchy ruined Poland; and we are greatly mistaken if our readers, before they reach the end of this history, do not arrive at the conclusion that it was the remote cause of the ruin of Hungary also.

At the death of a Hungarian monarch, a host of competitors to the throne arose on every side, and each set to work every engine of bribery and corruption within his reach to insure his own election. The quarrels thus raised were often protracted for years, or through the entire space of the succeeding reign, and entailed severe injury upon the commerce and industry of the country.

Upon the death of Ladislaus, three claimants appeared for the Magyar crown—Frederic III., emperor of Germany, and Uladislaus, son of Casimir, king of Poland, by Elizabeth, sister of the deceased king; and a diet having been convoked at Pesth, in December, 1457, Nicholas Gara there put forward his claims also, grounding them upon his relationship with the royal family, having married the sister of Count Cilly. But Szilagyi, the commandant of the fortress of Belgrade, determined not to suffer injustice to be done to the widow and surviving sons of John Hunyadi, and therefore marched upon Pesth at the head of forty thousand men, declaring that he entertained the utmost respect for the constitutional rights of the diet, and would not interfere with the exercise of their right of election; but at the same time stated his firm resolve not to allow the Hungarian sceptre to be grasped by the hand of a foreigner.

The foreign ambassadors next appeared to state the wishes of their sovereigns. Among them Charles VII. of France demanded the crown for one of his sons, or for the man upon whom he should bestow his daughter's hand. But Szilagyi cut short their deliberations by surrounding the place of meeting with an armed force; and whilst every one was expecting him to proclaim himself king, he disappointed all by proclaiming his relative, Mathias Corvinus, the youngest son of the great Hunyadi. A shout of assent from the majority of the diet testified their respect for the memory of the hero, and their sorrow for the untimely death of his son Ladislaus. For a few minutes Gara made desperate efforts to retard their decision, but the acclamations of the troops, "Long live King Mathias!" put an end to all hesitation.

CHAPTER XII.

MATHIAS CORVINUS.

A.D. 1457—1489.

Mathias was still a prisoner at Prague, when the news of his election reached him, in the keeping of Podiebrad, who refused to release him until he had received 40,000 golden florins, and extorted from him a promise that he would marry his daughter Catharine. Few men have ever had finer intellectual qualities, united with a more commanding personal appearance, than Mathias Corvinus; and when we take into account the greatness of the name which he inherited from his father, we may readily believe that few monarchs have ever ascended the throne under more favourable auspices. Passing over his able and upright suppression of the intrigues which disturbed the commencement of his reign, we find his administration of the internal affairs of his kingdom marked by an ability and broadness of view that were wonderful in so young a man, and procured for him from his people the title of Mathias the Just. Having calmed the internal discord in which he found the kingdom involved at his accession, he sternly refused the offer of an alliance made him by Mahomet II., and defeated the Turks in many brilliant engagements, and reduced all the dependent provinces, such as Servia and Bosnia, to complete subjection. These successes were, however, in some measure counterbalanced by the loss of the brave Szilagyi, to whom Mathias owed his throne. Having been taken prisoner by the enemy, he was remorselessly put to death. The coasts of the Adriatic, most valuable to the Magyar empire, as affording it an extensive sea-board, did not appear to possess their true value in the eyes of Mathias; for when reminded that this territory had formerly belonged to Hungary in the time of Louis the Great, and had been lost since his death, and that there was now a favourable opportunity of recovering it, he coldly replied, that he could not now offend the Venetians, as he hoped to form an alliance with them and the pope against the Ottomans.

By the death of Ladislaus, the emperor Frederick III. became sole possessor of the Austrian dominions, and under his rule they suffered from an unbroken series of calamities and misfortunes. His disposition was indolent and void of energy, and seemed formed rather to gratify in private life the refined taste of a *dilletante*, than face the storms of politics. He presented, in his single person, the strange combination of the most extreme autocratic pretensions, with the abuse of his understanding in the pursuit of exploded charlatanry. He discussed, with equal gravity and attention, plans of territorial acquisition and personal aggrandisement, and the mysteries of astrology and alchemy. Often, after having taken up arms for the realization of his ambitious projects, he suddenly abandoned the camp, and shut himself up in his laboratory to search mid the dross of the crucible for the philosopher's stone, or read in the motions of the stars the fate of himself and his courtiers. Had he been as warlike as he was covetous and avaricious, he would have proved a troublesome neighbour. The great feudatories in the interior of the empire were fortunately enabled to secure the peace of his dominions without his countenance or assistance, and he employed himself in the formation of empty projects against Podiebrad of Bohemia and Mathias, the former of whom actually aspired to the imperial crown.

His really weak and forlorn condition did not prevent Frederick from proclaiming himself king of Hungary, although the only actual ground for his claim was the possession of the Hungarian crown, and his hope that the youth of Mathias would render his kingdom an easy prey. Mathias had just returned from a successful expedition against the Turks when he received the news of his insolent assumption. He marched against him instantly, defeated him, and was already under the walls of Vienna, when the emperor sued for peace. It was granted, but only on condition that he should forthwith deliver up the crown; but Mathias was generous enough to pay him in return for it 60,000 gold florins, being about the sum which had been advanced upon it. The king then led back his army against the Turks, and, uniting his forces with those of Venice, he took the town of Jaicza, in Bosnia, by assault. The whole of the conquered districts were placed under the government of Emeric, duke of Szapolyai.

The satisfaction inspired by these successes was in some measure marred by the death of Catharine, the queen, without leaving any children. All the sovereigns of Europe hastened to express their sympathy with the king's bereavement. Numerous embassies were sent, laden with splendid presents, and bearing letters filled with expressions of condolement. Louis XI. of France distinguished himself above all others by the courtliness of his message, and the richness of his gifts. The short interval of peace which ensued was employed by Mathias in Transylvania, Moldavia, and Wallachia, all of which he reduced to subjection.

We have now to refer to an episode in the life of this great king, which must meet with unqualified condemnation. We doubt much whether even the notions of the age in which he lived, the influence of education and early prejudices, can extenuate a crime so repugnant to the dictates of Christianity. He undertook a war, which could in no way advance the interests of Hungary, and which, in point of morality, could not defend its shameless cruelty and injustice even by the poor plea of necessity. He was urged by the pope to set out on a crusade against the Hussites, then the advanced guard of the continental reformation, and to stifle the voice of opinion, and the freedom of religious worship, by the weapons which modern Rome has ever used so adroitly—the sword and the faggot. He undertook the task the more readily, because

Podiebrad, the king of Bohemia, seemed disposed to take them under his protection. At the diet of Agria, held in 1464, this war of extermination was formally declared, and Mathias took the field in person at the head of the Hungarian army, surrounded by the generals who had received their military training in the late conflicts with the Turks,—Emeric Szapolyai, an able and experienced officer, never at a loss for an expedient in the midst of the most unpromising circumstances, always cool and collected,—Blaise Magyar, a man of tremendous bodily strength and physical courage—no bad qualifications when gunpowder was in its infancy,—Paul Kinisi, the Murat of the Magyar army—fiery, brilliant, ostentatious, galloping to the charge with flashing sabre and in splendid costume, with kindling eye and brow of pleasure, like a lover to meet his bride. Like Murat, too, he had been raised for his valour from the ranks, looked upon the camp as his home, and death upon the battle-field as the necessary and only fitting exit from the turmoil of the world.

Wherever such men led, success was sure to follow. The Catholics of Bohemia flew to arms to aid them, and the Hussites were everywhere compelled to give way before the terrible attacks of the "black legions," as the Hungarian troops were called. As in all religious wars, the most terrible atrocities were committed upon both sides; and the Serbs, who followed the Magyars as auxiliaries, inflicted horrible devastation upon the districts through which they passed. In a few weeks, Moravia, Silesia, and Lusatia were all conquered, and, although Podiebrad still retained part of Bohemia, Mathias caused himself to be crowned king of the remainder, at Olmutz, the capital of the first of the above provinces.

In the meantime the sultan had been recruiting his strength, and again commenced the war by laying siege to Negropont, which he stormed. The Venetians, in consternation, appealed to the Magyars for succour, but Mathias refused to interfere, unless they gave him up possession of Dalmatia. He now began to perceive his error in neglecting to promote the growth of a maritime power, and to regret that, in expending his energies and strength in useless war against the Hussites, he had given breathing time to a far more formidable enemy.

Having quelled some internal tumults, he turned his attention in right earnest to the expulsion of the Turks. By their erecting a strong fortress at Szabacs, upon the confines of Sclavonia and Croatia, the whole country was laid open to them. It was absolutely necessary that this should be taken at all hazards. Mathias headed the besiegers in person, and the place was stormed after a desperate defence. This success was in a great measure owing to the personal valour of the king. Before the assault, he went alone in a boat by torch-light on the river, disguised as a fisherman, and reconnoitred the place. A ball struck the boat and extinguished the light, but he continued his observations, without the least sign of perturbation. He was the first to mount the breach, and animated his followers by his daring courage. The Turks were finally driven back to their own frontiers, and Mathias returned in triumph to Hungary, and celebrated his victory by his marriage with Beatrice of Naples, a woman devoured by pride and ambition.

He then raised a dispute with Venice, as an excuse for wresting Dalmatia from her; but no sooner had he set out, than the news arrived that the terrible Ali Bey was on the march towards the Hungarian frontiers with a large army. Mathias appealed to the nation to support him, and men of all ranks took up arms with the most fervid enthusiasm. Upon the plains of Kenyermezö, in Transylvania, then took place the most tremendous conflict recorded in the annals of Hungary. In the heat of the battle Bathori received six wounds, and fell under the hoofs of the horses. Paul Kinisi rushed forward, with a sword in each hand, and his armour broken, overthrowing every one who stood in his way, for the purpose of saving him. Making his way through the *melée*, he raised his fallen friend, and carried him out of danger. This exploit inspired the Hungarians with so much enthusiasm, that they precipitated themselves upon the Turks with such fury that they took to flight in a few minutes, their tents, baggage, and money-chest falling into the hands of the victors. In the midst of the rejoicings consequent upon this triumph, Kinisi was seen holding the body of a Turk between his teeth, and two others in his arms, and thus executing the Hungarian national dance.

Strengthened by this success, Mathias was enabled to detach the famous black huzzars to the assistance of his father-in-law, the king of Naples, who was threatened by the Mohammedans with another invasion. There was now a favourable opportunity for striking a heavy blow at the Turks, as two brothers were disputing the possession of the throne of the sultans. But, far from receiving any co-operation from the other sovereigns of Europe, Frederick of Austria invaded Hungary, and obliged Mathias to relinquish his designs against the Ottomans, and turn his attention to the defence of his own kingdom. An army was despatched against Vienna, under the command of Zelenyi and Szapolyai, which surrendered, after a short siege, in June, 1487.

Mathias continued to reside in Vienna for a considerable length of time, to the great regret of the Hungarians. He there concluded a treaty for the marriage of his natural son, John, with Blanche, of Milan, as he had no children by either of his wives. He soon after lost his old friend and companion, Emeric Szapolyai, and after his death he himself began visibly to decline. In the presentiment that his end was approaching, he bestowed the government of Vienna upon Stephen Szapolyai, who possessed but little claim to his confidence, and set out, in 1489, to meet the diet at Buda, where his son John was declared heir presumptive to the throne. He then took his departure, with the intention of returning to Vienna, in order to become reconciled with the emperor Frederick, but on his way was carried off by an attack of apoplexy.

Mathias was followed to the grave by the regrets, not of his own subjects only, but of the whole of Europe. His remains were transported with great pomp to the royal vault in the church of Alba Regia, and an epitaph, of which he himself was the author, was placed over the tomb.

"Mathias, jaceo rex, hâc sub mole sepultus
Testatur vires, Austria victa meas.
Terror eram mundo; metuit me Cæsar uterque;
Mors potuit tantum sola nocere mihi." *

Mathias was both a great statesman and a great general, but he by no means possessed that foresight for which Louis the Great was distinguished. Unlike him, he never attempted to assimilate the countries which his arms had subdued, so as, out of various races, to form a powerful, united, and progressive empire. Louis' great aim was the foundation of commercial prosperity, the only one which rests on a sure and lasting basis. It was for this that he expended so much blood and treasure in the attempt to acquire and retain the provinces bordering on the Adriatic; and had his successors followed up his line of policy, in all probability England would have found in Hungary a powerful rival in the race after material wealth in which she has been so successful. Mathias's genius was not of an equally practical turn. Whether it was owing to his supposed eastern origin, or the dazzling influence of his father's exploits, his efforts were oftener exerted to strike the imagination of his people by his prowess and magnificence, than to inspire them with a sense of their own strength and capabilities. His expeditions were all desultory, and often fruitless. The kingdom reaped no lasting benefit from any of his conquests or victories, because none of them were the result of a settled policy. He repelled the Turks more than once, but so repelled them, that in the following reign they were enabled to deal Hungary a blow from which she never recovered. He waged merciless war against the poor Hussite heretics, that he might gain the support of the Holy See, an acquisition which no really wise monarch ever valued, and no really powerful monarch ever needed. He humbled the house of Hapsburgh, but so humbled it that it was enabled to trample on the neck of the nation from his death down to the present time. His was not the steady light which shines more and more unto the perfect day, but a flash amid darkness, that shone only to blind and bewilder when it had disappeared.

As might be expected from his frank and chivalrous character, he was the idol of the people. No monarch in our history can be compared to him. In personal bravery and love of adventure he resembled Richard Cœur de Lion, but he had none of Richard's coarseness and ignorance. He was, above all things, a Magyar. He knew every fibre and corner of the national heart, and on this knowledge built up his popularity and glory. He gratified the pride and suppressed the jealousy of the nobles, by frequently convoking the diet, but was still adroit enough to retain every particle of power in his own hands. He won the

* "Here I, king Mathias, lie buried beneath this tomb. Conquered Austria attests my strength. I was the terror of the world; the two Cæsars feared me, and Death alone could subdue me."

affection of the common people by his never allowing lowness of origin to stand in the way of merit; he never forgot the obscurity of his own, for he knew that therein lay the greatest glory of his house. Above all, he was famed for his strict justice, so much so, that, when he died, men said, that "Justice was now gone."

From the time of Louis the Great, no Hungarian prince had ever displayed so much vigour in his administration. Little by little the nobles had been trenching on the prerogatives of the crown, and the great ones had gone far towards breaking up the equality which the constitution had established between all men of the order, by procuring the division of it into two parts—*status* and *ordines*. The *status* comprised the prelates and magnates who sat in the upper chamber; the *ordines*, or second chamber, included the nobles of the counties or the delegates of the towns to which Sigismond had granted the privilege of electing representatives in order to counterbalance the power of the nobility. Mathias, in order to flatter the grandees, retained these distinctions. It was in his reign that the powers and duties of the palatine were for the first time accurately defined. He was to govern the state during the absence or minority of the king, or during an interregnum, and his emoluments amounted only to 6,000 florins. The king's own revenues were, as might be expected, not very large, and were raised by the custom-house, the mint, and the contributions of the five free towns, amounting in all to nearly 400,000 ducats. This would have fallen far short of supporting his brilliant court, or supplying him with the expenses of his frequent wars, the means of rewarding and encouraging literary and scientific men, if he had not been aided by a subsidy which the diet voted and the nobility raised among themselves, but the king took good care never to show himself exacting, and thus worked upon the Magyar generosity to his own great advantage.

Sigismond had introduced into the military service of the country a more regular organization. By his arrangement, each county was bound to furnish a certain contingent of cavalry in proportion to the number of the inhabitants, amongst whom peasants, not noble, were admitted, and these received pay from the state. Mathias brought this system nearer to perfection, and was first amongst European monarchs to establish a regular army—a measure which gave a heavy blow to the military spirit of the nobility. As soon as the magnates found the duty of defending the country taken off their hands, they but too gladly betook themselves to the luxurious ease of their castles. The famous Black Legion, principally composed of Bohemians and Rascians, who gave to the Magyar army one of its most distinguished generals, Jaksics, carried terror wherever it showed itself, not less by its valour, however, than by its ferocity. Mathias, who was an enthusiastic admirer of every thing belonging to the ancients, endeavoured to model the discipline and tactics of the whole army upon those of the Greeks and Romans. The Black Legion cost the state 100,000 ducats; a hussar received forty ducats a year, and the entire army 1,060,000 ducats a year.

One of t e highest proofs of capacity afforded by Mathias was, however, his legal reforms. Besides the tribunals which sat quarterly, he established another permanent one to afford relief in cases of urgent necessity, and the decrees of which could be enforced even against the nobles, who claimed the right of being tried by the king alone. This was styled the *personalis presentiae regiae*, and answered in many respects to our King's Bench, as, by a fiction of law, the king was always supposed to be present in the person of the judge. He took vigorous measures to restrain and punish the robbery and brigandage of the great barons, who took possession of the property of their weaker neighbours without scruple, and upon the most frivolous pretences; as they refused to acknowledge the jurisdiction of the ordinary courts, the unfortunate owners seldom had much chance of its recovery, whilst the aggresssor, secure in his fortified castle, laughed at their remonstrances.

The higher classes in Hungary, in the reign of Mathias, stimulated by his example, began rapidly to acquire a love for lavish display. They showed no favour to commerce or manufactures except in so far as they supplied splendid dresses and equipages, harness, carriages, and arms, and delicacies of the table. This fatal tendency to extravagance was mainly due to Mathias himself. For the embellishment of his sumptuous palaces, and to do honour to the fine arts, he invited painters, goldsmiths, sculptors, and artisans of every trade from every country in Europe to take up their residence in his capital. But these strangers left but few traces of their stay in the diffusion of skill or a love of art amongst the Hungarians. They worked zealously for the king, to acquire fame and money for themselves, but as soon as he was gone they took their departure also.

The palace of Corvinus at Buda, of which the foundations had been laid by Sigismond, was radiant with ornaments of gold and silver; and the bishop of Castello, the Pope's legate, stated that fifty carriages could not contain the royal plate, all of massive gold, and set with precious stones. The outward pomp displayed at fêtes and ceremonies corresponded with the internal magnificence of the houses. When John Pruis was sent as an ambassador to France, he took with him three hundred horses of the same size and colour, ridden by young men belonging to the first families in Hungary, clothed in scarlet and sparkling with diamonds. "See what a display these nobles make," exclaims Fessler, "just before the dissolution of their empire." It seemed as if Mathias foresaw that he would be the last great king of Hungary, and determined that her sun should at least set in glory. It would be in vain to attempt, within the limits of our space, to give an accurate idea of the gorgeous splendour of the royal palace at Buda. Some of the first masters of Italy superintended its erection, or were employed upon the paintings that adorned its walls. It was there the king loved to retire from the fatigues of war or business, to revel amongst the creations of art, or to hang over the classic remains of the authors of antiquity. Having a passionate veneration for the works of the ancient Greeks and Romans, he never grew weary of reading them, and surrounded himself with statues modelled after their best sculptures; and at the great court festivals his guests found themselves surrounded by figures illus-

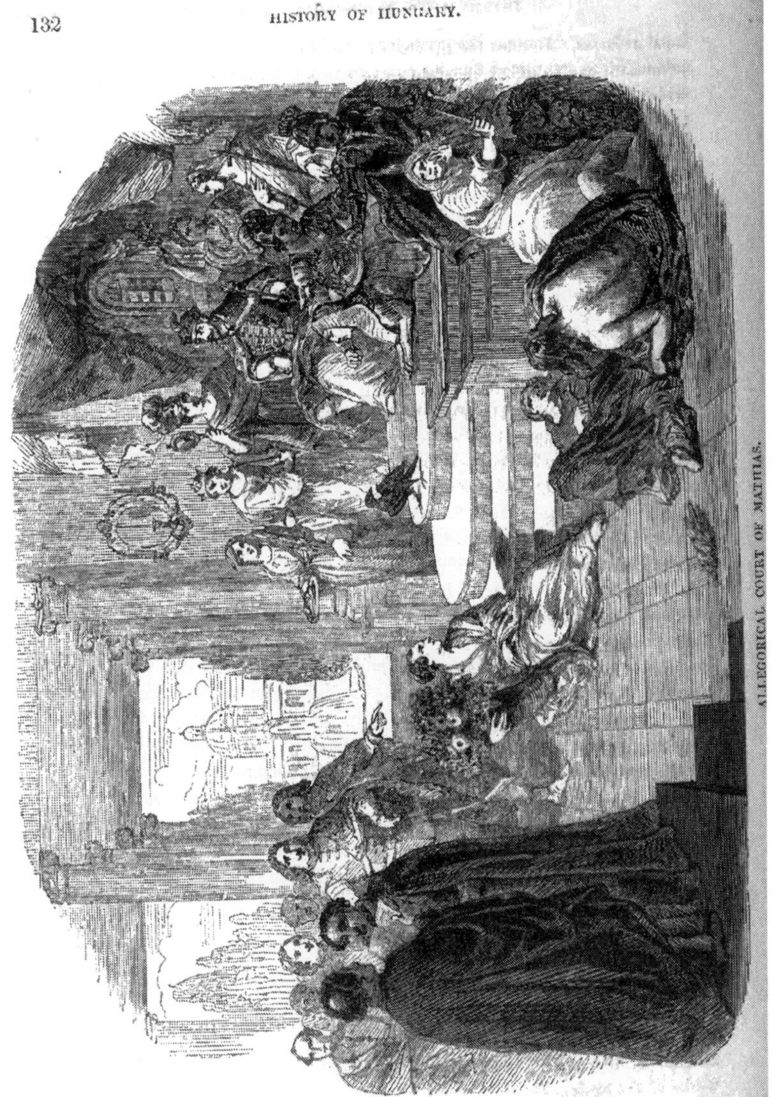

ALLEGORICAL COURT OF MATHIAS.

trating by their costume the mythology, customs, and traditions of the two great nations whose mutilated remains still excite the admiration and astonishment of mankind.

Mathias was not only a patron of scholars, but a scholar himself. Unlike many of the grandees of our own day, who imagine that their conventional rank can confer honour upon letters, he felt that the pursuits of literature would reflect lustre upon himself. Besides his native tongue, he spoke Latin, French, German, and Italian, with ease and fluency, and was familiar with the writings of Virgil, Cicero, Horace, Lucian, Pliny, Livy, and Sallust. He carried on correspondence with the greatest men of his day. He was the intimate friend of Bandini, of Ficini, and of Lorenzo de Medici. In laying the foundation of the great library of Buda, he left a striking monument of his wisdom and greatness. It contained the richest collection of oriental works that could then be found in the known world. Thirty copyists, of great skill in penmanship, were constantly travelling from one part of Europe to another for the collection or transcription of the rarest and most valuable books to enrich the king's collection.

Besides the universities of Buda, founded by Sigismond, Mathias erected another at Presburg, and commenced at Pesth the construction of a vast edifice capable of containing 40,000 pupils, the professors of which were to be supported by the state. It was by his direction, also, that the first printing-press was erected in Hungary, in the year 1470, under the management of an Italian. But in spite of all this patronage, the number of native Hungarians who achieved a position of eminence in literature and science was by no means great. One fact alone may serve to explain this seemingly strange phenomenon. No writer ever made use of the national language of the country. Latin was the tongue of the learned, and no fruit ever resulted from the teaching of it, as it was not understood by the masses. Science thus remained the exclusive possession of the few; and the best chronicles of Hungary, and in particular of the reign of Corvinus, are to be found in the works of two Italians whom he invited to his court, and who, in ponderous folios, and in a dead language, celebrated the glories of the nation, and heaped flattery upon their patron and his family.

CHAPTER XIII.

LADISLAUS IV. AND LOUIS II.—PEASANT WAR AND TURKISH CONQUEST.

A.D. 1489—1526.

THE only thing that was wanting to make up the sum of the good fortune of Mathias, was to have left a son to succeed him in the kingdom to which his father and himself had given so much prosperity and glory. This failure of legitimate issue produced, as might have been expected, five different pretenders to the crown. The first was John Corvinus, the natural son of the late king. He was supported by a powerful party among the nobility though he could put forward no reason in favour of his claim except his father's merit. The second was Frederick, emperor of Germany, whose ambassadors loudly declared that the kingdom could not be refused to him, or his son Maximilian, without manifest injustice. He founded his right upon the treaty which he had entered into with Mathias at the period of the restoration of the crown, in which the latter declared, that, if he died without leaving legitimate offspring, the kingdom should devolve upon him or his heirs. No regard was paid to this claim by the diet. The ambassadors were told that it belonged to the living and not to the dead to dispose of thrones; that their votes were free; and that before Frederick insisted upon the performance of their promises towards him, he should fulfil his to them; that those which had been made to him, in order to recover the crown which he unjustly detained, might be compared to those made by a man unlawfully imprisoned, in order to regain his liberty.*

The ambassadors of the king of Poland, whose son Albert was the fourth claimant, assumed a much more moderate tone. They confined themselves to dwelling upon the close proximity of Poland to Hungary, the alliance which had of old existed between the two countries, their power when united, and the precedents afforded by accession of many kings of Hungary to the Polish throne, and *vice versâ*, and they concluded by offering all the force at their master's command for the defence of the kingdom. The answer of the diet to these was much more favourable, and, in fact, held out some hope of success.

Beatrice of Arragon, the widow of Mathias, offered to decide the matter right speedily, by fixing on a husband who should reign jointly with herself, and to bring to the support of the nation the whole power of her father, Ferdinand, king of Naples.

* Bonf. Decad. ix. lib. 9.

But none brought to bear on the electors arguments so powerful as Ladislaus, king of Bohemia,—blood relationship, the proximity of the two kingdoms to each other, the advantages that would result from their union under the same chief, the great abilities of Ladislaus himself, and though last, by no means weakest, rich presents to the principal magnates. The suffrages were almost all in his favour; and a secret message was sent him, requesting him to present himself in Hungary, so as to anticipate his competitors, and promising that upon his appearance they would at once proclaim him king. He complied, and was crowned at Buda with more than ordinary solemnity.

The complaints of the unsuccessful candidates were loud and vehement, and by the intrigues which they set on foot they reduced the kingdom to the last extremity of weakness and disorder. One faction rallied round John Corvinus, but their own quarrels ruined them. Beatrice wished, at all hazards, to marry Ladislaus, and so clamorous did she become on that head, that he at last thought it best to comply.

Albert, the brother of Ladislaus, took arms to avenge his rejection, invaded Hungary, and laid siege to Cassovia. He was compelled to raise the siege, but not till Silesia had been ceded to him, on condition that he desisted from his pretensions. Maximilian followed his example, retook most of the Austrian towns which had been captured by Mathias, and some even in Lower Hungary. The former were left in his hands, and Vienna was surrendered to him, but he was compelled to deliver up the remainder of his conquests.*

A revolution in Turkey about this time deposed Bajazet; and Selim, his successor, being beaten by the Hungarians, was about to agree to a truce for three years, when Thomas Bakocz, the cardinal-archbishop of Strigonia, arrived in Hungary, bringing a bull from the Pope, calling upon the Hungarians to enter upon a crusade against the Ottomans. Some have ascribed this act of the cardinal to an overflowing zeal for the honour of the church and the spread of the Christian faith; while others have alleged, and with greater appearance of truth, that it was owing rather to a desire to be revenged upon the nobility for the frequent insults he had received from them on account of his low birth, as well as to the great influence which the successful issue of the enterprise would throw into his hands, particularly as he was already casting his eyes upon the triple crown.

At the call of the legate the peasants flew to arms, but this time it was not to march against the Turks. They declared that they had been ruined by the tyranny and exactions of the aristocracy, and that, as the nobles were more dangerous than the infidels, upon them would they wreak their vengeance. They chose for their motto, "God and Liberty," and assembling in immense crowds from every side, swore to exterminate their ancient masters. This revolt was the war of the peasant against his seigneur—of hunger against exacting riches

* Hist. des Revol. de Hongrie, liv. i. p. 33.

These men of labour and misery, whose life was a bitter cup of sorrow and trial, were the brothers in misfortune of the followers of William Longbeard, of Wat Tyler, and Jack Cade. Burdened with taxes, incapable of possessing hereditary property, daily exposed to the incursions of the enemy, and the no less terrible spoliation of their own landlords, they at length lost patience.

The king was feeble, inert, and cowardly, and had no resources within himself for any emergency. The nobles seemed to have lost their ancient military prowess, and many fled in terror to take refuge in the walled towns. There was no union, no organization, no foresight. Everything seemed to promise an easy

TORTURE OF DOZSA.

victory to the peasantry. Bakocz appeared to be the only one who had resolution enough to face the crisis, and put himself at the head of the nobility.

George Dozsa, a Szekler peasant, a straightforward, blunt, and sincere man, and full of courage, had been named by the cardinal commander-in-chief of the crusading forces, or, as it now appeared, of the insurgents; but a priest named Lorenzo, or Lawrence, was the soul of the insurrectionary movement. Though devoted to the interests of the people, he sought by his eloquence to induce the nobles to listen to their demands, and at least endeavour to come to an amicable understanding before proceeding to open force.

His efforts were unsuccessful; and, in a sanguinary engagement which soon afterwards took place, the peasants, though the artillery made lanes in their ranks, were victorious. The aristocracy perceived that its existence was at stake, and strained every nerve in preparations to continue the war. In a second battle, near the town of Temesvar, the steady discipline of the nobles triumphed over the rude and untrained valour of the rebels, who were totally defeated. Dozsa was taken alive by the victors, and in that awful hour, when all hope of mercy or relief was gone, he showed that he had a soul worthy of a higher station and a better fate. There was no pity for the base-born serf who had dared to rise up in arms against his lords. "To-morrow," said they, taunting him, "your majesty shall be crowned, but it will be with an iron crown, made by the blacksmith; your sceptre will weigh five pounds; your throne, too, will be large, and you shall recline upon it at your ease. You will then have need of a stout heart." Dozsa's face blanched for a moment, as he heard of the frightful punishment that awaited him; but, recovering himself quickly, he exclaimed—addressing the crowd whom he saw shuddering at his approaching doom—"Come back to-morrow, you miserable slaves, and see if I shrink in the midst of my sufferings! If a single groan escapes my lips, may my name be covered with eternal infamy!"

On the following day he was placed almost naked on a burning throne, and his head was encircled by a crown of red-hot iron. Fourteen of his followers had been kept without food for several days, and were then brought into his presence, and while he was yet living the flesh was torn from his bones and cast to them that they might satiate their hunger. "To it hounds!" was his bitter exclamation, "ye are of my own rearing!" And thus he died, enduring all with a stoical firmness that called forth the admiration even of his enemies.

The peasants were slaves before this revolt, but after it the yoke was laid heavier upon them than ever. They were deprived of the liberty which they had previously possessed of passing from the domains of one lord to those of another;* they had no longer any tribunals before which they could plead their cause, except those of the barons themselves, who were often parties in the suit.

The short interval of tranquillity which followed these storms was taken advantage of to present, in writing, to the king a collection of the *customary laws* which had been in force time out of memory, answering to the common law of England. One of the judges, named Verboczi, compiled and divided them into three parts, and called his work "Opus Tripartitum." The body of the Hungarian laws is contained in two volumes, of which this was the first, arranged according to the subject matter. The other is made up of the royal decrees. The whole was entitled "Jus Consuetudinarium Regni Hungariæ," or the Common Law of the kingdom of Hungary; a title which applies equally well to both, since the first, or the tripartite work, contains only the ancient customs, and the decrees of the kings, contained in the second, are in reality made with the consent of the two cham-

* The rigour of this was somewhat softened in 1556.

bers, and conformably to the principles of the common law. It is only by an occasional reference to this work that a correct idea can be given of the merits and bearings of the great controversy which has been going on between Hungary and the house of Hapsburgh now for full three hundred years.

This code was presented to Ladislaus in 1514, at a diet assembed in Buda. It was there solemnly confirmed by the king and the chambers.*

Ladislaus did not long survive the performance of this most praiseworthy act of his reign. He was born for a quiet, tranquil life, and always left the command of his armies to his generals; but he was, nevertheless, kind-hearted, equitable in his decisions, and generous to a fault. The diet, therefore, decreed the succession to his son Louis, who succeeded his father in 1516, when but ten years of age, to the thrones both of Hungary and Bohemia. In 1521 he assumed the administration, and celebrated his nuptials with Mary, the sister of Francis I. and Charles V., to whom he had been betrothed some years previously by the dexterous management of Maximilian I., who, at the same time, obtained the hand of Mary, Louis' sister, for Francis, thus rendering the succession of the house of Hapsburgh to the Hungarian crown doubly sure. Owing to the youth, inexperience, and neglected education of the monarch, both kingdoms began to suffer all the evils attendant upon an unstable and divided government—evils which were aggravated by the poverty and discontents of the Hungarian peasantry, and the quarrels and licentiousness of the nobility. His ministers could with difficulty maintain tranquillity in Bohemia, and, what is less wonderful, notwithstanding all their efforts, could not prevent the spread of the reformed doctrines, nor even perform the easier task of repelling the inroads of the Turks. Not that Louis himself was wanting in amiable qualities, or that there was in his character any defect so striking as to foreshadow the fate that awaited him. His stature was tall, and his appearance, even in youth, was majestic; his intellect was strong, and under better cultivation might have rendered him independent of the bad counsellors who surrounded him from his childhood; and his disposition was full of gentleness and generosity. He had in him all the materials of which a great man and a great king are supposed to be made, had it pleased Providence, so often apparently severe, but so surely ever wise and ever just, to have assigned him a longer reign, that he might have shown himself worthy of a better fate.

But even on the day on which he ascended the throne, the cloud from which the thunderbolt was to issue and crush him, was hanging in the sky. Ever since the reign of Bajazet the Second, but particularly under the short but brilliant one of the Sultan Selim, the Turkish power had been rapidly advancing. A striking instance of the vanity of human greatness is afforded by the fact that the

* In this work the animus of the noblesse against the unfortunate peasantry shows itself. In part iii. tit. 25, referring to the measures depriving the peasants of the right of seeking relief from any tribunal save that of their lords, the following passage occurs: "Hujusmodi libertatem propter seditionem et tumultuarium adversus universam nobilitatem, sub nomine cruciatæ, ductu cujusdam, scelerati Georgii Szekelii, insurrectionem, amiserunt."

empire, now so feeble that it requires all the efforts of European diplomacy to keep it from falling to pieces through sheer inanition, should, at no more distant period than the sixteenth century, have been the terror and the bugbear of Christendom, should have single-handed carried on aggressive wars against all the nations of Europe, and have furnished a rock against which the chivalry and fanaticism of the ablest warriors of the west foamed, fretted, and were broken. The religious zeal of the Mussulmans was then still at the height of its fervour, and it was animated and supported by centuries of great martial traditions, and found a rich harvest of conquest and glory in the discord and dissensions of their enemies. Christianity had lost among the Latins the binding power which, five centuries before, had driven 600,000 warriors to the maddest enterprise which human folly has ever conceived. Enthusiasm, no doubt, still burned as brightly in the breasts of many individuals as ever, but it had lost the power of combining, for a common object, those whose language, race, traditions, and desires, were widely different. The art of war, too, was still in its infancy. Gunpowder, though partially in use, had not yet seen the grave close over valour, and in the heady and tumultuous conflicts, by which the fate of kingdoms was then decided, the training, skill, experience and dexterity of the veteran janizzary, were but too often more than a match for the heavy panoply in which the Christian warriors encased themselves; and when we remember that to all these advantages were added the force and union derived from the controlling power of a single despotic will, and that, by rare good fortune, for a long series of years no sovereign ascended the throne who did not possess passing courage, energy, and skill, we can hardly wonder at the success which attended the Ottoman arms, both in Europe and Asia. Selim II. subdued Armenia, overran and humbled Persia, reduced the warlike tribes of Arabia, at least, to partial subjection, defeated the Mamelukes in two campaigns, annexed Egypt and Syria to his dominions. He then prepared to turn his arms westward, and in order that he might extend his empire in the Mediterranean and the Archipelago, built and equipped a fleet fully able to compete for victory with the maritime forces of the west—an achievement displaying no ordinary ability, when we remember that at the siege of Constantinople, the only naval armament which Mahomet II. produced for the defence of the straits of the Hellespont against the fleet sent to the relief of the city, was a crowd of open and unwieldy boats, which the Christian sailors broke and dispersed by the mere force of their motion through the water. He next turned his arms against Rhodes, as one of the bulwarks of Christendom, but was baffled by the valour of the knights of St. John, and was then about to try his fortune on the side of the Danube, when his schemes were suspended by his untimely death. They were revived by his son, Solyman the Magnificent, who, to all his father's bravery and activity, united learning and accomplishments which no Ottoman prince had ever boasted, and no Mussulman since the days of Al-Raschid. Immediately after his accession to the throne, he sent an embassy to Louis, offering to continue the treaty of peace which his father had entered into, but upon conditions so harsh, and couched in language so imperious and menacing, that the king, either carried away by youthful ardour, or instigated by bad counsels, maltreated the ambassadors and drove them from his presence. Solyman, but too glad of the excuse for recommencing hostilities, immediately made preparations to avenge the insult, and crossing the frontier, laid waste Rascia, Sclavonia, Moldavia, and Wallachia, and, worse than all, took Belgrade, the key of Hungary, which Hunyadi had so valiantly defended against the assaults of the bravest of the Ottomans, led on by Mahomet II. After this achievement, however, which took place on the 29th of August, 1521, he returned to Constantinople with the intention of making another attack upon Rhodes, which proved successful. After a short interval, during which he was occupied in suppressing an insurrection in Egypt, he again turned his attention to the conquest of Hungary, a project which was favoured by the dissensions of the Christian princes, and by the indecision, maladministration, and licentiousness which prevailed at the Hungarian court. He passed the winter of 1525 near the frontiers, making preparations for the invasion.

The young king in vain looked around him for assistance. Charles V., the emperor of Germany, and Francis I., of France, were engaged in that long and bloody contest for the crown of the Cæsars, which ended in the overthrow and capture of the latter upon the bloody field of Pavia, and all the minor states of Europe were breathlessly watching the tremendous game which these two master-players had in hand. It was in vain to call upon the pope to preach for another crusade. The Church had then more to fear from enemies within her own bosom than from the fiercest onslaughts of Paynim or pagan. Luther had begun to preach against indulgences, and Germany was labouring in the throes of a great religious revolution. The Holy Father could offer nothing but his prayers and blessing, and these he sent; and from Henry VIII. came a sum of money.

Louis, having failed in all his efforts to obtain foreign aid, turned his attention to the internal resources of the kingdom, and ordered a general rising of the nobles and their vassals, by sending round a bloody sabre to every house, in accordance with the ancient Scythian custom. The rendezvous was fixed at Tholne, and hither the prelates and magnates repaired with small and badly equipped troops, and with scanty contributions in money towards the expenses of the war. The regular army, so large and well-organized in the time of Mathias, was now but a shadow of its former self. When a muster was made of all the forces, there were scarce found twenty-four thousand men in all, undisciplined and badly officered, to meet the two hundred thousand strong, flushed with victory, whom Solyman was leading across the frontier. The nobles made light of the disparity, and in all the pride of folly swore roundly that the Turks would fly at the first onset; and this false confidence was encouraged by Paul Tomori, who, from the humble rank of a Franciscan monk, had arisen to the archbishopric of Colocza, and who, owing to his success in a few trifling skirmishes with the Ottomans, was, in conjunction with George, count of Scepuze, appointed general of the forces. John Szapolyai, the waywode of Transylvania, as well as some others, led a body of cavalry to the aid of the Hungarians, but, owing to the precipitation of the leaders, was never able to come up with them until it was too late.

Stephen Verboczi, an experienced soldier, feared the issue of an engagement, and strongly advised the king not to risk his person in the field, but shut himself up in the citadel of Buda, where, in case of reverse, he could abide in safety; but this prudent counsel was scouted by the nobles, who declared that if they could not fight beneath the banner of the monarch, they would not fight at all. Inde-

DEATH OF LOUIS IN THE MARSH.

cision for a long time reigned in the camp. The more prudent wished to wait for reinforcements, and not to risk the fate of the kingdom in a single action where the odds were so largely against them; but this was met by charges of cowardice and pusillanimity; and at last the news arrived that the Turkish army, after taking Peter Varadin, were encamped on the plains of Mohacs, a town lying between the Danube and the Drave, in the neighbourhood of the Five Churches; and it was unanimously resolved to offer battle. The two armies lay in the presence of each other for three days without the occurrence of anything beyond light skirmishes, in which the Hungarians always had the advantage. The Turks wished to fatigue them, and, if possible, to outflank them. Paul Tomori, anxious to take advantage of a movement made by them with this object, assured the king that the time for the attack had now arrived, and that victory was certain. Brodercis, the chancellor of the kingdom, advised him to await the arrival of the Transylvanian corps, and the Croats under Christopher Frangepan, but in vain. "Sire," said Perenzi, bishop of Great Varadin, "twenty-six thousand Hungarians will now fall martyrs for the faith, under the conduct of our dear brother, Paul Tomori. There remains only one thing more to be desired,—that the chancellor Brodercis, who is known at Rome, should survive the carnage, and plead before the pope and cardinals for their canonization." At last, on the 29th of August, 1526, Paul Tomori gave the signal for action, after placing the king in the rear, surrounded by a guard of chosen cavaliers. The army advanced to the attack with loud shouts and beating of drums; and the cavalry charging with their usual impetuosity, overthrew and routed the first of the enemy's battalions, and committed such havoc, that Andrew Bathori flew to the king to announce that the Turks were flying, and that the victory was won; to request him to advance with his reserve, and aid the conquerors in the pursuit. Louis, full of youthful ardour, obeyed the imprudent summons, and galloped forward; but only to find the flower of his army broken by the main body of the Turks, commanded by Solyman in person, and flanked by three hundred pieces of cannon, which vomited death amongst the ranks of the Christians. The right wing, unable to bear up under the storm of shot, turned and fled. The left continued the engagement with unshaken courage, charging up within ten paces of the batteries, in the chivalric, but vain, attempt to storm them. At last, blinded by the smoke and dust, and weakened by the incessant carnage, the survivors gave way; and in attempting to return across a marsh were engulphed by hundreds. The Turks, astonished by the resistance that had been offered them, could scarcely believe in their victory, and it was not till after hours of silence that they were fully convinced that the Hungarian army was indeed annihilated. Paul Tomori did not survive his defeat, and with him seven bishops, twenty-eight of the higher nobility, and 22,000 men were left dead upon the field.*

As soon as the king found that the day was lost, he reluctantly rode off the field. On arriving at the village of Czetze, he was stopped in a marshy plain watered by a rivulet; a Silesian nobleman, who was mounted on a light steed, passed without difficulty, and Louis instantly attempted to follow, but his horse, being heavy and loaded with caparisons, sank in the morass, and in struggling to reach the opposite bank fell back on his rider. The noble flew to his assistance, drew him from the slough, and unbuckled his armour, but he was mortally bruised, and expired in a few moments. The Turks came on rapidly; the body was cast

* Knolles's History of the Turks, art. "Solyman the Magnificent," *passim*. Historie of the Troubles in Hungary (London, 1600). Histoire des Revolutions de Hongrie, liv. i., p. 35; an account abridged from Bradeuth, who was present in the battle.

aside and lost, and was not discovered till two months after, when it was buried at Alba Regia.*

Immediately after the battle, Solyman marched upon Buda, which was surrendered to him without striking a blow, and while encamped upon the Danube the heads of the seven bishops who had fallen at Mohacs were presented to him with great pomp and ceremony, and on learning the names of the owner of each, he passed remarks upon them according to what he had previously heard of their character and ability. He stayed at Buda about twenty days, and during the whole of that period squadrons of cavalry overran the whole kingdom, plundering and burning the houses, and slaughtering the inhabitants without distinction of age or sex. Such was the terror inspired by their atrocities, that mothers killed their children, and husbands their wives to prevent them falling into their hands alive. Wherever they passed they left nothing behind but a howling waste without food or shelter for living creature. Before Solyman took his departure, Buda was plundered, the splendid library of Mathias Corvinus was committed to the flames, and the bronze statues of marvellous workmanship which adorned his palace were carried to Constantinople, and there cast into cannon, and two hundred thousand Hungarians were led into captivity.†

The battle of Mohatz was even more disastrous to Hungary than that of Flodden Field to Scotland. It decided her fate. She had been for a long time envied by Austria, and looked upon as a legitimate prey by some of her own nobles. To the former she fell a victim. With this fatal day the bright pages of her history end. The record henceforth is that of a contest between liberty and power, between law and the arbitrary will of the monarch, between the defenders of the constitution to which more than fifty kings had sworn, and the adherents of a foreign ruler, whose language, race, and sympathies were not those of the nation over whom he was called to reign.

* Coxe's Hist. of the House of Austria, chap. 33.

† Knolles's Hist. of the Turks.

CHAPTER XIV.

FERDINAND I. AND JOHN SZAPOLYAI.

A.D. 1526—1564.

THE Hungarian monarchy was essentially elective. The right to choose their own ruler was a right of which the diet never lost sight. The crown had, upon the death of the sovereign, it is true, in more than one instance been placed on the head of his son and heir; but no claim to the succession based upon inheritance was ever for a moment acknowledged, and in their treatment of their king, the Hungarians took every means to prevent the idea gaining ground that he was anything more than the first amongst a nation of equals. Upon the real nature of the constitution at the period when the house of Hapsburgh first ascended the throne, the dispute which has raged between it and the nation for three hundred years altogether turns. The history of Hungary since the battle of Mohacs is, in reality, as we have already remarked, the history of this dispute; and it is only by setting out with a clear knowledge of the people's rights and sovereign's duties when it commenced, that the reader can judge between the contending parties. This is to be found in the "Opus Tripartitum," to which we have already referred. It is there expressly provided, though in general terms, that all measures should be submitted to the assembly of the people, and receive the sanction of their votes; and, if proposed by the people, should in like manner be submitted to the prince for his approbation, before they could have the force of law; but a special clause is inserted to define the meaning of the word people as the *populus* of the Romans, the prelates, magnates, barons, and other nobles, and expressly excluding the *misera plebs*, the serfs and others not noble, from taking any benefit under the constitution.*

The laws bound the king even in a greater degree than the people, as the most prominent of their makers and promulgators, and he was compelled to answer before the palatine to any charge or complaint which might be made against him; the only instance of royal responsibility to the claims of subjects to be met with, we believe, in the history of any modern country, except Poland. He was held liable, also, for the repair of all wrongs or damage caused by his

* "Nomine autem Populi, hoc in loco, intellige solum modo Dominos, Prelatos Barones et alios Magnates atque quoslibet nobiles." Part iii. tit. 4. In this appears the worst feature of the Hungarian constitution.

officers or by his peasants,* and he was bound to provide for the defence of the kingdom against all its enemies or oppressors out of the revenues of the domains of the crown; but in case these did not suffice, it devolved upon the prelates, barons, and the nobility, and all others of every rank and condition, to make up the deficiency. And if at any time such an emergency should arise, that the ordinary resources of the kingdom would not be sufficient to meet it, then a general diet of all the Magyars was convoked in the plain of Rakos, and any extraordinary contribution which might be called for was granted, but only by the unanimous consent of the whole of the prelates and nobles; and in order to guard against the influence of faction or favouritism upon the king, it was expressly ordained, that if any particular county, of its own accord, granted any supplies or subsidy above and beyond what was voted by the general assembly, in the ordinary grant of the chamber, the nobles of that county should be held guilty of perjury and treachery, and should be cut off from all intercourse and communication with the other nobles of the kingdom. The palatine, as the first personage in the realm after the king, had a right to the first vote at the election, and was, by virtue of his office, general and commander-in-chief of all the armies of the kingdom, and whenever any difference arose between the king and the nobility, he was bound to act as mediator and endeavour to reconcile them. The king had not the right of making war, or of introducing foreign troops into Hungary, without the express consent of the assembly, but was bound to use every endeavour to keep peace and make others keep it. He was prohibited from calling upon any freeman to answer to any charge beyond the boundaries of the kingdom, even before the ordinary and lawful judges, and from condemning any one upon any accusation whatsoever, until he had been indicted and convicted with all the necessary legal forms. He was also expressly forbidden to commit to the hands of foreigners any charge, dignity, office, or appointment, and was bound to place in command of the fortresses Hungarians only, who had distinguished themselves by their services. Four of the privileges of the nobility are, in this summary, singled out from a host of others as of prime importance, the observance of which is strictly insisted upon:—

First, that no matter upon what charge, complaint, or accusation, no gentleman (*nobilis*) was liable to arrest or detention, until he had been tried and convicted by the ordinary tribunals.

Secondly, the nobility were subject to no authority save that of the king lawfully crowned.

Thirdly, they possessed the power of enjoying without let or hindrance all the revenues of their lands and hereditaments, situate within the boundaries of their lordships, and were exempt from all conditional service, and above all from rent, tribute, or tax.

* *Jobbagiones*, a barbarous word, originally applied to all the nobles of the kingdom, but afterwards to the serfs on the king's domains.

Fourthly, they had the power of resisting by force of arms any attempt on the part of the king to destroy, modify, or in any way interfere with the rights and privileges of the nobility, as set forth in the general decree of Andrew II., surnamed *Hierosolymitanus*, without being liable to any charge of treason or felony.

The oath by which the kings at their election swore to observe these articles is worthy of translation.* "We swear by the living God, and by the blessed Virgin Mary His mother, and by all the saints, that we will preserve the churches consecrated to God, the lords, prelates, barons, nobles, and free towns of Hungary, and all the inhabitants of this kingdom, in all their immunities, rights, privileges, franchises, all good customs, ancient and generally approved, that we will do justice to all, and that we will keep inviolate the decree of the most serene King Andrew."

The foregoing abstract may serve to give the reader some notion of the manner in which the supreme authority was divided between the king and the nobles, and the pains taken in framing the constitution to guarantee to the latter the full enjoyment of their liberties. It is upon the articles above cited, that the Hungarians ground their complaints against the house of Hapsburgh. The adherents of the latter ever since the accession of Ferdinand I. have never ceased to charge the Magyars with being animated by a restless mutinous spirit, with being fond of change, turbulent and averse to a settled government. The latter have in reply pointed to the digest of their laws in justification of their acts, and have asserted that as these laws were in operation for more than seven centuries, and had been confirmed and sworn to by every monarch who had ascended the throne, the Hapsburgh family were bound to accept them with all their consequences, and threw upon those who sought to infringe them the blame of all the dissensions and violence which the kingdom had suffered.

The house of Austria grounded its claim to the kingdom upon the double right of succession and conquest. The right of succession was derived from the various matrimonial alliances contracted between members of that family and the Hungarian princes, and upon the treaties of alliance and succession entered into between Mathias Corvinus and Ladislaus II. with Frederick, by which it was agreed that in case either of the former died without legitimate issue, the crown should revert to the latter, or to Maximilian his son, or to Ferdinand. The accompanying table, taken from the work of the able and learned historian of the house of Austria, will present a clearer view of the grounds upon which this claim was based than any other explanation that can be furnished.†

* Nos, N. N., juramus per Deum vivum, per ejus matrem S. Mariam Virginem, per omnes sanctos, quod nos ecclesias Dei, dominos, praelatos, barones, nobiles, civitates liberas, et omnes regnicolas in suis immunitatibus, et libertatibus, juribus, privilegiis, ac antiquis bonis et approbatis consuetudinibus conservabimus, omnibusque justitiam faciemus, serenissimi quondam Andreæ Regis Decretum Observabimus, &c.

† Coxe's History of the House of Austria, vol. i. part ii. p. 546.

TABLE ELUCIDATING THE CLAIMS OF FERDINAND I. TO THE THRONES OF HUNGARY AND BOHEMIA.

Mary, d. of Louis the Great, king of Hungary, d. 1395. = SIGISMOND, son of Charles I., king of Bohemia; king of Hungary in right of his wife, Mary, 1386; Emperor 1411; king of Bohemia 1419; d. 1437. = Barbara, d. of Herman, count of Cilly.

Hedwige, 2nd d. of Louis the Great; married Ladislaus II., king of Poland, d. 1434.

Elizabeth, d. 1412. = Albert II., duke of Austria, king of Hungary 1437, king of Bohemia and emperor 1438, d. 1439.

Ladislaus III., king of Poland 1434, king of Hungary 1440, d. 1444.

Ladislaus IV., *Posthumus*, b. duke of Austria; king of Bohemia 1440, king of Hungary 1444, d. 1457.

Elizabeth, d. 1503 = Casimir, king of Poland 1444, d. 1492.

Ladislaus, king of Bohemia 1471, king of Hungary 1490, d. 1516. = Anne.

John I. Albert, kings of Poland.

Sigismond, king of Poland.

Anne = Ferdinand I., archduke of Austria.

Louis II., king of Hungary and Bohemia, d. 1526. = Mary of Austria.

Isabella, d. 1559. = John of Szapolyai, prince of Transylvania elect, king of Hungary 1527, d. 1571.

John Sigismond, d. 1571.

The grounds of the right of conquest have still to appear in our narrative.

The career of the house of Hapsburgh presents one of the most remarkable examples upon record of continued good fortune. No other of the reigning families of Europe has withstood the shocks and revolutions of the last ten centuries with the same audacious confidence in its own destiny, and with equal exemption from all the ordinary consequences of folly, injustice, and oppression. A thousand storms have rolled over its head. It has bowed before them all, and survived to rejoice in the sunshine of restored tranquility and prosperity. Its descent can be traced up through all the changes and revolutions of the middle ages to the

HUNGARY IN MOURNING.

earlier centuries of the Christian era, when one of its heads is found among the robber barons of Germany, perched in a tall castle upon an inaccessible cliff. From that day, when the inheritance did not equal in extent the estates of many an English gentleman, to the present, when it has absorbed a third, at least, of northern Europe, every member of it has been distinguished by the same grasping imperious spirit, the same indifference to means in the pursuit of personal power and gain. Most of the earlier counts were distinguished by great ability, great tact, and great military bravery, but we can hardly point to one who displayed any proper sense of his responsibilities to the people whom he governed. They were singularly tenacious of their rights, powerfully animated by the love of acquiring. The consequence is that Austria has for many centuries been governed as private patrimony rather than as a state. Other constitution than the will of the monarch, or the traditions of the monarch's ancestors, no Austrian subject has ever known. And this policy, strange to say, has so far been singularly successful; not, indeed, as regards the welfare of the people, but as regards the stability of the reigning family. How many dynasties has this family seen extinguished and forgotten!—how many governments overthrown—how many "battles, sieges and fortunes" has it passed through in safety, while monarchies in which military genius seemed hereditary, whose thrones were based on the affections of united, fond, and brave people, whose existence, in some periods of their history, seemed a thing to last for ever, have been blasted, like an oak by lightning, and their heirs sent to wander in indigence and exile, and to build their hopes upon the misfortunes of their successors and the fickleness of the crowd.

Neither the training nor temper of the Hapsburghs fitted them for reigning as constitutional kings. A monarch whose will has been his law, frets against the restraints of the parliamentary system, like an imprisoned lion against the bars of his cage, and break them he will by force or stratagem. There are a thousand examples of the truth of this in the history of every country in Europe; there is hardly one to prove it false. Hungary had experienced many disasters before the battle of Mohacs, but none which struck so deadly a blow at her liberties. Her spirit was broken by the ravages of the Turks; and torn by dissensions from within, she was forced to cast herself at the feet of Austria, and merge her history in that of a family of despots. The principle of election now gave way to that of hereditary descent, and more than this, singular complications arose in the working of the legislative machinery, from the fact that the king was no longer a national monarch. He had other states and other interests to attend to; he resided at a distance from the seat of government; he could if necessary, by the subsidies and military force of his other dominions, render himself quite independent of the supplies or remonstrances of the diet. The consequence of this was, that the national assembly had its attention altogether diverted from its proper sphere of duty. It felt itself responsible for the rights and liberties of the nation. It felt that these liberties were viewed with a jealous eye by a powerful and ambitious neighbour, the head of a foreign nation—and that neighbour their own king. It directed its whole energies, therefore, to the single task of watching him, of counteracting his intrigues by other intrigues not less mischievous. From standing constantly on the defensive it became violently conservative, and saw in every change an attack upon its privileges. The written constitution was an object of deep dislike to the Austrian emperors, who in their hereditary states were accustomed to no such restraint; but the more they sought to overturn it, the more fondly and fiercely did the Hungarians cling to it. To the latter its very defects became objects to be revered and admired. They thought only of preserving, never of improving it. Progressive legislation, that should improve the condition of the people and develop the resources of the country, became a thing unknown. The ravages of the Turks, and the scarcely less terrible ravages of the rival parties who contended for the throne, were left to be repaired by time, which heals all wounds to be sure, but seldom without leaving behind ineffaceable scars. In the contests with the Ottomans, the Magyars had risen to the level of heroism; in their contests with Austria they never displayed the same energy and activity, and in their long disasters, in their many grievances we see a striking proof of God's watchful guardianship of the rights of humanity. These oligarchs who thundered against the oppressions of Austria, were themselves grievous oppressors. Their boasted constitution and laws were formed for the benefit of one section of the population only. The real people, the serfs who tilled the soil, who bore the brunt of the Turkish ravages, who toiled generation after generation upon soil to which they had no claim save in death, who heaped up riches that others might enjoy them, who starved that their lords might revel in luxury, who knew no law but the will of the baron, and to whom no political changes brought freedom or relief, had no interest in this struggle. They fought the battles of their masters, that their masters might crush them more effectually. When they rose under George Dozsa, they rose in obedience to one of those instincts of human nature which no slavery can ever utterly extinguish. Borne down by skill and force they resumed their old life of hardship and endurance. The code which governed them was one which for ingenious cruelty and wrong has no parallel in history, save the penal enactments by which England sought in the eighteenth century to extirpate Catholicism in Ireland, or those by which it is now sought to perpetuate negro slavery in America. In Hungary, these odious distinctions proved the ruin of those who upheld them. In the serfdom of the peasants lay the seeds of the national downfall. To outrage liberty daily in the persons of their vassals before the eyes of their children, was not the way to train up good citizens to love and defend the state. It is thus that God in all ages defends the interests of truth and justice, by infusing into oppression poison for the oppressor. The strength of the vanquished and wronged may fail them; but the laws of morality are ever the same, and make known in unseen and hidden ways the watchful providence of God over his creatures.

Immediately after the battle of Mohacs, and death of Louis, Ferdinand laid claim to the two crowns of Hungary and Bohemia, to the latter in right of his wife Anne, the only sister of the deceased monarch, and the other in virtue of the compact which gave him the reversion of the crown in case of the failure of male issue in the reigning family. But as both these countries repudiated all claims founded upon any right but that of election, he prudently waived them, and put himself in competition as a candidate before the diets. His only opponent in Bohemia being the duke of Bavaria, he was elected by a committee of twenty persons, who were appointed by the states to choose a king. In his letter of thanks to the states, he promised to preserve inviolate all their rights and privileges, to observe the religious compacts, to raise no foreigners to any office in the state, to issue good money, to govern the kingdom according to the ancient laws and customs, and to reside at Prague. He also, by a public act, acknowledged that he owed the throne to the free choice of the barons, nobles, and states of Bohemia, and disclaimed all other pretensions. He soon after repaired to Iglau, where he took the usual oaths, and continuing the journey to the capital was crowned in the cathedral with Anne, his wife. After taking possession of Moravia, Silesia, and Lusatia, at that time dependencies upon the Bohemian crown, he proceeded to Hungary.*

Here he had a more formidable rival in the person of John Szapolyai, the wayvode of Transylvania, who had led 40,000 men to the aid of Louis, but was unable to reach him till it was too late. His family was partly of German origin, and were distinguished by their brilliant services in the reign of Louis the Great, and changed their original name of Heems or Kapol of Deákfalua to that of Zapolya, their estates in Sclavonia. It then received the addition of the final *i*, a termination which has the same value when attached to the name of a noble, as *de* among the French *gentilshommes*. Modern historians, however, call them Szapolyai.† Upon hearing of the result of the battle of Mohacs, John remained inactive at the head of his army near Szeguedin, while Solyman was overrunning the country. He had already begun to aspire to the throne, and was waiting for an opportunity to advance his claims. He was very popular amongst the nobles on account of the active and successful part he had taken in suppressing the insurrection of the peasantry, and he sought to ingratiate himself with them still further, by sending messages to all the leading men, representing to them the disgrace it would inflict upon the country, if any other than a native were elected to wear the crown. His pretensions were favoured also by Peter Perenyi, who had at that time the crown in his possession, and in an assembly of the states held at Tokay he was unanimously elected king by a large party of the nobles, who were averse to the rule of a foreigner. He was afterwards crowned at Alba Regia with great pomp. After the fêtes and rejoicings attendant upon the ceremony were over, he bestowed the principal dignities and offices of the state upon his chief supporters, amongst others upon Verboczi, who was related to him by marriage, a man, who had gained immense popularity in the country, owing to his ardent patriotism and brilliant eloquence.

Immediately upon hearing of this, Ferdinand wrote to his sister Mary, the widow of Louis, imploring her to use all means in her power to procure his election to the throne of Hungary, to prevent that monarchy, which was in reality the bulwark of Christendom against the Ottomans, from going to dissolution. She, therefore, summoned another diet at Presburgh, where a party of nobles declared John's election illegal, because the assembly at Tokay had not been summoned by the palatine, and, in their turn, elected Ferdinand. The latter

* Coxe's Hist. of the House of Austria, vol. i. part ii. p. 551.

† Paul Száy.

instantly prepared to support his claim, by marching a large army of Germans and Bohemians to Buda, having previously taken the usual oath to observe the rights and privileges of the nation. He was joyfully received by his supporters, who were mostly made up of magnates, who plumed themselves upon their long descent, and were jealous of John's election, and, therefore, hailed Ferdinand as "the saviour and restorer of Hungarian liberty." Another assembly of the states was summoned at Buda, who confirmed the decision of that of Presburgh; and Ferdinand was proclaimed king, and John and his adherents

JOHN SZAPOLYAI.

were declared traitors, if they did not make their submission within twenty-eight days. John undoubtedly occupied a proud position as the champion of the national rights, and, in the hands of an able and energetic man, it would have been so used as to vindicate Hungarian independence for ever. But he was wanting in decision and self-reliance, and in many instances gave strong evidence of pusillanimity. By the persuasion of the more valiant of his followers, he once offered battle to the Austrian forces, but being defeated, took refuge in Poland, leaving Ferdinand undisputed master of the kingdom. There he was received with great kindness by Lasky, a wealthy and powerful noble, who advised him strongly to seek the aid of Solyman to recover his rights. Lasky himself accordingly set forward to Constantinople as his ambassador, and there won the support of the vizier and the bashaws by his presents, and by the grace and suavity of his manners, so that the sultan was already influenced in his favour before he had obtained an audience. He offered to Solyman, on John's behalf, to hold the crown of Hungary as a Turkish fief, and to pay him an annual tribute, in case he assisted in driving out Ferdinand, and he represented to him that the relationship of the latter with Charles V., and many other powerful monarchs of the west, would render him a dangerous neighbour in case he succeeded in retaining Hungary. The sultan listened with attention, and, after some consideration agreed to support John.

Very soon after, Ferdinand bethought himself of sending an embassy to Constantinople also, as he was not without fears that John would seek Turkish aid. John Oberdansch was, therefore, despatched for this purpose, but on his arrival, he at once perceived by the cool demeanour of the officials that he had been anticipated, and it was, therefore, not without some misgivings, that, after making professions of a desire for peace, he required the restoration of Belgrade, and other places wrested from Hungary. This demand, contrasting so strongly with the humble offers of submission which had been made by Szapolyai, roused the ire of the sultan to the highest pitch. He started from his seat and exclaimed, "Belgrade! Go tell your master that I am collecting troops, and preparing for my expedition. I will suspend at my neck the keys of my Hungarian fortresses, and will bring them to that plain of Mohacs, where Louis, by the aid of God, found a defeat and a grave. Let Ferdinand meet and conquer me, and take them after severing my head from my body! But, if I find him not there, I will seek him at Buda, or follow him to Vienna!" *

While he was preparing to execute his threat, Szapolyai collected a corps of Polish troops, and entering Hungary defeated the Austrians at Cassau, and was soon joined by partizans from Hungary, Transylvania, and Sclavonia.† Shortly afterwards Solyman appeared on the frontiers with 300,000 men, and pitching his camp on the plains of Mohacs, was joined by John and a great crowd of the Hungarian nobility; the former did him homage for his kingdom, by kissing his hand, and the sultan promised speedily to put him in possession of all he had lost. After leaving Solyman's tent he paid his respects to Louis Gritti, the son of Andrew Gritti the doge of Venice. The former was a hired spy of Solyman, and stood high in his favour, and thus enabled to render John important service.

The sultan soon after began his march, took Buda, and the citadel having been surrendered to him by treachery, he delivered it to John. He then despatched a corps of irregular cavalry to ravage the country as far as the Lintz. Visegrad,

* Hist. Rerum. Gest. inter Ferdinandum et Johannem, Scriptores Rer. Hung. vol. ii. p. 394.

† Coxe's History of the House of Austria, vol. i. part ii. p. 563.

Gran, Comorn, Raab, and Altenburg fell before him in rapid succession, and he at last arrived at Vienna, having pillaged the inhabitants on the line of his march.

Ferdinand was by this time thoroughly alarmed; and had made every exertion to save his capital. The fortifications were old, and had been built before the invention of gunpowder, and consequently though fully able to resist the attacks of unaided valour, they could offer but small defence to a well served park of artillery; the ditches were dry and shallow, and there were no flanking towers. By the exertions of the emperor, however, all these defects were in some measure remedied. He caused the wall to be repaired as well as time would permit, travelled himself in person to many of the principal towns of Germany to request aid against the infidels, and succeeded in procuring reinforcements to the extent of 20,000 men, and Frederick, the count palatine, advanced at the head of a large corps of troops raised by the German states, and though too late to enter the city, contributed to its relief by keeping the Turks in a state of continual alarm.

The latter spread their camp around the whole city in four divisions, three of which were commanded by bashaws of tried skill and valour, and the fourth, containing the janizaries, by the sultan himself. The first few days of the siege, while awaiting the arrival of the heavy artillery, which was being brought up the Danube on rafts, were employed in pouring in showers of arrows thick as hail, without any other effect, however, than compelling the garrison to keep under cover. But as fate would have it, the artillery never came. When passing Presburgh, the boats which conveyed it were assailed by Wolfgang Oder, the governor, with a battery of artillery concealed amongst the trees on the bank of the river, and the greater part were sunk or destroyed, and the guns thrown into the water.

Solyman, though greatly chagrined by the loss of his artillery, still did not give up hopes of success. By mining in every direction, he sought to effect breaches in the walls, but his efforts were frustrated by the diligence of the garrison, who discovered the position and extent of the works by placing dice on drums laid upon the ground and basins filled with water to exhibit the vibrations caused by the sound of the besiegers' tools. Countermines were then made with great rapidity, and in this way 9,000 of the Turks were either slain or overwhelmed. One mine was, however, at length completed before it was discovered, and on being exploded made a wide breach in the walls, and a large body of the besiegers instantly rushed to the assault, covering their approach by a discharge of arrows. The Viennese met them in the opening with unshaken courage, and after a sharp hand-to-hand conflict, compelled them to retire. Two more breaches were soon after effected in a similar manner, and a second and third time the assailants were driven back with tremendous slaughter. Solyman made a fourth attempt, in which his whole army took part, but with no better success than before, and still greater sacrifice of life, and, at last, finding the winter at hand, and fearing the arrival of fresh succours, he raised the siege, and retired to Buda, after having wasted thirty days before the walls. The joy of the Viennese at their deliverance was somewhat damped by learning that the Turkish army had laid waste the whole country in its retreat, and had led more than sixty thousand persons into captivity.* At Buda John Szapolyai was solemnly proclaimed king in the midst of a numerous assembly of Turkish and Hungarian nobles, and the crown of St. Stephen and the other regalia which the sultan had hitherto retained in his possession were delivered to him. A body of Turkish troops were then left in the garrison, and Solyman returned in triumph to Constantinople, committing such frightful havoc on his way, that John, who owed him his throne, shed tears when he heard of it.

At his departure Solyman left Louis Gritti, to whom we have already referred, a renegade Venetian, the son of the doge, to be the confidential adviser of Szapolyai. He soon after recalled him to Constantinople, and sent him back invested with still more extensive powers as lieutenant-governor in his name of the kingdom of Hungary. Gritti made his entrance into Wallachia at the head of a large body of troops, and passing thence to Transylvania, caused a proclamation to be made through the Hungarian provinces, to king John's great chagrin, ordering all the prelates, magnates, and free towns, to have recourse to him as arbitrator and lieutenant of the grand seignor, and as sole judge of all their debates, strifes, and quarrels. Emerik Cibacy, bishop of Varadin, the wayvode of Transylvania, who was already at enmity with Gritti, was greatly disgusted by his sudden elevation, made no haste to pay his respects to him, and when he did receive him, it was at the head of an armed force in an open plain. This demeanour so greatly incensed the latter, that, being urged on by other aspirants for the office of wayvode, he caused Emerik to be assassinated in his tent, and had his head carried to him suspended by one of the ears. Roused into fury by the murder of their wayvode, the Transylvanians rose in arms, and having defeated Gritti and taken him prisoner, they put him to death, as well as his sons, whom they surprised and overpowered.

After having passed the winter of 1529 in tranquillity at Constantinople, in the following spring Solyman renewed his preparations for the subjugation of Austria, and, with a larger army than ever he had assembled before, set out late in the spring; and after a march of fifty-six days reached Belgrade. The extent of his armament, and the remembrance of the sufferings endured by the inhabitants of the countries through which he passed on the former occasion, spread terror throughout Germany; and the religious dissensions by which that country was then torn and divided, incapacitated Ferdinand from making so gallant a defence as before. Succours were voted by the diet to the full extent of its ability, but by no means sufficient to stem the torrent which threatened to overwhelm the whole of western Europe. Ferdinand sent ambassadors to Solyman with rich

* Knolles's Hist. of the Turks, art. Solyman the Magnificent. History of the Troubles in Hungary, p. 50.

presents and proposals of peace; but they met with a haughty and insolent rebuff, and were ordered to follow his march and await his pleasure. Having crossed the Save, he left the Danube (on which he embarked his artillery in a flotilla of three thousand vessels) on his left, and turning a little to the right, poured his hordes through the western provinces, till on arriving on the frontiers of Styria, he stopped before the little town of Guntz, since so famous, but till then almost unknown. It was a small place, square built, badly fortified, and garrisoned only by eight hundred men, under the command of Nicholas Jurissitz. Solyman encompassed it round about with five hundred thousand men, and a battery of three hundred field pieces; and called upon the governor to surrender. The summons was disregarded, and the Turks commenced the attack by making three separate breaches in the walls by the explosion of mines, while the cannon from a neighbouring hill rained shot incessantly upon the interior. Jurissitz, nothing daunted, constructed a curtain of earth and boards, which shut out the ramparts from the sight of the Turkish gunners, and thus allowed his soldiers to give their whole attention to the defence of the breaches against the assaults of the janizaries; and succeeded in repairing, in one night, all the damage done by the enemy in three days. At last Solyman threw up two mounds of such height that they not only overtopped the walls, but enabled the gunners who were stationed with cannon on the top to pick off every one who showed himself in the streets; and thus covered, the besiegers once more rushed to the assault, and once again were beaten back with great slaughter. Bribes, promises, threats, and entreaties were all employed in vain; and the sultan was at length compelled to accept a feigned submission, and leave Jurissitz in possession of the fortress, after a siege of twenty-eight days. The gallant example afforded by the little garrison of Guntz, aroused the ardour of all the warriors of Christendom; and the check experienced by Solyman, gave time to Ferdinand to concert measures for the defence of his dominions.

The troubles in Germany were composed by the treaty concluded by Charles V. at Ratisbon, and enabled both Protestants and Catholics to unite their forces against the common enemy with extraordinary vigour and unanimity. Charles drew his veterans from the Low Countries; Ferdinand collected troops from Bohemia and the neighbouring provinces; Sigismond of Poland sent succours; and the ablest officers from all parts of Europe flocked to volunteer their services, and, if need were, to serve in the ranks. The emperor and Ferdinand having united their forces, consisting of 90,000 foot and 30,000 horse, encamped under the walls of Vienna to await the approach of the Turks. A great battle was then daily expected which should finally decide the fate of Europe.

But Solyman was disheartened by the unexpected resistance he had met with at Guntz, and was astonished by the wonderful and unusual harmony of the Christian powers. His baggage and heavy artillery had not yet arrived, being unable to get past Presburgh, and instead of fighting he determined to retreat. He, therefore, despatched his irregular cavalry to lay waste the country, and retired through the mountains to Gantz, the capital of Styria, where he remained for a short time inactive, but winter approaching, he was at last compelled to return precipitately to Constantinople, discomfited and humiliated, and he had scarce arrived when the news reached him that his light-horse which had penetrated as far as the Ems, had been surrounded and cut to pieces on the way back, in September, 1532.*

A favourable opportunity was now afforded to Ferdinand to conquer the whole of Hungary and expel John, if he could have but secured the support of the huge army which Charles had under his command. But as soon as Solyman had abandoned the field, it was found impossible to keep together the heterogeneous materials of which it was composed. Winter was approaching, provisions were becoming scarce, and disease was breaking out in the camp, and Ferdinand soon found himself left with little more than his own forces.

With these he for several years carried on a desultory warfare with John, which brought no positive advantage to either, while it devastated and impoverished the country. At last, the latter, tired of the dispute, chagrined and humiliated by the reproaches which were cast upon him, on account of his alliance with the sultan, and despairing of ever being able to recover the provinces bordering on Austria, consented to divide the kingdom with Ferdinand. By the mediation of Charles, a treaty was concluded at Great Varadin, by which it was stipulated that John was to retain the title of king, together with Transylvania, and all that part of Hungary which was then in his possession, and Frederick was to hold the remainder, and at John's death his male issue was to inherit his paternal dominions and the wayvodeship of Transylvania only; and he was to renounce all alliances against the house of Austria, and both were to unite in a league against the Turks. It was not without indignation that the Hungarians beheld the cool manner in which the kingdom had been divided by the two potentates, without the participation of the states, just as if it was the patrimony of either, of which he had the full and entire disposition. But such was the misery and desolation which prevailed, that they had neither the courage to remonstrate nor the strength to resist. The arrangement was apparently very advantageous for Ferdinand, as John was childless, unmarried, and well stricken in years, but no sooner was the treaty concluded than he married his cousin, Isabella, daughter of Sigismond, king of Poland, a young and beautiful princess. A great number of enemies now rose up against him amongst the members of his own party, and the remainder of his life was spent in combatting their intrigues. He died on the 21st July, 1540, of a stroke of apoplexy, but not before he had received the welcome intelligence that his wife had been delivered of a son, at Buda, who was called John Sigismond, after his grandfather.

Ferdinand's rule had already disgusted those amongst the Hungarian nobility who had raised him to the throne. They had been terrified by the frightful

* Knolles's History of the Turks.

disasters which foreign invasion, civil war, and divided rule, had brought upon their country, and the constant and insidious attacks which Ferdinand was making upon their laws and liberties inspired them with sorrow and remorse for the part they had taken in supporting him. There is still extant a remonstrance which they addressed to him, clear, succinct, and forcible, and worthy of record, as the last groan of expiring liberty. They declared that before taking into consideration his principal demands, bowed down by the load of their grief, they could not refrain from addressing him in as few words as possible upon the subject of their many grievances—the crying injustice and oppression which they had for so long a time endured, in the constant infringements of their liberties and privileges. They had undergone terrible injuries from the Turks, murders, burnings, and cruel tortures, but these were but trifling in comparison with what they had suffered from the soldiers of the king, who had desolated the country by plunder, rapine, and violence, and justified their outrages by complaining of the delay in the payment of their wages, though the diet had invariably shown the utmost willingness to grant supplies. They declared also that the greater part of the troubles and ravages to which the kingdom had been exposed were the work of the officers commanding the foreign troops, whom Ferdinand, contrary to law, had introduced into the kingdom. The fortresses were all in their hands, and they made a practice of pillaging the farms in their neighbourhood, and added insult to the injury by speaking of the Hungarian people in the vilest and most contemptuous terms. These foreign soldiers were the terror of the districts through which they passed, as they acted as if in an enemy's country, and for all these reasons the states and orders of the kingdom implored Ferdinand to put a stop to the disorders, so that they might no longer be treated as outlaws or aliens by those whose duty it was to succour and protect them.*

Upon John's death, Ferdinand thought he had nothing to do but to enter into possession of the whole kingdom, according to the terms of the treaty, but to his astonishment and chagrin the adherents of the late king refused to acknowledge his claims, and crowned John Sigismond almost immediately after he had been baptized, using in the ceremony the royal crown, of which they had retained possession.* Ferdinand sent a message to Isabella, his mother, requiring the delivery of the regalia and the acknowledgment of his right to the succession; but Isabella was a woman of too high a spirit to surrender one tittle of her son's claims. All the historians of the period join in eulogizing her character and her accomplishments. From her mother, Bonna Sforza of Milan, she inherited the grace and acquirements for which the Italian women in that age were famous, and she added to them beauty and tenderness, which were by no means so general. But these were the least of her charms. She had, though cradled in prosperity, armed herself against the severest reverses. She was not only versed in classic lore, but had studied the science of government with a zeal which humanity

* Art. 2—5, of 1559. Art 36 and 37, of 1563.

nursed and kept alive. Those details of poverty and hardship, which so often disgust and repel the high-born and fortunate, were to her a source of interest and attraction. Throughout the whole of her life she was the friend and consoler of the wretched serfs, who seldom had any other. She inquired into their wants, listened to the rudely told story of their grievances, and became their advocate and intercessor with their seigneurs. After her husband's death, it devolved entirely upon her to act as guardian of her son, and to fill the duties of the office which the diet had conferred upon him; and her position, difficult under any circumstances, was rendered doubly difficult by a declaration of hostilities on the part of Ferdinand. She felt the necessity of having a coadjutor, whose firmness, experience, and sagacity might support her through the storms and rials of a civil war.

This she found in George Utjssenovitz, usually styled Martinuzzi, one of the most remarkable men of his day. He was the son of Gregory Utjssenovitz, and was descended from a poor but noble family of Croatia. He was born in 1482, in the castle of Namiezas in that province, of which place his father bore the title of count. But the castle or the title were the only inheritances which descended to George, and owing to the impoverished circumstances of the family, he had not received in his youth the education suitable to his rank. His mother was left a widow a few month after his birth, and as unaided merit had, in that age of the world, but few paths open to it, she took care to provide him with a powerful and influential godfather, in the person of her brother, James Martinuzzi, bishop of Scardona in Dalmatia, and that she might interest the bishop still more in his *protegé*, she made the latter adopt his surname, which he bore during the remainder of his life. Nevertheless, his uncle soon after refused to acknowledge him, and to save himself from destitution he obtained a subordinate office in Szapolyai's household. Martinuzzi's proud spirit, however, could ill brook the indignities and petty slights to which his position exposed him, and he lost no time in entering the monastery of the monks of St. Paul, where John took a refuge after one of his defeats by the Austrians. Martinuzzi made himself known to him, wormed himself into his favour and confidence, and ended by becoming his ambassador or rather his spy. The cowl, then more respected than the purple, preserved him amidst the many hazards to which his new calling exposed him. When Szapolyai, by the aid of the sultan regained his throne, he did not forget the friend of his adversity. He made him bishop of Great Varadin, created him treasurer, and by his testament nominated him one of the guardians of his son. Martinuzzi, in his new sphere, displayed the most extraordinary versatility of character. He in many respects was a counterpart of Cardinal Wolsey. He had the same pride, the same audacious ambition that thought no pinnacle in the state too high for him to stand upon, the same austere devotion to his ecclesiastical duties, combined with the same pomp of power. But unlike Wolsey, he was not merely an artful, selfish churchman, with just ability enough to push himself forward. Martinuzzi could, when occasion required, fling off the monk's habit, and assume the arms and carriage of a soldier. He was too prudent to seek danger, but when it came he knew how to brave it, and in the field displayed all the skill, courage, and fortitude of an accomplished general. In the transaction of civil business, he was acute prompt, and energetic. He was gifted with commanding eloquence, and was distinguished by the dignity of his deportment. He had but little regard for the sanctity of an oath; gave it and broke it, with equal facility. He was skilful in discovering the designs of others, and equally skilful in veiling his own mystery. He had in short most, if not all the talents which make a man famous, and but few of the virtues which make a man good. By his enemies he is depicted as a

ISABELLA SZAPOLYAI.

monster; by his friends as a hero and a saint. Both are alike far from the truth. His great faults were his perfidy, his inordinate ambition, and his impatience of control, and these were too common in the middle of the sixteenth century amongst men of his class, to warrant us in judging him by the light of our own time.*

By his advice the young king was proclaimed under the revered name of

* A memoir of Martinuzzi was published in Paris in 1715, from which the facts of his history are principally derived

Stephen, and he and his mother were placed in security in the castle of Buda, and an embassy was despatched to Constantinople to seek assistance from the sultan—a fatal and inexcusable step, which entailed a century of suffering and disaster upon Hungary. Ferdinand, hoping to prevent another civil war, sent an embassy also to Constantinople, offering to hold Hungary as a fief of the Porte and pay tribute like his predecessor, in case the sultan acknowledged his claim to the crown. But it by no means accorded with the policy of the crafty Solyman to receive as his vassal a powerful monarch in the prime of life, who might, ere long,

VERBOCZI.

not only have the will but the strength to set him at defiance. He secretly wished to annex Hungary to his own dominions, and no better opportunity of effecting his purpose was ever likely to occur than while her destinies were entrusted to the hands of a woman, a child, and a priest. He haughtily rejected Ferdinand's proposals, and called upon him not only to relinquish all claims to the Hungarian crown, but to acknowledge the Austrian territory as a fief of the Turkish empire. The archduke, however, had not placed his whole trust in the success of the negotiation. Before the return of his ambassadors he had despatched an army to Buda, in 1540, which besieged the queen and her son in the citadel, under the command of General Fels. The skill and courage of Martinuzzi caused the failure of the enterprise. In the following year the attempt was renewed by Roggendorf, when a traitor, to whom Martinuzzi had given some cause of offence, sold the pass, and the Austrian troops had already entered the gates, when the sentinels gave the alarm. The garrison rushed to their arms, and under the command of Urbain Batthyanyi drove them back sword in hand. In the heat of the engagement, a watchman on the tower announced the appearance of the Moslem standards on the plain close to the city. The sultan had sent his vizier, Mehemet Pasha, to the relief of the queen, with a large body of troops. The Austrians were taken by surprise, but after some hesitation, Roggendorf determined to offer battle. He accordingly shifted his camp. The Turks harassed him by constant assaults, and, at length, in a general engagement, his army was utterly routed. Great numbers were forced into the Danube and drowned, others in attempting to escape in boats fell under the fire of the janizaries; and the garrison of the citadel sallying forth to take part in the conflict, added fresh horrors to the scene. Roggendorf, mortally wounded, sought in vain to rally his terror-stricken troops. The tide of battle soon rolled into the streets of Pesth, and in the melée neither age nor sex was spared. Soldier and citizen, friend and foe, were hewed down by the Turks in one indiscriminate massacre. The Danube was choked with the bodies of the slain, and the blood, rushing down from the high ground, dyed its waters for miles. Three thousand soldiers were slaughtered in the church of St. Gerard, in which they had taken refuge; and many more perished in the flames of the royal stables, which Martinuzzi ordered to be set on fire on hearing that they were occupied by Ferdinand's troops. The latter lost thirty pieces of siege artillery and one hundred and fifty field pieces, and nearly 25,000 men in killed and wounded, besides those who were taken prisoners. Roggendorf made his escape to the island of Czalókoz, and there died.

Solyman had followed in the track of his vizier with a large army, and arrived under the walls of Buda soon after the victory, where he was joined by other corps which had been employed in wresting Transylvania from Ferdinand. He sent some presents to the queen and her son, and expressed the most lively desire to see the infant for whom he had undergone so much toil and trouble, and whose interests he had so deeply at heart, and requested her to send him to his camp. Isabella, with all the suspicious tenderness of a mother's love, hesitated to commit him to the hands of one whom she could not but regard more as a relentless conqueror than as an ally, and made a thousand excuses for refusing to comply. But Martinuzzi impressed upon her the danger of offending the sultan, soothed her fears, and offered to guarantee the king's safety by accompanying him in person. He was accordingly magnificently dressed, placed in a splendid carriage, and thus conveyed to the Turkish camp. Solyman received him with all outward marks of affection—took him in his arms, caressed him, and desired his own sons always to regard John Sigismond as their brother. The ladies and nobles who formed the royal suite were received with equal courtesy and were sumptuously entertained at the sultan's own table. While the festivities were proceeding, the janizaries entered Buda in large bodies, but without order or regularity, under pretence of seeing the town. The Hungarian garrison suffered them to pass without suspicion, but, to their surprise, within a short time afterwards, they suddenly seized upon all the principal posts, disarmed the guard, and issued a proclamation, warning the inhabitants to confine themselves to their own houses, and to deliver up their arms peaceably, and as a measure of still greater precaution, a Turkish soldier was billeted in every family. The infant prince was then sent back, but Martinuzzi and all the others who accompanied him were detained prisoners. The queen, on hearing of these acts of gross perfidy, was seized with consternation, and fearing some still worse outrage, wrote humbly to Solyman, beseeching him to liberate her friends and restore to her the possession of her capital. The answer was short, but decisive. She and the other guardians of her son were required to renounce in his name all right to the throne, and, in return, he was invested with the principality of Transylvania, as the tributary and feudatory of the Porte, and Isabella was required to quit Buda and repair forthwith to her new dominions. A garrison of 10,000 janizaries was then placed in the citadel, and Verboczi, the eminent lawyer who had formed the code, was appointed supreme judge of the inhabitants of Buda, but he did not long enjoy his doubtful honours, as he died some months afterwards, bitterly regretting on his deathbed the equivocal part which he had played towards the close of his career. The queen was more attached to her son than to the crown, and she set out without hesitation, but no sooner had she arrived upon the frontiers of Transylvania than the nobles of the principality, fearing that by receiving her they might draw on themselves the anger of the Turks, wished to oppose her entrance. She was consequently compelled to call Martinuzzi, who had regained his liberty, and been appointed by the sultan to act as her adviser, to her aid, though his pride and ambition had made her fear and hate him. He hastened to her assistance, put down her enemies, seized upon the treasury, and soon surrounded himself by a powerful party, to whose intrigues and machinations she could only oppose a small number of faithful friends.

Having mastered Buda and Pesth, Solyman soon captured all the other principal fortresses, extended his arms on both sides of the Danube, and annexed to his dominions all the southern provinces of Hungary. Ferdinand, disheartened by the defeat of his army under Roggendorf, and despairing of obtaining any aid from his brother Charles, who had schemes of his own to attend to, and finding his territory exhausted and his treasury half empty, determined to sue for peace, in the hope of being enabled to retain, at least that portion of Hungary which was still in his hands. He, therefore, sent rich presents to Solyman and requested the investiture of the kingdom. Solyman received the presents but refused the investiture, and required him thenceforth and for ever utterly to renounce all claim to the kingdom of Hungary. From that moment Hungary became the theatre of a contest which, happily, has had few parallels in history, between two foreign armies, to whom victory seemed but a secondary object, and the ruin and misery of the inhabitants the chief. Austrians and Turks both acquitted themselves of their horrible task with equal fury. A new force, furnished by the electors of Germany, also made its appearance on the scene, and added to the violence and outrage which the unfortunate Hungarians had to undergo. Ottoman or Christian made little difference. The Catholic prince and Mahometan sultan adopted without scruple the same means of securing their conquests—burning, massacre, and pillage. At last, the Five Churches, Strigonia, and Alba Regia, were all carried by the Turks, and half the country was groaning under the arbitrary rule of the pashas, when Ferdinand was forced to request a truce of five years, which he obtained upon the humiliating condition of paying an annual tribute of 30,000 ducats, and becoming a feudatory of the Porte.*

Martinuzzi was, in the meantime, carrying things with a high hand in Transylvania. He had seized upon the revenues, and refused to allow the queen even what was sufficient for her personal wants. He used every means in his reach to attach the nobles to his party; or if any one gave open signs of aversion to his schemes, his enmity pursued him to the death. The unfortunate Isabella for a long time bore his arrogance and injustice with patience and in silence, hoping that time and Providence, in whose watchful care her simple and earnest piety taught her to repose the most implicit trust, would, in the long-run, deliver her out of his power. At last, however, finding his insolence and tyranny increasing from day to day, she was driven to complain to the sultan as the only one powerful enough to afford her redress. Solyman wrote to Martinuzzi, ordering him to alter his manner of dealing with the queen, or he would make an example of him for the benefit of others who might be equally presumptuous. The bishop now perceived that his only resource, if he meant to preserve his power and influence, was to throw himself into the arms of Frederick, and betray his trust as the guardian of the orphan child of his best friend and benefactor. He was the more inclined to this step by the continual vexation he underwent from Solyman, who, in addition to his yearly tribute, was constantly demanding of him victuals, ammunition, and supplies of every description for his enormous army. He therefore opened up negotiations with an Austrian emissary for procuring the fulfilment of the treaty entered into by the late king John. The intrigue speedily came to the knowledge of Isabella, and she immediately apprised Solyman of it, who despatched a message to Buda ordering the pasha in command to arrest Martinuzzi alive or dead, and sent letters into Transylvania depriving him of all state, office, and authority, and ordering his subjects to kill him as a traitor. He also wrote to the wayvode of Wallachia, and his other officers in the Hungarian provinces, desiring them to aid the queen with all the forces at their command. Martinuzzi received timely notice of the measures that were about to be taken against him, and retired from the queen's court to a well-fortified town

* Isthuanfuis, p. 47.

called Sassebessa, and there determined to defend himself. He called around him all his partizans from various parts of the kingdom, and raised and equipped four thousand soldiers from amongst the hardy and warlike Szeklers. Petrowitz, John Sigismond's other guardian, who took the queen's part in the quarrel, began also to assemble an army, but before taking any decisive step determined to await the arrival of the Turks; but, finding there was no sign of their appearance, Isabella became desirous of a reconciliation, and George feeling doubtful of the security of his position threw no obstacle in the way, and it was speedily effected. In a very short time, however, the quarrel broke out afresh, but before it came to an open rupture, Ferdinand succeeded in inducing his brother Charles V. to lend him his aid. The latter accordingly gave directions to his general, Castaldo, to place himself at the head of the Austrian forces, and march upon Transylvania. The army left Vienna in May 1551, and on its arrival at Agria, Castaldo caused the town to be fortified and resumed his march, crossed the Teyss and reached Debreczin without accident. He was here joined by Andrew Bathori, and some other Hungarian magnates, with a troop of cavalry. In the meantime, Isabella summoned a diet, composed of her adherents, to advise her what measures she should take for the expulsion of Martinuzzi from the kingdom. He was at that time at Varadin, the seat of his bishopric, and on hearing what was going on, set off full speed towards Transylvania. On the way the carriage was overturned, and he himself was nearly drowned in passing a small stream. His attendants looked upon the accident as an evil omen and advised him to return. His reply at once rebuked them for their superstition, and betrayed the height of his own ambition. "It is not this chariot," said he, pointing to the vehicle which lay shattered in the water, "which rules my destiny; but that glorious one that you see shining in the heavens!"* Upon reaching Torde, he wrote to the principal nobles, both of the queen's party and his own, calling upon them, if they wished to save the kingdom from falling into the hands of the Ottomans to repair forthwith to him, that there they might provide for the common good of all. Within a short time he was joined by a considerable number of irregular troops, both infantry and cavalry, and putting himself at the head, he marched rapidly to Egnet, dissolved the diet, and caused the queen and her son to take refuge in Alba Julia, which Petrowitz had garrisoned and fortified; but fearing that it might not prove strong enough to resist the bishop's army, she left it and removed to Sassebassa. Martinuzzi immediately laid close siege to the former place, and was using every effort to take it when Castaldo crossed the frontier and advanced into the heart of the country. Upon hearing of the approach of the Austrian forces, Isabella despaired of success, and surrendered Alba Julia. Negotiations were then opened between the contending parties, and at length, partly by threats and partly by persuasion, the bishop induced her to yield Transylvania and her possessions in Hungary to Ferdinand, and to renounce her son's claims to the crown, in exchange for the

* History of the Troubles in Hungary, p. 99.

principalities of Oppelen and Ratibor in Silesia, with the sum of 100,000 ducats, and she, at the same time, surrendered the crown and regalia, which had been allowed by the Turks to remain in the possession of the family of Szapolyai. For himself, Martinuzzi demanded the government of Transylvania, the archbishopric of Gran, 1,500 horse as a private guard, and 4,000 crowns yearly, as a salary attached to the office of treasurer, and though last not least, that Ferdinand should use his interest with the pope to procure him a cardinal's hat. Every one of his requests was complied with. Having now got everything he wanted, satiety brought on regret. He saw with chagrin, that great as were the honours and dignities with which he was loaded, his real influence in the affairs of the kingdom must end with the deposition of the queen, for Ferdinand was not a man to admit of dictation from a priest, let his talents be ever so great. He therefore began to endeavour to persuade the queen to hold out a little longer, and delay her consent to the articles of the treaty. She was disgusted by his perfidy, and refused his counsel, and at last seeing no other recourse, he announced to Castaldo that he was ready to carry the agreement into execution.

At last the day arrived, on which the last act in this sad drama was to take place. The diet was summoned at Kolosvar to witness the resignation of the queen, and the surrender of the crown, the symbol of Hungarian liberty and glory. A curious superstition had connected in some measure at least, the right to the throne with the possession of the regalia. In the eyes of the multitude they had been made sacred by the touch of St. Stephen, and carried with them the sanction of the church, and the blessing of heaven. Fraud or violence had in one or two instances previously, transferred them to the hands of strangers, but without shaking the popular faith; but now for the first time, the nation was to witness the transference, with all the legal and necessary forms, not only of the outward and visible signs of the sovereignty, but the inward and unseen grace which their possession conferred upon the elect of the people. Isabella rode on horseback to a celebrated abbey, about eight miles from Kolosvar, attended by a crowd of nobles, and in the great hall the ceremony took place. A dense multitude filled the room and awaited her appearance in dead silence. She entered leading her son by the hand. The regalia lay on a table before her—the crown, the ivory sceptre, the mantle of cloth of gold bespangled with diamonds, the gown or robe, the shoes of gold, and the stockings. Taking the crown in her hand, she burst into tears, but speedily recovering her self-possession, she turned towards Castaldo, the Austrian general, and addressing him in Italian, bewailing her misfortunes, and committing herself and her son to the care and protection of Ferdinand, delivered it to him amidst the cries of the young prince, who seeing his mother's grief, stretched his little hands towards the glittering bauble, as if to seize and retain it, doubtless prizing it, in his innocence, more highly than the authority of which it was but the emblem. Castaldo received it and thanked her, and forthwith forwarded it, under a strong escort, to Ferdinand, to whom the Hungarians, thinking all controversy now at an end, swore allegiance. A few days after, despatches were received from him, ratifying the treaty which had been entered into by Castaldo, and giving instructions to have the betrothal of his daughter Johanna with John Sigismond celebrated by proxy without delay, which was accordingly done with great pomp and apparent rejoicing. These being concluded, on the following day, the ninth of September, the queen departed from Kolosvar, accompanied by an escort of 400 Hungarian cavalry. The Austrian general rode at the head of the cavalcade two miles out of the town, and when he took his leave, she made a vain effort to conceal the marks which grief had but too plainly left on her face.

All parties seemed now heartily sick of contention, and everyone looked forward to a long interval of peace. But Ferdinand's bad policy disappointed their hopes. He disgusted Martinuzzi, and wounded his pride by conferring the chief military command upon Castaldo, a Spaniard, who possessed all the punctilious haughtiness of his nation. This division of power between two spirits so fiery and discordant, led to the usual consequences—a continued series of jars. Martinuzzi used all the arts in which a long course of intrigue had made him an adept, to thwart and disappoint his colleague, and Castaldo in his turn forwarded daily complaints to Vienna, of the rapacity and insolence of the cardinal, and accused him of harbouring designs for the introduction of the Turks into the country.

To complaints such as these, Ferdinand was well prepared to listen. He had already had ample proof of the audacity and tergiversation of which Martinuzzi was capable. He was jealous of the influence he exercised in Transylvania, and perhaps still more jealous of the signal ability which he displayed in the government of the province; he hated him for the opposition he had experienced from him in times past, and he feared him for his ambition. Martinuzzi would clearly never prove an useful or submissive servant, and Ferdinand was determined he should never become a rival or an equal. But the means he chose to carry his determination into effect were such as could only suggest themselves to a base mind.

Solyman was indignant at all that he saw going on in Hungary, and at the utter disregard of his real or imaginary rights in the division and allotment of the territory which had been made by the queen and Ferdinand, and accordingly assembled a large army to avenge the insult, and chastise those who had proved traitors to his government. He had no sooner approached the frontier than Martinuzzi opened a communication with him. The intrigue was discovered and reported to the Austrian government, and orders were instantly sent to Castaldo to get rid of him in the best way he could. The Spaniard received the command without surprise, and proceeded to carry it into effect with characteristic coolness and dissimulation. He displayed no change in his manner towards Martinuzzi, save by an increase of cordiality. He consulted him upon public affairs with more than ordinary confidence and harmony. He listened to his advice, and adopted his suggestions even in matters in which the latter had no authority or jurisdiction. The archbishop was at that time staying at his country house at Lintz, a strong castellated residence, serving equally for pleasure or security. Castaldo had access to him at all hours, and Martinuzzi received him with that blind confidence which a long course of good fortune too often inspires. Pavacini, Ferraro, Monino, Piacentino, and Scaramoncia, were the instruments selected to pour out Ferdinand's vengeance. The day appointed for the deed was the 19th of December, 1551. The previous night was dark and cloudy, as if the elements wished to portend the tragedy. The wind blew fiercely, and the rain beat heavily on the turrets and battlements of the castle, and the doors inside slammed, and the windows shook, as they never had slammed or shook before. At daybreak the gates were opened, to let the cardinal's baggage waggons pass out, as he was to change his residence at noon. Twenty-four harquebusiers, who had been concealed outside, seized the

ASSASSINATION OF MARTINUZZI.

opportunity to enter, and distributed themselves over the castle, having their arms concealed under long Turkish robes. The marquis Sforza then went up towards Martinuzzi's chamber, accompanied by Ferraro, Castaldo's secretary, and the other conspirators. The servant opened the door without suspicion and admitted them. Ferraro approached the bedside and handed him some papers for his perusal and signature. Martinuzzi rose and sat down at the table, and while intent upon the documents, Ferraro stabbed him in the neck with a dagger. The wound was not mortal and he instantly sprang to his feet, with all his ancient courage and promptitude, and snatching a poignard from his breast, defended himself with such energy that his assailant retreated to the lower end of the table; but Sforza, who was

SIEGE OF AGRIA.

standing close at hand, fractured his skull with a blow of his sabre. He fell, but was not dead; and on seeing the harquebusiers enter the room, he cried out in

Latin, "What means this, my friends?" They discharged their pieces into his body, and exclaiming, "Jesu Maria!" he expired. Thus perished one of the great men of his age, a child of poverty and neglect—a man whose energy and talents made sovereigns fear and hate, and at last kill him. Assuredly when Ferdinand caused his assassination, it was less as a supporter of the Turks, than as a champion, wavering, vacillating and faithless often it may be, of Hungarian liberty. He was ambitious in the highest degree, but he was often the supporter of the national cause in spite of himself. Priest, cardinal, conspirator, he was still a Hungarian. He was a good statesman, as statesmen went at that day, an able general, and an intrepid soldier. He knew how to unite salutary caution with dauntless courage, to be prompt without being rash. When he fell the hopes of th e Hungarians fell with him, for of all their defenders and leaders, he in both force and policy possessed the highest ability.

He had no sooner breathed his last, than the castle was plundered and deserted by the attendants, and his body lay naked and bloody on the floor of his chamber for many days,—"none so poor as to do him reverence." At last, some of his friends recovered from their panic, and conveyed him to the church of Alba Julia, where he was buried side by side with John Hunyadi.*

Ferdinand saw at once what disgrace this murder would bring on his name, and published a long manifesto in justification of it. But the pope, Julius II., was not to be so easily put off, when so foul an offence as the assassination of a priest of the church had been committed. The only answer he returned to Ferdinand's pleas, was the fulmination of a bull of excommunication against all who were in any way concerned in the murder, and he laid claim to the cardinal's property, as he had died intestate. Castaldo and his adherents had, however, seized upon all Martinuzzi's personal effects, and appropriated them to their own use,—amongst other valuables a large collection of antique coins, and it was no easy matter to induce a hired soldier of the sixteenth century to disgorge his plunder.† Ferdinand used every means in his power, threats, entreaties, bribes and intrigues, to get the excommunication taken off, but for a long while in vain. At last he was successful, but the sacred college took care to add to their absolution, a condition which must have destroyed its spiritual efficacy—"*If* the defence and allegations made by Ferdinand be true."

The thunders of the Vatican, after all, were by no means so terrible as the thunders of the Porte. The sultan irritated by the efforts that had been made to deprive John Sigismond of the province of Transylvania, prepared to invade Hungary, at the head of two large armies, and Isabella took refuge with her father, the king of Poland, to await the issue. The Transylvanians, also, were exasperated by the foul crime which had deprived them of so able a governor. The nobles retired to their castles, and the Szeklers actually rose in rebellion, and were pacified

* Martin Fiume, p. 171.

† History of the Troubles in Hungary, p. 171.

with difficulty. Castaldo found himself at the head of a mutinous and disaffected force, and surrounded by a hostile population. The Turks advanced without opposition under the command of the bashaw of Belgrade. The queen, hearing of their arrival, hastened to join them, and was followed by a powerful party of nobles. Temesvar, Lippa, and other places speedily fell before them. Buda bid defiance to the attacks of the Austrians. Castaldo in vain asked for succour, and was at last obliged to take refuge in the Austrian territories.

The courage of the Spaniards and Austrians was, however, at length restored by the arrival of Duke Maurice of Saxony, who came to Ferdinand's aid with an army of 15,000 strong; but Mehemet Pasha, the Turkish general, nothing daunted, proceeded to lay siege to Agria, with 60,000 men and sixty pieces of artillery. The place was protected by an old castle, without any of the defences which the invention of gunpowder had rendered necessary. The walls were low and weak, and were overlooked by a high hill at the distance of a pistol shot. But these defects were well supplied by the valour of the garrison, consisting of 2,000 Hungarians, headed by 500 gentlemen of the highest rank.

The soldiers and the inhabitants both took a solemn oath, which fanaticism only could have dictated—"That whosoever spoke of capitulation should be put to death; that all the provisions should be fairly divided, and husbanded with care, but that as soon as they were gone, the besieged should eat one another, the victims to be chosen by lot, and that the women should labour in repairing the walls, and should support their husbands and brothers in the breach and on the ramparts.

At last the Turks made their appearance, (1552,) and were hailed with defiant shouts. Mehemet sent a flag of truce offering honourable terms of surrender. The bearer was not admitted within the gates, and the only answer was the elevation of a coffin covered with black, on the point of a lance, signifying the determination of the garrison to die at their posts. On the following morning fifty pieces of artillery opened their fire upon the castle and walls, and speedily dismantled the one and laid the other in ruins. The choicest of the Ottomans then made three separate and simultaneous assaults, but such was the desperate courage of the besieged that they were driven back with the loss of 8,000 men. Four divisions of the jannizaries, led on by the bravest of the Moslem officers, now advanced to the attack, and succeeded in mounting to the top of the breaches. The whole population of the town turned out to meet them. The women threw scalding water and huge stones upon the heads of the foe, and in many cases came on to the charge with sabre and buckler, torn from the lifeless hand of a father or lover, who had fallen shattered at their feet. Mothers, for the first time in the history of the world, with more than Spartan heroism, or Spartan ferocity, saw their daughters swept down by the artillery without a sigh or tear, and advanced without misgiving to fill up their places. Those whom age or disease had enfeebled were often seen standing ankle deep in the blood of their nearest and dearest relatives and friends, encouraging the fainting soldiers to support the conflict. After several ineffectual attempts during a siege of forty days, the bashaw was at last obliged to abandon his enterprise, terrified and disheartened by the furious valour of the Christians, who were so far from being exhausted, that when making his retreat, they attacked him in the rear, killed a considerable number, and carried off a large quantity of booty. The siege was raised on the 18th of October, 1552.*

The Turkish army was, however, generally successful, and defeated the forces of Ferdinand in several encounters. Isabella made repeated applications to Solyman for the restoration of her government, and though he gave her several promises of redress, the Austrian oppression of the Transylvanians proved in the end a more effectual ally. In 1556, she made a triumphant entry into the province, accompanied by her son, while the Austrians retired before the victorious arms of the Turks, and followed by the execrations of the inhabitants; she was received with transports of joy. Her misfortunes seemed to have sent her new charms and new claims to the support and fidelity of her adherents. Her son was now old enough to win the hearts of the people by evidences of courage, generosity, and fortitude. They swore allegiance to her enthusiastically, and kept their oaths in spite of the intrigues and disturbances set on foot by Ferdinand and his lieutenant Castaldo. A diet was convened at Hermanstadt, where all the nobility did her homage. The Austrians, however, still retained the fortress of Erlau, and a large portion of the district to the east of the Teyss.

On the 7th of August, in the same year, Charles V., emperor of Germany, the most powerful prince and successful warrior which Europe had seen since the death of Charlemagne, disgusted with the emptiness of his titles and the real insignificance of his greatness, resigned his crown and retired into a monastery, leaving Spain, the Low Countries, and all his possessions and claims in Italy to his son, Philip II. Ferdinand was elected emperor, but in consequence of some difficulty as to the manner of accepting the resignation, the voluntary abdication of an emperor being a new event in the history of Germany, he was not proclaimed for two years afterwards. His attention had been directed in the meantime to the destruction of Bohemian liberty, and the attempt to reconcile the religious sects, by whose rancorous dissensions his Austrian dominions were torn. From his elevation to the imperial throne, he expected to derive an increase of strength, that would enable him finally to subdue Hungary, and secure the darling object of his ambition—the hereditary settlement of the crown in his family. He had already effected this in Bohemia by a *coup d'etat*, characterised by unexampled ferocity, and his new schemes were favoured by the wavering and indecision of Isabella.

She was not yet forty years of age; but a life of bitter anxiety, care and fatigue, had prematurely wasted her powers, exhausted her strength and played havoc with her beauty. The load of disappointment and chagrin which her precarious posi-

* History of the Troubles in Hungary, p. 236.

tion, and her son's vassalage to Solyman, imposed upon her was a weightier one to bear than ten additional years. The slights to which her dependence upon the Turks exposed her, joined with her declining health, made her anxious once more to retire into private life, and she had again made proposals to Ferdinand, for the surrender of Transylvania, when the negotiations were cut short by her death on the 20th of September, 1559. Her son, John Sigismond, preferred the protection of the Ottomans, declining any dealings with Ferdinand, and therefore assumed the title of king of Hungary, and demanded the cession of the district between the Teyss and Transylvania, as well as the principalities of Oppelen and Ratibor.

A predatory warfare followed the refusal of the latter to comply, in which the Turks occasionally interfered, and which the Poles vainly endeavoured to bring to an end by offers of mediation. At length, however, Ferdinand became anxious to secure an interval of tranquillity for the purpose of procuring the quiet succession of his eldest son, Maximilian, to the throne, and with this object concluded a truce with Solyman for eight years, upon promising not to disturb Sigismond in the possession of Transylvania, and to renew the tribute to the Porte. Maximilian was accordingly elected with all the ordinary formalities by the magnates and nobles of the provinces which Ferdinand still possessed. He was required to take the customary oath to observe all the established laws and usages of the kingdom, including those which his father had broken and set at defiance.

John Sigismond refused to agree to the treaty into which Ferdinand had entered with the sultan, and began to make frequent incursions into the Austrian dominions. Ferdinand fearing to call down upon himself the anger of Solyman, contented himself with standing upon the defensive, and even made frequent offers of reconciliation, which he proposed to strengthen and confirm by the gift of his daughter's hand in marriage. John Sigismond refused them all, and at the instigation of the Turks kept up the guerilla warfare, in the midst of which Ferdinand died, on the 25th of July, 1564, of a fever which was brought on by chagrin. In private life his character was estimable in the extreme. He was a good husband and a good father. His religious opinions were sincere, and were singularly free from all taint of intolerance, as was evidenced by the wisdom and impartiality of the measures he adopted for the reconciliation of the Protestants and Catholics in his dominions. He was handsome, affable in his deportment, learned and fond of study. His acquaintance with the modern and classical literature was greater than any monarch of the day could boast, and he was an efficient patronizer of science and art. But there were defects in his character which these light and common virtues can never counterbalance or even palliate, though it is too much the habit of historians to overlook them, or at most visit them with but a gentle reproof. Lust of power and acquisitiveness carried to excess are vices which in private individuals the laws of society will punish or restrain, but when displayed on a large scale by those above all rule, except the laws of God and the unchanging canons of morality, those whose duty it is to condemn, too often approve or are silent. But assuredly the absence of visible retribution does not imply the absence of guilt. The enormity of a crime is not in an inverse ratio to its magnitude. The wresting of a kingdom from the lawful owner is a more brilliant exploit than the forcible seizure of another man's field, but it is a no less heinous wrong. To do it triumphantly is no excuse either in the one case or the other. To break an oath solemnly sworn to a whole nation, is not less a perjury than to break one sworn to a neighbour. Nay, it is greater, because the evil and mischief and suffering which follow it are greater. When public opinion and public teachers affect to see a distinction and a difference between acts like these, they show themselves forgetful of the principles of true Christianity and of sound justice. When princes say, they can with a good conscience perpetrate acts, which as private individuals they dare not, and would not attempt, they either lie grossly or their moral sense is hideously depraved. Better for a man that he were sunk in the darkest depths of paganism, than that, in the light of Christianity and civilization, he should seek to hide his crimes beneath the gorgeous tapestry of success. Better for a people that the sea rolled over their dwellings, than that they should ever confound right with possession. Ferdinand swore to maintain the Hungarian laws and constitution, and every hour of his after life he sought as far as in him lay to infringe them, and brought a century and a half of war upon the kingdom. He swore also to maintain the Bohemian laws and constitution—he destroyed them by a *coup d'etat*, and massacred all those who dared to protest or fight against his usurpation. Martinuzzi stood in his way, and he murdered him without scruple or remorse. But he did all this with impunity, and therefore men say he was a good prince, a good husband, and a good father, and that he lent new lustre to the house of Austria. Perhaps so; but he was none the less a traitor and a murderer.

CHAPTER XV.

JOHN SIGISMOND, MAXIMILIAN, AND STEPHEN BATHORI.

A.D. 1564—1586.

When Maximilian ascended the throne the war was carried on with renewed vigour. John Sigismond was ever active and ever aggressive, and his opponent had at last no resource but to take arms for the defence of his share of the Hungarian territory. His forces under the command of two of the ablest generals of the day, Swendy and Count Salm, after recovering the captured places, reduced Tokay, Kovar, Erdad, and Bathor. Maximilian sent an embassy to Solyman, offering to continue the payment of the tribute, and demanding continuance of the truce concluded with his father. But the conditions proposed by the latter were too imperious to be accepted, and war again broke out with the Turks. Solyman headed his army in person, and advancing towards the scene of hostilities, he was preparing to ascend the course of the Danube, when the aggressions of the garrison of Zigeth, a town on the frontiers of Sclavonia, who in a sally killed one of his favourite bashaws, induced him to select it as the first object of his vengeance. It lay in the midst of a marsh, and was approachable only by a narrow causeway. The garrison consisting of but 3,000 men, was commanded by Nicholas, Count Zrinyi, the descendant of an illustrious Croat family, who resolved, feeble as were his means, to resist to the last extremity. The attack was commenced on the 6th of August, 1566, and at first was attended with partial success. The Turks went through enormous labour, making roads across the marsh, and erecting huge mounds for the artillery, and succeeded in battering down the greater portion of the outer wall, and after twenty assaults, obtained possession of the old town, and forced the garrison to retire into the fortress. The number of the defenders were now reduced to six hundred, but such were their valour and fortitude, that they repulsed the Ottomans in a series of bloody combats. Solyman's patience was beginning to be exhausted. He called before him his principal bashaws, reproached them in the bitterest terms with cowardice and incompetency, and threatened that, if they failed to take the citadel in the next attempt, he would cause their heads to be struck off, and march to the assault over their dead bodies. The ungovernable fury of his passion rendered vain both his threats and his promises. He was seized that same night, (Sept. 4, 1566,) by an attack of apoplexy, which carried him off in the forty-sixth year of his reign, after a career of unexampled splendour and prosperity, during which he raised Turkey to a pitch of power and pre-eminence, from which she has ever since been steadily declining.

The death of their leader would have filled the Turkish soldiers with discouragement and consternation, and might perhaps have altogether marred the success of the enterprise, if the grand vizier, acting, it is said, upon his deceased master's instructions, had not taken effectual means to conceal it from them. The physician who attended the sultan in his last moments, and the servants who waited upon him, were all strangled before ever they had quitted the tent, and the inanimate corpse, clothed in the imperial robes, was placed upright upon a throne, the curtains were drawn aside, and the army, defiling before it at a distance, were animated and encouraged by the belief that the eye of their sovereign was upon them. The artillery, which had been playing upon the castle without intermission, had laid the interior in ruins, and had effected a wide breach in the outer wall. The enemy were preparing to storm it, when a fire broke out which consumed most of the provisions and ammunition, and buried a large number of the garrison in the ruins of their habitations. Of the six hundred who had survived the repeated attacks of the besiegers, there now remained but one hundred and seventy, exclusive of sick and wounded. There was nothing left for these but death,—the speedier the better. Zrinyi drew them up in the courtyard, and appearing in full uniform, took of each an affectionate farewell, and drawing his sword, led them across the lowered drawbridge, against the enemy. The Turks astonished at the temerity of the small party which they saw advancing, at first hung back fearing a stratagem, but at last became reassured and rushed to the attack. Zrinyi defended himself with courage and dexterity. A pike thrust in the breast caused him to waver for a moment, but he still fought on, sternly rejecting all offers of quarter. A blow of a sabre in the leg rendered him unable to stand, and he then maintained the combat on his knees, until at length he was laid prostrate by a musket ball passing through his head. All his followers, except four who surrendered, died sword in hand upon the spot, and the Turks entering the fortress found nothing but blackened ruins to reward them for a siege of thirty-four days, and the loss of 20,000 men.*

During the greater part of this siege, two of the Austrian armies were encamped within a short distance of Zigeth, and never moved to the assistance of the garrison, one of 10,000 men, under the Archduke Charles, and the other of 100,000, under the emperor himself, composed of volunteers from every country in Europe, and veteran soldiers who had been trained in the wars of Charles V. Maximilian calmly remained upon the defensive, fearing to risk the safety of his forces in a pitched battle, which, if the event proved adverse, might lay Hungary, and perhaps Austria, at the feet of the sultan. He recked little of the fate of the little garrison under Nicholas Zrinyi, but the bashaw of Buda had a better estimate of

* History of the Troubles in Hungary, p. 328.

† History of the Turks (Knolles's,) Art. Solyman the Magnificent.

the loss the Austrian cause had sustained, when in forwarding the Zrinyi's head to Count Salm, he wrote, "As a proof of my generosity, I forward you the head of one of your greatest and bravest generals, whose loss you may long regret; his remains have been interred with all the honours due to a hero."

The inertness of the Austrian armies led also to the fall of Gyula, defended by Kerecsenyi, and a third of Hungary was soon laid open to the ravages of the Turks, who carried away 80,000 of the inhabitants into captivity. Two diets addressed remonstrances to the emperor upon this deplorable policy, and complained bitterly of the excesses and extortions of Swendy, the Austrian general, and of the violation of the constitution, daily perpetrated, in the appointment of foreigners to the highest offices of the state. Maximilian, however, turned a deaf

STEPHEN BATHORI.

ear to their complaints, as he relied upon the renewal of the truce by the new sultan Selim. He was not deceived. Negotiations were opened, Selim withdrew his armies, and the result was a treaty of peace, in which it was stipulated that John Sigismond should continue to be the waywode of the sultan and of the emperor in Transylvania; that a half of Hungary Proper should continue in the possession of Maximilian, and that the other half, with Buda the capital, should be annexed as a dependent province to the Turkish empire. No sooner did the terms of this infamous bargain become known, than many of the principal magnates protested against it in the only way that the misfortunes of their country had left them—by retiring to their castles, and refusing to take any part in the transaction of public affairs. Others, possessing more fire and energy, passed into Transylvania, to the camp of George Bocksai, and entered into a conspiracy for throwing off the yoke of Maximilian. The plot was discovered and the authors banished, and this failure, united with the intrigues of a confidant of John Sigismond, named Bekessi, who had secretly sold himself to the Austrians, induced Sigismond, at length, to consent to enter into a treaty of peace, by which he agreed to renounce the title of king, and take that of most serene prince; that Transylvania Proper should become his patrimony, and that portion of the frontier of Hungary which he then occupied should remain in his possession during his lifetime, but at his death should revert to the house of Austria; and in case the sultan should refuse his consent to an agreement of which he had no cognisance, and should expel him from his dominions, the castle of Oppelen in Silesia should be his asylum; and lastly, if he died without male issue, the states of Transylvania should elect a prince dependent upon Austria.

Maximilian had in return promised him one of his nieces in marriage, and afterwards displayed some reluctance in giving consent. John insisting, new troubles were on the point of arising, when the dispute was ended by the death, some think violent, of the latter.* The Transylvanian diet chose, as his successor, Stephen Bathori, a man whose birth, eloquence, military services, and winning manners, disarmed all opposition from whatever quarter. Unfortunately, however, his reign was not long confined to the narrow limits of Transylvania, and doubtless, Maximilian, when confirming his election, little foresaw that he would successfully compete against him for the crown of Poland. The house of Austria was already, by consecutive elections, for more than one hundred years in possession of the German empire. During the whole of that period, Hungary also occupied a prominent place in all its ambitious schemes. The desire of each monarch was to make that kingdom, as Ferdinand had often declared it to be, hereditary in the family. This it was found impossible to accomplish, but in order to open the way to it, the father often took care to have his son elected during his lifetime. Ferdinand had in this way secured the succession to Maximilian, and Maximilian in like manner secured it to his son, Rodolph. But he pushed his plans of aggrandizement still farther, and pretended to have an incontestible right to the Polish crown, which had been left vacant by the voluntary abdication of Henry of Valois, who, on receiving the news of the death of his brother, Charles IX, fled precipitately from the kingdom, like a thief in the night. Some of the nobles were gained over and declared Maximilian king, but the diet meeting immediately after, pronounced their proceeding null and void, and elected Stephen Bathori in 1576. Maximilian never afterwards bore any good-will to the Poles; and he would undoubtedly have shown it in a substantial manner, if his attention had not been absorbed by subjects of more pressing importance nearer home. Bathori appointed his brother Christopher to govern Transylvania as his lieutenant, and fixed his residence in Poland.

* "*Seu fato, seu veneno, properata mors abstulerat.*" Florus, Polon. de Porchit, lib. i.

Maximilian did not long survive to regret his loss. His health had been for some time declining, and his death was hastened by anxiety and over-exertion. He expired at Ratisbon, where he had been holding a diet, October 12, 1576, in the fiftieth year of his age and the twelfth of his reign. He was, on the whole, a wise and just prince, though Coxe's panegyric is certainly open to doubt. "No stronger proof," says he, "can be given of his amiable qualities, than the concurring testimonials of the historians of Germany, Hungary, Bohemia, and Austria, both catholics and protestants, who vie in his praises and in representing him as a model of impartiality, wisdom, and benignity; and it was truly said of him, what can be applied to few sovereigns, that in no one instance was he impelled, either by resentment or ambition, to act contrary to the strictest rules of moderation and justice, or to disturb the public tranquillity. Germany revived in his favour the surname of Titus, or the Delight of Mankind; and if ever a Christian and philosopher filled the throne, that Christian and philosopher was Maximilian the Second."*

Bathori's reign was distinguished by wisdom, courage, and impartiality. He signed the *Pacta Conventa*, the imperious charter, or rather bond which the Polish nobles were in the habit of exacting from their kings,—and better still, he faithfully observed them. He subdued or conciliated the Austrian party, repressed the invasions of the Muscovites, changed the Cossacks from turbulent neighbours into useful allies, allayed the rancorous dissensions between the catholics and protestants,† reformed and purified the administration of justice. He was the constant benefactor of science and learning. He founded the University of Wilna, and stimulated the industry of the students by holding out to the most successful the prospect of honourable employment. He was himself a proficient in several languages, had a profound knowledge of history, and was master of a Latin style unequalled by that of any scholar in his kingdom for purity and elegance. But by nothing was he so much distinguished as his spirit of enlightened religious toleration. This principle, so glorious in its results and so noble in its origin, has had greater difficulties to contend against, in obtaining a recognised place in the policy of human legislators, than any other. It has been fighting for existence since the world began, has outlived a thousand generations of its enemies, and will, in the long run, assuredly be triumphant. But a few hundred years ago, to recognise its truth, was a proof of extraordinary intelligence, sagacity, and foresight. Bathori acknowledged it in a saying as remarkable for its wisdom as for its high-toned piety, when urged to take severe measures with the dissidents—"I reign over persons," said he, "but it is God who rules the conscience. God has reserved three things to himself,—the creation of something out of nothing, the knowledge of futurity, and the government of the conscience." He died suddenly at Grodno, in 1586.

* Coxe' House of Austria, vol. i., part ii. p. 648—9.

† *Dissidents* they were called in Poland.

CHAPTER XV.

TROUBLES UNDER RODOLPH II.—BOTSKAI'S INSURRECTION.

A.D. 1586—1619.

About the time of Stephen Bathori's death, two other sovereigns ascended the throne of their ancestors; Amurath III. at Constantinople, and Rodolph II. at Vienna. The latter, as we have already said, was crowned by the Hungarian diet with great pomp at Presburg, in 1572, during his father's lifetime, and at his death entered upon the government of his dominions. Few men have ever been more wanting in the qualities needed by a ruler. He was vain, fickle, variable, and had a natural distaste for the duties of his office. Instead of devoting his chief attention to the cares of government, he principally occupied himself in the study of natural history, astronomy, and chemistry. He had been very intimate with Tycho Brahé, the celebrated astronomer, who, with all his talents, was weak enough to attach importance to alchemy and judicial astrology. By him Rodolph was warned that his life would be attempted by one of his own blood, and this prediction had a most powerful effect upon the weak mind of the king, and brought about that change in his character and habits, which, as will be seen, afterwards caused his downfal.

His first object, on ascending the throne, was to secure his dominions against the attacks of the Turks, and for this purpose, and at the same time in order to diminish the enormous expense of keeping up the fortresses on the side of Croatia, he transferred that country as a fief of the empire to his uncle Charles, duke of Styria, who, from the proximity of his own diminions, would be better enabled to provide for its security. The fortress of Carlstadt, which afterwards became the capital of Croatia, a military station of the highest importance, was built by him. He also split up the frontier territory into a number of fiefs, which he bestowed upon all the vagabonds, marauders, and *condottieri* from all parts of Europe who chose to settle upon them, upon condition of doing military service against the Turks. These colonies gradually extended along the frontiers of Sclavonia and Croatia, and from them were drawn the ferocious hordes of irregular troops, known as Croats and Pandours,* by which Austria was for a long time enabled to spread

* "When leagu'd oppression poured to northern wars,
Her whisker'd pandours and her fierce hussars."
Campbell's Pleasures of Hope.

terror among her neighbours, and which, even so late as 1849, played an important part in the army of the Ban Jellachich. Another nest of freebooters was established at Clissa, in Dalmatia, during the reign of Ferdinand, composed of christians who had been driven from those provinces which had been conquered by the Turks, and had settled in the Austrian territory. They received a settlement, upon condition of continually bearing arms against the infidels; and so faithfully did they fulfil their mission, that under the name of Uscocks* they became the terror of the Ottomans. The latter, however, before long expelled them from their original seat. They then settled at Senga, in Croatia, on the coast of the Adriatic gulf, and here received a vast accession of strength and numbers from the Italian robbers and pirates. They now extended their ravages to the sea, and their christian zeal diminishing as their forces and cupidity increased, they began to deal out equal treatment to all sects and nations, by plundering every ship that came in their way, to whomsoever it belonged. At last the Turks determined to extirpate them. Predatory warfare was constantly raging on the frontiers: it was trifling in extent, and was winked at both in Austria and Constantinople, because both governments looked upon it as encouraging the growth of a military spirit among their subjects; but the outrages committed by the Uscocks were too great to be overlooked. The truce concluded between Amurath and Rodolph was accordingly broken by the former in 1591. The bashaw of Bosnia invaded Croatia, captured the fortresses of Wihitz and Petrina, and in the following year laid siege to Siseck. The Austrians here attacked them and defeated them with a loss of 12,000 men, amongst whom were the bashaw himself and a nephew of the sultan. Amurath was enraged beyond measure at this disaster; formally declared war, and crossed the frontiers of Hungary and Croatia at the head of a numerous army. The two following years were passed in sanguinary hostilities, but the Turks had the advantage by taking Siseck and Raab. In 1595, however, the tide of success again turned in favour of the Austrians, and the cause of this brings us back to the affairs of Transylvania.

On the removal of Bathori to Poland the government of the province had been committed to his brother Christopher. He in his turn transmitted it to his own son Sigismond, at his death, in 1582; placing the latter, who was but an infant, under the protection of the Porte. Sigismond, when he came of age, managed for some time to balance the influence of Turkey and Austria, one against the other, with great adroitness. The diplomacy of the latter, at length, however, proved triumphant. Sigismond concluded an alliance, defensive and offensive, with Rodolph; he was to retain Transylvania as an independent principality, that part of Hungary which was still in his possession, Moldavia and Wallachia, and to hold the rank of a German prince. Any territory which might be wrested from the Turks, or others, was to be equally divided; and if Bathori should be expelled from his dominions, he was to receive

* Wanderers.

compensation in some other quarter, and if he died without male issue, his inheritance reverted to the house of Hapsburg, and the alliance was strengthened by his marriage with Christina, daughter of the duke of Styria.

Austria was thus delivered from all fears on the side of Transylvania; she had lost an enemy and gained a friend, and was now enabled to pursue the war against Turkey with redoubled vigour: in it Sigismond distinguished himself by his romantic bravery. By uniting his forces with those of the waywodes of Moldavia and Wallachia, who had acknowledged his supremacy, he was enabled to defeat the grand vizier, recapture Turgovitz, and send the Ottoman armies in full retreat towards Constantinople. The Austrians, thus aided, were likewise successful, and distinguished their arms by the taking of Visegrad and Gran* (Sep. 6, 1595).

Mahomet, the son and successor of Amurath, thought it was now high time to take the field. He entered Hungary at the head of his forces, took Erlau, defeated the Archduke Maximilian, and had he not been prevented by the approach of winter, he would have carried his arms into Upper Hungary, and Austria itself. In the following season, however, the sultan was unable to tear himself away from the allurements of the harem, and for the next two years the campaigns were little else than a succession of desultory skirmishes, which, while they contributed nothing either way to the final decision of the contest, had a terrible and disastrous effect upon the country, by destroying all security for life or property, and exposing the peaceable or helpless inhabitants to the violence and outrages of a brutal and licentious soldiery. In 1596, Sigismond, always acting under the influence of caprice, gave up his territory to Rodolph in exchange of Oppelen and Ratibor, and an annual pension. The emperor was acknowledged by the States, and sent his brother Maximilian to act as his governor; but no sooner had he arrived than Sigismond changed his mind, and once more reappeared in Transylvania. In 1599 he again became disgusted by the troubles attached to his office, and once more abdicated, but this time retired into Poland, where he resided with his brother-in-law the great chancellor Zamoiski. He had transferred the government of Transylvania to his uncle Andrew, the cardinal archbishop of Wermia, who, however, was speedily dispossessed by Michael, the waywode of Wallachia. The latter had thrown off his allegiance, and again joined the Turks, immediately after Sigismond's first resignation. He was gained over by the emperor, and joined his forces with those of the imperialists, for the purpose of expelling Andrew, who, in the conflict, was defeated and killed. Michael now laid claim to the principality on his own behalf, and in his turn was routed by the Austrian general Basta. Sigismond seized this opportunity of once more reappearing upon the scene of his former exploits. Michael now united his forces with those of his enemies, against the new competitor, and Bathori was totally routed with the loss of 10,000 men. Basta then caused Michael to be assassinated, and another treaty was entered into with Sigismond, by which he

* Coxe's House of Austria, ch. xlii.

agreed to retire to Lobcovitz, in Bohemia, with an annual pension from the emperor. The remainder of his life was passed in tranquillity till his death in 1618.*

The war between the Austrians and Turks had in the meantime been raging in Hungary with unabated fury. Ferat Pasha had just returned from a campaign in Persia, and was sent to take the command of Buda, that by following up the attacks upon the christians, he might occupy the attention of the janizzaries, whose turbulent and mutinous spirit had already made them the dread and terror of their own government. Croatia now became the principal theatre of their ravages; and, notwithstanding, the devotion of the people to the house of Hapsburg, they found themselves abandoned, without aid or pity, to a cruel and relentless enemy. Relief, at last, came from Hungary. During the whole of these troubles many of the magnates and nobles of the latter country, paying no attention to the disputes between the diet and Austria, devoted their lives and fortunes to carrying on a crusade against the Turks; and, from year to year, amidst all changes and reverses, remained constantly in arms at the head of their vassals. Foremost in valour and energy, at this period, were Nicholas Palfi, George Zrinyi, and Forgatz. After having driven the Ottomans from several towns, Palfi, under the orders of Schwartenburg, laid siege to Arabon. Upon summoning the pasha who commanded the place to surrender, the latter replied, that when the weathercock, on the spire of a neighbouring church, was heard to crow thrice, the Hungarians might begin to hope to take the place, but not till then. Within a few hours afterwards, the principal gate was blown open by a petard, and Palfi entering at the head of his followers, routed the Turks with great slaughter (1598). The town of Pesth, feebly defended, was likewise captured by the Austrian forces under Russvarm, aided by a great crowd of Hungarian officers. The general result of all this warfare was not, however, very advantageous to either party. Mahomet III., the sultan, was too much occupied by troubles in Asia, and intrigues and conspiracies in his own capital, to be able to carry it on with vigour or energy. The imperialists, on the other hand, were disabled by the want of money, which rendered it necessary to disband the troops at the end of each campaign, so that in the beginning of every spring, a new force had to be raised, composed of raw levies, who knew nothing of war and were unused to the climate and diet of Hungary.

It was upon the Hungarians themselves, upon the farmers and peasants, and country gentlemen, who each year saw their fields desolated, their substance wasted, their houses plundered, their wives and daughters insulted or led into captivity by one or other of the contending parties, whose sleep after days of watching and anxiety was filled with troubled dreams, and who rose every morning with terror and foreboding, that the burden of the war fell. The youth of the country, as fast as they grew to man's estate, flung away their

* Isthuanfius, lib. xxii. xxiii.

lives and energies in this disastrous contest, and left crowds of widows and orphans in the towns, and villages, and castles. And all these sacrifices and trials, terrible as they were, were borne with unfaltering courage and constancy. Murmurs and complaints against Austria, in truth, there were many; for her object was clearly the overthrow of the national institutions, and the absolute and entire subjugation of the inhabitants of every rank. But there were no reproaches ever cast upon the supine indifference of the other nations of Europe, who, for two centuries, beheld a gallant people combatting the advances of Islamism with a heroism and devotion which has few parallels in

NICHOLAS PALFI.

history, in the noble and successful effort to save christendom from forcible imposition of a fatalist creed, which must have stayed the progress of civilization and paralyzed the energies of the west. From protracting this conflict the Magyars themselves had little to hope. A peace under Turkish rule would, at least, have brought security to life and property. A peace under Austria promised no more—hardly so much. This long and bloody war was waged in obedience to higher instincts than those which prompt men to seek material comfort or prosperity; those which teach them that there are worse evils than death, or poverty, or exile, than captivity or imprisonment,—the degradation attendant upon forgetfulness of glorious traditions, and the dishonour of flinching from the performance of a duty which Providence, when it placed them on the confines of christendom and civilization, had clearly marked out. The march of the nation in this era of blood and violence was marked every step by unheard-of suffering, and self-sacrifice, and devotion. The history of each family became a romance in itself—full of moving incidents, hairbreadth escapes, stern tragedy, and noble endurance.

Rodolph had long lost the confidence of his Hungarian subjects. He never, as was the custom with former sovereigns, made his appearance at the sittings of the diet, nor paid any attention whatever to the internal affairs of the country. He placed foreigners in the chief civil and military employments, and he suffered the office of palatine, to the due administration of which the Hungarians attached great importance, to remain unfilled after the occurrence of the first vacancy during his reign. The complaints and remonstrances of the diet were treated with contempt or indifference; and the German troops whom he called to his aid were a more dreadful scourge than the janizzaries of the sultan.* By his own narrow-minded religious bigotry he now introduced new complications into the long-standing quarrel between him and his subjects. To enable the reader to understand the merits of this new dispute, we must digress a little.

The ancient laws of Hungary entailed severe penalties upon any one who attempted to introduce or inculcate, within the kingdom, any doctrine contrary to those established by St. Stephen when he embraced Christianity. It was in conformity with these enactments that Louis II. and John, upon the requisition of the diet, condemned to be burnt all those innovators who, under the name of *Lutherans*, had appeared in large numbers, not only in Germany, but in all the adjacent countries.† Ferdinand of Austria, however, gave proof of good sense or moderation in not following their example. Religious dissensions were at that time raging in his German dominions, and it required all the skill and management he had at command to soothe them; and, doubtless, the fear of offending the protestant party in the German States had much to do with his leniency towards their confrères in Hungary; but, nevertheless, his conduct in this regard fully entitled him to the praise of history. He confined his attention solely to the preservation of his secular power, and the repression of the conspiracies which arose from time to time against his authority; and suffered the various sects to propagate their doctrines in whatever manner pleased them. He gave a signal proof of his toleration in 1561. In that year a great number of Hungarian protestants assembled at Agria, for the purpose of making a public profession of their faith. Ferdinand feared that it was a meeting of conspirators against the government, and hastened thither to disperse them; but on learning

* Coxe's History of the House of Austria, chap. xlii. p. 635.

† Art. liv. of the year 1523, and Art. v. of the diet of 1524.

on the way the real nature of the convention, he turned back and suffered them to proceed without molestation.*

Maximilian followed the same course. If the protestants were faithful to his government they were sure of his protection; but all this favour and toleration was rendered utterly worthless—"a mockery, a delusion, and a snare"—by the establishment in the kingdom of their most implacable enemies, the Jesuits. The encouragement bestowed upon the latter, the attention paid to all their maxims, filled the Lutherans with a feeling of uncertainty and insecurity, and straitened them in the exercise of their religious worship. The Jesuits very speedily performed their usual feat of worming themselves into the highest offices of the state, and managed ere long to obtain great influence over the councils of the prelates and magnates; and it may be readily believed that this was invariably exerted for the damage and detriment of the new religion and its professors. Rodolph did not, by any means, follow a consistent course with regard to them. At first he openly favoured them, despite the complaints of the clergy; but in 1604, to appease these very murmurs, all the rigour of the old law was put in force.

Cassau, a seat of government in Upper Hungary, was the first place in which these barbarous decrees were carried out. It was remarkable for the number, industry, and prosperity of its protestant inhabitants; but neither peaceable demeanour nor honest toil could save them from the lawless violence of those in power. Twenty villages belonging to the town were occupied for the maintenance of the military. The governor Belgioioso expelled them from their church, prohibited the exercise of their worship, and added insult to injury by parading the streets with executioners in his train, and inflicting instant punishment upon all who murmured against his brutality.

Things were in this position when a diet was convoked at Presburg, ostensibly to consider the best means of making head against the Turks. The deputies of the states, however, seized the opportunity of demanding a redress of grievances, before proceeding to the transaction of any business whatever. Some complained of the outrages of the foreign troops; others of the bestowal of the offices and dignities of the state upon strangers; and others sought reparation for injuries inflicted upon themselves or their families during the war. The protestants, relying upon the toleration granted by Frederick, and the positive edicts issued in their favour by Maximilian, declared that they had an established position in the kingdom which the laws had recognised, and complained of the persecutions at Cassau. But all joined in the standing, repeated, and now time-honoured declaration, that "Besides various kinds of death and violence which they had to fear from the Turks, his majesty's troops were the cause of incredible evils to the whole kingdom." The court of Vienna, which has been ever remarkable for

* Letter of the Protestants of Hungary, dated from Agria, 6th February, 1562, recorded in the Hist. Diplom. part i. p. 39.

its tenacity in carrying out what it has once taken in hand, thought that by temporizing, the fervour of the malcontents would cool down. The grievances complained of were, therefore, laid aside for examination at a more convenient season; but in the meantime Rodolph poured out his vengeance upon the protestants, by issuing a decree, in 1604, which rebuked them in severe terms for interrupting the transaction of public business, and forbade the diet, henceforth and for ever, to discuss questions affecting religion. Some private individuals were, at the same time, singled out for more substantial marks of disapprobation.

All this added fresh fuel to the flame of discontent which had been already kindled. An appeal to arms was now the only resource, and looking around for a leader, the choice of the insurgents fell upon Stephen Botskai, the principal magnate of Upper Hungary, and the uncle of Sigismond Bathori, a man of great eloquence, courage, and military skill. He had made frequent visits to Prague, to represent to Ferdinand in person the deplorable situation of the country; but he had never been admitted to the royal presence or even that of the minister, but was suffered to stand for hours in the antechamber, exposed to the insults of the court minions.* Such treatment naturally had the effect of irritating and enraging him to the last degree, and his resentment was still further increased when, on his return home, he found that Belgoioso had ransacked his castle and laid waste his estates during his absence. He instantly issued a spirited proclamation, setting forth the grievances under which the nation laboured, and called upon the people to wrest by force of arms those measures of redress which had been denied to remonstrance and entreaty. Crowds of volunteers instantly flocked to his standard from every side, of all ranks, nobles as well as peasants. Great numbers of heyducs, as the head foot-soldiers in the imperial service were called, were scattered over the country, after having been disbanded. All these flocked to join, upon being promised four crowns a month and as much booty as they could obtain on the estates of the Austrian partizans. Six thousand of them deserted in a body from the Austrian army and joined him. On receiving intelligence of the outbreak, Belgoioso, the imperial general, immediately prepared to march to suppress it; but the heyducs in his army all deserted to join their brethren, and the Germans were consequently defeated with great slaughter, and the loss of two of their generals. Basta, Rodolph's lieutenant in Transylvania, sought in vain to persuade Botskai by fair means to lay down his arms and disband his forces. The latter expressed his willingness on several occasions to do so, if the government of Transylvania were committed to his hands alone, and that of Hungary to a native of the country, as also the command of all the garrisons; if no Walloon or French soldiers should ever be admitted into Hungary; if the German troops should be compelled to confine themselves to their quarters, and prevented from harassing and plundering the poor country-people in their vicinity; if the authors of all past outrages should be delivered up

* Coxe's History of the House of Austria, ch. xlii.

to the proper authorities, to receive the punishment due to their offences; if the emperor should appear in person at the sittings of the diet; and if the free exercise of his religion were granted to every one. These conditions were all refused by Basta, and the war continued. The leading adherents of Botskai all assembled on the 29th of March, 1605, in the castle of Szerencza, where all the great families of the patriotic party were represented by one or other of their respective members—the Bethlens, the Rakoczis, the Drugets, the Toroks, and the Szecsis. Their chief was here proclaimed prince (*fejedelem*), and found his strength greatly increased by a considerable accession of forces from Transylvania. After the

THE HUNGARIAN CROWN.

assassination of Michael, the waywode of Wallachia, and the abdication of Sigismond Bathori, Basta, the imperial general, had taken possession of the entire province, received the allegiance of the natives, and, in the emperor's name, confirmed all their rights and privileges. He did not long observe them, however, and the ferocious cruelty which characterized his administration soon drove the people into insurrection. They chose a magnate named Moses Tekeli, who, with several others, had taken refuge among the Turks, to act as their leader. Tekeli entered the country at the head of a large auxiliary force of Turks and Tartars, was joined by the inhabitants, took the principal fortresses, and was soon after elected and proclaimed prince of Transylvania. Before the Germans were completely expelled, however, he was attacked, defeated, and killed, by the new waywode of Wallachia. His followers then dispersed or went into exile, and the country once more lay at the mercy of Basta. Under his rule it again became the scene of all the horrors which military despotism, famine, and disease could produce. The terrible results which Sheridan ascribed to the British rule in the province of Oude, after the death of Sujah Dowla, were here to be seen on every side—"plains unclothed and brown, villages depopulated and in ruins, churches unroofed and perishing, vegetables burnt up and extinguished;" as if some monster had stalked across the length and breadth of the land, tainting and poisoning with pestiferous breath what his voracious appetite could not devour. All traces of industry or civilization disappeared: the inhabitants lay in the ruins of their dwellings, whining and greedy skeletons. Corn was sold at its weight in gold; the horses and dogs were greedily consumed, and at last the putrid bodies of the dead were torn from their graves, and the pestilence brought on by the wretched sustenance thus afforded, finished the work which famine and the sword had begun.* The remnant who, on the death of Tekeli, had sought refuge across the frontier, now appealed to Botskai to put an end to these horrors, and, under the command of Gabriel Bethlen, ranged themselves under his standard.

Assisted by the Turks, both with men and money, Botskai speedily expelled the Austrians from Transylvania, and returning victorious into Hungary, was received by the Turkish army on the plains of Rakos with royal honours. Achmet, the sultan, sent him a club, a sabre, and a standard; and the grand vizier placed on his head a royal diadem, which had been worn by the despots of Servia, and proclaimed him king of Hungary, and prince of Transylvania. Botskai, however, was too patriotic or too prudent to accept from the Turks honours which the nobles of his own country alone had the right to confer, and which, if received from the Ottomans, would render him dependent upon them. He declared, therefore, that he looked upon them as but proofs of the sultan's friendship, and as a means of recovering the liberties of his countrymen. He now prosecuted the campaign with vigour. Szathmar, Hust, Newheisel, Nitria, and almost all the posts of Upper Hungary speedily fell into his hands; while the Turks, profiting by these troubles, took Gran, Visegrad, and Novigrad, and his irregular troops threatened Styria and Moravia. The country was now in a deplorable state. The emperor's soldiers plundered for want of pay, and the heyducs because it was their habit. The peasantry in many places had wholly abandoned their habitations and fled to the mountains or into Poland, often dying of hunger on the way. The flocks and herds were abandoned; all cultivation or tillage ceased. Austria itself was not much better off. The Turks and Hungarians ravaged it without scruple or remorse. From the towers of the churches at Vienna, fifteen towns or villages

* Knolles's History of the Turks, art. Achmet.

might be seen on fire, all at once, in the surrounding country, lighted either by the rebels or the emperor's own soldiers.* Everywhere was confusion and disorder.

During all this time Rodolph displayed the utmost apathy and indifference. It was his intolerance and bigotry which had kindled the flame, but he left it to other hands to extinguish it. While the Turks and Hungarians were ravaging his dominions, he was secluded in his palace at Prague, pursuing his favourite studies, surrounded by astrologers, chemists, painters, turners, engravers, and mechanics. He became irritable almost to frenzy, drove his confidential ministers from his presence, and suffered himself to be guided entirely by his mistresses, whom he changed with every moon.* He had a brother Mathias, who was as much distinguished by his vigour, activity, talent, and magnanimity, as he for his indolence, sloth, and suspiciousness of temperament. Rodolph feared and persecuted him; his early life was one of trial and vicissitude, but his abilities gradually asserted themselves, and he was at last, appointed to the governorship of Hungary, where he greatly distinguished himself against the Turks. In 1605 he became heir presumptive to Rodolph by the death of his brother Ernest. Rodolph, however, still refused to allot him a proper establishment, or permit him to marry; but Mathias bore all these slights and insults with patience and good temper, and used every means to make himself popular with all parties, both in Hungary and in Austria. As Rodolph sunk into contempt and ridicule, he rose in importance; and in the commencement of the year 1606, when the Austrian monarchy seemed on the point of dissolution, the other members of the Hapsburg family acknowledged him the head of the house, and promised him their support and assistance in all things. Before, however, taking any decisive steps for taking possession of the crown, he determined to use his best endeavours to restore peace in Hungary. For this purpose he gained over Illeshinsky, Botskai's prime minister, and by his advice offered his master most liberal terms, from the knowledge that he was labouring under a mortal disease. Peace was, therefore, concluded upon the following terms:—"First, that the question of religious toleration should remain in the same state as in the reigns of Ferdinand and Maximilian, and that the arbitrary clause introduced into the decrees by Rodolph should be suppressed; secondly, that Mathias should be lieutenant-general of the kingdom, having under his orders the palatine still to be elected; thirdly, that Botskai should preserve the title of prince of Transylvania and a part of Hungary; and fourthly, that on the failure of his male issue, these territories should revert to the house of Austria." To these special articles a general clause was added, declaring that the king should hereafter observe the ancient laws and immunities of the kingdom; that the palatine should be elected by the Hungarians, in the manner prescribed by the laws; that the governments, the administration of the finances, and all other charges and offices whatsoever, should be confided to the Hungarians; that all property pledged to

* History of the Turks, art. Achmet, *passim*.

foreigners should be redeemed, and that all foreigners should be required to take their departure.

A truce of twenty years was, at the same time, concluded with the Turks, on condition that both parties should remain in possession of the territories which they then held; and the dishonourable tribute which the two preceding Austrian sovereigns had been paying to the Porte was to cease by the presentation to the sultan of a voluntary gift of 200,000 dollars. This treaty, at last, restored peace to Hungary, but at the expense of her unity and independence. Some idea may be formed of the state of weakness and lassitude to which these long wars had reduced the country—a century before so powerful—by a statement of the divisions into which it had been split up by the various factions.

Hungary with Croatia, Sclavonia, and the frontiers, was then reckoned to cover an area of 4,427 square miles, and Transylvania one of 736. Of these 5,163 miles

Turkey possessed - - - - -		1,859
Botskai in Hungary -	1,346	2,082
in Transylvania	736	
And Austria only - - - - -		1,222
	Total	5,163*

Botskai died in 1606, and was succeeded by Sigismond Rakoczi, who, however, soon abdicated in favour of Gabriel Bathori.

This treaty, called the "Pacification of Vienna," was concluded on the 23rd of June, 1606, by the Archduke Mathias and by the ministers of Botskai. It had the force of law in Hungary, and was inserted in the body of laws under the above title. The emperor ratified it in the August following, but not without much delay and great reluctance. Although he had given Mathias full power to conclude it, he expressed himself greatly dissatisfied with its tenour, and even went so far as to call a diet of the empire to demand succours for continuing the war. He had doubtless discovered the secret compact which had been entered into between Mathias and the other princes of the family, and his jealousy being roused, he began to use every means in his power to bring about his destruction or downfal. By a series of intrigues, he managed to separate the interests of his other kinsmen from those of his brother; and the latter, at last saw that if he meant to accomplish his schemes, there was no resource left but an appeal to force. Before resorting to open violence, however, he took every means to avoid all risk of failure. He summoned a meeting of the Hungarian states at Presburg, conciliated the protestants by a confirmation of all their rights, and induced them to enter into a confederation with deputies of Austria, binding themselves to consider as enemies all who should offer any opposition to the Pacification of Vienna. They granted him troops; he marched into Bohemia: and Rodolph, after a feeble resistance, found himself abandoned by all his supporters, and compelled to resign

* La Hongrie Historique, p. 163.

into the hands of Mathias, Hungary, Austria, and Moravia, and to guarantee to him the succession to the crown of Bohemia; Mathias in the meantime bearing the title of king elect of that kingdom, with the consent of the states. Rodolph, at the same time delivered up the Hungarian regalia, which for some time past had been kept at Prague.

The reputation which Mathias had acquired in the Hungarian wars, the evident superiority to his brother in all the qualities which form a ruler which he had displayed, and the repeated attempts which Rodolph had made for the destruction

GEORGE THURZO.

of their liberties, made the Hungarians hail the change with delight; Mathias was, therefore, elected and crowned with great pomp and solemnity. But the diet, with a wise indifference to the glare of fêtes and pageantry, determined not to lose sight of the opportunity which was now afforded them, of recovering and securing their rights and privileges. All their demands were therefore drawn up in a regular capitulation, and presented to the new king for his consent, and Mathias yielding to necessity, assented to their proposals and signed a compact containing the following stipulations:—1. Religious liberty was guaranteed to all. 2. The king should propose to the diet four candidates for the office of palatine, two

GABRIEL BETHLEM.

catholics and two protestants; one of whom the diet should elect. 3. The crown and regalia should be committed to the keeping of two laymen. 4. The Chamber of Finances of Hungary should be independent of that of Austria, and be presided over by a native of the country. 5. The jesuits could not possess real property in the country. 6. All offices and employments should be filled by natives. 7. The king should reside in the country, and during his temporary absence should be represented by the palatine, who should be gifted with full powers, &c." If these conditions were considered exorbitant, Mathias did wrong in accepting them if he afterwards had any intention of making efforts to evade them. But as the emissaries of Rodolph were busy in the diet bidding against him for popular favour, he had neither time for consideration nor for hesitation.

The catholic priesthood no sooner heard of the concessions which had been made to protestantism and religious liberty, than they commenced to storm and protest. At the head of this party was Peter Pazmány, the archbishop of Strigonia, and through his influence every effort was made to rouse the coarse passions and prejudices of the multitude against the Lutherans. Their intrigues were counteracted, however, by the firmness and ability of George Thurzo, the palatine, himself a protestant. He was not content, however, with protecting their freedom in Hungary only. He induced the diet to interfere with the emperor on behalf of Austria, which was then torn by religious dissensions. In Croatia, however, he was less fortunate. Protestantism had there never made much progress. The people were of a coarse and superstitious temperament, and were in complete subjection to the priests. They declared, "that they would sooner separate from Hungary than have their country invaded by that abominable pest called Lutheranism."* The clergy, always indefatigable, patient, and persevering, when the interests of their own order are in danger, lost no opportunity of stirring up discontent in the minds of their adherents, and new fuel was added to the flame which they had kindled, by the outbreak of another revolution in Transylvania. Gabriel Bathori, who had succeeded Sigismond Bathori on the throne of the principality, had suffered his licentiousness to tempt him into insulting the wives of some of the nobles, who instantly fell upon him and murdered him; and in his place Gabriel Bethlem, a brave warrior and an able statesman, was unanimously elected, with the consent and approbation of the sultan. Under his government his dominions enjoyed a full measure of peace and tranquillity, and began to recover from the horrible devastations of preceding years. He did not, however, assume his dignity without dispute. Transylvania had been secured to the house of Austria, on the death of Botskai, by the Pacification of Vienna, and Mathias was, of course, now anxious to enforce his rights, and he considered the present opportunity (1617) favourable, as the Turks were engaged in wars on the side of Asia and Poland. He therefore summoned a diet of the empire, to the throne of which he had succeeded in 1612 by the death of Rodolph, for the purpose of obtaining succours to enforce the fulfilment of the treaty of Vienna, and to expel the Turks from Moldavia and Wallachia, where they had recently established waywodes dependent on the Porte. But the diet refused all aid. The

* Fessler's History of the Hungarians, vol. vii. p. 679.

protestants were dissatisfied with his conduct towards them, and succeeded in outvoting his adherents. He met with no better success on applying to a general assembly of the states of the whole of his dominions, and at last was obliged to save his dignity by taking advantage of the presence of Turkish ambassadors in Vienna, to conclude a peace with the sultan for a further period of twenty years, with additional explanatory articles, and no mention being made in it of Tran-

GEORGE BOTSKAI.

sylvania, the rights of Gabriel Bethlem were thus tacitly recognised. Mathias died soon after, in 1619, leaving his crown to his cousin, Ferdinand II.

CHAPTER XVI.

WARS OF GABRIEL BETHLEM AND FERDINAND II. AND III.

A.D. 1619—1654.

A MAN less qualified for the duties of the office he was called upon to administer, probably could not have been found in the whole range of the Austrian dominions, than Ferdinand II. When he was elected to fill the throne he found the state labouring in the throes of a religious revolution, his subjects divided into two great parties of polemical combatants, who made every town, and even house, an arena for their ferocious and fanatical quarrels. The safety—nay the very existence—of the Church of Rome was threatened. The rise of the reformation had astonished her; its successes had exasperated and alarmed her. There was no engine of fraud or violence that was not put in motion to crush it at once and for ever. The new doctrines were rushing over her domains like a flood, obliterating all the old bulwarks, which she had erected in a thousand years of conquest, to circumscribe and extirpate freedom of thought. Reason had long ceased to be her friend; for centuries before she had declared war against it as a traitor to God, and the handiwork of the devil, with which no good christian, could have any dealings without running the risk of an eternity of roasting. She therefore, bid complete defiance to it; and it, in its turn, never worked but for her damage and detriment. She had gone on building her claims on tradition, till tradition, like an ancient pile, began to topple and give way, amidst the jeers and laughter of the profane heretics, who could see no necessary connexion between truth and antiquity. Long trained in habits of command, accustomed to implicit obedience, on proceeding to punish the rebellion of the deserters, she was astonished to find force repelled by force, authority by argument. The course of a prince who found himself called upon to arbitrate between her and her revolted subjects, was sufficiently clear to any mind which prejudice or the spirit of party had not clouded. He should have proclaimed liberty of conscience to all, and contented himself with confining the combatants to a war of words, and preventing their dogmas merging by an easy transition into blows. He should have raised the law out of the mire of faction, and abashed the howling bigots by placing them face to face with justice—calm, passionless, inflexible. He should have made security for life and property independent of all opinions, and paid no more attention to the thunders of Rome than to the rancorous denunciations of the Lutherans. The former had no vested interest in men's opinions—she might as well talk of a vested interest in a wave of the ocean; and the latter, in claiming full liberty for themselves, were bound, as a duty of prime importance, to respect the liberty and the convictions of others.

Instead of being a mediator between these parties, Ferdinand showed himself, from the first moment of his reign, a violent and unscrupulous partisan. His mother was a pious catholic; his guardians the archdukes Ernest and Maximilian, who had charge of him after his father's death, were bigoted catholics; and he completed his education at the university of Ingolstadt, under the care of the Jesuits, and came out a full-blown bigot. He declared that had he been as free as his brothers, he would have entered the order; but without submitting himself to their rules, he possessed a full measure of the intolerance and hatred to protestantism which at that time characterised them. He frequently declared that he would sooner live with his family in banishment, or beg his bread from door to door, and submit to every possible injury and insult, than yield an inch of ground to the perverse principles of Lutheranism. When he ascended the throne, he refused to confirm the privileges which his father Charles had granted to the protestants of his dominions in Styria. He made a pilgrimage to Loretto, and vowed on his knees before the image not to desist from his efforts until he had extirpated heresy in his dominions; and at Rome his zeal was fired and confirmed by consecration at the hands of Pope Clement VIII. On his return, he banished all protestant preachers and schoolmasters. In place of protestant seminaries, he founded colleges of Jesuits; and commissioners, by his orders, traversed the whole country, restoring the old churches to the catholics, and demolishing the new ones and the school-houses which the reformers had erected. Notwithstanding their knowledge of his antecedents, little opposition, strange to say, was offered to his election in Bohemia, and still less in Hungary. He was crowned at Presburg in 1618, as successor to Mathias. The latter died in March, 1619, leaving the whole of his dominions in a state of terrible agitation: and when Ferdinand ascended the three thrones to which he had succeeded, he saw nothing around but discord and rebellion. The protestants were everywhere ready to take up arms for the defence of their rights, which Ferdinand, during the latter years of Mathias's reign, had grossly outraged. The storm was already brewing, which, when it burst, raged for thirty years in the celebrated war, which during nearly the whole of that period turned the fairest countries of Europe into a smoking battlefield; but which has derived interest, and even lustre, in the eyes of the present generation from its forming the subject of two of the finest productions of Schiller's pen.*

The German protestants rose in insurrection under the celebrated count Thurn, a man of great military skill, daring enterprise, and deep ambition. He speedily formed relations with those in Hungary and Bohemia, and the whole of the latter country was soon in the power of the insurgents. Ferdinand had not yet been raised to the imperial dignity, and the protestants hastened to use every means to

* "History of the Thirty Years' War" and "Wallenstein."

depose him from the throne of Bohemia. A general diet of delegates from the various states of the kingdom was held at Prague, in July, 1619, in which a list of grievances was drawn up, charging him with having broken his coronation oath by interfering in the government during the life of Mathias, with having commenced war without the consent of the diet, and with having devastated the country with foreign troops, and having sought by transferring the eventual succession to the Spanish princes to reduce them under a hateful and despotic yoke, and ended by offering the imperial crown to the elector palatine Frederick, who accepted it with fear and trembling. He was crowned at Prague, and acknowledged by all the protestant states of Europe.

No sooner was this done than Gabriel Bethlem entered Hungary, in answer to the call of the protestants of that country, at the head of a large army—took Cassau, Tiernan, Newhasel, dispersed the imperial forces under Homonai, sent 18,000 men to enforce count Thurn, got possession of Presburg by treachery, and seized upon the regalia. The fate of the unfortunate Frederick is well known. Overwhelmed by the vigorous measures of Ferdinand, his armies were driven from one post to another by the imperial forces, under the duke of Bavaria and the famous count Tilly, until they made their last stand under the walls of Prague. The Bohemian army in vain sought to throw up defences amongst the ravines of the White Mountain. They were furiously attacked; the Hungarian cavalry were routed in the first onset, and after a battle of an hour's duration, in which the Moravian troops, under the prince of Anhalt and the young count Thurn, displayed the most indomitable valour, were utterly routed, with the loss of 5,000 men, 100 standards, and all the artillery.

When the armies were on the point of engaging, Frederick, instead of placing himself at their head and setting his life and fortune upon the issue, sat down to preside at an entertainment given in honour of the English ambassador. It was in vain that messengers from the field came to say that it was absolutely necessary that he should encourage the troops by his presence. He steadfastly refused to quit the scene of the festivities; and it was only when a courier came to announce to him, that fortune was declaring against him, that he consented to mount and ride forth. He ascended the ramparts on the side next the White Mountain just in time to see his army flying in mad confusion towards the city before the victorious legions of the emperor. His officers offered to collect the remnant of the troops within the city, and the burghers armed and volunteered to defend it to the last extremity, but in vain. Nothing could induce Frederick to remain. He fled in the night, and died some time after in indigence and exile.*

* The battle of Prague excited great attention all over Europe. In the days of our grandmothers no young lady was considered to have completed her education till she could perform on the harpsichord the well-known piece of music, which imitates the charge of the cavalry, the roar of the artillery, the groans of the wounded, and the trumpet of victory, as heard on that famous field. It is only within the memory of the present generation that young gentlemen have ceased to ask for it, and young misses to simper and comply.

Gabriel Bethlem for a long time supported the prestige acquired by his earlier successes. He was proclaimed king of Hungary, and obtained considerable advantages over two generals of ability and reputation whom the emperor had opposed to him. A treaty of peace was, however, at last concluded, upon the conditions that he withdrew his garrisons from the places he had captured during the war, surrendered the crown, and abandoned the title of king. The emperor, on his side, agreed to assign him the duchies of Oppelen and Ratibor in Silesia, and to allow him to retain for life Cassau, Tokay, Mungatz Szathmar, and Esseck, with seven counties of Hungary, and to grant the protestants complete toleration; but, as a set-off against this latter concession, he insisted upon the restoration of the Jesuits, who had been expelled in the reign of Mathias. In consequence of this peace, Ferdinand soon after held a diet at Presburg, where he restored the regalia with great pomp, and had the satisfaction of witnessing the coronation of his empress Eleanora, whom he had recently married. As he was well aware that it was only by maintaining Hungary in a state of tranquillity that he could hope to make head against the powerful confederacy which the German protestants had formed against him, he not only granted a general amnesty and fulfilled his promise of toleration, but approved of the choice of a protestant palatine.

He did not long adhere to his good intentions. His *animus* against the reformed party, still further inflamed by the war he was now carrying on with the king of Denmark, soon began to show itself once more in a series of acts of petty hostility, more remarkable as omens of what was to follow than for their real mischief. Bethlem complained that the duchies that had been promised him in Silesia had not been given him; that due respect had not been shown to his ambassadors; that Jagerndorf and others of his friends had been persecuted and harassed; and finally, that the stipulations inserted in the treaty relating to the protestant religion had not been carried into effect.* He therefore collected an army of 45,000 men, joined his forces with those of Mansfeldt, the general of the confederacy, after his victory over the imperialists at Presburg; and at the same time the bashaw of Buda entered Lower Hungary at the head of a large force, captured various fortresses in the district of Gran, and laid siege to Novigrad. They were opposed by two able generals, the famous Wallenstein and Swartzemberg, but without checking their progress. Wallenstein, however, followed Mansfeldt into Hungary, where the two armies remained for some time inactive in the presence of one another; but famine, disease, and the approach of winter at last brought the contest to a close. The king of Denmark had been defeated, and Gabriel Bethlem began to fear that the whole force of the Austrians would now be directed against him, and concluded a truce. The bashaw of Buda feared the winter, and followed his example; and Mansfeldt, finding himself thus abandoned, disbanded his soldiers, sold his artillery and military stores to the

* Histoire des Revolutions de Hongrie, p. 62.

Turks, and set out for Venice through Bosnia with only twelve officers, but died at Zara on his way, and thus rid the house of Austria of one of its most formidable enemies.* The treaty of peace was again renewed, the truce with the Turks prolonged.

Ferdinand II., following the practice of his predecessors, caused his son Ferdinand III. to be elected and crowned king of Hungary in 1625. Bethlem once more seized this opportunity of renewing the hostilities. His disposition was restless, and his ambition boundless; the feelings of the Viennese court towards the Hungarians were known to be anything but kindly; the protestants were in a state of continual insecurity and alarm, everything seemed favourable for commencing another campaign. His courage was greater than his fortune. He at first obtained some successes over General Schlick, near Presburg, but his star soon paled its fires before the more redoubtable genius of Wallenstein, and he was compelled once more to sue for peace. He pledged himself to furnish no more aid to the Bohemian rebels, and Ferdinand promised on his part an adherence more strict than ever to the Pacification of Vienna. Bethlem survived this truce only three years, and his death in 1629, relieved the Austrians from a load of anxiety.

The Transylvanians elected George Rakotski to fill his place, and during nearly four years Hungary and Transylvania enjoyed the blessings of peace and tranquillity. At last, Ferdinand believing that the Turks, in consequence of the recent confirmation and prolongation of the truce, would not attempt to interfere, determined to reduce the latter into the form of a province of the Austrian dominions.† He justified his enterprise by the plea that Transylvania was formerly dependent upon Hungary, and that in accordance with treaties which had been several times renewed and confirmed, it should of right revert to the house of Austria upon the death of Bethlem. But there was reason to fear that he had other objects in view than a mere assertion of the rights of the archducal crown. If Transylvania were re-united to Hungary, it would form a powerful ally for the patriotic party in their struggles against Austrian domination. But if, on the other hand, it were annexed to Austria, it would facilitate the execution of any designs against the Hungarians which the emperor might entertain. The palatine, Nicholas Esterhazi, accordingly received orders from Ferdinand to attack Cassau and Transylvania, and compel Rakotski to relinquish his claims to the principality, and deliver it up to the Austrian general. The war ended as might be expected, where the attacking party was only half in earnest. No sooner did Rakotski appear on the banks of the Teyss, than the palatine took flight, and justified his apparent pusillanimity, by assuring the emperor that the enterprise

* Coxe's History of the House of Austria, vol. i. part ii. p. 806.

† "Cæsar Esterhazum Palatinum anno seculi decimi septimi trigesimo, cum instructâ manu ut Transylvaniam in provinciæ formam redigeret et septem comitatus ad Patiscum amnem, una cum urbe Cassovia reciperet, misit."—*Chronicle of Parchitius under Ferdinand III.*

could not end well, and that on the whole it would be much better to leave prince George in the peaceable possession of his dominions. Ferdinand now saw that he must choose other agents than the Hungarians for the execution of his design, and determined that the next time, the Germans alone should be the agents of his will. But this nation, the ever ready tool of despots, were hateful to the Magyars, and doubly hateful to the Transylvanians, and their very appearance on the frontiers would have been sufficient to have kindled the flame of revolt from one end of the kingdom to the other. This was not the only difficulty that the emperor had to contend against. He was at that moment engaged in a contest with Gustavus Adolphus, the chivalrous and unfortunate king of Sweden, which threatened the security of his throne and the integrity of his empire, and which needed all the resources at his command for its maintenance. He was, therefore, reluctantly obliged to postpone his designs against Transylvania to a more convenient season, and Rakotski had time to take measures for his defence, and for compelling Austria to acknowledge his title by soliciting foreign aid. The sultan had the strongest possible interest in supporting him, and, therefore, readily consented to despatch a large force towards Newheisel, whose presence extorted from Ferdinand a promise to abstain in future from all interference in the internal affairs of Transylvania.

(1632.) Whether it was that Rakotski did not think himself justified in relying upon Ferdinand's promises, or that the measure of success, which had as yet marked his career, had awakened within him bolder and more ambitious hopes, he now seemed resolved to push his pretensions beyond the bounds of his principality, and to profit by the favourable disposition which was evinced towards him by the Hungarians. Either with the desire of augmenting the number of his partizans, or of lending lustre and sanctity to his quarrel, he made religion the pretext of a new outbreak. He accordingly raised a large army, and set out on his march towards Hungary. Unable to oppose him with its own forces, the court of Vienna was compelled to raise up enemies against him by intrigues, which were remarkable for their success. Csaki, the general of the troops of Gabriel Bethlem's widow, who still held possession of the fortress of Tokay, kept him for a long time engaged; and Stephen Bethlem, who had killed one of his relations, sought to protect himself from his vengeance by collecting a horde of Tartars and Turks, and for a long time harassed and annoyed him by a series of irregular attacks. In addition to this, the sultan, to his great surprise and chagrin, held out some threats of invading his dominions. Thus foiled, Rakotski was not only compelled to solicit a reconciliation with Ferdinand, but to seek it with a show of cordiality which he was far from feeling.* Tranquillity was thus again restored.

In 1635, the peace of Prague gave a death-blow to the protestant confederacy, and rendered Ferdinand's influence paramount all over Germany. Wallenstein,

* Histoire des Revolutions de Hongrie p. 64.

the extraordinary man whose talents, courage and ambition made him the dread and envy of his contemporaries, and made the Austrian emperor fear the successes of his armies almost as much as their defeats, had been removed by assassination; the young king of Hungary had given incontestible proofs of valour and conduct, by defeating the Confederates in a bloody battle at Nordlingen, and had been elected king of the Romans; John de Wert, and other Austrian generals, had repelled the attacks and humbled the pride of France; the Thirty Years' War, originated by the worst of passions of the human heart, supported by the ruin of nations, a lavish expenditure of treasure, and the blood and bereavement of two generations, was now all but at an end; everywhere the star of the house of Hapsburg was in the ascendant. But in this uprise of Austria, Hungary saw the prospect of her own downfal. The weakness of the one was the strength and opportunity of the other, and Hungarian liberties were never more in danger than when the Austrian eagle was fluttering its pinions in victory.

On the 15th of February, 1637, in the midst of all these successes, Ferdinand died, in the fifty-ninth year of his age, of a decline brought on by incessant anxiety and continual fatigues of mind and body—after one of the most eventful reigns recorded in history. He was brave in danger, firm in adversity, sagacious, persevering, and energetic; but he was a blindly and childishly superstitious devotee, an inveterate bigot, and was devoured by an ambition which allowed no obstacles founded on humanity, justice, or good faith to stand in its way.

Ferdinand was succeeded by his son Ferdinand III. This prince had, when crowned king of Hungary, entered into the same engagements as all his predecessors, to govern the Hungarians according to the laws and constitutions of the kingdom; but it soon became apparent that he treated these engagements with the utmost contempt, and there was hardly a single article in the code against which he did not direct an attack. Nevertheless, as the Hungarian protestants had now become obnoxious to him in the extreme, in consequence of their connexion with the German protestants, the sworn enemies of his house, it was against them that he gave most evidence of enmity and repugnance. He took every means in his power to diminish their number, and expelled many of their ministers. As Rakotski had several times proclaimed himself the protector of protestantism and of Hungarian liberty in general, to him they naturally looked for aid in this emergency. Before undertaking their defence, however, he determined to assure himself against all contingencies by seeking assistance from the Turks. The sultan, Ibrahim, gave them every promise of support. He next drew up a statement of Hungarian grievances—those of the protestants in particular—and laid it before Ferdinand. The Austrian cabinet perceiving, however, that the sultan was occupied by the czar of Muscovy, who had taken the fortress of Azov, and by the knights of Malta, and still more by his projects against the Venetians, and relying upon the truce of seven years, which had been concluded sometime previously, paid no attention to the document whatever. This irritated Rakotski, who forthwith issued a manifesto, complaining "that the house of Austria, in violation of several treaties heretofore entered into, was placing Hungary amongst the number of its hereditary provinces; that contrary to the same treaties, it had removed the protestants from places of trust and dignity, deprived them of their livings, and expelled their ministers; that in making a point of establishing Austrians in the kingdom, it violated all law, neglected the care of the frontiers, and everything that was of profit or importance to the nation." All this enlisted the sympathies of the Hungarians on his side; but a victory gained over Bonchaim, the Austrian general, speedily increased his army to 60,000 men. He took Cassau, Neusohl, Chemnitz, and several other places, and advanced as far as Eperies, where he published a proclamation exhorting the Hungarians to insurrection. Ferdinand was at first greatly embarrassed. The flower of his forces were engaged in a distant war in Jutland, but he managed to collect together 10,000 men, who kept Rakotski's numerous but undisciplined and predatory hordes in check, and at the same time renewed the truce with the Turks for twenty years. Rakotski, finding he was not likely to meet with the support which the French and the sultan had promised him before setting out on his enterprise, was compelled to desist from hostilities, and fall back within his own frontiers. In the following year, 1645, he formed a league with the Swedes, who were pressing Austria so hard that Vienna itself was threatened, and entering Hungary at the head of 25,000 men, sent his son to Bounn, which Tortenson with 8,000 was besieging, and detached 6,000 to join a corps under the Swedish general Douglas, which spread such alarm to Presburg, that the crown and regalia were removed.*

Ferdinand was now in desperate straits, but taking advantage of some bickerings between Rakotski and the Swedes, he brought about a negotiation with the latter, which ended in a treaty of peace, which would have been most advantageous, not only to the Rakotski family in particular, but to the Hungarians in general, had Ferdinand been as faithful in fulfilling his promises as he was ready in making them. The articles are recorded in the acts of the diet for the year 1647, and lay down an obligation on Ferdinand's part to observe Andrew's decree, forbid the alienation of crown property, determine the choice of deputies for the diets and the manner of giving their suffrages, banish from the kingdom all foreign troops, and forbid the drafting of Hungarians for military service into foreign countries; interdict the bestowal of offices upon foreigners (how often was this done in vain!), and make it indispensable on the part of the sovereign to make known to the diet all treaties entered into with the Porte or other powers on their behalf. Nor were the protestants forgotten. The record contains an ample list of the churches, schools, &c., which were then restored to them, or bestowed upon them newly in the different provinces, towns, and villages of the kingdom. Rakotski was formally recognised as the legitimate prince of Transylvania; the seven counties which had been held by Gabriel Bethlem were ceded to him, as

* Coxe's History of the House of Austria, vol. i. part ii. p. 938.

well as the duchies of Oppelen and Ratibor in Silesia, and the title of prince of the empire was conferred upon him and his descendants for ever.

This treaty was confirmed at the diet held in 1647; and at the same time Ferdinand caused his son of the same name, and elder brother of Leopold, to be

ANCIENT BUDA.

elected and crowned king. During his short reign, the country was tranquil; but in 1654 he died, leaving his rights to Leopold.

CHAPTER XVII.

THE REIGN OF LEOPOLD.

A.D. 1655—1697.

THE reign of Leopold was a period which witnessed events more important to Hungary than any which preceded it, or have followed it, save only the revolutionary years, 1848 and 1849. No monarch of the house of Austria had ever made so determined attacks upon Hungarian liberty, and to none did the Hungarians oppose a braver and more strenuous resistance. Nothing was left untried on the one side to overthrow the constitution; nothing was left untried on the other to uphold and defend it. Few in England know anything of the result; fewer still the steps which led to it; and even those whose position or pursuits have made them acquainted with the facts, have formed their judgment not so much from an impartial weighing of them, as in obedience to the dictates of passion or hereditary prejudice. The Hungarians look upon their struggles against Leopold as a patriotic defence of privileges legitimized by a thousand years of possession; and the partisans of the house of Austria, on the other hand, inveigh against them as the efforts of a restless and tumultuous people to free themselves from the control of their lawful rulers. Unhappily, this is not one of those questions upon which the present generation, looking at it in the light of history, can form an impartial and unbiased opinion. Blood has flowed in our own time in the old quarrel of the seventeenth century. Neither party has retreated from the struggle in despair, and poured out its sorrows and regrets in the bosom of tradition. The vanquished are not subdued; the conquerors are not triumphant. Success has not lent lustre and legitimacy to rebellion; but the sword cannot root out the chagrin of defeat, and the hope of revenge.

Leopold was elected to the throne of Hungary at Presburg, in 1655, during the lifetime of his father, when but fifteen years of age. The usual conditions were offered for his acceptance by the diet, before conferring the crown upon him, and he accepted and swore to observe them, and embodied them in a special diploma which he caused to be inserted in the public records:*—

I. That he would preserve inviolate all and singular, the franchises, immunities, privileges, laws, statutes, and customs of the kingdom.

* Arts. of the year 1655.

II. That in each diet (which he would assemble as often as possible, at the farthest at intervals of no greater length than three years), he would redress all sound grievances (*gravamina*).

III. That he would administer the affairs of Hungary by means of Hungarian ministers, and would deliberate upon them with them; and that for no reason, and upon no pretence whatsoever, would he suffer his Hungarian subjects to be sent, taken, or carried before foreign tribunals.

IV. That he would confer the government of the frontiers, and all other offices in accordance with Article XI., of the year 1608.*

V. The fifth article, which is rather lengthy, relates to tribunals prescribed by law, and the abolition of the long and intricate forms of pleading, by which justice was delayed and the suitors injured, and of the decision of controversies by extraordinary commissioners assuming arbitrary powers, which, till the accession of the house of Hapsburg, were unknown in Hungary, and were utterly opposed to the spirit of her laws.

VI. That for the better preservation of the tranquillity of the kingdom, religious affairs should remain upon the same footing as fixed by the Pacification of Vienna, and should not be disturbed either by his serenity or by others.

VII. That he would observe all the ordinary forms in the election of the palatine, and would support and maintain him in the exercise of his authority, office, and jurisdiction.

VIII. That he would provide for the security of the frontiers.

IX. That the free towns, and those of the mountains, should be secured in the enjoyment of their rights, liberties, and privileges.

X. That he would not remove the Hungarian crown out of the kingdom, upon any pretext whatsoever, nor by any address or artifice.

XI. That he would not alienate any part of the kingdom, but on the contrary, would regulate the differences existing between Hungary, Poland, and Silesia, upon the question of boundaries, and would use every endeavour to restore to the former all that she might have lost, or have been unjustly deprived of.

XII. The alliances entered into with Bohemia, Transylvania, and with the other provinces, should be maintained in full force, in accordance with the treaty of Vienna.

XIII. That he would faithfully observe all that was contained in Article II. of the diet of the year 1608, relative to the means of preserving the public peace, and the prohibition against declaring war without the knowledge of the states, or introducing foreign troops into the kingdom.

XIV. That the castles of Pernstein, Kobersdorff, Gintz, Forchvenstein, Eisen-

* "The command of the frontiers, as well in this as in the above-mentioned kingdoms (Croatia, &c.), shall be conferred upon natives of Hungary, or upon those of the provinces dependent on her."

stadt, and Hornstein, should remain under the jurisdiction of the Hungarian crown.*

XV. The fifteenth has reference to the redemption of some towns mortgaged to the Poles.

XVI. The soldiers who had obtained any privilges from his majesty the emperor, should enjoy them under the reign of his serenity the king.

XVII. His serenity promised the states that, during the life of his imperial and royal majesty the emperor, the latter should in no way interfere in the government of Hungary.†

These express stipulations were dictated on the part of the Hungarians by a distrust which their experience of the bad faith of the Austrian court more than justified. The folly of trusting to these precautions, however, when not backed up by more powerful weapons than oaths or arguments, soon became apparent. Leopold acting under his father's advice and direction, subscribed to the compact without hesitation, and without any formal retractation laboured all his life after to nullify it. The means he employed for this purpose, as will be seen in the progress of our narrative, were such as appear in the history of every attempt made by despotic princes to deprive a democracy of its liberty; constant watchfulness to take advantage of anything in the course of events that might favour his schemes; sometimes open and undisguised oppression, at others subtle intrigues scarcely less lamentable and odious in their results than oppression itself; constant sowing of division among the nobles; corruption by promises of places at court, pension and emoluments—menaces, bribes, and threats of every description.

The first two years of the young king's reign passed over without the occurrence of any event of importance. In 1657 his father died, and during the whole of that year he was occupied in procuring his election to the imperial crown, and combating the intrigues set on foot by France and Sweden to deprive him of it, Cardinal Mazarin wishing, on behalf of the former, to obtain it for his youthful sovereign Louis XIV., who had but just then ascended the throne, and the latter willing to sacrifice anything to humble the house of Hapsburg. Leopold had no sooner secured it, than he found his attention called to the affairs of Poland, which had been invaded by Charles Gustavus, king of Sweden, aided by George Rakotski, the second of that name, prince of Transylvania, who had succeeded his father, with the consent of the states and approbation of the Turks, who then exercised a more powerful influence in the affairs of the principality than they had done for some years previously. Great confusion had for a long while prevailed at Constantinople, in consequence of the turbulence of the janizzaries, who, like the prætorian guards at Rome, frequently held in their

* These castles had been detached from the hereditary provinces and incorporated with the kingdom of Hungary by ancient treaties with the house of Austria.

† Histoire des Revolutions de Hongrie, pp. 70, 71.

hands the destinies of the empire. In 1648 Mahomet IV. ascended the throne, in the fifth year of his age; and the usual evils attendant upon a minority were aggravated by the contentions of the women of the harem, each of whom aspired to the supreme management of affairs. Their strifes at last led to the outbreak of a long and bloody war between the two great military bodies of janizzaries and spahis, which for some years filled the empire with violence and bloodshed. The authority of the sultan was, however, at length restored, and the disorders quelled by the ability of two grand viziers, Achmet and Mahomet Kiupruli. Under their rule the aggressive policy of the Porte was resumed, and, as usual, its attacks, covert or overt, were directed chiefly against Austria.

FRANCIS VESSELENYI

Rakotski's administration, both at home and abroad, had been remarkably successful until his alliance with Sweden against Poland, formed in the hope of obtaining for himself a reversion of the crown of the latter kingdom. Leopold was, however, enabled to counteract his schemes by inducing Denmark to declare war against Sweden—a measure which caused Charles Gustavus to return precipitately to his dominions. After his departure Rakotski found himself overwhelmed by the attacks of the Poles and Tartars, supported by 10,000 Austrian infantry and 6,000 cavalry, whom Leopold had sent to their aid, and was compelled to retreat in confusion. He had scarce regained his own dominions when the Turks, wishing to profit by his weakness, sent him a stern reprimand for invading Poland, and announced their intention of dethroning him as a refractory vassal. He instantly appealed to Leopold for aid, who, in accordance with the 12th article of the compact he had entered into at his election, was bound to afford it. He not only refused, however, but forbade the Hungarians to meddle in the contest, lest it should furnish a pretext to the Ottomans for the invasion of the kingdom. He then sent an army of Germans into Hungary under the command of General Souche, with orders to seize upon those places in Hungary that were held by the Rakotski family, and garrison them.* This order was promptly executed, and the unfortunate Rakotski, abandoned on every side, was attacked by the bashaw of Buda with an army of 25,000 men, while he had but 6,000 to oppose to him. He did not decline the combat, but was killed and defeated, after fighting with heroic bravery, in a battle fought near Clausemburgh, leaving a widow and a son, Francis, aged fifteen, who had been appointed his successor, and who was entrusted to the guardianship of John Kemeny, one of his most successful generals. The Turks forced the states of Transylvania to elect in his stead two princes in succession, Redei and Bartzai, whose temporary elevation forms their only claim to notice. General Souche managed by force or fraud to obtain possession of Tokay, Szathmar, Erschit, and Onod; but he was unable to prevent Great Varadin from falling into the hands of the Turks.

The young prince Francis, shortly after his father's death, embraced the Roman Catholic religion, which was not then dominant in Transylvania, and thus alienated the affections of the great mass of the people. Kemeny, forgetful of his trust, took advantage of the circumstance to secure his own election, and having deposed and assassinated Bartzai, called upon Leopold to aid him against the Turks, in which he was warmly seconded by the Hungarians, who were alarmed by the capture of Great Varadin.† Leopold was but too glad to comply, but the force which he sent to his assistance was again a German army, under the command of foreign officers, in direct violation of the articles of his capitulation, and which the Hungarians and Transylvanians resented by refusing quarters and supplies. This force was under the command of the famous

* Coxe says that this army was sent into Hungary at the request of the diet. It is possible that this request was made with the view of saving Transylvania, but most improbable that the diet desired the seizure and occupation of some of the most important towns in the kingdom by German troops, of whose presence, under any pretence whatsoever, they had the greatest abhorrence, particularly when we find the second article of their proceedings in 1659 (the year following), expressly forbidding their introduction into the country; and making it essential that those stationed on the frontiers should be officered by Hungarians. It is stated in the Memoirs of Montecuculli, that though the states of Hungary had asked for the army, it was badly received when it entered the kingdom; and they murmured greatly because the German general wanted garrisons to place his troops in. This goes to confirm the Hungarian account of the transaction.

† Coxe's History of the House of Austria, vol. i., part ii. p. 988; Histoire des Revolutions de Hongrie, p. 74.

Montecuculli, who, in his memoirs, tells a doleful story of the refusal of the Transylvanians to receive any assistance from him, and of their obstinate persistence in asserting that they were quite able to manage their own affairs. The Turks had expelled Kemeny, and, with the consent of the states, had put Michael Apaffi in his place. Montecuculli,* after one or two slight successes, was compelled to fall back upon Upper Hungary, after leaving 1,000 horse with Kemeny, and a garrison in Clausemburgh. Leopold assembled the states at Cassau, and demanded of them quarters for the German troops and liberty to place a garrison in Cassau, under the pretence that there was some danger of a war with the Turks, and that it was necessary to have a force to oppose them on the spot. They refused to comply, and in the meantime the troops had passed into Lower Hungary and found quarters there. The states immediately called upon the emperor to withdraw them, and settle the question either by declaring war at once against the Turks, or by taking measures for the prolongation of the peace. A diet was therefore summoned at Presburg in 1662, which sat from May till September, without coming to any conclusion upon the subjects in dispute. It charged Leopold with having violated the constitution, in not having supported the war by contributions from the crown domains, and in employing foreign officers and soldiers instead of the army of the insurrection, the only force which was strictly legal. They also alleged that negotiations had been carried on between the courts of Austria and Vienna without their cognizance. After weeks of useless recrimination, Leopold proposed, by way of compromise, to withdraw 9,000 of his troops to the frontier, to pay the remainder at his expense, and subject them to the laws of Hungary and the jurisdiction of the palatine. But when this offer came to be taken into consideration, the protestants brought forward complaints of renewed persecutions which had been lately set on foot against them, and getting in a dispute with the catholics, the diet broke up in confusion, without coming to any decision, one way or other. The field was thus left free to Leopold to act for the present as he pleased, and he availed himself of

* Raymond, count of Montecuculli, was one of the most extraordinary men of modern times. He was of noble Italian family, and was born at Modena in 1608. He entered the army early, and distinguished himself in the imperial forces during the war against the Swedes. He was taken prisoner and kept in confinement during two years, the whole of which period was devoted to the study of works bearing on his profession. On his liberation he served under John de Werth in the war in Bohemia in 1657. He was raised to the rank of a field-marshal, and until 1664 he was constantly engaged with the Turks in Hungary and Transylvania, and closed the campaign by a signal victory gained at St. Gothard in the latter year. In 1675 he was selected to command the German army against France, as the only general worthy to be matched against Turenne. Between the two they reduced war to an art, and their marches, countermarches, manœuvres, and encampments, were the delight of the military connoisseurs of the day. Upon the death of Turenne he was opposed by Condé, and closed his military career by the siege of Philisburg. He passed the remainder of his life in retirement, occupied in the composition of his memoirs and other literary works. He died in October, 1681, aged seventy-two. His books upon the science of war were considered unquestionable authority till Napoleon upset his system, and proved that it was possible to conquer against all rule.

the opportunity to enter into negotiations with the Turks, which ended in the conclusion of a treaty of peace at Temesvar,* but left the grievances of the Hungarians completely unredressed. The chief command of the Austrian troops remained in the hands of Montecuculli and German officers, without any regard whatever being paid to the claims of the palatine.

The truce, however, had hardly been concluded, when the vizier Kiupriuli, wishing to take advantage of the defenceless and distracted state of Hungary, burst across the frontier at the head of 100,000 men, and meeting with no opposition from the forces of Montecuculli, which were small in number, and were weakened by the hardships of the preceding winter, crossed the Drave at Esseck, and the Danube at Buda, cut off a corps stationed at Parkun, captured several fortresses of great importance, and detached a predatory corps of Turks and Tartars, who extended their ravages as far as Olmutz and threatened Vienna itself. Kemeny had in the meantime been defeated and killed in a skirmish with the Turks, and Apaffi, whom they had nominated as his successor, now attacked and captured Zekelheid and Clausemburgh, and would have subdued Croatia and Styria, had he not been baffled by the valour of Nicholas Zrinyi the worthy descendant of the hero of Sziget. The news came like a thunderclap upon Leopold, who was lying sick of the small-pox at Vienna. Montecuculli was barely able to save himself from destruction, by shutting himself up in the strong position of the Schut, and it was found almost impossible to raise the army of the insurrection in the presence of an enemy who swept across the country like a whirlwind. There was no resource left, but an appeal to the states of Christendom for aid against the common enemy. The German diet was then sitting at Ratisbon, and after some hesitation, agreed to postpone the consideration of all other questions for the present, and take measures for aiding the emperor, and consented to maintain a body of 6,500 men for a year. The other princes of Europe were equally liberal. Pope Alexander VII. forwarded 700,000 Roman florins, and allowed the emperor to tax the ecclesiastical property in the Austrian dominions. The king of France sent 6,000 men under the command of the Count de Coligny, and the Marquis de la Feuillade. The king of Spain, though his resources were impoverished, furnished money or magazines to the full extent of his means; the king of Sweden added 2,500 men to the contingent, which as a member of the empire, he was already bound to furnish.

At the opening of the campaign, the army under the command of Count Hohenlohe took the field, and a great number of trifling combats took place between him and the grand vizier, but without any decisive result. The energies of the Christian forces were paralysed by the quarrels between Montecuculli and Zrinyi, the ban of Croatia; the former was as cautious and calculating as the latter was fiery and impetuous, and he was exasperated against the Hungarians, on account of the poor reception they had given him the preceding campaign.

* History of the House of Austria, vol. i. part ii. p. 992.

Their differences aided the Turks effectually. They failed in an attack on Canisia, and Zrinyi had the mortification of witnessing the reduction of a fortress which he himself had built on the Mura, for the express purpose of repelling the incursions of the infidels. Irritated by this ill success and also at Montecuculli's delay, he left the army in disgust to lay his complaints before the emperor.

Kiupriuli now directed his march towards the frontiers of Styria, and Montecuculli drawing together the whole of the Christian forces, amounting to 60,000 in all, took his stand behind the Raab in the strong position of St. Gothard, to oppose his progress. The emperor's own troops were stationed on the right, those of the empire in the centre, and the French and other auxiliaries on the left, to dispute the passage of the river. A body of janizzaries crossed without hesitation, and the rest of the army followed, but owing to a sudden rain, a part was left on the farther shore. The janizzaries were attacked early on the following morning and thrown into confusion, but being supported by fresh reinforcements which crossed the river, the Christian forces were repulsed and broken, and some fugitives flying to Gatz, announced that the day was lost. But the skill of Montecuculli restored the fortune of the combat. His cavalry kept the spahis in check, and the janizzaries were routed by the steady discipline of the Germans and the indomitable valour of the French: 8,000 were slain, and many more were lost in attempting to climb the rugged banks of the Raab. Among the killed on the side of the Turks were the bashaw of Buda, and a son of the khan of Crim Tartary; but they did not on this occasion lose merely in their irregular troops accustomed to flight; but in the disciplined corps of the janizzaries, Albanians, and spahis, who, in the figurative language of the east, were styled the sword and shield of the empire.*

A success so great, and in some measure unlooked for, led the Hungarians to expect that it would be attended by the total expulsion of the Ottomans from the kingdom. But it was no easy matter to keep together the heterogeneous materials of which the Christian army was composed, and the jealousy evinced by the Hungarians themselves at the presence of foreign troops within their territory warned Leopold of the necessity of bringing the war to a speedy close. To the astonishment of everybody, however, he concluded a truce for twenty-one years with the grand vizier. The battle was fought on the 1st of August, 1666, and the treaty was signed on the 17th of September. The Turks were to retain Great Varadin and Neuheisel, and Apaffi was recognised by the emperor as the legitimate prince of Transylvania. Leopold held all the towns, fortresses, and counties in Hungary which he had wrested from Rakotski; and the garrisons which had been received in various places during the war were maintained there; and in addition to all this, to render himself still more secure, he built a new fortress, Leopoldstadt, on the Waag. The Hungarians, who knew

* Histoire des Revolutions de Hongrie, p. 76.

nothing of the treaty and took no part in framing it, were irritated by it in the highest degree; and denounced it as a flagrant violation of Leopold's capitulation. They even arrested the secretary of the imperial resident in the Turkish camp as he was conveying the treaty to Vienna, and were with difficulty induced to liberate him and restore his papers. After great delay the states were at length persuaded to ratify the conditions of the truce, upon the emperor's promising to replace the German troops by Hungarian levies, and to grant no state office or trust without their knowledge and consent. He, at the same time, restored the crown of St. Stephen to Presburg, which, during the war, had been carried away to Vienna.

The Hungarians now found themselves in a more lamentable position than ever. The Turkish bashaw commanding the garrison in Neuheisel began to levy tribute over the whole of Hungary, to the very frontiers of Moravia; and the people, unable to resist, were compelled to pay it. On appealing to the court of Vienna, orders were sent down to them to refuse it in every case; but no mention was made of protection or support, though the German troops still occupied the garrisons. The imperialists, secure in their fortified posts, abandoned the open country to the ravages of the Ottomans, so that it was kept in a state of continual warfare. During this so-called peace, no less than 60,000 men perished upon the frontiers of Vezprim and Papa alone.* Applications were at last made to Leopold for permission to send a minister to the Porte to complain of these outrages, and of the infraction of the treaty; but this was refused. Such was the posture of affairs when the diet assembled at Presburg and Neusohl, in 1668, in a state of the highest irritation. The emperor sent down commissioners to demand subsidies for the support of the foreign troops still remaining in the country, and the erection of new fortresses. The deputies steadfastly refused compliance, and complained in bitter terms of the scenes of violence which were daily witnessed throughout the kingdom, worse by far in their results than open and avowed hostilities, of the levying of the tribute, and carrying off the inhabitants into captivity practised by the Turks. The palatinate had lately become vacant by the death of the illustrious Wesselenyi, who had been for a long while the prophet and guide of the patriotic party, and who was on the point of forming a party to rise in insurrection against the emperor, in accordance with an express article in the constitution which Leopold himself had sworn to maintain.

The states now called upon Leopold to fill it up, as they had now more than ever need of a mediator between him and them. As this office was always an obnoxious one to the Austrian court, and as the palatine was always looked upon with distrust and suspicion, Leopold refused to comply, though this was one of the duties which he had expressly engaged to perform. This inflamed the discontents of the diet, and they were wrought up to the highest pitch of agitation, by hearing of the death of Nicholas Zrinyi, while out boar-hunting, some said by

* Histoire des Revolutions de Hongrie, p. 78.

accident, but the majority attributed it to the machinations of the Austrians. Alarms now spread on every side. Rumour and excitement magnified every incident, however trifling, into importance. It was confidently stated and believed, that it was the intention of the government to remove, either by open or covert violence, every man who was bold and honest enough to offer any opposition to its tyranny and exactions. Peter Zrinyi, the brother of Nicholas, placed himself at the head of the malcontents, and by his energy and activity speedily placed all things in train, ready for action. He attached to his party, amongst others, count Frangipani, a young magnate of great talents and influence; Tattenbach, governor of Styria, and Nadasdi, president of the high court of justice, and he gained over the young count Rakotski, by bestowing upon him his beautiful and accomplished daughter, Helena, in marriage. They now began to assemble troops, and called upon the emperor once more to summon a diet, and fill up the office of palatine; but he not only again refused, but actually connived at the excesses of his troops, and encouraged the catholics in their persecution of the protestants. The chiefs of the national confederacy thereupon entered into relations with Apaffi, the prince of Transylvania, sought aid from the Porte, and in accordance with article III. of the year 1608, convoked a diet at Cassau for the performance of the duty which the sovereign had declined to fulfil. Previous to this, the Viennese court had been so irritated by the refusal of the diet of Presburg to comply with the requirements of the royal commissioners, that they pretended to regard it as an act of treason, and actually summoned the principal members to Vienna, there to undergo the confiscation of their goods, and receive the punishment due to their disobedience and rebellion. There was clearly no resource left but an appeal to arms, a step which was in such cases expressly authorized by a clause in the *Bulla Aurea*. They, therefore, consolidated their union. Rakotski assembled 2,000 of his retainers, and was joined by a large force of insurgents from various parts of the kingdom, and made an attack upon Tokay, but was repulsed by the garrison, and was prevented from occupying Mungacs, which contained his father's treasure, by the prudence or timidity of his mother, who ordered the artillery of the place to be turned against his troops.

By means of intercepted letters and spies at the Ottoman court, Leopold had obtained timely warning of what was in contemplation long before the actual outbreak of the insurrection, and took prompt measures for its suppression. Troops were sent against Rakotski in Upper Hungary, and against the others in Croatia and Styria. Tattenbach, Zrinyi, Frangipani, and Nadasdi, were secured by treachery, and in direct violation of law were dragged away to Vienna out of the jurisdiction of the national tribunals, and there imprisoned, and shortly afterwards executed. The sons of Zrinyi were sentenced to perpetual imprisonment, and, in the hope of rooting out the memory of the leaders and destroying the influence of their families for ever, their property was confiscated, their children were ordered to change their names, those of Nadasdi into that of Creutzberg, and those of Zrinyi to Gunde.

Rakotski was saved by the influence of his mother, and the more potent influence of his own wealth, which was lavishly poured into the Austrian coffers, and procured him liberty to lay down his arms and retire in peace. He did not, long survive his overthrow.

An amnesty was proclaimed on the 6th of June, 1671, excepting by name, however, a crowd of leaders, who had escaped into exile. The offices of palatine, supreme judge, and ban of Croatia, were formally abolished; the monarchy was declared hereditary in the house of Hapsburg; thirty thousand additional troops were quartered in the kingdom; the people were loaded with extraordinary taxes, besides being burdened with the maintenance of foreign soldiery. In another proclamation, published shortly after, the constitution was declared changed; the government was vested in a council nominated by the emperor, and John Gaspar Amprugen, a Hungarian, indeed, but a bigoted catholic, blindly devoted to Austria, and grand master of the order of Teutonic Knights, was appointed president and governor-general of the kingdom. Every effort was now made to extirpate the protestant religion. Courts were established for the punishment of heresy; the protestant churches were shut up, a general decree of proscription issued against the ministers, and such as were taken were cruelly tortured or sent to the galleys. Two hundred and fifty of these unfortunate men were sentenced to be stoned or burnt, but their sentence was commuted into hard labour and perpetual imprisonment. Their fortitude under these dreadful sufferings, their piety, and magnanimity filled all who saw them with pity, and the authorities, in order to remove them from the public gaze, sold them at fifty crowns each to work in the Neapolitan galleys. They were at length liberated by the intervention of the Dutch admiral, De Ruyter. The vengeance of the court was even extended to women. Secszi Maria, the widow of the late palatine Wesselenyi, in whom the hopes of the patriots had been centred, was not shielded by her bereavement. An army under the duke of Lorraine besieged her in her castle of Murany, and at last forced her to capitulate, upon the express condition that she should retain the keys and be left in peaceable possession of the place. No sooner had the besiegers entered than she was arrested, placed in close confinement, and soon after sent to Vienna, where she died in a dungeon.

(1672.) The oppression and cruelties of the Austrians at last became intolerable. Protestants and catholics forgot their differences, and united against an enemy to whom everything Hungarian seemed hateful. "Better die on the battle-field," was the cry on every side, "than linger in misery, and be slaughtered or starved in our own houses!" Disputes broke out very soon between Leopold and the prince of Transylvania, and a rising having taken place in Hungary, the insurgents were assisted by the former, as well as by the Turks and French, with supplies of arms and ammunition, and money. In several encounters with the imperial troops, they were partially successful, and took some towns and fortresses—amongst others, Eperies. Leopold then sent into Hungary a reinforcement of 10,000 men, under the command of General Kops, aided by

Esterhazy, a Hungarian noble. The malcontents were led on by Petroczi, Suchai, Szepezi, and many other magnates of high standing and influence, who had taken refuge in Transylvania; but their undisciplined forces were easily routed by the trained soldiers of Austria. This abortive attempt increased the miseries of those of the Hungarians who still remained in their unhappy country. The imperial troops wreaked their vengeance, which they were unable to pour out upon their armed opponents, upon the unfortunate peasants and gentlemen, who vainly sought safety in peaceful submission. Thousands who could no longer endure the brutal insolence of the soldiery, the desolation of their households, and the insults offered to their wives and daughters, fled to the mountains, or crossed

FORTRESS OF MURANY.

the Transylvanian frontier, and swelled the ranks of the insurgents. The situation of Leopold was now becoming perplexing in the extreme. He was engaged in an arduous contest with Louis XIV. of France, which left him neither time nor resources for carrying on the war in Hungary. He vainly offered terms to the insurgents, upon condition that they laid down their arms and returned home; but they had too much and bitter experience of his perfidy to trust themselves defenceless in his hands. By the aid of the new levies that were daily joining them, they were enabled to obtain several considerable advantages over the imperial forces. They were at last placed in a position of decided superiority by the arrival of an army of 6,000 Poles and 8,000 Magyars from Poland, under the command of a French general, the Count de Boham, and thus reinforced, they defeated the Austrians under General Schmidt, in two pitched battles. These successes were, however, after all, but temporary, and the malcontents would have been obliged once more to give ground (1677), had they not found in the youthful Emerik Tekeli a leader worthy of the cause and equal to the crisis.

His father had been associated in the former conspiracy with the unfortunate

EMERIK TEKELI.

Frangipani, Nadasdi, and Tattenbach, but, more fortunate than they, had died sword in hand, fighting in defence of his castle, leaving an avenger in the person of his son, who, at the early age of sixteen, found himself a fugitive in Poland, bereft of his property, which Leopold had confiscated, and left without friend, support, or counsellor. It was in vain that he demanded from the court of Vienna the restoration of his property: his remonstrances and entreaties were treated with contempt or indifference, or were met with threats and reproaches. Hatred to Austria now became the ruling passion of his life, and by its intensity seemed to develop all the powers of his mind into precocious activity.

His father's wrongs had left an indelible impression on his mind, but sorrow for his loss was now absorbed in the desire to avenge it in vindicating the liberty of his country. When he repaired to the court of Apaffi, the prince of Transylvania, though scarce eighteen, he had all the ardour and enthusiasm natural to his years, combined with the courage, firmness, foresight, and self-reliance which are usually found in conjunction with maturity alone, and which nothing but adversity can confer upon youth. He distinguished himself amongst the crowd of refugees who now filled Transylvania, by his wit, cheerful disposition, and undaunted valour. He soon gained the favour of the prince Apaffi; and after serving as a volunteer in the forces which the latter sent to the aid of the Hungarian insurgents, he found himself, before he had reached the age of twenty, placed in the chief command, by the unanimous consent of all, except Wesselenyi, the brother of the late palatine, who was jealous of his talents and affected to despise him for his youth. Upon assuming the leadership, he placed on the broad folds of his banner, worked in letters of gold, the proud and appropriate motto—"*Pro aris et focis,*" and crossed the frontier at the head of 20,000 men, mostly volunteers, to whom union and enthusiasm supplied the place of discipline.

Shortly after beginning his march he held a council of war, to take into consideration the plan of the campaign, and it was there resolved that after waiting for some reinforcements of the frontier guard, which were on their way to join them, they should cross the Teyss, and then act as circumstances might dictate. He then took the road into Upper Hungary, being joined by great numbers of volunteers on his way, and approached Mungacs for a purpose altogether foreign to the object of his expedition. Helena, the beautiful daughter of the unfortunate Count Zrinyi, had, as we have already said, been married to the young prince Rakotski, with the view of attaching him more firmly to the revolutionary party. She was now a widow, and in the bloom of her youth, and Tekeli had seen and loved her. A union with her became one of the secondary aims of an ambition which success and flattery was rendering stronger and more daring; and amidst all the care and anxiety with which his position surrounded him, she seldom ceased to occupy his thoughts. But the great obstacle in his way was Rakotski's mother, who, being a zealous Roman Catholic, was strongly opposed to the marriage of her daughter-in-law with a Lutheran, and was in command of the fortress of Mungacs, which contained the treasures of the family. Tekeli brought the army into the neighbourhood, in the hope of being able in some way to arrange an interview with the young princess; but her mother-in-law no sooner heard of his approach, than she sent all the force at her command to attack him: but, after an obstinate conflict, he came off victorious, with great slaughter, and amongst the prisoners he made upon that occasion was the brother of his inamorata.* His success was, however, so dearly bought, that he was compelled

* Histoire des Troubles de Hongrie, depuis 1656 jusqu'en 1687, vol iii., pp. 310-11.

to silence, for the present, the whisperings of the tender passion, and prosecute the campaign in another quarter. He soon extended his conquests towards the Danube, and pushed his predatory parties into Styria, Moravia, and even Austria herself, which were greatly aided by a certain Father Josa, an ecclesiastic, who had abandoned the altar for the field, and gathered round him a great number of country gentlemen whom the troubles of the times had deprived of all means of livelihood but pillage. With the view of making a diversion in Transylvania, an Austrian army, under the command of General Lesley, who divided his army into three battalions, and proudly boasted that the rebels would melt before him like snow before the sun. His presumption received a signal check. Each of the three corps was utterly routed, and the strength of the insurgents now became so formidable, that Leopold was fain to open negotiations with them, with the view of gaining time to recruit his diminished armies. He, therefore, offered Tekeli to restore his estates, to consent to his marriage with the princess Helena to grant toleration to the protestants, and an amnesty for all engaged in the insurrection. While these proposals were under consideration, Generals Wurm, Schmidt, and Dunewald, were rapidly collecting forces to strengthen the garrisons of the various important posts which were threatened by the Hungarians. Tekeli, finding himself deceived, abruptly broke off the negotiation, recommenced hostilities, and seized upon the towns and rich mines in the mountains. While here, they heard of the approach of the three Austrian generals at the head of 18,000 men, with the design of forcing the passage of the river of Altsohl, where it ran through a gorge among the hills. After a sharp conflict the imperialists proved successful, but Tekeli retired in good order. On receiving some reinforcements he again returned, and offered battle; but the Austrians once more renewed their proposals for a truce upon condition that they should retain the mountain towns, and the Hungarians those upon the Turkish frontier. Tekeli accepted them, and consented to a cessation of hostilities for three months.

This truce was extremely advantageous for the emperor, as it brought Tekeli into discredit with his own followers, who began to mourn loudly that he was sacrificing the public good to his private interests, and had concluded a dishonourable peace with the view of promoting his marriage with the princess Rakotski, and deserted in crowds to join the forces of Wesselenyi, his rival and detractor. This was exactly what the Austrians desired, and after a month of delay they declined to continue the truce any longer, unless they were put into possession of the Turkish frontier. Tekeli now saw that he was their dupe, and that, far from entertaining any real desire for peace, they wished merely to gain time and to sow division amongst their enemies. The war was once more renewed; and Tekeli, smarting with chagrin, displayed such energy and courage in carrying it on, that he completely regained the confidence of his adherents. But the plague was at this time raging both in Austria and Hungary, both armies were reduced and disheartened by its ravages, and the operations of the Hungarians were now, for the most part, confined to making mere forays into the enemy's territory. To add to their difficulties the intrigues of Wesselenyi divided their forces into two hostile factions, who wasted upon each other the strength and courage which should have been reserved for the enemy. Wesselenyi was at last overpowered, arrested, and sent prisoner to Clausemburg, and Tekeli once more, allured by the promise of the princess Helena, concluded a truce.

(1680.) This truce had no better object in view than either of the preceding. Leopold hoped to gain time to recruit his army and finances, and to strengthen and establish his absolute rule over Hungary. Tekeli began to open up negotiations with the Turks, and to keep up the spirits of his followers, assured them of the influence he possessed in Constantinople; and resuming hostilities, gained a considerable advantage over the imperial forces at Leutchau, in Upper Hungary, which induced Leopold at last to make propositions which seemed to strike at the root of the discontents. Delegates from both sides assembled at Presburg, and those of the Hungarians laid down the following demands as the basis of all negotiation. 1. The election of a palatine, with the full power and authority attached to his office by the laws. 2. The consequent dismissal of the grand master of the order of Teutonic Knights from the office of viceroy of the kingdom, with which the emperor had invested him, after he had declared himself absolute sovereign of Hungary. 3. The expulsion of all foreign troops from the kingdom, unless they were placed in subjection to the laws, and to the authority of the palatine. 4. The convocation of a general diet, in which the states should have complete liberty of speech. 5. The reinstatement of the protestants in all the rights and privileges of which they had been unjustly deprived, and the possession of which had been repeatedly guaranteed to them by the princes of the house of Austria in formal diplomas. For himself, Tekeli stipulated for nothing but the restoration of his property.

The Viennese cabinet was unwilling to accede to propositions like these, which would have undone the whole work of the previous five years, and left the emperor more powerless in Hungary than ever. It temporised, promised, retracted, intrigued, warned the catholics that if a diet were assembled, the whole of the church property would be thrown into the hands of the protestants, but steadily avoided coming to any conclusion. Tekeli was fast becoming disgusted, and renewed his negotiations with Turkey. The sultan promised to support him with all the power of the empire, in case he chose to break with Leopold. Rumours of an armament on a vast scale in Constantinople reached Vienna. A war seemed imminent. The emperor became alarmed, and at last agreed to summon a diet at Oedenburgh, in February, 1681. But the remedy came too late, too late for the pacification of the kingdom, too late for the consolidation of Leopold's power as a constitutional king, and above all, too late for the fair fame of Emerik Tekeli. Had this proposal been made half a year sooner, his name would have come down to us the most brilliant, most revered, and most unsullied of all those in the long list of patriot heroes. He was already too far gone in his negotiations with the Turks to recede without difficulty and danger.

Perhaps he feared to trust to Leopold's promises, and if he did, he had but too much reason; perhaps he feared the anger of the sultan, who would never have laid calmly aside his preparations for war without seeing the face of an enemy; and if he did, he had reason too. But, however it be, it is certain that he refused to be a party to the assembling of the diet, or to have any part in the negotiations, and covertly continued to solicit the intervention of the Ottomans. The consequences proved disastrous for Hungary; and none had more reason to regret them than Tekeli. Obloquy has ever since been heaped upon him by the partizans of Austria, as the ally of the deadliest enemy of the Christian name, and as the betrayer of Europe to the Turks, and the attacks of political malice have been but too warmly supported by the violence of religious bigotry. With our knowledge of the circumstances in which he was placed, we dare not judge him harshly. He was overwhelmed by one of those misfortunes which for six hundred years have clung to Hungary like a curse—the misfortune of being weak and divided in the midst of united and powerful neighbours, and of often finding, in times of difficulty, no better refuge from the rage of one, than the scarcely less dangerous friendship of another. The only ally powerful enough to protect Hungary against the power of Austria was Turkey, and the fact that Turkey was Mahometan has blasted Tekeli's reputation. It was his misfortune, no doubt, that such was the case, but was certainly not his fault that at Constantinople he found all the cardinal virtues of Christianity at least as well practised and exemplified as at Vienna.

When the diet assembled, Leopold conceded nearly every point in dispute. Paul Esterhazy was selected palatine, the new form of government was abolished, a general amnesty was published, the illegal imposts were removed, the frontier militia was re-established, liberty of conscience was granted to the protestants, the confiscated property was restored, the heirs and descendants of the nobles who had suffered for the former conspiracy were permitted to reassume their family names. The disputed points relative to the maintenance of the foreign troops, and the subjection of the nobles to their own tribunals, were to be settled in accordance with Leopold's oath at his coronation, and the constitutions of the kingdom. In short, every grievance which had arisen during recent troubles was provided for and redressed.

With all this, Tekeli, and a large party with him, distrusting Leopold's promises, or relying upon Turkish aid, refused to have anything to do, but, at the request of the diet, he consented to prolong the armistice which had been entered upon, for six months.

Leopold took advantage of this interval to send an embassy to Constantinople to solicit a renewal of the truce of 1664, which was now on the point of expiring. But he was foiled by Louis XIV., who everywhere proved his most powerful enemy. By his influence the emperor's requests were refused by the divan, unless upon condition that he paid an annual tribute, demolished the fortifications of Gratz and Leopoldstadt, yielded Neutra, Eschkof, the Isle of Schutz, and the fortresses of Murany to Tekeli, and restored to the Hungarian nation all its ancient rights and privileges. To such proposals as these there was of course no reply but the one—war.

As soon as Tekeli heard of the result of the negotiations, he married the princes Helena, who had been freed from restraint by the death of her mother-in-law, and thus obtained possession of the fortress of Mungacs, and then made every preparation for the approaching campaign. His alliance with the Turks rendered his name odious throughout Europe, and alienated him from a great body of his own countrymen. He was accused of being animated by insatiable ambition, which made him ready to sacrifice everything to what he believed to be his own interests, and he was held responsible for all the evils resulting from the tremendous struggle now impending. He declared, in his defence, that the promises of Leopold had been so often and so shamefully violated, that he dared not then trust to them; that in the course he was taking he saw the only road to safety, and that without an alliance with Turkey, neither Hungary nor any other power in Europe could offer a successful resistance to the aggressions of Austria. As soon as the truce expired, he once more took the field, and being joined by the forces of Apaffi, the prince of Transylvania, entered Buda in triumph, where he was inaugurated prince of Upper Hungary by the bashaw (1682), who gave him the investiture in the oriental manner, with sabre, vest and standard. He was soon after joined by numbers of protestants, who were irritated by the attempts of the emperor to evade the fulfilment of his promises regarding the restoration of their rights; and being assisted by the bashaws of Buda and Varadin, he sent a predatory corps into Moravia, and attacked and captured Zathmar, took the castle of Cassau by escalade, and the town also. Eperies fell in like manner, and all the towns occupied by German garrisons. The diet, however, and the great body of the nation, took part with the emperor. The German troops, under the pressing necessity of the case, were suffered to remain in the kingdom, upon condition that they were kept in strict discipline and were withdrawn at the close of the war. Such of the national forces as still survived the carnage and troubles since 1664 were embodied for the defence of the kingdom, the hussars and heyducs were under the command of Esterhazy, the palatine, in Upper Hungary. Bathyanyi, Palfi, Kohari, and other Hungarian nobles, raised their vassals and fought stoutly against the Turks in Lower Hungary and on the frontier of Croatia, though the German garrisons in most instances surrendered their posts after a slight resistance.

During the year 1682, however, no open rupture between the Turks and the emperor took place. The former merely served as auxiliaries in the army of Tekeli, and by their skill and experience gave him a manifest superiority over the Austrian generals, whose operations were, however, completely paralyzed by the weakness and vacillation of the Viennese cabinet. Leopold made several attempts to treat with Tekeli, in the hope of bringing down on him the suspicion and distrust of the Turks, but without success. He then began to occupy himself more usefully in calling the attention of the other nations of Europe to the danger which threatened Christendom, and imploring their aid against the common enemy. He was strenuously supported by the pope, for more reasons than one. The papal nuncio travelled into Poland, and prayed for succour in an agony of entreaty; all the weapons of the spiritual armoury at the Vatican were flourished before the faces of the catholic potentates, to persuade them to unite against the infidels. The Austrian ambassadors at the various German courts employed all the arts of policy and intrigue to rouse the religious ardour of the princes. There were glory and plunder for the ambitious and warlike, everlasting salvation for the devout and superstitious, and threats and vengeance for the laggard or indifferent. All this was not without its effect. The electors of Bavaria and Saxony promised the greater part of their forces, and several other members of the empire followed their example. Leopold began to recover from his fears and take heart again. Negotiations with Tekeli were no longer spoken of, and his name was now never mentioned but as that of an insolent rebel, who would soon lie at the mercy of the emperor.

In the meanwhile the most stupendous preparations were being made in Turkey. All Asia seemed to be preparing to overrun Europe. Towards the close of 1682, the sultan repaired in person to Adrianople, and raised the horse-tail standard, and 300,000 of the true believers were soon gathered around it, panting to be led against the christians. A treaty was entered into with Tekeli, by which it was stipulated that he should be elected prince of Hungary; that the sultan should restore to the Hungarians all their ancient liberties, defend them with all his power, make no treaty to their detriment, put them in possession of all their towns and fortresses, establish free trade between the two countries, receive their ministers as those of crowned heads, and never exact a greater tribute than 40,000 gold ducats annually. In the commencement of the year 1683 Tekeli convoked a diet at Cassau, at which the envoys of the emperor were present, and some futile attempts were once more made to bring about a reconciliation, and the assembly broke up without coming to any conclusion. The Ottoman army, under the command of the grand vizier, Kara Mustapha, shortly after commenced its march towards Belgrade, and Tekeli issued a proclamation calling upon the Hungarians to repair to his standard, promising them the protection of the sultan and security for their lives and property, and threatening with fire and sword all who neglected or refused to obey.

He joined his forces with those of the Turks at Esseck, and advanced rapidly towards Austria. The German troops terrified by his proclamation and unprepared for a defence against so formidable an enemy, hastily abandoned their posts at his approach. Papa, Vesprim, and various other towns, surrendered without resistance. To all who submitted to his authority Tekeli gave letters of protection, to protect them from the violence of the invading army; and many of the nobles, whom the long and apparently interminable broils had rendered indifferent to the claims of party or the fate of their country, availed themselves of those safeguards to remain quietly upon their estates. Others joined the insurgent chief and stood by him to the last; but a great number, and particularly the Roman catholic prelates, followed the Germans in their retreat. The more timid, who wished to abide the issue in safety without committing themselves to the cause of either party, took refuge in castles of their friends in remote districts, or left the country altogether.*

Leopold had in the meantime stipulated for succours from John Sobieski, king of Poland, whose very name already made the Turks tremble, and had employed the palatine Esterhazy to raise in Hungary the army of insurrection; but such was

CHARLES OF LORRAINE.

the apathy of the imperial court, the tardiness of the German succours, and the desertion of the soldiers, that when the emperor reviewed the troops in person at Presburg, on the 7th of May, he had but 40,000 in all, the command of which he committed to Charles, Duke of Lorraine. On the 11th, Leopold returned to Vienna, and Lorraine opened the campaign by laying siege to Neuheisel, but was compelled to abandon it by the approach of the whole Turkish army, and fearing they might cut off his retreat, retired forthwith to Vienna, laying waste the country on the line of his march, having thrown some of his cavalry into Raab and Comorn.

* Histoire des Revolutions de Hongrie.

THE SIEGE OF VIENNA BY THE TURKS.

He found the city in a terrible state of confusion and dismay. On the 7th of July the emperor, empress, archdukes and archduchesses of the imperial family, with many of the nobles, had fled precipitately to Lintz, and the news of their departure filled the citizens with consternation. Thousands packed up their goods in carts, carriages, and waggons, and poured forth into the open country, going they knew not whither; many broke down, and others, losing their way, wandered about the roads till captured by the advanced guard of the Turks. Wailing and lamentation filled the streets and houses. The doors of most of the mansions of the dastardly courtiers and nobility lay wide open, the furniture scattered about in confusion, their jewels even having, in many instances, been abandoned in their terror. On the 12th and 18th the suburbs were burned, and on the 15th the huge army of the vizier encamped about the city, and commenced the siege. The churches were filled with weeping suppliants for the mercy and protection of heaven; in the streets the citizens were pouring out maledictions upon the emperor and the Jesuits. The fortifications were dilapidated, and the garrison small and inefficient. The only hope lay in the Poles and the duke of Lorraine. The latter did everything that skill and valour could suggest. He threw a reinforcement of 8,000 men into the city, and then retiring beyond the Danube with his cavalry, harassed the vizier, and marching rapidly to Presburg, there defeated Tekeli, who had been detached to secure the passage over the river at that point. But in the meantime the Turkish artillery had effected a breach in the dilapidated walls of the city; they were already in possession of the outworks, and the unfortunate citizens were in hourly expectation of an assault, with its attendant horrors. The German succours had not arrived, and the Polish army was only beginning to assemble on the frontiers of Silesia. The duke of Lorraine was sending message after message to hasten their march; the emperor was in a state of despair in his retreat at Passau, and implored Sobieski to make no delay. "My troops," said he, "are now assembling; the bridge over the Danube is already constructed at Tuln, to afford you a passage. Place yourself at their head; however inferior in number, your name alone, so terrible to the enemy, will ensure a victory!"* Sobieski was touched by his entreaties, and immediately started at the head of 3,000 cavalry, leaving the rest of his army, numbering 30,000, to follow; and traversing Silesia and Moravia with the rapidity of a Tartar horde, arrived at Tuln, but found the bridge unfinished and no troops assembled, save those of the duke of Lorraine. He was stung with chagrin; but, on the solicitations of Lorraine, consented to await there the arrival of the main body of his forces. They reached the Danube on the 5th of September, and in two days after they were joined by the German succours. The united armies, consisting of Poles, Saxons, Bavarians, and Austrians, amounted to 70,000 men, and by unanimous consent the chief command was conferred upon John Sobieski;—the duke of Lorraine, who had been his rival as a candidate for the throne of

* Coxe's History of the House of Austria.

Poland, setting a noble example of magnanimous disinterestedness by zealous obedience to his orders. The night of the 11th had been a night of terrible anxiety in Vienna. The garrison was exhausted, the breach was practicable, and it was feared the Turks would advance to storm it on the morrow. To their relief and delight, at the dawn of day the Polish hussars were discerned by the aid of telescopes on the heights of Kalemburg. On the same morning the Christians began their attack, and though throughout the day they had the advantage, the vast masses of the Turkish army remained unbroken. Towards nightfall the Polish king had fought his way to the entrenched camp of the vizier, and perceived him in his tent, sipping coffee with his sons, in a state of tranquil indifference. Provoked at this display of nonchalance, he rode forward, surrounded by a chosen band of followers, shouting out the warcry of "God for Poland!" and repeating, at intervals, the well-known verse, "Non nobis, non nobis, Domine exercituum, sed nomini tuo, da gloriam!" The lancers, as they charged, responded by loud cries of "Sobieski! Sobieski!" No sooner had this dreaded name caught the ears of the Ottomans than they were seized with consternation. "Allah!" exclaimed the Tartar khan, "the king is with them, sure enough!" Still they made a stout defence, but the Poles committed terrible havoc in their ranks; and six pashas having fallen, the vizier and his forces fled precipitately, leaving his camp and baggage, which contained immense riches, in the hands of the victors.

On the following morning, Sobieski entered Vienna, amidst the acclamations of the inhabitants, who hailed him with the titles of Father and Deliverer, and struggled to kiss his feet, or touch his garment or his horse. So great was the crowd of his almost adoring admirers, that it was with difficulty he made his way to the church of St. Stephen, where he offered thanks to God on bended knees for the success which had attended his arms. After dining in public, he returned amidst the same rejoicings to his camp, declaring that that was the happiest day of his life.

When Leopold returned to his capital, the clamours and execrations of the populace met him on every side. All the humiliating circumstances attendant on his flight, and which in the terror of the moment had been forgotten, now rose up vividly before him—his precipitancy, his cowardice, his traitorous desertion of his subjects. His enemies were now scattered, but he owed his delivery to the valour of a foreign king; and as he rode along the streets of Vienna, he could hear the booming of the cannon which proclaimed to the world Sobieski's triumph and his own disgrace. His manner of meeting the Polish monarch added to his humiliation. "How should I receive him?" he inquired of the duke of Lorraine. "With open arms," was the magnanimous reply, "for he has saved Christendom!" Instead of this, however, his greeting was stiff and formal to the verge of insult: a few words of thanks were hastily muttered, and Sobieski withdrew in disgust.

In five days after, the allied armies set out in pursuit of the enemy, and overtaking them, again defeated them, and captured Gran, which had been in possession of the Ottomans for seventy years, as well as Visegrad, Eperies, the Five Churches, Szeguedin, and other important fortresses. All the towns which had submitted to the Turks in the first panic of the invasion now surrendered, and again acknowledged Leopold. The sultan, enraged at the reverses of his army, recalled Kara Mustapha, and invested Solyman Pasha with the chief command. The latter instantly marched to the relief of Buda, to which the imperialists were now laying close siege, but was repulsed, and had the mortification of witnessing the surrender of the place, after it had been in possession of the Turks for a century and a half. The latter, after suffering a signal defeat on the plain of

SOLYMAN PASHA.

Mohacs, now precipitately retreated to Belgrade, and abandoned Hungary. Throughout the whole of the campaign, a crowd of Magyar nobles, amongst whom were Esterhazy, Batthyanyi, Nadasdi, Palfi, and others, had displayed the most indomitable valour, and had in no small degree contributed to the successes which attended the Christian arms. Instead, however, of feeling grateful for devotion, which was certainly inspired by no hope of imperial favour or reward, but simply by the hatred of Turkish domination, Leopold and his ministers repaid them by cruelty and ingratitude. "They forgot," says the historian Fessler, "that it was the Austrian generals who had lost the most important posts; that it was the blunders and oppressions of the Viennese court which had caused the Hungarians to throw themselves into the arms of the Turks, their ancient and implacable enemies; and that the Magyars, after having borne the whole weight and evils of these continual wars, were now at last compelled to purchase the victory by the sacrifice of their property and even of their lives."*

The Christian army soon after separated, and the German auxiliaries returned home. Sobieski was irritated by the jealousy of the emperor, who was offended at his attempts to bring about a reconciliation between him and the malcontents, and suspected him of intriguing with Tekeli to obtain the crown of Hungary for his son. He therefore withdrew his troops and returned to Poland, and declared

ARREST OF TEKELI.

that he would fight against the Turks, but not against the Hungarians. The imperial forces which remained, however, were amply sufficient to prosecute the war with success; and many of Tekeli's followers, despairing of his cause, and seduced by the emperor's promises of pardon, abandoned him and laid down their arms. Intrigues against the insurgent chief were set on foot at Constantinople and upon his failing to relieve Cassau, he was arrested by order of the sultan, and sent in chains to the capital. The chief who succeeded him surrendered to the imperialists; the fall of Cassau placed the greater part of northern Hungary in

* History of Hungary, vol. ix. p. 405.

the power of the emperor. Tekeli found means to justify his conduct before the sultan; proved to him that the charges made against him had been the result of German intrigues; and his accusers having been strangled, he was restored to his command, and indemnified for his injuries and losses. But it was impossible to restore courage to his party, who had been disheartened by his arrest, or to make amends for the loss of Cassau. Still he might once more have made head against his enemies, and restored the prestige of his former successes, had he not been abandoned by the prince of Transylvania. His dominions were fertile, well peopled, and abounded in provisions of every sort, and would prove an invaluable storehouse to whichever of the contending parties gained him over to its side. This was accomplished by exertions of the Austrian ministers, and a treaty was concluded at Vienna between Apaffi and the emperor, in which the former agreed to receive German troops into his territory, to supply them with forage and provisions, to cede to the Austrians the two important fortresses of Clausemburg and Deva, and to maintain an offensive alliance against the Turks. Leopold, on his side, acknowledged the claims of Apaffi and his son to the throne of the principality, and promised, after their death, to abstain from all interference with the free choice of the diet in electing a successor. Both the Hungarians and Transylvanians afterwards complained of the infraction, on the part of the emperor, of nearly all the articles of this treaty; but for the present it had the effect of completely ruining Tekeli. His partisans deserted him in crowds, and finding his cause completely lost, and being hourly exposed to the persecution of the Turkish pashas, he retired to Nicomedia, in Asia Minor, there to lament in silence the calamities which had fallen on his country. In a distant corner of Hungary, his wife Helena, the widow of Francis Rakotski and the daughter of Peter Zrinyi, was the first to check the victorious march of the imperial forces. In 1686, she remained in command of the fortress of Mungacs, with her two children (by her former marriage), and bid defiance to the Austrian army. It was in vain that they informed her of the defeat and captivity of her husband; she treated their threats and promises with equal indifference, and made such a vigorous defence, that after a siege of five months, General Caprara was forced to content himself with the possession of the town, and leave the fortress in the hands of its intrepid mistress.*

Hungary now lay vanquished once more at the feet of Leopold, and he prepared to carry out without hindrance his long-cherished project of incorporating it with his hereditary dominions. The circumstances were more favourable than ever they had been before, but he and his ministers were still fully aware that it was no easy task to destroy the constitution in opposition to the wishes of a people so devotedly attached to their liberties as the Hungarians. Experience had taught him that his sudden assertion of "absolute power, acquired by the laws of war," in 1671 had been a false step, as the result had proved. To declare that

* The story of Tekeli's courtship with this lady is quaintly told in a curious little book, entitled "The Amours of Count Tekeli." London, 1686.

Hungary and Transylvania were two provinces dependent upon the Austrian crown, was not simply to state a falsehood (for that was a small matter), but to contradict treaties and capitulations which both Leopold and his predecessors had signed and sworn to observe, and the existence of which was known to all the world. To assert a right of conquest was absurdity, for he could not bear arms against his own dominions, nor could the suppression of a rebellion release him from his solemn obligations. These arguments suggested themselves in 1671 to every man in Hungary, and with such powerful effect that the outburst of the rage and discontent had involved the kingdom in a bloody war, and placed Leopold's own capital in danger. It would now have been a flagrant outrage upon the public opinion of Europe to overthrow the Hungarian constitution by the aid of hired armies collected avowedly for the expulsion of the Turks. A *coup d'état* was manifestly impolitic, if not impracticable. He therefore resolved to cloak his designs under a show of legality, to break the spirits of the people by cruelty and oppression, and terrify them into the surrender of their liberties. All that was wanted was a plot, an engine of oppression which ever despot finds ready at hand.

Even those of the Hungarians who had formally submitted to Leopold were disaffected, for they found their lot no better than when they had been in arms against him. The German troops treated the country as a conquered territory, and the imperial officers ruled with all the rigour of martial law. All security for life and property and liberty was at an end. Whether those severities had the desired effect of driving the people into another conspiracy for the overthrow of Austrian domination, or not, will in all probability never be satisfactorily decided. The Austrian accounts of the transaction distantly allude to the cruelties of the military, paint the conspiracy in glowing colours as a daring attempt to deprive the illustrious house of Hapsburg of its just rights, and find the origin of it in the inherent turbulence of the malcontents, and their impatience under any rule, however lawful or impartial. The Hungarians deny the existence of the conspiracy, and point to the subsequent acts of the imperialists as the best possible proof of the truth of their assertion, alleging that those whose ends are infamous are seldom choice in the selection of means ; that those who wade to power through the blood of the innocent will not hesitate to justify their crimes by slandering their victims. In the early part of the year 1687, Tekeli was said to be still in the neighbourhood of Mungacs, the fortress in possession of his wife—deserted by his followers and with little to sustain him but hope. About this time, also, it was said that his sister, the Countess Nadasdi, whose husband had died during the siege of the place, left the castle with an imperial passport, and repaired to Cassau, where she used every effort to induce the inhabitants once more to take up arms and repair to the standard of their old leader, and that she visited various parts of Upper Hungary upon a similar errand. A rumour to this effect having got abroad, the commander of the garrison at Cassau caused two women, the wives of soldiers, to be arrested, upon pretence that they were emissaries in the

THE PRINCESS HELENA RAKOTSKI.

employment of the disaffected. Upon their information it was suddenly discovered that all the principal persons, not only in Cassau and Eperies, but in Altsohl, Neusohl, Leutsch, Oedenburg, and Presburg were in correspondence with Tekeli and his wife, and were engaged in a conspiracy for the overthrow of the emperor's authority. Thousands were accordingly arrested and thrust into prison. A tribunal was established at Eperies for the trial and punishment of the accused, composed of Count Caraffa, a foreign general of sanguinary disposition, as president, assisted by officers as ignorant and brutal as himself, and a few renegade natives. Troops of dragoons were sent out into every part of the country to arrest and bring in all those whose property or rank rendered their condemnation desir-

THEATRE OF EPERIES.

able. Upon the evidence of the two female informers, they were put to the torture to wring from them confessions of guilt. After a short examination, conducted in secret, those who refused to condemn themselves were either distended upon ladders until every joint in their bodies was dislocated, or were burnt on the side and back with red hot iron, or had iron bands placed round their foreheads and compressed by a screw till their eyeballs started from the sockets. Atrocities such as these were of daily occurrence both at Debreczin and Cassau, but it was at Eperies that the persecutions displayed the full extent of their ferocity. It was in the latter that Caraffa established his head-quarters. Though he at first declared that it was amongst the protestants that the conspiracy had originated, it soon became apparent that the hatred of the Austrians was not directed against any creed or party, but against all who bore the name of Hungarians. Four noblemen of great wealth and influence, two of whom were catholics, resident in Eperies, were selected as the first victims of his vengeance. Partly upon the evidence of the two women and partly from confessions wrung from them in the midst of excruciating torments, they were condemned to have all their property confiscated, to have their fingers cut off, to be then beheaded, their bodies divided into quarters and flung on the high road, and their heads placed on stakes on a gibbet. To facilitate the work of destruction, a permanent scaffold was erected in the centre of the town, which has ever since been known in Hungarian history as the "Bloody Theatre of Eperies." Thirty executioners dressed in green uniform were employed night and day in torturing, mutilating, and decapitating. Crowds of the gentry were daily brought in from all parts of the country by the soldiers, catholics as well as protestants, arrested wherever found, without warrant and without inquiry—some in the churches, some in the streets, some in the fields, some in the bosom of their families, and some when out hunting, unconscious of danger. Not one was taken with arms in his hands; upon none were found any proofs of participation in a conspiracy. Those who had taken no part whatever in the recent war met with no greater mercy than those who had. It was enough that they were wealthy, powerful, influential, of high descent. It was in vain that they asserted their innocence or produced the letters of amnesty which had been granted them upon laying down their arms and making their submission. They were charged with having corresponded with Tekeli and his wife. They asked for proofs—for the production of the letters, or copies of them, they were answered with insults. If they refused to acknowledge themselves guilty of all that was alleged against them they were put to the torture, and every incoherent remark or explanation that escaped them in their agony was noted down as proof, and upon it they were condemned and executed. Those whom greater strength of nerve, or powers of physical endurance, or consciousness of innocence supported through the terrible ordeal, and sealed their lips, were too happy if they escaped with the loss of their property and were liberated from their dungeons, and thrown upon the world mutilated and beggared. Sisters, wives, and friends often cast themselves at Caraffa's feet, and implored for their relatives a fair trial in open court, according to the laws of the country. He invariably referred them to Vienna, but never delayed the proceedings. The application was made, and after an agonizing interval of suspense, the answer came, perhaps it was favourable, but it was always too late, for when it reached Eperies the accused were no more.*

Caraffa's tribunal continued to sit from the month of March until the close of the year, and during that period there were but few families of distinction in the kingdom who did not witness the loss of their property or one or other of their

* For full details regarding this horrible tragedy, see "The Life of Leopold," by Posterla, one of his panegyrists, and the "Histoire des Revolutions de Hongrie." No nation in

members. Happy were they who, by enormous bribes, early offered and judiciously distributed, saved their households from the ravages of the destroyer. But it was only in poverty and obscurity that there was safety. No sort of influence, however great, was sufficient to save those whom fortune had raised above the rank of the peasantry, from the daily and nightly fear of arrest and condemnation. "If," says the biographer and eulogist of Leopold; "the Hungarians repented of having submitted to the emperor so soon, and recommenced their old practices, it must be confessed, either that the yoke imposed upon them was extraordinarily harsh, since they preferred embracing the cause of a desperate party, to remaining for ever in subjection,—or they were extraordinarily fickle, since they so quickly became desirous of a change."

As soon as all the leading men in the kingdom were dead or intimidated, the country prostrate at the feet of the soldiery, and Turkey rendered incapable of interference by the outbreak of disturbances at Constantinople, the Austrian ministers, prompted by the Jesuits, strongly advised Leopold to take advantage of his successes, establish arbitrary government, and abolish the protestant worship. Either from fear or prudence, however, for he had already shown himself regardless of the claims of justice, he contented himself with seeking to obtain from the diet an acknowledgment of the hereditary rights of his family to the crown. As a preliminary step, he summoned to Vienna a few of the principal nobles who had escaped the persecutions of Caraffa, and restored to them the crown of St. Stephen, which, contrary to law, had been carried from Presburg, and then convoked a diet in the latter town, to place it upon the head of his son Joseph, as "the only means of restoring his ancient kingdom to its pristine splendour and felicity." The diet accordingly assembled, though with little hope of freedom of discussion, for the troops of the emperor occupied every post in Hungary and Transylvania, and the Theatre of Eperies was still standing, to which one unguarded word might any moment have consigned the proudest of them all.

When the members found themselves once more assembled, however, courage, so much of which is traditional and well nigh ineradicable amongst a people unused to slavery, returned, and when the emperor submitted demands, they ventured to remonstrate. They declared that, though quite willing to elect and crown the archduke Joseph, they could never abandon their ancient right to choose their own sovereign, nor acknowledge any hereditary claims to the throne, by whomsoever preferred; and they required him, so soon as peace with Turkey should be concluded, to withdraw the German troops from the country, and examine and redress all their grievances before the coronation.

Singularly enough, Leopold replied by conciliation. Dignities and honours were distributed amongst the magnates; the protestants were promised liberation, if they gave in their adherence to the emperor. Upon the more obstinate or more

Europe expressed greater horror at the erection of the permanent guillotine in Paris during the revolution than Austria. The recollection of her own atrocities in Hungary a century previously should have moderated her wrath.

inflexible, less legitimate influence was brought to bear. Count Drascovics, the judex curiæ of the kingdom, distinguished himself by his opposition to the court party, and his staunch adherence to the ancient constitution. One of the ministers of the emperor paid him a visit at his own house, and found him at dinner with a number of his friends. He took him aside, assured him that his majesty was clement and merciful, and wished well to the Hungarian nobility, but to merit his favour they should avoid his displeasure; and he warned Drascovics, in particular, to provide for the safety of himself and his family by an entire acquiescence in the orders of his master. The count replied, that when these orders were contrary to law, he must needs obey the law. The minister then handed him a paper, and notwithstanding the pressing solicitations of Dracovics, refused to join the party at dinner. The latter then withdrew into another room, to peruse the document which had been left in his hands, but had hardly finished reading it, when he dropped down dead.

This event created a great sensation in Presburg, and the impression it produced amongst the Hungarians was anything but favourable to the court. The more moderate ascribed it to natural causes; the more violent felt certain it was the work of the Jesuits, to whom they imputed the deepest skill in the stealthy and mysterious removal of their enemies; while the partisans of Austria, on the other hand, pointed to it in triumph as a manifest mark of God's disapprobation of those who set themselves in opposition to their sovereign. As soon as the agitation caused by it had subsided, the diet sent a deputation to the emperor, headed by Paul Szechenyi, archbishop of Kolocza, offering to make the crown hereditary in the male line in his family, but steadfastly refusing to admit the female line to any share in the succession; and stipulating, that whenever the former should become extinct, the right of election should again revert to the diet, and that in the meantime they should continue in the enjoyment of all their ancient rights and privileges. To all this the emperor consented, but refused to sanction the thirty-first article of the decree of Andrew II., which gave the nobles the right of offering armed resistance to the king, in case he infringed upon any of the other articles of the charter, without being liable to a charge of high treason. The diet allowed the reservation, in order to avoid coming to an open rupture, and nothing now remained but to proceed with the coronation of the archduke. Just as the archbishop was about to administer to him the customary oath to observe all the established laws and customs of the kingdom, a sealed paper was put into his hands, which, on being opened, was found to contain a new formula* forwarded from the court, differing from the ancient one in that it made the observance of the rights, liberties, privileges, and customs of the kingdom

* The words marked in italics are those inserted in the new formula. Nos, &c. juramus, &c. quod nos ecclesias Dei, dominos prelatos, barones, &c. in suis immunitatibus et libertatibus, juribus, privilegiis, et antiquis bonis et approbatis consuetudinibus, *prout super eorum intellectu et usu, regio ac communi statuum consensu dictaliter conventum fuerit*, conservabimus, omnibusque justitiam faciemus, &c.

dependent upon the sense in which the states and the king should agree to receive them.

As the king was bound to convoke the diet at least at no greater intervals than three years, but in reality did convene it only when he pleased, it will be perceived that the insertion of this clause enabled him to put his own interpretation upon the laws.

The coronation, however, took place, with all the usual solemnities, on the 9th of December, 1687, with great pomp and magnificence, and with a minute observance of all the ancient forms and ceremonies. The tribunal at Eperies was suppressed, a general amnesty was granted for all past offences, and it was arranged that the pay and quartering of the troops, both Hungarian and foreign, should be settled by Hungarian and German commissioners, and that a chamber of finance, composed of both nations, should be established at Buda. This year, 1689, saw Leopold everywhere triumphant. Tekeli's wife had surrendered the strong fortress of Mungacs, and thrown herself and her two sons upon the emperor's protection. Her husband's party was totally subdued. Hungary was pacified, Transylvania had entered into an alliance, Joseph had been crowned king upon more favourable conditions than he had ventured to expect, even the natives of Wallachia offered their submission, and of all the possessions which the Ottomans had once held to the north of the Danube Great Varadin and Temesvar now alone remained. Tekeli had retired beyond the Teyss, and remained for a long time in the neighbourhood of Gyula, unable to make any effort to retrieve his misfortunes. He protested vainly, but not without show of justice, against the concessions of the diet at Presburg, as contrary to the spirit of the constitution, and as obtained by the influences of coercion, an armed force being present in the place of their deliberations, and the scaffold standing at Eperies. In this protest he was joined by a considerable number of nobles who had gone with him into exile, and though Austria affected to treat it with contempt, there can be no doubt it was not without its effect upon the minds of the natives.

The Turkish empire was at this period shaken to its very foundation. The ill success of the first campaign, and the defeat before Vienna, caused the deposition of the khan of Tartary, the execution of four bashaws, and even of the grand vizier himself, Kara Mustapha. The battle of Mohacs led to the resignation of another vizier, and the discontents which these misfortunes occasioned at Constantinople, caused another revolution. Mahomet IV. was deposed, and his brother Solyman placed on the throne; the pride of Turkey was completely humbled, and the new sultan attested his weakness by the earnestness with which he sued for peace.

Leopold was, however, too much elated by success to lend a very favourable ear to his proposals, and imprudently demanded such concessions as would have involved the abandonment by the Ottomans of all their dominions in Europe. The sultan indignantly refused, and Louis XIV. encouraged him by promises of support, which he fulfilled by making an irruption into the empire. Thus seconded, the Turks began to take heart, and under the leadership of the new vizier, another Kiupriuli, once more restored the glory of their arms. He relieved Temesvar and Great Varadin, which were blockaded by the imperial troops, and after having retaken Nissa and Widdin, laid siege to Belgrade, which had been captured the preceding year by the elector of Bavaria. The fortress only held out six days, owing to the negligence of the imperialists, who had never repaired the breach by which they themselves had entered. Tekeli, on the other hand, burst into Transylvania with a Turkish army, defeated the Austrian general Heisler, and made him prisoner. Michael Apaffi had died a short time previously, and his son of the same name, a youth of fourteen, had succeeded him in the principality. The latter was now driven out, and being joined by some of the counties, Tekeli declared himself prince of Transylvania, and sustained his claims with vigour. He defeated the combined Austrian and Transylvanian forces, and killed the prince of Hanover, who was in command of them. His fortunes were once more in the ascendant, but he owed his successes less to his own skill, than to the folly and weakness of Austria. The latter was compelled to divide her forces by sending a large army into the empire to support the claims of the archduke Joseph to the imperial crown, and she had treated the inhabitants of the newly-acquired provinces of Servia and Wallachia with such cruelty and oppression that they were ready to rise up against her upon the first signal from the insurgents, finding the yoke of the Turks no worse than hers.

The preparations for following up these successes in 1691, owing to the troubles in Constantinople, were conducted without much vigour or activity. Tekeli had, at first, been promised an army of 50,000 men to put him in a position to accomplish the total reduction of Transylvania; but finding himself deceived, and being unable to maintain his ground against the Margrave of Baden, who left the Danubian provinces to their fate, and forced the passes of Transylvania, he was driven back into Moldavia, and Apaffi reinstated upon the throne of the principality. He then joined his forces with those of the grand vizier at Semlin, and in 1691 they both entered Hungary at the head of 100,000 men. Their progress was stayed, and their hopes for the moment blasted, by the battle of Sulankémen. The Margrave of Baden, who commanded the imperial forces, found himself outmanœuvred by Tekeli, who cut him off from his supplies by rendering himself master of the Danube, so that his only hope lay in an action, notwithstanding the vast numerical superiority of the enemy. His right wing was at first obliged to give ground with great loss, and he was beginning to despair of the day, when General Dunewald assailed a weak point in the Turkish entrenchments at the head of the German and Hungarian cavalry, and with such effect, that the Turks were thrown into complete disorder. Their confusion became a rout, when the sudden lowering of the standard of the prophet informed them that the vizier himself had fallen. 20,000 of the Turks were left upon the field, but the lateness of the season and the heavy losses by which the imperialists themselves had purchased their victory, prevented them following up their success.

Tekeli's services did not protect him from shafts of envy and malice at the Turkish court, and no small portion of his time was taken up in endeavouring to counteract the intrigues which were set on foot for his ruin. Care and anxiety were fast making inroads upon his health; but in the ensuing year (1692) his position was rendered more comfortable by the restoration of his wife, who, ever since her surrender of Mungacs, had been shut up a prisoner in the Ursuline convent at Vienna. The pressure which was made upon the emperor's resources by the successes of the French, made him now more inclined to listen to offers of accommodation, and as a preliminary step, the Countess Tekeli was exchanged for General Heisler, and joined her husband at Constantinople in January of this year.

The margrave of Baden soon after quitted Hungary to succeed the duke of Lorraine in the command of the German army, leaving Generals La Croix and Caprara to carry on the war; but nothing of any great importance took place during the campaign which followed his departure, though the emperor had received large reinforcements from the electors of Brandenburg and Hanover, the bishop of Munster, and particularly from the Irish soldiers who took refuge on the continent after the surrender of Limerick. The sultan was embarassed by disturbances at home, and was unable to give his serious attention to affairs in Hungary. Tekeli was daily soliciting a force sufficiently large to enable him to penetrate into Transylvania, where he had a powerful party of adherents; but he soon found that the divan was intent upon the proposals made on behalf of the emperor by the ministers of England and Holland, and that they were quite ready to sacrifice him, if by so doing they could advance their own interests. Instead, therefore, of profiting by the inactivity of the imperial army, the vizier quietly suffered them to take possession of the Five Churches, Great Varadin, and Gyula. The campaign of 1694 produced results of no greater importance. The continued changes and contentions which were taking place amongst the Ottoman ministers had reduced the Turkish empire to such a state of weakness, that had it not been for the war which Louis XIV. was carrying on against the empire in Germany and Flanders, there can be little doubt that the Porte would have been reduced to the necessity of soliciting peace upon any condition its enemies chose to offer. In the month of August a feeble attempt was made by the grand vizier at the head of an army of 50,000 men to blockade the imperialists near Petervaradin; but the approach of winter and the want of provisions compelled him to relinquish his design, and on his return to Constantinople he was strangled for his pains.

In 1695 the Turks took the field once more, and were this time opposed by Augustus, the elector of Saxony, at the head of the imperial armies, but met with some success. They directed their attack against Transylvania, took Lippa, and near Lagos defeated a large body of cavalry which was on its march to join the imperial forces, and killed their leader, General Veterani. This mishap rather deranged the elector's plans, and the Turks might have effected an entrance into Transylvania without molestation, had they not adhered to their old rule of going into winter quarters without fail in the first week of October. The sultan Achmed the Second died this year, and was succeeded by Mustapha, his brother, who, early in 1696, took the field in person, with the view of saving Temesvar, which the imperialists were besieging. He succeeded in defeating the elector in a feebly-contested action,—the allied armies being decimated by disease brought on by using the water of the marshes.

In 1697 affairs assumed a very different aspect. Early in the year a person named Francis Tokkay put himself at the head of a number of bandits and peasants whom they forced to join them, surprised the fortress of Tokay, and put the garrison, amounting to two hundred men, to the sword. Patak shared the same fate, and Tokkay then sent a circular to the principal nobility, in which he styled himself a colonel in the service of Prince Tekeli, inviting them to take up arms for the recovery of their liberty. No person of note gave him any sort of countenance, and Prince Francis Rokotski, who was shortly to play so distinguished a part in Hungarian history, hearing that it was the intention of the insurgents to carry him off by force and put him at their head, retired to Vienna. They were soon after defeated and dispersed, and the fortresses they had captured recovered.

The outbreak, however, had the effect of drawing the sultan Mustapha to the frontier at the head of a powerful army. He was undecided whether to cross the Teyss in search of the Germans and offer them battle, or to invade Transylvania, and took counsel of Tekeli, who accompanied him. The latter advised him to open the campaign by laying siege to Great Varadin; and then, in case the imperialists came to the succour of the place, they would be compelled to fight under a disadvantage, being drawn away from the Danube, by which alone they received their supplies. He was overruled, however, by the grand vizier, who persuaded the sultan to adhere to his original plan, and he accordingly advanced against the Germans, who were encamped on the northern bank of the Danube above Petervaradin.

The famous Prince Eugene who had learnt the art of war in these Turkish campaigns, and who now, for the first time, found himself in the chief command, was at the head of the imperial forces, and inflicted a total defeat upon the Turks in the battle which followed. The grand vizier did not survive the defeat. The sultan fled precipitately to Temesvar, placed garrisons in that town and in Belgrade, and hurried to Constantinople to suppress the commotions which his defeat was likely to excite amongst his own subjects. Eugene poured his troops into Bosnia, and captured Serai, the capital, out of the plunder of which he paid his troops, and then retired into winter quarters. On his return to Vienna, instead of being thanked for his success, he received a cold rebuke for disobedience of orders from the punctilious emperor.

The peace of Ryswick would now have enabled Leopold to follow up his successes against the Turks, but his treasury was exhausted, and the prospect of a vacancy in the Spanish succession made him anxious to conclude the war and give his whole attention to Europe. Plenipotentiaries from all the powers in alliance against the Turks, accordingly met the sultan's ambassador in the little village of Carlowitz near Petervaradin, and through the mediation of England and Holland a treaty was concluded, after a negotiation of two months' duration. The emperor retained possession of Transylvania, which, though nominally subject to Michael Apaffi, had in reality been an Austrian province ever since the expulsion of Tekeli; all Hungary north of the Morosch, and west of the Teyss, and all Sclavonia, except a small district between the Save and the Danube in the neighbourhood of Belgrade. The Turks were permitted to continue the protection they had granted to Tekeli, but were prohibited from affording any future assistance to the malcontents, and both parties agreed to deliver up

ENVIRONS OF BUDA.

the rebel subjects who might escape into their respective territories.* This treaty, which was concluded in November, 1691, was the most memorable and most important in the history of the house of Austria. Hungary, and Sclavonia, and Transylvania, were at length secured and made hereditary in the family, and the Turks from being the most powerful and most terrible of European nations, sank to a position of feebleness and obscurity from which they have never since emerged.

* Coxe's History of the House of Austria, vol. i. Part II.

(A.D. 1687—1691.) During the greater part of the foregoing chapter we have been wholly occupied with the wars carried on between Austria and Turkey, and of which Hungary and Transylvania were generally the theatre. In following the march of armies, and chronicling the triumphs of tacticians, the miseries of the people, whose vitals are eaten up by the demon of discord, are necessarily in some degree lost sight of. To gain a proper idea of the state of Hungary and the position occupied by the diet at the period of the treaty of Carlowitz, we must go back to the year 1687, in which the states surrendered their right of election, and made the crown hereditary in the family of Hapsburg.

The reader may remember that Tekeli protested against the proceedings of the diet of Presburg upon eight grounds:—1. Because the court of Vienna had used illegal and coercive measures to force the diet into a compliance with its will, by the presence of an armed force, by bribes, promises, and threats. 2. Because the whole nation was labouring under the intimidation caused by the bloody Theatre of Eperies, and the county assemblies were unable to deliberate freely. 3. Because a fixed and positive determination to carry the imperial will into effect was shown in the terms of the decree by which the diet was convened. 4. Because while the members voted under constraint, those who protested acted from their own free will. 5. Because in the absence of a great number of the nobility the states were not competent to pass a law binding their posterity, and surrendering a portion of the liberties which had been in existence for seven centuries. 6. Because the house of Austria having been for centuries hateful to the great body of the nation, it was not probable that such concessions would have been made spontaneously. 7. Because the form of the coronation oath was illegally altered. 8. Because the Archduke Joseph broke his promises.

This protest was treated with contempt or indifference, but it is worthy of attention as being an able defence of the rights of Hungary, and as having been fully confirmed in every particular by the subsequent conduct of Austria. From the assembling of the diet at Presburg till the peace of Carlowitz, during the whole period of the Turkish war, Hungary was treated in every respect as a conquered country. The nobles met with insult and outrage, and the peasantry were exposed to all the tyranny and violence which a rude and licentious soldiery could inflict. The privileges of the municipalities were abolished or disregarded, the concessions made to protestants were nullified, the laws were set aside, and the country was governed solely by despotic orders from Vienna, or by the will and pleasure of the officers in command of the troops. The palatine was reduced into the mere agent of the court. He was summoned to Vienna, and there, without convoking or consulting the diet, the sum was fixed which Hungary was called upon to contribute to the imperial exchequer; and to him was committed the task of apportioning it amongst the different counties. Thousands of families were defrauded of their property by the officers of the revenue. Their estates were first seized, and then they were called upon to prove their right to possess them.

The troops were quartered on the people at their own discretion or that of their commanders. Every individual in the middle class, after furnishing a fixed contribution to the commissariat, was often compelled to maintain an officer and one man in his house and amongst his family. All lucrative employments or offices were bestowed on foreigners. All the money of the kingdom was gathered into the imperial treasury, and the natives were left to effect the exchange of their commodities by barter. The primate, grand chancellor and king lived at Vienna, and thither was the final resort in all suits and causes; but so expensive, tedious, and doubtful was the process of appeal, that there were few Hungarians who did not prefer submitting to the most cruel injustice, to running the gauntlet of long and vexatious litigation in a foreign country, and before a foreign tribunal. The Hungarian chamber of finance, which the emperor, with a show of favour and concession, had established at Presburg, had in reality no other duty than to register the decrees of that of Vienna, and to transmit to the Aulic Council all the money which the excisemen and farmers of the revenue could wring from the people. Many of the proudest families in the kingdom, who could trace their descent from the days of Arpad, and who lived amidst their vassals in regal splendour, had been utterly extirpated by Caraffa, and their houses left desolate, or occupied by troops. Their places were now filled up by the German minions of the court, or by brutal soldiers who had distinguished themselves by their unrelenting ferocity, and who, void of all sympathy with the people, did everything in their power for the overthrow of the constitution. The administration of justice in the courts became "a mockery, a delusion, and a snare." Bribery, corruption, and intimidation took the place of law. The Jazyges and Cumans, who had been entitled to all the privileges of the nobility, and the inhabitants of many of the free towns and boroughs, were sold into serfdom to the Teutonic Knights, who exacted their dues with such terrible severity, that mothers disposed of their children to the Turks to procure funds to meet them. Thousands of peasants every month crossed the Turkish frontier, preferring to brave all the insolence and oppression of the Moslems, to living under the tyranny of those of their own faith.

Previous to commencing the negotiations for the peace of Carlowitz, whether it was that the emperor wished to destroy the remnant of liberty which the diet of Presburg had left untouched, and that he wished to take away from the nobility all excuse for ever again resorting to foreign aid for the redress of their grievances, he summoned at Vienna an assembly of the deputies of the states. Amongst the number were the primate and grand chancellor, cardinal Colonitz, prince Esterhazy the palatine, Paul Szechenyi, archbishop of Kolocza, and many others of the principal magnates of the kingdom. The cardinal was employed by the court to make known to them the emperor's object in calling them together. He was a devout catholic, and no less devoted adherent of the house of Austria, whose interests and those of the church he believed to be identical; and when any opportunity of serving either of them presented itself, no other considerations were allowed to stand in his way. Patriotism was nothing to him; catholicism everything. He was willing that Hungary should be ruined rather than she should be heretic. Amongst his private friends, when he uttered the real sentiments of his heart, he frequently made use of an expression which has since become famous—"*Faciam Hungariam captavam, postea mendicam, deinde catholicam.*"* Leopold could not have chosen a more faithful exponent of his will.

At the first conference he had with the deputies he informed them that his imperial and royal majesty, in his great and paternal goodness, was anxious to assimilate Hungary in every respect to his hereditary dominions—in manners, language, customs, and laws; and he, therefore, called upon them to reject their Corpus Juris, and accept at his hands a constitution which certain persons of ability had framed at his request. He then remarked upon the great number of nobles in Hungary who, contrary to all received maxims of government, claimed exemption from taxation, and proposed that for the future, whilst all who really possessed the advantage of illustrious birth should receive due consideration, they should lay aside their exorbitant pretensions; and that those of them who possessed the means of living in a certain style, should receive at his hands the titles of counts, barons, and chevaliers, and thus be placed on a footing of equality with the Austrian nobles; and, lastly, that for the variable and uncertain subsidies by which the expenses of government were then met, they should substitute a fixed and invariable contribution, to be called *Contributio Continua*, which should be assessed with strict impartiality. He did not doubt, at the same time, that Hungary would cheerfully take upon herself a third of the revenues of the whole of his majesty's dominions.

The pith of the entire proposition was, in short, the abolition of the constitution; the substitution of laws framed by Palm, the secretary of the council of war at Vienna, and a monk named Gabriel, both creatures of the emperor,—the "persons of ability" referred to in the cardinal's address; the creation of a distinction between the Magyars, lowering the poorer into the rank of commoners, and raising the rich into the ranks of the Austrian nobility, and thus abolishing the equality which was their proudest boast; and last and most important, the surrender of the last safeguard of liberty, the right of voting the supplies, and the substitution of a fixed tax, which would render the emperor totally independent of the people and indifferent to their complaints.

The audacity of the proposals at first struck the deputies dumb with astonishment; but recovering from their surprise, they made Paul Szechenyi, the archbishop of Kolocza, a brave, able, and patriotic prelate, their mouthpiece, and through him informed the emperor, that they had no power to comply with his requests; that

* I will make Hungary first captive, then a beggar, then catholic.

it was illegal to discuss them even beyond the boundaries of the kingdom; and that if they could, they would not. The efforts of the palatine Esterhazy to induce them to consent, were met with indignant reproaches, and after a violent altercation, the meeting was broken up and the deputies returned home. Though thus foiled, however, Leopold did not abandon his illegal courses until they led to another outbreak, as we shall shortly see.

We cannot conclude this chapter without alluding to the fate of Tekeli. After the peace of Carlowitz, he passed the remainder of his days in retirement. The emperor refused to restore to him his confiscated property, and as a substitute the sultan bestowed on him Caransebes and Widdin, as a feudal sovereignty. Mahomet, Mustapha's successor, transferred him to Nicodemia, in Asia Minor, where he allowed him a handsome pension. He was afterwards neglected by the Ottoman court, and falling into great poverty, lived for a long while in one of the vilest streets in Constantinople, amongst the Jews and Armenians, receiving a miserable pittance to support himself and his family, and obliged to eke out his livelihood by carrying on the trade of a vintner. Towards the close of his life, singularly enough, he, who had roused the protestants of Hungary to take arms in defence of their religion, became a Roman Catholic. He lamented bitterly to the last hour having committed his fortunes to the keeping of the Turks, whose policy, he said, was as wavering and fickle as the crescent in their arms. Overcome by chagrin, poverty, and disappointment, he died at the age of fifty, in 1705, and lies buried in the Greek cemetery. He was a brave, able, and energetic man, full of enthusiasm, and actuated all through life by two great passions—love of country and hatred of Austria. Even his enemies acknowledged his sincerity, however much they might condemn his judgment.

Happily, his beautiful and accomplished wife, the princess Helena, did not live to see the close of his career. She died in 1703, after sharing all his trials and reverses. She had left an avenger behind her in the person of Francis Rakotski, her son by her former husband.

CHAPTER XVIII.

REBELLION OF FRANCIS RAKOTSKI.

A.D. 1700—1711.

What to do with Hungary after the peace of Carlowitz was a question of no ordinary difficulty to the Viennese cabinet. To pacify it was absolutely necessary, as the emperor was now about to throw all his strength into the war of the Spanish succession, and when contending against an enemy so powerful as Louis XIV., it would have been in the highest degree dangerous to have left another, weaker perhaps, but no less watchful and energetic, in his rear. All classes of the population were in the highest state of irritation. Every insult and injury that could rouse the hatred and indignation of a high-spirited and turbulent race had been heaped upon them. The clergy had been treated with studied neglect, or open and marked contempt; the nobles had been harassed and outraged by the government officials in every possible manner; the free towns had been despoiled of their privileges; great numbers of the peasantry had been sold into slavery, and those who remained were suffering from religious persecution. There was clearly no hope of lasting tranquillity. The ink was scarce dry on the treaty of Carlowitz, when another storm began to lower. There were but two ways of arresting it: either to redress all the grievances of which the Hungarians complained, or to deprive them of all means of resistance. To have adopted the former would have been to undo all that Austria had been fighting for more than a century to accomplish; but, in the present posture of affairs, a no less costly and less troublesome process presented itself, and it was resolved to try it. Some native commissioners were accordingly appointed to take into consideration, in conjunction with the imperial officers, the best means of removing the most serious of the evils complained of, and through their instrumentality many of the nobles obtained compensation for private injuries; but the state of the country, and of the people generally, was in no way improved.

The emperor determined, therefore, to render insurrection impossible, by a total disarmament, and by dismantling all the fortresses in the kingdom which might prove troublesome in case of an outbreak. A general search for arms was accordingly commenced in Upper Hungary, and for some time carried out with great vigour, but afterwards abandoned, for what reason was not known. Many of the principal castles were razed to the ground, and an endeavour was made to weaken the resources of the malcontents, by raising several native regiments, and draughting them out of the kingdom for foreign service, a measure which had been already adopted with regard to the hussars.

All this, however efficacious Austria might think it, only irritated the people still more, and animated them with a still greater desire to throw off a yoke which was every day becoming more irksome. The feeling of discontent was stimulated by the intrigues of France, which pursued Leopold with an animosity which neither time, nor distance, nor failure could damp. Everything was ripe for a rising; nothing was wanting but a leader, and as the fittest person to fill that office, the eyes of the government and of the disaffected were both turned to prince Francis Rakotski.

He was the third of that name, and was born in 1676, at Borshi, a country house not far from the fortress of Patak.* He was the son of Helena Zrinyi, daughter of the unfortunate Peter Zrinyi, and of Francis Rakotski. He had a brother of the same name, who died in infancy, and a sister, Juliana, four years his senior, of whom we shall speak hereafter. His father died when he was but five months old, and to his mother, so celebrated for her beauty, her misfortunes, and her heroism, was committed the care of his inheritance and his education. Helena, finding no safety for herself or her children in either of the castles of Patak or Makovicz, into which she had been compelled to admit German garrisons, took refuge in that of Mungacz, which was occupied by her mother-in-law, Sophia Bathori, the widow of George Rakotski. The latter was a warm partizan of the emperor, and her harsh temper and stern bigotry made Helena's life at Mungacz a weary one enough. At length she was relieved from constraint by the death of Sophia, and was now enabled to bestow her hand and fortune upon the insurgent chief, Tekeli, who, during the lifetime of her mother-in-law, had been a warm but unsuccessful suitor. Her gallant defence of the fortress against the imperial forces has been already mentioned, as well as the long negotiations carried on by Tekeli with the imperial court, before he could obtain the consent of Austria to his marriage. Helena had but too much reason to hate the house of Hapsburg, and cling to her native country. The revolutionary leader could not have chosen a wife better fitted to sympathize in his hopes and efforts, and cheer his drooping courage. There was a dark shade of sorrow running through all she remembered of her early youth, and which lent new bitterness to her detestation of foreign domination. Her father, count Zrinyi, and her uncle, Frangipani, had died on the scaffold at Vienna, amidst the sneers and curses of an alien soldiery; and the harshness of her mother-in-law had but

* The following table traces his descent from Geo. Rakotski I.:—

George Rakotski, prince of Transylvania, elected 1630; died 1648.
|
George, succeeded 1648; killed 1660.
|
1. Francis, b. 1645; d. 1667.=Helena, d. of Peter Zrinyi, d. 1703.=2. Emerik Tekeli.
|
Francis Leopold,=Charlotte Amelia, princess of Hesse Rheinfeld,
d. 1735. d. 1722.

nursed the memory of her wrongs. Whether her zeal for the national cause was heightened by her affection for Tekeli, or her affection for Tekeli was deepened by her devotion to the interests which he fought to defend, must be left to the decision of those who claim accurate knowledge of the workings of woman's heart; but it is certain that her blind submission to his will was the means of doing serious injury to her infant son. The counsellors of her husband saw in him a rival of their master, who might one day prove powerful enough to grasp and secure a sceptre which they were seeking to render independent by slow and painful efforts. By their intrigues, therefore, Francis, in his early boyhood, was exposed to a thousand dangers and fatigues, from which his tender age ought to have saved him. He was dragged from one part of the kingdom to the other, in the march of the armies of his father-in-law, and compelled to undergo all the hardships which fall to a soldier's lot in active service. The vigorous constitution, and the patient temperament with which Providence had gifted him, brought him safely through an ordeal which few children could have undergone; and his disappointed persecutors, in order to get rid of him, formed the design of cutting him off by poison. One of his servants was offered a bribe of a castle and large estates in case he became the minister of their will; but he had the manliness to repel their proposals with indignation, and thus preserved his master for a more stirring and ambitious career, than even the fear-haunted imaginations of his enemies had ventured to depict.*

After the defeat of the Turks at Vienna and Parkani, Tekeli retired to Great Varadin, but, while there, found that the intrigues of his enemies at the Ottoman court were leading the sultan to entertain strong suspicions of his fidelity. As a means of allaying them, he bethought him of sending his step-son Francis as a hostage to Constantinople, and preparations were already being made for the boy's departure, when the prayers and tears of his mother saved him from an exile from which, in all likelihood, he would never have returned.

After the surrender of Mungacz, the princess Helena found herself at the mercy of Austria, for although an article in the capitulation reserved to her the right of residing in any part of Hungary she pleased, and, as guardian of her children, of disposing of all the domains which still belonged to them, no sooner had she laid down her arms, than she received orders to repair forthwith to Vienna. Refusal might have been dangerous, resistance was impossible. She set forward on her journey, and on her arrival at the gates of the capital received the first taste of the insults which were still in store for her. She and her suite were for three hours kept waiting at the barrier, exposed to the gaze of a mob whom the news of her approach had collected, and was then conducted without ceremony to a convent in the suburbs. She was now informed that it was his imperial majesty's desire that her children should be taken from her and committed to the care of cardinal Colonitz. That he might enter upon his new office with the least possible

* Histoire des Revolutions de Hongrie, p. 150.

delay, the cardinal sent his carriage that same evening to bring them away. They had no sooner entered his house and saluted him, than he carried off Juliana to an Ursuline convent in the neighbourhood. Terrified by the lonely and secluded aspect of the place, knowing little of her conductor and nothing as to whither he was leading her, the young girl at first refused to enter. To overcome her reluctance, Colonitz had to resort to force, and was brutal enough to push her in with his foot. Her brother was at the same time shut up in a private house, where for three days he heard nothing of his relatives. At the end of that period he was permitted to bid his mother a hasty farewell, and was hurried off into Bohemia, where he remained for five years, partly in Prague and partly in the little town of Neuhaus, under the tuition of the Jesuits.

The great object of the cardinal was to induce him and his sister to assume the cowl and the veil, and bid adieu to the world, either with the view of his extinguishing the Rakotski family, which for many generations had been one of the firmest bulwarks of Hungarian freedom, or of securing their large possessions for the church. Probably neither motive predominated. Colonitz had cunning sufficiently comprehensive to make the same means conduce to two great ends, and, doubtless, sought to strike down with the same blow the enemy, both of his faith and of the detestable policy by which Austria sought to propagate it.

It is, however, satisfactory to know that, whatever his design might have been, it was totally unsuccessful. Renowned as the Jesuit fathers were even then for their skill in moulding the minds of youth after their own hearts, Francis was proof against all their influence and persuasions, and evinced an obstinate attachment to the vanities of the world, and an obstinate dislike to the religious seclusion of the cloister, which filled his instructors with holy indignation.

His sister proved equally intractable. Whatever want of firmness and resolution her sex might have entailed upon her, was supplied by an ally which, more than once in the world's history, has proved triumphant over all restraints, whether civil or ecclesiastical, and has many a time carried its point in spite of fire and sword and flood. The fame of her beauty, and her wealth, had spread far and wide through the kingdom. Her forced confinement in the convent had surrounded her with romance, and inflamed the ardour of many a man, who, had she been free and happy, would have looked coldly on her charms. Full a hundred nobles fell in love with her, for no better reason than that they had never seen her and could have but small hopes of winning her. Count Aspemont-Reckheim, the commandant-general of Upper Hungary, proved himself the ablest and most adroit of them all, and in a case like this, tact and ability were *prima facie* evidence of worthiness. He heard of the absence of the cardinal at Rome, whither he had repaired to take part in the election of Pope Alexander VIII., and hurrying to Vienna, managed to obtain the permission of the emperor to pay his addresses to the young princess in person, and to ask her mother's consent to his marriage. He was successful in each step, and when Colonitz returned, he found, to his infinite chagrin, that the bird had flown, and the cage was empty.

Francis no sooner heard of his sister's marriage than he quitted Prague, and suddenly arrived in Vienna. The cardinal declared that he had no business to come, that he had given him full power to manage his property, and desired him to return to Prague in three days. Rakotski declined to comply, and thanking the cardinal for his zeal for his welfare, signified his intention of henceforth assuming the direction of his own affairs himself. Colonitz then, as a last resource, obtained an order from the emperor commanding the prince to travel in Italy, in the hope that during his absence his stewardship would still continue. In this he was again disappointed, for the Countess d'Aspemont, aided by Count Bathyanyi, took that office upon herself.

His travels lasted for a year, and upon his return he married Eleonora, princess of Hesse Rheinfeld, and in consequence incurred the extreme displeasure of the emperor, who still claimed the right of acting as his guardian, and caused him to be arrested on his return to Vienna. The production of a patent, however, which had been granted him a year previously, declaring him of full age, procured his release, and once more finding himself his own master, he determined to take up his abode upon his paternal estates in Hungary. He lived here for some time in complete retirement; but he soon found that, go where he would, or act how he might, Austria was resolved to give him no peace.

An irreconcilable jealousy already existed between him and the imperial court. The history of his family was no very pleasant story to brood over: all the wrongs it had suffered from the house of Hapsburg—the execution of his grandfather and great uncle, the condemnation of his cousin to perpetual imprisonment, the degradation of his father from his office and authority, his forced retirement into private life, the banishment of his father-in-law, and the imprisonment of his mother, in defiance of the terms upon which she had capitulated,—were calamities which might well sour the sweetest temper, and nurse in the tenderest heart hatred of the oppressor and hope of revenge. On the other hand, Austria regarded him with a mistrust for which her own injustice had given good foundation, and she evinced it by a series of petty annoyances which soon brought matters to a crisis. German garrisons were placed in all his castles and fortresses, and the commanders not only encroached upon his seigneurial rights, but treated his tenantry with so much cruelty that they at last rose in insurrection, though without the knowledge or co-operation of their landlord, and were not reduced without some trouble. Spies constantly watched him in every direction, and his correspondence with his mother, who had rejoined her husband at Constantinople, was regarded with extreme suspicion.

About this time overtures seem to have been made to Rakotski on the part of France, with the view of inducing him to take up arms against the emperor, and he seems to have listened to them, and entered into some arrangements with others of the discontented nobles for that purpose. It is, however, extremely difficult to arrive at the exact truth of the matter. The existence of a widely extended conspiracy, centring in Rakotski, is as stoutly affirmed by the Austrians as it is stoutly denied by the Hungarians; but there can hardly be any doubt there existed at all events some thoughts of an insurrection, and that it was instigated by France.

There was a Fleming, named Longueval, at this time in Hungary, a man of considerable ability, and very winning manners and extended information, who managed to insinuate himself into Rakotski's confidence—all the more easily, as the latter was extremely fond of conversing in the French language, which Longueval spoke fluently. After a long course of intimacy, during which Longueval is said to have acted as the prince's confidential agent in carrying on his negotiations with France and the Hungarian malcontents, he took his departure for the purpose of visiting Liege, his native town. Three months afterwards, Rakotski received from his sister the news of his arrest at Lintz, and the discovery upon his person of letters implicating himself and Sirmay, and several other nobles. What followed proves, either that the prince was labouring under the influence of extraordinary, if not incredible infatuation, or that the whole story of the conspiracy was a fabrication, Longueval a lying informer, and the letters forgeries. Upon receiving this news he made no attempt to escape, although he was but eight leagues distant from the Polish frontier, and he displayed equal phlegm or indifference upon learning the arrival of General Solari at Eperies the same evening. The latter had orders to arrest him, but some kindness shown him by Rakotski's mother, when a prisoner in the Seven Towers at Constantinople, made him hesitate to execute his task in person. He, therefore, sent two captains at the head of a battalion of infantry. They placed a cordon round the castle in which the prince resided, broke open the gates, disarmed the guard, and mounting the staircase, at the head of fifty men, forced an entrance into his chamber where he lay in bed with his wife, who was then in an advanced state of pregnancy. The soldiers formed a circle round the room with levelled arms, and the two officers approached the bed with cocked pistols in one hand and lighted candles in the other, and called upon Rakotski to surrender. Resistance was out of the question. He rose, dressed, and was conducted in his own carriage to Eperies, and thence to Neustadt, where he was shut up in the same dungeon which had formerly contained his maternal grandfather, Count Zrinyi. He was confined here for six weeks, in ignorance of the nature of the charge which had caused his arrest, and at last two officers were sent down from Vienna to examine him. He protested against being called upon to answer their interrogatories, and claimed the right, which by the Hungarian constitution was secured to every Magyar magnate, of being tried by the diet only, but at length consented under protest to answer, as a proof that his reluctance was not owing to his guilt. He was then confronted with Longueval, who was abashed by the presence of his injured benefactor, and stammered out with hesitation and difficulty, a list of overt acts of treason, all of which Rakotski solemnly denied. Guilty or innocent, made, however, little difference. His condemnation was resolved upon in any case. As a last resource, he gained over one of the officers commanding the troops which kept guard over him, and through his instrumentality, made his escape in the uniform of a dragoon, and took refuge in Poland, after numerous romantic adventures and hairbreadth escapes. His friend, Sirmay, was arrested the same day as Rakotski, but Berczeny, another noble, who was compromised by Longueval's information, reached Poland in safety.

The government now proceeded to pass sentence of condemnation upon the prince, without any further delay. He was found guilty of the crime of high treason; his property was confiscated, and large rewards were offered to any person who would secure and deliver him up, dead or alive. His position in Poland, consequently, became one of considerable danger, for at that period the agents of the powerful were not over scrupulous as to the means they made use of to accomplish their ends. Mere residence in a foreign country was not, as at present, a guarantee for the personal safety of those who were obnoxious to their own government. He was, therefore, obliged to change his residence frequently, and to assume a variety of disguises. No efforts were left untried by the Austrian ambassador in Warsaw to procure his extradition, but all his proposals were indignantly rejected by the Polish nobility, most of whom looked upon the Hapsburgs as the sworn enemies of all free nations.

After a year and a half of retirement in Poland, Rakotski had brought his negotiations with France and with the Hungarian nobility to such a state of maturity, that he thought he might safely venture upon an invasion of Hungary. The state of affairs in Europe was highly favourable to the execution of his design. The war of the succession was still raging with varied success; but so far the balance seemed to incline in favour of France, although England and Holland had joined the ranks of her enemies. The emperor's ministers were alarmed by the successes of Charles XII., an old ally of Louis and a fast friend of the Rakotski family, against Poland, and by the fear that, in case any disturbances broke out in Hungary, the insurgents would receive aid from Turkey. At last the emperor withdrew the principal part of his troops to defend himself against the attacks of the elector of Bavaria, who had espoused the cause of Louis XIV., and finding the coast clear, Rakotski determined to issue from his retreat and raise the standard. He accordingly commenced his march at the head of a few Polish guards of the palatine early in June, 1703. He had already sent out emissaries through the whole of Hungary to apprise the people of his coming, and risings of the peasantry had already taken place in many parts of the kingdom. On the sixteenth of June he crossed the Caparthians and was then joined by a riotous horde of peasants headed by persons of their own rank, and mostly armed with scythes and forks. This motley band of recruits hailed him with shouts of joy, and immediately agreed to obey him in everything and follow him everywhere. His first care was to introduce some sort of disci-

PRINCE FRANCIS RAKOTSKI.

pline, to appoint officers, and restrain their wild licence and brigandage. Having reduced them at least to partial order, he began his march, and was speedily reinforced by crowds of volunteers from every quarter. In the duchy of Mungacz, where his mother's memory was still cherished and revered, the inhabitants of the villages thronged to his quarters with bread, and wine, and meat, and supplies of every description. The women knelt down by the wayside, and, according to the custom of the Greek churches, saluted him with the sign of the cross, and pointed him out to their children as their deliverer. Few of the men entered his camp without enlisting under his banner. Half armed, unorganized, and badly officered, such was their confidence in their own rude courage, and their devotion to the cause, that they declared their readiness to march wherever he led, and live or die by his side.

His army now amounted to about five thousand infantry and three hundred cavalry, and rumour doubled the number. With this force he determined to push on and attack the fortress of Mungacz, which was garrisoned by five hundred Germans, many of whom were worn-out veterans, and many more secret adherents to his cause. He had scarce entered the town, however, when he was surprised by the imperial forces, was repulsed, and made his escape with difficulty. He reached the frontiers of Poland in safety, and there remained inactive till joined by Bercsenzi with additional supplies of men and money from Poland and France, and descending once more into the plains of Hungary, issued a manifesto setting forth his grievances, calling upon the inhabitants to repair to his standard, drove before him several small detachments of the enemy; and the courage of his troops being roused by these successes, he determined to pass the Teyss, though the heavy rains had inundated the whole district in its vicinity. His infantry were but half clothed, and were marching day after day along roads where the mud rose to the knee at every step, or wading across marshes up to the middle in water. Still, in spite of all these toils and hardships, and in defiance of all difficulties, thousands daily thronged to his standard, abandoning houses, goods, and family, to combat for liberty. The river was passed by the aid of small wherries; and upon the news of his arrival in Upper Hungary spreading abroad, those nobles whom fear had hitherto kept quiet, hastened to declare for the invader, and led their vassals to his camp. He now laid siege to Kalo; but, owing to the want of artillery, a furious assault made by his troops was repulsed, and it was not till firebrands had been cast into the town, and many of the houses were in flames, that the inhabitants rose and compelled the garrison to surrender. By this success, Rakotski gained possession of four pieces of artillery, a very seasonable accession to his armament. Somlio fell before him in like manner, and before the close of the year he was at the head of twenty thousand men, had captured all the smaller forts in the east of Hungary, and had reduced Zolnoc and Tokay on the Teyss, and the central fortress of Erlau.

The court of Vienna was thunderstruck by a movement at once so sudden and unexpected. There was nothing but confusion and division in its councils. The elector of Bavaria, aided by France, had made himself master of Passau and Lintz, and was already threatening Vienna itself. Amongst all the Hungarian magnates, count Simon Forgacz was the only one whose fidelity to the imperial cause promised to throw many obstacles in Rakotski's way. Count Berczenyi had in the meantime overrun the mountainous districts of Upper Hungary, taken Scepuse and Levitsch, obtained possession of the towns in the neighbourhood of the mines, and sent his marauding parties even into Austria and Moravia. Early in the year 1704, count Karoly, a powerful magnate of Lower Hungary, alienated by the neglect of the court, went over to the insurgents, roused the peasantry, occupied all the open country below the Danube, and established a communication with Berczenyi on the other side. The emperor was anxious to treat for peace as the only means of saving his crown, and commissioned the archbishop of Colocza to open negotiations with Rakotski for this purpose. The latter consented to an interview, and appointed Gyöngos as the place of meeting, and towards the close of the month of March he left the siege of Agria, which he was then carrying on, in order to attend the conference. To all proposals, on the part of the archbishop, Rakotski replied, that he would consent to no peace the maintenance of which was not guaranteed by foreign powers, as the Hungarian people had suffered too much from Austrian perfidy ever to place any trust in her oaths or promises. To such a treaty Leopold, of course, had no thoughts of agreeing, and the negotiations were consequently broken off in a few days. During their continuance, the Austrian envoy several times inquired with an air of surprise, what was the cause of all this violence and bloodshed, and talked, as of old, of clemency, benignity, mildness, and oblivion in case the insurgents laid down their arms; but Rakotski silenced him by an explicit declaration that nothing less than a positive redressal of each grievance complained of in the manifesto, which he had issued on commencing the war, would satisfy him.

He had scarcely returned to Agria, when he was joined by count Forgacz, hitherto a major-general in the emperor's service. After having sworn allegiance to Rakotski, he recounted to him all the injuries he had experienced at the emperor's hands, all the false charges and suspicions which had been heaped up against him at Vienna, and for which he was on the point of being arrested when he escaped.

The consternation at Vienna had now reached its height, General Heuster was dispatched with a large body of troops to the south of the Danube, and the garrison was drawn out from Passau under General Schlick, to oppose the insurgents in the north. After a few feeble efforts, however, to maintain their position, they were compelled to fall back, as they found the whole nation in arms. The one took refuge in Presburg, and the other continued his retreat to Vienna, for the purpose of protecting the capital. Another attempt at negotiation was now made. On the part of the Hungarians the same conditions were still adhered to. 1. The acknowledgment of Rakotski as independent prince of

Transylvania, to which dignity the states had unanimously elected him a short time previously. 2. The abolition of the hereditary monarchy, and the revival of the article in the oath of King Andrew, which authorised armed resistance, in case the king in any way infringed upon the constitution or upon the privileges of the nobility. 3. The expulsion of the Jesuits and all other religious orders which were considered dangerous to the peace and freedom of the country. 4. The removal of foreign officers and foreign garrisons. 5. The appointment of Berczenyi as palatine. 6. The complete toleration of the protestant worship, and the restoration to that sect of the four hundred churches of which it had been deprived. But this conference had no better result than those which had gone before it, and when it was broken up, the insurgents secured passages over the Danube, joined the French in preparing an attack upon the capital, and while

FAC-SIMILE OF THE SIGNATURES OF RAKOTSKI AND BERCZENYI TO THE MANIFESTO.

the Bavarian army hung upon the opposite frontier of the empire, Karoly so closely menaced Vienna that the citizens prepared for flight.

Leopold now determined to make a desperate effort to drive his French and Bavarian enemies from Germany, and prevent their co-operating with Rakotski, and having obtained the aid of Great Britain, the splendid victory obtained by Marlborough at Blenheim once more placed his star in the ascendant. He was enabled to send all his forces against the Hungarians, and General Heuster having obtained a signal victory over them, drove them back from the Austrian frontier, and compelled them ever afterwards to confine their operations to their own country.

In October, 1705, Leopold, the emperor, died, after one of the longest reigns recorded in the annals of his house, during the whole course of which he had displayed an amount of perfidy, cruelty, and injustice, towards Hungary, which no arguments could justify, and no turbulence on her part could palliate. Joseph, his son and successor, had been, as we have already said, crowned king of the Romans and king of Hungary at an early age, but, with childlike deference to his father's will, never attempted to take any part in the government. He always displayed great courage, great magnanimity, and a disposition towards mildness and conciliation, which he certainly did not inherit from Leopold. The latter, however, had the good sense to perceive how much he himself had suffered from the instruction of the Jesuits, and took care not to submit his children to the same training. Joseph, therefore, was not slow to observe how much the empire suffered from the troubles in Hungary, and showed himself disposed to put an end to them by granting an amnesty, and redressing many of the grievances of which the insurgents complained. His designs were favoured by the successes obtained by his forces over Rakotski, and possibly might have succeeded, if the Maygars had not already suffered too much, easily to forget or readily to forgive.

His offers were rejected, and that this might be done with greater pomp and show of legality, Rakotski summoned a diet at Setzim, to which all the magnates and prelates of his party repaired, and deputies from all the counties and free towns, except four or five, which contained German garrisons. A large tent was erected between two lines of the army, in which the assembly was to take place. The proceedings were opened in the usual way, by the celebration of mass by the bishop of Agria, and after a short address from Rakotski the deliberations commenced. After lengthened discussions they resolved to form a regular confederation, similar to that of Poland, with a responsible chief, or head, whose title should convey the idea, not so much of a master as of an administrative officer. They, therefore, determined to name him *Dux*, or leader, and elected Rakotski to fill the office, and agreed that he should be assisted by a council of twenty-four senators, whom they called upon him to name. Fearing, however, to make himself obnoxious to the many whom he might offend by passing them over, he for a long while declined to accept the power which they assigned him, but at last consented, upon their agreeing to present him with a list of those whom they thought worthy of the office. Being now proclaimed dux, and chief of the confederates, a mass was sung, and Rakotski, placing his hands between those of the bishop of Agria, took the oath in the form drawn up for the occasion, and then, according to the ancient Germanic custom, was elevated on a buckler by the principal magnates; who, with the prelates, senators, and the deputies of the counties and the free towns, swore to obey and be faithful to him, and to fulfil and keep all the statutes of the confederation.

They then replied to Joseph's proposals by offering to acknowledge him as king in case he abandoned his claim to the throne as a hereditary possession, ceded Transylvania to their leader, revived the oath of King Andrew, and, in fact, yielded to all the demands which they had before made. The emperor, of course, rejected their conditions, and the war was carried on with renewed vigour. The insurgents had again rallied, had driven the Austrian army into the island of Schutz, blockaded all the fortresses held by German garrisons, and ravaged the frontiers of Austria, Styria, and Moravia, and shut up the imperial general

Rabatin in Transylvania. As a last resource, Joseph sent General Herbeville, with orders to recover Transylvania at all hazards. Herbeville, accordingly, raised the blockade of Great Varadin, forced the entrenched pass of Sibo, and entering Transylvania, reduced the whole country and re-established Austrian rule. On the other hand, Styria and Moravia were still molested by predatory hordes, and Vienna itself kept in a state of continual alarm, as the insurgents pushed their incursions to the very walls. Joseph once again made great exertions to pacify the insurgents. He proposed to Rakotski to give him the margravate of Bengau in exchange for Transylvania, and to restore him his estates in Hungary, and make him a prince of the empire; and sought to support his offer by calling in the aid of his wife and sister, who had been shut up in prison by Leopold, but were now liberated. He at the same time acknowledged the confederacy, and agreed to confirm all the rights and privileges he had sworn to maintain at his coronation. But Rakotski's wife, with Spartan courage, instead of advocating peace, encouraged her husband never to lay down his arms until he had achieved the objects for which he had taken them up; and then he himself resolutely refused to listen to any proposals made to him personally apart from the states. The latter, at the same time, would not abate one jot of their original demands, and hostilities were consequently resumed, after a short truce.

In June, 1707, an assembly of the confederate states, to which thirty-one out of the fifty-two sent deputies, met at Onod, and although Rakotski showed himself disposed to conclude an honourable peace with the new emperor, the house of Austria was formally deposed and the throne declared vacant. Almost before the assembly had broken up, Rakotski received a message from the czar of Russia, informing him that he intended to use his influence to procure his election to the throne of Poland. This proposition caused him great uneasiness, as it promised to involve the affairs of Hungary in very serious difficulty. To have aspired to the throne as the nominee of a foreign despot would have justly roused the ire and opposition of the nobles, and would have given deep offence to the Swedish king, whose enmity to Russia was implacable. He therefore declined the dangerous honour with a firmness, and, at the same time, with a prudence and delicacy which did him the highest credit.

These negotiations ended, the war continued with varied fortune. The materials of which the national army was composed necessarily militated against its success. The supplies were uncertain, the levies fickle, impatient of discipline, and badly armed. The nobles, as soon as their bursts of enthusiasm passed away, grew tired of the marching and countermarching, the hardships, perils, and fatigues of guerilla warfare, and sighed for the repose of their castles. Those who had led their peasantry into the field saw with alarm that their estates were lying uncultivated and their rents unpaid, and trembled lest the triumph of independence, if it did triumph, should find them beggared. Others were jealous of their leader's fame, and accused him of studying his own interests more than the national welfare, and of seeking to found a dynasty upon the ruins of public liberty. The peasantry were worn out and impoverished by the protracted hostilities, and no longer displayed their former ardour. The boasted succours which France had so often promised never came; the assurances of other sovereigns proved equally deceitful, and Rakotski found himself obliged to contend against the whole force of the empire with a mere handful of followers.

Joseph, in the early part of 1708, summoned a diet at Presburg, composed of those magnates and deputies from the towns who still adhered to him, and by opening it with ordinary formalities, sought to give an air of legality to his proceedings. The confederates looked with contempt on the small number who obeyed the call; and the emperor had reason to regret the step he had taken, when he found that religious differences were the only subject which his diet would discuss, and that after a long session they broke up without result.

General Heuster soon after assumed the command of the Austrian armies, and issuing from the island of Schutz, crossed the Waag, and came up with Rakotski's forces near Trentsin. The latter were badly organised; had no confidence in their officers, and the leaders were quarrelling with each other. When Heuster commenced the attack they were taken by surprise. The insurgent cavalry gave way before the Rascians. Rakotski galloped off to rally them and lead them back into action; but on his way his horse missed his footing in leaping a ditch, fell, and was killed on the spot, throwing his rider to some distance. The prince was picked up senseless, and carried to the edge of a neighbouring wood, and when he recovered his consciousness he found that all was lost. Six thousand men were left dead on the field; as many more were captured; and the rest, except two brigades of cavalry, amounting in all to 4,000 men, were dispersed amongst the neighbouring woods and mountains. From this time Rakotski was never able to make head against the enemy. Many of his best officers deserted him; those who remained were suspicious and desponding; the whole of Lower Hungary had been reduced. He still, however, continued to maintain the contest with as much vigour as his diminished resources would allow, but was compelled, for the most part, to confine his operations to desultory skirmishing.

He was at last induced to open up negotiations with John Palfi, who had embraced the imperial cause, and was placed in the chief command of the German troops. He accordingly wrote to him towards the close of the year 1709, representing the advantages that would result from an honourable peace, and asking him to enter upon a negotiation for that purpose. After despatching the letter, he found that the czar was shortly to arrive in Poland, and that if he obtained an interview with him, he might possibly obtain some assurance of timely assistance, that even yet might retrieve his cause. He therefore, as soon as he had received a favourable answer from Palfi, appointed a place of meeting, and in the mean time started for Poland in all haste. He arrived on the 5th of December at Mungacz, and a few days afterwards received the disheartening intelligence, that Agria, which he had captured after great labour and loss, had surrendered to the enemy almost without resistance, owing to the intrigues of some refugee monks.

Pope Clement XI. had sent a circular to all the clergy, ordering them to recognise the emperor Joseph as the legitimate sovereign of Hungary, and abandon the confederation upon pain of excommunication. The clergy obeyed, and the Catholic officers and nobles giving way, suffered their fears or their piety to get the better of their patriotism, and followed the example of their spiritual instructors. Upon hearing of these misfortunes, Rakotski stayed his progress, and went to Kichvarda to review all the cavalry which were still left him, where he found 12,000 men. He addressed them at some length, giving his reasons for opening up negotiations with Palfi, and warning them, that if he failed in bringing them to a favourable conclusion, they must then either succumb to the Austrian yoke, or die in defence of their liberties. He then proceeded to Vaga, where he met General Palfi. They lodged in the same house, and conducted their proceedings with great show of cordiality. Palfi assured him of the emperor's good will and esteem, and advised him to write to him, making his submission, in which case there was no doubt that his master would confirm the Hungarian people in all their laws and liberties, grant a general amnesty to all who had been concerned in the late troubles; and as for Rakotski himself, there was no honour, or dignity, or favour that he might not look for, except the principality of Transylvania. He besought him at the same time to reflect upon the perils of his position, warned him that if the Hungarian people now neglected to secure their rights by a timely surrender, they would be treated, when vanquished, as the Bohemians had been after the battle of Prague.

Rakotski consented to write the letter, but declined entering into any treaty without the knowledge, advice, and consent of the states and the senate, or to accept any favour for himself personally. Towards the end of January, 1710, he convoked a meeting of all the senators who were within reach, at Schalank, about three leagues from Mungacs, and laid before them the state of affairs, informed them of the emperor's proposals, and offered to release them from their oath of fidelity if they chose to accept them. They unanimously refused, declared that they were bound by their oaths not to lay down their arms until they had recovered their liberties, and that they would stand by him till death. He accordingly set out for Poland to seek for assistance, leaving the troops in command of Karoly. The latter no sooner found himself at the head of affairs, than he entered into a convention with Palfi at Szathmar, which stipulated for a general amnesty, the restitution of confiscated property, the liberation of prisoners, and the exercise of the protestant religion—the confirmation of all the rights and privileges recognised by Joseph at his coronation. When this was signed, then the insurgent army laid down their arms, and the war was at an end. Joseph offered to receive Rakotski as a reconciled enemy worthy of his esteem and friendship; but the proud chief sternly spurned his proposals, and would have nothing to do with a treaty which had been entered into, not only without the consent of the states, but by the treachery of a subordinate.

All hope of re-kindling the insurrection being now at an end, Rakotski dismissed the few followers who still adhered to him, and passed over from Dantzic to Hull, and sailed thence to France. He never again returned to Hungary. After taking up his abode in France, the government settled on him a pension of 100,000 livres, and 40,000 for the support of his exiled adherents, and for some time he sought to drown the memory of his misfortunes by taking part in the gaieties and dissipations of the court, then in the height of its splendour. The implacable enmity, which for nearly two centuries had subsisted between France and Austria, made Paris the natural asylum of all against whom the indignation of the emperor was directed; and so old are the absolutist tendencies of the Hapsburgs, that two centuries and a half ago numbers of unfortunate men were wandering as now over the earth houseless and penniless, the wronged and outraged victims of their tyranny. Paris was then what London is now, the city of refuge, to which all the vanquished fled. In the many memoirs and letters which chronicle the doings of the court of Louis Quatorze, we find frequent mention of names which would have sounded barbarous in the ears of the polite world of the day, if the monarch's smiles had not made them fashionable. The Hungarian and Transylvanian nobles were found at all the fêtes, both at Paris and Versailles, by which the great king sought to hide the chasm of ruin and convulsion which daily was widening at his feet; they were the admired of all admirers at the gorgeous reunions at Marly; Monsieur invited them to accompany him whenever he went to hunt; Condé entertained them with the splendid hospitality for which Chantilly, in his day, was famous; boots were worn *à la Transylvaine;* and the unfortunate Zrinyi, who was beheaded at Neustadt, gave his name to a sort of coat which was long the delight of the Parisian *elégants*.

St. Simon tells us that Rakotski lived in intimacy with all those of the nobility who were remarkable for wit, intellect, or bravery. Madame du Maintenon made him her special favourite; and Madame Dunoyer writes, that no assemblage of the *beau monde* was considered complete or select in which he was not included. But this was a weary life;—the pensioner of a court, and the idol of fashion, fêted and caressed through the caprice of the moment, and liable to be abandoned at any time for some new star, Rakotski soon grew disgusted, and, in 1718, went to Spain, upon the representations of Alberoni, in the hope that he might, by his aid, be enabled to effect a new revolution in Hungary. Disappointed in this, he set out for Constantinople, and after a vain attempt to induce Turkey to continue the war which she was then carrying on against Austria, he spent the remainder of his life in complete tranquillity at the Castle of Rodosto, on the Sea of Marmora. He died in 1735, at the age of sixty, thoroughly wearied of the world and its pursuits. He has left behind him several works, most of them of a religious character—hymns, soliloquies, and meditations. The most valuable and important is his memoirs of his own life and actions, from his birth till the close of the war in Hungary. It is dedicated to Eternal Truth, and is written in a spirit of candour and impartiality, which has called forth the admiration of all parties. Besides being the best account extant of the events of the period, it is an able vindication of his own name and memory, and of the motives and acts of the patriots. Rakotski is one of the finest examples in history of unconquerable devotion to a cause. He united the most winning simplicity with the astuteness of a statesman, and the indomitable energy of a soldier. An aristocrat by birth and rank, he was still a republican formed on the Roman mould, austere and truthful, a lover of equality and liberty; but yet, not of a liberty which should pervade all ranks, noble as well as peasant. He was, undoubtedly, the champion of a democratic noblesse, but such a champion, that plebeian sympathies, respect, and adoration followed him in all his enterprises. He is entitled to be placed amongst the foremost in the noble army of martyrs whom Hungary has furnished to the cause of freedom. None was more regardless of self, none ever showed more loyal devotion to duty, to patriotism, and to honour. In the closing year of his life, his intellect seems to have given way under the influence of seclusion and disappointment, and to have sunk into a state of monastic gloom. But even at the last he was a noble wreck.*

Joseph died in April, 1711, but three months after the pacification of Hungary.

* He left two sons, Francis and George. They were educated at the Austrian court, but were not permitted to assume the family name. They both died young, and without issue.

CHAPTER XIX.

CHARLES III. AND MARIA THERESA.

A.D. 1711—1777.

JOSEPH was succeeded by the archduke Charles, his brother, who had disputed the crown of Spain with Philip V. The resources of the empire were now exhausted; Charles himself was sick of war, and he therefore confirmed the treaty of Szathmar with a very good will, and restored to the Hungarians the crown and regalia which had been kept for a long time at Vienna. He declared his intention, notwithstanding the opposition of his Austrian counsellors, to rule in accordance with the laws; and in spite of the opposition of the catholics, he granted complete toleration to the protestants. His reply to the remonstrances of those who saw danger in all opinions but their own, is worthy of record: "Although I approve of your zeal, and am ready to defend the church of Rome at the peril of my life, yet justice, policy, and my own interest, require that I should not leave my protestant subjects without a ray of consolation." *

This policy of concession had the desired effect. The Hungarian people sank into a state of political lassitude, after their long troubles, which nothing occurred to disturb until 1715. In that year the Turks broke through the treaty of Carlowitz, declared war against Venice, and, having conquered the Morea, laid siege to Corfu. The Venetians instantly called the attention of Charles to the infraction of the treaty which his father had been mainly instrumental in bringing about, and sought his aid. The latter accordingly made preparations to commence hostilities. An offer of mediation was made to the Porte, but he rejected it with contempt; and Prince Eugene was immediately despatched towards the scene of his early triumphs with a small, but well-disciplined army, which was flushed by successes in the Netherlands and on the Rhine. He was joined, on entering Hungary, by a large force of the insurrection; and the cheerfulness and good will with which the Magyars volunteered their services, were the best evidences that could have been afforded of the wisdom of the policy which the emperor had pursued towards them. The palatine, John Palfi, commanded the Hungarian cavalry, and a crowd of nobles, of the highest distinction, served under his orders. Eugene crossed the Danube near Petervaradin, and encamped, in sight of the Turkish army of 150,000 men, behind the very entrenchments which he had

* Memoires de Lamberti, as quoted by Coxe, tom. vii. p. 561.

thrown up twenty years before. He immediately commenced the attack in the new village of Carlowitz, in which the treaty had been signed, on the 5th of August, 1716, overthrew the mighty but undisciplined hosts of his enemies, killed 30,000, including the grand vizier, and captured fifty standards and 250 pieces of heavy artillery. Temesvár, the last of the ancient possessions of the Turks in Hungary, was taken, and the fertile plain of the Banat was thus effectually secured.

In the following year, Eugene again took the field, and in the month of June laid siege to Belgrade. The fortress was garrisoned by 30,000 men, and offered a vigorous resistance. After a blockade of two months, a large army under the command of the grand vizier, marched to its assistance, and encamped in the form of a semicircle, stretching from the Danube to the Save, and thus confining the imperial army to the marshy ground between the two rivers. Disease and famine now began to press heavily on the latter. The enemy threatened by the fire of their batteries to break down the bridge over the Save, which was their only means of a retreat; and the hourly ravages of sickness making the odds, in point of numbers, still more disheartening. There was no resource but to offer battle. The imperial army numbered 60,000 men, of whom only 40,000 could be brought into action, while the Turks were 200,000 strong, and were encamped behind formidable entrenchments which bristled with artillery. To engage under such circumstances was a risk which nothing but extreme necessity could justify. The attack was made at midnight, under cover of thick darkness. The whole of the right wing advanced in silence, and surprised the guards of the enemy's works; but the obscurity which had favoured their first onset, afterwards caused them to fall into confusion, and they were on the point of being overwhelmed, when the rising of the sun showed them their position, and gave them light to conquer. Eugene reorganised his forces, and, placing himself in the front rank, led them once more to the assault, sword in hand. His example inspired the troops with such enthusiasm, that in their fury they bore down all opposition. They burst across the entrenchments in a solid body, seized upon the artillery, and turned them against the confused masses of the Turks, who, in a few minutes, fled in dismay, the hindmost killing those before them to facilitate their escape. The victory was complete; Belgrade surrendered immediately afterwards, and a treaty, concluded at Passarovics, a village in Servia, in July, 1718, established a truce for twenty-five years, and secured to the house of Austria the Banat of Temesvár, the western part of Servia and Wallachia, and the town and territory of Belgrade, and part of Bosnia.* From this period, the military frontiers have always remained under the control of the Viennese ministry of war, instead of the Hungarian palatine, a usurpation against which the diet has never ceased to protest.

After the cessation of hostilities with the Turks, scarcely anything occurred in

* Vie de Prince Eugene.

Hungary to disturb the tranquillity which prevailed amongst all classes, but which was owing, perhaps, as much to exhaustion and the desire of repose, as to the existence of general satisfaction and contentment—until Charles summoned the diet to meet at Presburg, in 1722, for the purpose of giving in its adherence to the Pragmatic Sanction, a measure which, at that time, began to occupy the attention of all Europe, and was destined to prove the cause of many calamities, not to the imperial family only, but to the empire at large.

Leopold had formed a new family compact, to which both his sons, Joseph and Charles, gave their assent, by which the succession was entailed upon the daughters of Joseph in preference to the daughters of Charles, in case they both died without male issue. When Charles ascended the throne, he reversed the order of succession, and so altered the compact that his daughters should take precedence of those of his brother, with remainder to the queen of Portugal and the other daughters of Leopold. To this new arrangement he gave the name of the Pragmatic Sanction, and made it his first object to obtain for it the recognition, first of the states of his own dominions, and then of the various European powers. After its promulgation, three daughters were born to him; Maria Theresa, Maria Anne, and Maria Amelia, and he fixed upon the eldest of these as the heiress of his vast dominions, and compelled his nieces to renounce all claims to the crown, founded upon any previous compact, as soon as they married the electors of Saxony and Bavaria. Though the choice of a female sovereign was in some measure repugnant to the spirit of the Hungarian constitution, the diet readily consented to proclaim her the successor to the throne. The foreign policy of Charles, during the whole of the subsequent portion of his reign, was altogether based upon the desire to obtain from the states of the empire, and the various foreign powers, a similar recognition of her claims; and to this most of the diplomatic squabbles which arose during the ensuing twenty years owe their origin. To enter into them in detail would be foreign to the nature of the present work. In 1736, the archduchess Maria Theresa was married to Francis Stephen, duke of Lorraine and Bar, grandson of Charles's sister Leonora. By this match, the two branches of the ancient house of Alsace, both of which claim descent from duke Etticho in the seventh century, and formed the two branches of Hapsburg and Lorraine, were reunited. Though these nuptials were the result of Charles's own desire, he took care, when ratifying them, to neglect no precaution necessary to secure to his male issue, in case he should ever have any, the succession to his own dominions. In the marriage contract, Maria Theresa solemnly ratified the Pragmatic Sanction, and promised faithfully to make no pretensions to the crown, if at any time her father should have a son; and the duke, her husband, promised on his part, never to put forward any personal claim to the succession whatever.

Charles was induced by Russia, in 1736, to break through the peace of Passarovics, and enter into an offensive alliance against the Turks. A more unpropitious moment could not have been chosen for such an enterprise. Eugene, who for many years had been the animating spirit of the Austrian army, was dead, and there was apparently—and as the event proved in reality—not one worthy to succeed him. The fortresses were dismantled, or mouldering to decay; the troops badly disciplined and discontented. The result was such as might have been expected. In the campaigns of 1737 and 1738, the imperial generals were one by one defeated; and, after a war displaying almost unexampled incapacity, dissension, and poltroonery, a peace equally disgraceful was concluded in November, 1739, by which the emperor ceded the fortresses of Belgrade and Szabatch, as well as the whole of Servia, Austrian Wallachia, and a small district on the banks of the Danube, retaining the Banat of Temesvár, but only on condition that he should demolish the fortifications of Mendia. During the whole of this, the Hungarian magnates looked on with indifference. They felt little interest in the quarrel, and were more anxious to preserve their property than to save the honour of the imperial arms. The inferior nobles had but small attachment to the Hapsburg family, and rather rejoiced than otherwise at witnessing its disasters; while the peasantry, loaded with taxes, and treated by all parties with equal cruelty and oppression, cared not whether the Christian arms were triumphant or not; because, as victory would make their lot no better, defeat could make it no worse. Charles did not long survive his disgrace. He died on the 20th of October, 1740, from an attack of gout, aggravated by imprudent exposure to the severity of the weather in hunting, in the fifty-sixth year of his age, and the thirtieth of his reign. In him the male line of the house of Austria became extinct.

He was succeeded by his daughter Maria Theresa, known in Hungary under the name of Maria II., when but twenty-four years of age. She was one of the most remarkable sovereigns who have ever appeared in any age or in any country. There are few graces whether of mind or body, which can lend a charm to womanhood, that she did not possess. Her figure was tall, symmetrical, and commanding; her features regular and beautiful; her countenance full of intelligence and animation; her voice soft, musical, and displayed marvellous facility of adaptation to entreaty, command, or invective. To all these feminine charms she added strength of understanding such as all men do not possess, and of which any man might be proud; and an energy of will sufficient to triumph over any obstacle or difficulty. No woman ever knew better how to subordinate the charms of her person to the accomplishment of great deeds of policy; and certainly none ever had greater need of all the skill and resources at her command. The state of the empire at her father's death cannot be better described than in the words of the English ambassador at his court, and from them some idea may be formed of the perils by which the young queen was surrounded. "Everything in this court is running into the last confusion and ruin; where there are as visible signs of folly and madness as ever were inflicted on a people whom Heaven is determined to destroy no less by domestic divisions than by the more public calamities of repeated defeats, defencelessness, poverty, and plague." The treasury contained only 100,000 florins, and these were claimed by the empress dowager; the army, exclusive of troops in Italy and the Low Countries, did not amount to 30,000 effective men; there was great scarcity of provisions, and consequently great discontent amongst the populace in Vienna, and reports were widely circulated that the Austrian empire was at an end, and that the elector of Bavaria was about to enter and take possession of the imperial dominions. Notwithstanding all the adhesions which Charles had received from the various European states, during his lifetime, to the Pragmatic Sanction, hardly one of them, except Hungary, now proved faithful to its promises. Claimants of the crown started up upon every side. Poland, Prussia, Russia, and Holland, certainly transmitted assurances of support; but when the time came for showing their sincerity, they were found wanting. France, upon whose decision most depended, answered by polite equivocations.

Maria Theresa had hardly ascended the throne, when a rival appeared, in the person of the elector of Bavaria, who asserted that the will of Ferdinand I. bequeathed the kingdom of Bohemia and his Austrian dominions to his daughters and their descendants in case of failure of male issue; and as this contingency had now occurred, he claimed the crown as the lineal descendant of Anne, Francis' eldest daughter. To this Charles, in whose lifetime this claim had first been propounded, replied that the clause in Ferdinand's will devised his dominions to his daughters only on failure of legitimate issue, and did not exclude the female heirs of the male line. The elector, however, was not convinced, and refused to recognise the Pragmatic Sanction. He now prepared to dissolve it by force of arms. But the first attack on the new sovereign came from a quarter in which it was least expected.

Frederick II., the king of Prussia, had been amongst the first to write to the queen on her accession, assuring her of his friendship and support; but, either with the view of distinguishing himself or of extending his territory, he suddenly and unexpectedly entered Silesia on the 23rd of December, 1740, at the head of twenty battalions and thirty-six squadrons, all the while pretending that it was for the benefit of the empress that he should occupy a portion of her territories, in order to prevent them falling into the hands of any other power. After a series of fruitless negotiations for the purpose of inducing him to withdraw his forces, an Austrian army, under the command of marshal Newperg, was hastily collected and sent against him, but was totally defeated at Molowitz, on the 8th of April, 1741. France now set intrigues on foot for the dismemberment of the Austrian empire. The elector of Bavaria commenced hostilities in the July following; Russia looked coldly on; fruitless attempts were made by the British minister to mediate between Frederick and the queen, and the throne of the latter seemed tottering to its fall. England alone remained faithful to her in her distress. The utmost enthusiasm on her behalf seemed to pervade all classes of the community, and the parliament voted her £300,000 as a subsidy to aid her in defending her dominions against her enemies.

France now openly commenced hostilities, and sent two powerful armies into Germany, extorted a declaration of neutrality from Hanover, and prepared to co-operate with the elector of Bavaria. The electors of Cologne, Saxony, and the palatine, joined the confederacy; Spain prepared to make a descent from Italy; Frederick was about to join his forces with the allies; and Russia was involved in a war with Sweden, which prevented her interfering on either side.

PETERVARADIN.

In this extremity, Maria Theresa had but one resource to fall back upon, and that was an appeal to the Hungarians, and to this she resolved to betake herself. All the world looked forward to finding her deceived. It was thought a thing impossible that this turbulent noblesse, so jealous of control, so enamoured of liberty, so prone to fret against foreign domination, and so renowned for their indomitable spirit, would not now seize upon the most splendid opportunity that

MARIA THERESA BEFORE THE DIET.

had ever presented itself of throwing off a yoke which had ever been hateful, and to break which they had already shed torrents of blood. But all the world was wrong. The Hungarians seemed to have reserved their hatred for despotism only when the despot was prosperous and powerful. When misfortunes came, their animosity was disarmed, and their rage turned into pity. All the wrongs they had suffered from the Hapsburg family were forgotten when its representative was a young and beautiful woman, with Europe in arms against her. Maria Theresa had too much feminine tact and penetration not to detect the existence of this chivalrous weakness in their character, and her confidence in her own judgment was sufficiently strong to save her from the doubts and misgivings which were daily uttered by the Austrian ministers. Grown gray in falsehood and intrigue, they could neither understand nor appreciate the high generosity of soul which could make a brave and proud people the protector of an unfortunate enemy.

In May, 1741, deputies were sent to Vienna by the Hungarians to swear fidelity to the new sovereign, and to invite her in the name of the nation to repair to Presburg and there receive the crown of St. Stephen. She immediately set out accompanied by her husband the archduke, and on her arrival her first act was a concession which had the effect of conciliating the whole nation. Charles VI., after the death of the palatine Count Palfi, in 1732, had refused to allow the election of a successor, and had appointed the grand duke lieutenant-general of the kingdom. The queen now gave directions for the immediate election of another palatine, and promised never to allow that office to remain vacant for more than a year. Count John Palfi was accordingly proclaimed by the unanimous voice of the diet, and count Joseph Esterhazy succeeded him in his office of judex curiæ. The twenty-fifth of June was the day appointed for the coronation, and on that day Maria repaired to the church of St. Martin, where she was solemnly consecrated and the crown placed on her head by the archbishop of Strigonia and the palatine. She then proceeded on foot to the church of the Franciscans, and there conferred the honour of knighthood of the order of St. Stephen upon forty-four of the principal magistrates, and immediately afterwards rode in a magnificent carriage, surrounded by a vast concourse of people, to the great square, where a lofty throne had been prepared for her reception. Taking her seat, she placed her hands between those of the primate, and solemnly swore to preserve inviolate all the rights and immunities of the Hungarian people,—never to carry the crown beyond the frontiers of the kingdom, and never to confer upon foreigners any office, appointment, or dignity; and in conclusion she pledged herself to observe the decree of Andrew the Second, with the exception of the thirty-first clause, which gave power to the nobles to take arms against the sovereign for the defence of the fundamental laws of the kingdom, without incurring the penalty of high treason.* The whole ceremony was magnificent and well-ordered, and on descending from the throne she mounted on horseback, and rode slowly to the foot of the barrow, known as the Royal Mount, which overlooks the Danube, and

* I have already given the form of the oath, as well as the excepted clause.

then, armed with a sabre of St. Stephen, she galloped to the top, and according to the ancient custom defied the four corners of the globe with the drawn sword, and amidst the acclamations of the people. "The antiquated crown," said the English minister, who was present at the ceremony, "received new graces from her head, and the old tattered robe of St. Stephen became her as well as her own rich habit, if diamonds, pearls, and all sorts of precious stones can be called clothes.

'Illam quicquid agit, quoque vestigia vertit,
Componit furtim, subsequiturque decor.'" *

A new charm was lent to her beauty by the air of delicacy which her recent confinement had given to her countenance, and the heat of the weather, the excitement of the ceremony, had flushed her cheeks with an animated glow, while her beautiful hair flowed in long ringlets over her shoulders and bosom. Every movement and look filled the Magyars with enthusiasm, and drew fervid oaths of allegiance from the armed throng of cavaliers who witnessed the solemnity. So great a display of devotion filled the queen with delight; and she would gladly have prolonged her stay in Presburg, if the news from Austria had not necessitated her return to the capital.

The elector of Bavaria had seized upon Passau, as well as on the chateau of Oberhaus, and was soon after joined by the French army. The allied forces, after the capture of Lintz, advanced to St. Poelten, within eight leagues of Vienna. Terror reigned in the city. The grand duke closed the gates, and determined to resist to the death; while the queen, accompanied by her infant son, set out once more for Presburg. On her arrival, she summoned the diet to the castle, and, as soon as the members were all assembled, she entered, clad in deep mourning, wearing the crown of St. Stephen on her head, and bearing her child in her arms. She traversed the great hall with slow and majestic step, and, having ascended the tribune, paused for a moment amidst awful silence, and then addressed the deputies in Latin. "The disastrous situation of my affairs," said she, "induces me to lay before you the recent hostile invasion of my hereditary dominions, the imminent danger in which this kingdom is now placed, and a proposal for the consideration of a remedy. The very existence of the kingdom of Hungary, of my person, my children, and my crown, are now at stake. Forsaken by all, my last hope is placed in the fidelity, arms, and tried valour of the Hungarians; exhorting you, the states and orders, to deliberate without delay on the most effectual measures for the preservation of my person, my children, and my crown, and to carry them into immediate execution. As far as I am concerned, you may rely on my hearty co-operation in all things that may conduce to the national honour and the pristine happiness of this ancient kingdom." †

* Mr. Robinson's letter to Lord Harrington, June 28, 1748.

† Coxe gives this address in the original Latin, which he extracted from the records of the diet.

MAGYARS OF JASZBERENY.

The youth, beauty, and distress of the queen, who was then a second time pregnant, produced an overwhelming impression on the deputies. For a moment after she ceased speaking there was profound silence; and then, as if by a sudden impulse, they all sprang from their seats, drew their sabres, flourished them in the air, and, returning them to their scabbards with a loud crash, exclaimed with one voice, "Vitam et sanguinem; moriamur pro rege nostro Maria Theresa!" *

Great as was Maria's confidence in the influence of her charms and manner, she had by no means expected so lively a demonstration of attachment, and as the shouts of the nobles rang through the chamber, overpowered with gratitude and joy, the dignified deportment which she had hitherto preserved quite forsook her, and she burst into tears. The deputies instantly hastened to the diet, and voted men and money sufficient for carrying on the war with vigour. The same scene was repeated a few days afterwards, when the duke of Lorraine took the oath as co-regent of the kingdom, the deputies repeating their exclamation, "We will die for the queen and her family; we will die for Maria Theresa!"

The elector of Bavaria, Charles Albert, who had assumed the command of the Gallo-Bavarian army, had abandoned his project of besieging Vienna, and had now made Bohemia the theatre of the war. The French had already entered Prague; the grand duke had advanced against them at the head of 30,000 men, but the rigour of the weather had retarded him. On the 24th of January, 1742, Bohemia was entirely subdued, and Charles Albert was proclaimed emperor of Germany at Frankfort.

These reverses but inflamed the ardour of the Hungarians. The worse the aspect of Maria Theresa's affairs the greater was their devotion. Three thousand nobles were already in arms in Silesia against the king of Prussia. The palatine raised the red standard, the signal for levying the insurrection, and instantly every Magyar rose in arms. Twelve thousand Croats, and various other tribes from the banks of the Save, Drave, and Teyss, answered to the appeal and poured their hordes westward to the queen's assistance—Pandours, Sclavonians, Tolpachs, whose strange costume, curious arms, and ferocious valour, struck terror into the disciplined armies of France and Germany. Freedom was offered by the queen to all serfs who bore arms in her defence; and the clergy, who even in the most critical posture of affairs seldom contributed anything to the necessities of the state beyond their prayers, now broke through their usual rule, and contributed a large subsidy towards the expenses of the war. The ladies of London sent a sum of £100,000 for the same object, which had, in many instances, been raised by the sale of their jewels,† as a tribute of their admiration; but Maria declined to accept it. The Bavarians were beaten by the Austrians soon after, and Lintz taken; but to counterbalance this success, Count Saxe seized on Egra, and the duke of Lorraine was defeated at Czaslow by the king of Prussia, and prince Lobkovitz at Sahay by marshal de Broglio.

The king of Prussia was, however, by this time tired of the war, and opened

* Our lives and blood at your service; we will die for our *king* Maria Theresa!

† Lacy. Vol. ii. p. 482.

up negotiations, by which he agreed to desist from hostilities upon receiving possession of Upper and Lower Silesia, with the county of Glatz, except the towns of Troppau and Jagerndorf, and the high mountains beyond Oppau. A treaty to this effect was signed at Berlin, under the guarantee of the king of England, on the 28th of July, 1742. Augustus III., elector of Saxony, was included in it, and agreed to withdraw his troops from the French army and recognise the Pragmatic Sanction—a promise which he fulfilled. Success was now everywhere on the side of the Austrians. Charles of Lorraine joined his forces with those of prince Lobkovitz, and forced marshal de Broglio to retire from Frauenberg, destroyed his rearguard, and captured his baggage, while the Croats and other irregulars harassed him in his retreat. The garrison of Piseck refused to surrender to a detachment commanded by Nadasdi, and the Croats immediately swam across the river with their sabres in their mouths, and climbing each other's shoulders, scaled the walls and made the garrison prisoners of war.* Cardinal Fleury, the prime minister of Louis XV., who had been always averse to the war, now made overtures for peace, which, however, were rejected by Maria Theresa on any other conditions than that the French troops should lay down their arms. This proposal was, of course, treated with scorn, and marshal Maillebois left France at the head of 40,000 men, to march to the rescue of his countrymen. But the way was 600 miles in length, and lay through a country full of defiles and overrun with the enemy's troops. The sufferings of the army shut up in Prague were dreadful, and marshal Belleisle resolved to effect his retreat from the city, and hasten to meet Maillebois. He accordingly quitted it, on the 16th of December, at the head of 11,000 infantry and 3,000 cavalry; and after a forced march of 100 miles through a mountainous district covered with snow, in which his soldiers underwent almost incredible sufferings, he succeeded in reaching Egra. He had left behind a detachment to guard the sick and wounded, under the command of an officer named Chevert, who made so gallant a resistance that he forced prince Lobkovitz to suffer him to march out of the town with all the honours of war. Bohemia was now once more in the power of the Austrians; and though Maria Theresa was chagrined by the escape of Belleisle's army, she celebrated the surrender of Prague by a magnificent entertainment, at which a chariot-race took place, in imitation of the Greeks, in which ladies alone were permitted to contend, and amongst that number were the queen herself and her sister. Her coronation took place soon after. She proved herself an able administrator, and while her husband was in the field she carried on negotiations with her allies with signal success.

The campaign of 1743 was opened by the entrance of prince Charles of Lorraine into Bavaria, where he attacked and put to flight the imperial army, and took the general Minuzzi and his principal officers prisoners. He then advanced against the French and compelled Broglio to fall back upon the Rhine, while Nadasdi,

* Mr. Robinson's Letter to Lord Carteret. June 11, 1742.

the Hungarian general, harassed him in his retreat. The unfortunate emperor, seeing himself abandoned on every side, lost all courage, renounced his pretensions to the Austrian succession, and yielded his dominions to the queen of Hungary, to be held by her until the close of the war. This treaty gave Maria a complete superiority, and the battle of Dettingen soon after removed all doubt as to the fortune of her arms. The king of England, George II., had for a long time been in a state of uncertainty as to whether he should take any active part in the quarrel. But at length relieved from his apprehensions for Holland by the march of Maillebois into Germany, he declared openly for Austria and came to her aid with an army of English and Hanoverians. His forces, however, got into a position at Dettingen from which there was no escape, except by cutting their way through the enemy. The nature of the ground, the choice of posts, and the place of battle, were all in favour of the French, but all these advantages were lost by the impatience of the duke de Grammont, who issued from his lines, and thus caused the route of the whole army. The allies, however, derived no advantage from the victory beyond securing their own safety.

Prince Charles of Lorraine now penetrated into Alsace, but was repulsed by marshal Coigny, and retired to Brisgau. This reverse did not, however, prevent the queen of Hungary from repairing to Munich, where her beauty, grace, and the remembrance of her recent trials, caused the Bavarians to forget that they were the subjects of Charles Albert, and to swear allegiance to her. Cardinal Fleury, who had so long ruled France with so much wisdom and discretion, was now dead, and Louis XV. was his own master. Count Saxe had been created marshal of France, and four armies were despatched at once; one to defend the passage of the Alps, the other to seize upon that of the Rhine, and the others to defend Flanders (1744). They had made some conquests in the latter province, when the news arrived that prince Charles had penetrated Alsace, had driven Coigny into his lines at Vecssemburg, and that 9,000 Hungarian hussars and Pandours had crossed in boats under the command of Nadasdi and Trenk, and had already appeared in sight of Luneville. Louis XV. immediately renounced his projects in Flanders, left marshal Saxe to maintain his conquests, and hastened with 80,000 men to the relief of marshal Coigny, when he was seized at Metz with an illness which threatened his life. This event, however, did not suspend the operations of the war. Marshal Coigny entered Friburg in triumph; and various other corps advanced to his aid from different quarters. A new turn was now given to affairs by the king of Prussia, who again took up arms against Austria, at the same time justifying himself in a manifesto, which he caused to be distributed through Europe. He was jealous of Maria Theresa, and dreaded her ambitious schemes with regard to the other German states. His measures were taken with his usual secresy and promptitude. Almost immediately after the declaration of war, he appeared in Bohemia, and captured Prague, and made himself master of the whole country to the east of the Moldau. At the same time a corps of Bavarians and Hessians, under Seckendorf, made an irruption into

Bavaria, and reinstated the emperor in the possession of his capital and the greater part of his electorate.

Maria Theresa was not daunted by these unexpected disasters. She once more made an appeal to the Hungarians, and received the same answer as before. The aged palatine, count Palfi, called upon the insurrection to rise, and forty-four thousand men instantly took the field, while thirty thousand held themselves in readiness as an army of reserve. "This amazing unanimity," says Tindal,* "amongst a people so divided amongst themselves as the Hungarians, especially in point of religion, could only be effected by the address of Maria Theresa, who seemed to possess one part of the character of Elizabeth of England, that of making every man about her a hero." We have, in this respect, a true picture of her character in a letter she wrote to old Palfi, with a present of her own horse, richly caparisoned, with a gold-hilted sword, ornamented with diamonds, and a ring of considerable value.

"FATHER PALFI,—

"I send you this horse, worthy of being mounted by none but the most zealous of my faithful subjects; receive at the same time a sword to defend me against my enemies; and take this ring as a mark of my affection for you.

MARIA THERESA."

The enthusiasm which was displayed in every part of the kingdom was as great as ever, and a large force was speedily sent to the relief of Bohemia. Prince Charles hastened back from Alsace. His march through Germany won the admiration of all the tacticians of the day; and though he arrived too late, he was enabled to reconquer what he had been unable to preserve. He deceived Frederick by a series of able manœuvres, beguiled him into abandoning his position, and the latter did not perceive his mistake until the Austrians were masters of Prague, and he himself compelled to retreat before them from post to post in all but confusion (1745).

Things were in this position, when the unfortunate emperor died, after witnessing the miscarriage of all his schemes, and the downfall of his most ambitious hopes. One great element in the quarrel was thus removed, and Maria Theresa found her party strengthened by the addition of Holland, who entered into an alliance against the French, with England and Austria. France now appeared in a position almost as precarious as Austria had been at the commencement of the war; but the genius of marshal Saxe, and the courage of the king, restored her drooping fortunes, and the victory of Fontenoy, which was mainly due to the valour of the Irish brigade, was the first in a series of brilliant successes. This unexpected turn in affairs was not, however, sufficient to make the elector of Bavaria, the son of the late emperor, forgetful of the lessons which his father's misfortunes had taught him. He refused to accept of the imperial crown which was offered him, renounced all claim to the states of Maria Theresa, and confined

* Vol. xxi. p. 76.

his attention to the wise government of his own. Prince Charles received a severe repulse, on the 4th of June, at Friedberg, from the king of Prussia; but this did not prevent Maria Theresa from procuring her husband's election to the imperial dignity, proving then, as on every other occasion during her lifetime, that his happiness and welfare were the great objects of her ambition. Her troops were again defeated, in September, at Prandnitz; and after a second victory, Frederick entered Dresden with as much pomp and rejoicing as if it had been his own capital. At length, however, through the mediation of George II. of England, a peace between Austria, Poland, and Prussia, was once more concluded, on the 25th of December.

But in the meantime, the Infant Don Philip had entered Milan; the Pretender had landed in Scotland in search of a crown, and, after filling the English government with alarm, had found only defeat, danger, and disappointment, and narrowly escaped a shameful death. The capture of Brussels, and several victories gained by the French, seemed to more than counterbalance the advantages derived from peace with Prussia. But fortune was more favourable in Italy—and the losses there sustained by France were as signal and as rapid as her victories in the north. The Austrians had already passed the Alps, and ravaged the frontiers of Provence, when they were compelled to retreat by marshal Belleisle. The Piedmontese repulsed the chevalier de Belleisle, the marshal's brother, with great courage, at Exelles, where the French commander himself was killed, after giving a display of the most desperate valour. Various successes attended the French arms in the Low Countries during the early part of 1748; and at length, both parties being heartily tired of the war, concluded a peace at Aix la Chapelle, in the autumn of that year (Oct. 8).

By this treaty Maria Theresa was confirmed in the possession of all her father's dominions in the low countries; the king of Sardinia, the republic of Genoa, and the duke of Modena, recovered all that they had lost in the course of the war; the Infant Don Philip remained master of the duchies of Parma, Placenza, and Guastalla; and, lastly, the Pragmatic Sanction was fully recognised in reference to all the hereditary dominions of the emperor Charles VI., except so much as Maria Theresa had ceded to Don Philip and the king of Prussia. To the latter was guaranteed the possession of the duchy of Silesia and the county of Glatz.

Thus ended this famous war. It was begun through injustice and ambition, for the purpose of overwhelming Maria Theresa, and dismembering her empire; but, to the confusion of its promoters, it had the effect of rendering her greater and more powerful than ever, of consolidating her resources, and causing a tide of chivalric enthusiasm to rise in her defence. She had shown herself courageous in misfortune; when success and prosperity came, she proved herself worthy of them, by prudence, moderation, and generosity. Even her enemies were compelled to pay homage to her virtues and graces. We have given but a rapid sketch of the events of the war, because it has, in reality, but little connexion with Hungarian history, except in so far as the Hungarian troops gave, on every battle-field, proofs of indomitable valour and constancy; and as the Hungarian people were the first to bid defiance, on the queen's behalf, to the trained armies of three of the most warlike kingdoms in Europe, led on by generals who had grown gray in the service. It was their good fortune also, that in none of these campaigns did a hostile force put foot in their territories, and they were thus enabled to pursue in peace the various operations of commerce and agriculture, which each generation, for centuries previously, had seen interrupted, either by internal disturbances, or by foreign invasion, and that they aided building up a power whose fostering protection gave them repose after their troubles, and introduced reforms and ameliorations, the effects of which have not yet ceased to show themselves, even in our own time. It is to these that we shall now direct attention. To attempt to follow the empress queen through the various "battles, sieges, and fortunes" by which her career was agitated, and the various disturbances which her relations with neighbouring princes underwent, would be foreign to our present purpose, and, from the outline sketch in which our space would compel us to present them, would be necessarily uninteresting to the reader.*

The great and leading idea of Maria Theresa's reign was, the establishment of one law and language throughout the whole of her vast empire. Some of the earlier kings of Hungary fancied that differences of race, language, and manners amongst their subjects were a source of national strength; and in this they were undoubtedly wrong. But the Austrian monarchs too generally erred in the opposite direction. In their eagerness to reign over a united people, amongst whom the tongue, manners, and costume of the governing power should prevail, they overlooked the difficulties which lay in the way of a "consummation so devoutly to be wished." The mingling of races, and the obliteration of distinctions, is the slow work of time, of equal laws, and of a community of interests. The arms of a conqueror may overcome, but a people's manners and mother-tongue, bid defiance to cannon and bayonet. A petty tribe, of obscure origin, and without a single ennobling memory, will cling to them with a tenacity which survives a dozen dynasties and a hundred revolutions. A great nation, loving its independence, whose history is a line of light, and whose traditions breathe of liberty and glory, may be conquered in a single campaign, but will take centuries for its subjugation. Those very distinctions which were the objects of Maria Theresa's aversion, were the pride and glory of the Hungarians. In attempting to remove them, she overrated her power. But, nevertheless, she was not wholly unsuccessful. In her day, as at a more recent period, it was the common opinion in Vienna, that the Hungarians were barbarians—proud, courageous, and indomitable, certainly, but still barbarians—and, as a matter of course, greatly in need of civilisation. The possibility of a humanising process, in which the introduction of the German language, manners, habits, and costume, did not form a part, never

* The foregoing narrative of the events in the earlier part of Maria Theresa's reign has, in great part, been condensed from Lacy's Histoire de Hongrie, Voltaire's Siécle de Louis XIV., and Coxe's History of the House of Austria.

occurred to the Austrians, and does not seem to have occurred to Maria Theresa; but she found time enough, amidst the distractions of foreign war, to endeavour to carry out her project. She had too much tact, however, to offer violence to deeply-rooted and honest prejudices; and instead of resorting to the measures of coercion which her predecessors had so often vainly employed with the same object, she sought to subdue the nobles by the fascination of her beauty and her conversation, just as she had subdued the diet, in the early part of her reign, by the romance of youth and beauty in distress. She was witty, intellectual, and dignified. Every look, and attitude, and tone, was full of power and of seduction. Burke's description of her ill-fated daughter, might be applied to her with far greater truth and accuracy, "that never lighted on this orb, which she scarcely seemed to touch, a more delightful vision, * * * decorating and cheering the elevated sphere she moved in—glittering like the morning star, full of life, and splendour, and joy!"

She knew how to gather illustrious men around her, and then to mould them, as it were, after her own will and pleasure; to impress them, at a glance, with the consciousness that they stood in the presence of one mightier than they. She made her court the resort of all the gay, the brave, the accomplished of the day—a galaxy of splendour, of which she was the brightest star. The influence of a married woman who unites personal charms with mental power, is, perhaps, the strongest under which young men can fall; her position, more especially if rank be one of the elements in it, renders passion hopeless or impossible, and makes her dominion a mixture of the intellectual and æsthetic solely. None knew this better than Maria Theresa, and none ever made better use of it in advancing her own schemes. The youth of the Magyar noblesse were constantly invited to court, were flattered, amused, were inspired with all the *spirituels* tastes which the French philosophers were then diffusing through Europe. What wonder if, surrounded by so much that was brilliant, attractive, and withal so elevating, they forgot what it most behoved them to remember and love, the liberty and glory of their native land. They neglected their language, cast aside their splendid and becoming costume, and speedily became more German than the Germans themselves, and at last sunk into a state of sybaritic carelessness, more fatal to all earnest purpose and high endeavour than open and avowed renegadism.

The queen, however, managed very ably and judiciously to hide her insidious attacks upon the constitution by the introduction of a number of really useful reforms. She expelled the jesuits from the kingdom; she provided a better system of education for the masses, abolished a number of barbarous usages which had been handed down from the early days of feudalism, such as the use of the rack, and right of sanctuary in particular places, and at last so thoroughly connected the cause of enlightened reform with German institutions, that many of the Magyars began to get ashamed of their own. So thorough, in short, was the influence which this wonderful woman gained over them, that she never summoned the diet more than three times during her long reign of forty years, and habitually disregarded those constitutional forms which the natives had ever preserved with the most watchful jealousy.

One of her measures, however, displayed talent so far-seeing and comprehensive, and so wise a regard for the welfare of the very poor and helpless classes, that it must for ever redound to her honour, and more than compensated for any slight breaches of the forms of the constitution. This was the *Urbarium*, or code of laws regulating the relations between landlord and tenant.

The very existence of the Hungarian peasant was hardly recognised by the law until the year 1405. He was his master's serf, and this was all that the diet knew or cared about him, though he was at the same time not a mere slave. In the above year liberty was accorded him of leaving the place where he was born, in case he could obtain his lord's consent, and the latter was not allowed to refuse it without good and sufficient reason. In 1548 the insurrection under Docza so exasperated the nobles, that all the peasants were reduced to absolute serfdom, but this law was repealed soon after, and at last, after various changes, the peasant's charter, which, for the first time, placed his rights on a firm and well-defined footing, came from the hand of Maria Theresa.

In 1764, at the last of the three diets held during her reign, she caused strong representations to be made regarding the grievances which pressed upon the peasantry, but nothing was done. An insurrection soon after broke out, and great excesses were committed in various parts of the country before the troops could put down the disturbance. Maria instantly resolved to take advantage of the excitement to remove the abuses of which she complained by her own arbitrary act, and though she thereby committed a breach of the constitution, she excused herself by the plea, that the end she aimed at more than justified the means. The result was the famous *Urbarium*, which remained in force till 1835. The leading provisions of this code have been thus enumerated by Mr. Paget:—

"1. The peasant was no longer attached to the soil, but could leave his farm and landlord whenever he thought fit, having first given due notice to the magistrate, and paid his debts.

"2. An entire peasant's fief consisted of a house and garden-ground, to the extent of an acre; of an arable and pasture farm, varying in different countries, and according to the qualities of the soil, from sixteen to forty acres of arable, and from about six to twelve of meadow land. The landlord could only dispossess the peasant, nor that without due process of law, in case he had absolute need of the land to build his house upon, or in case of incapacity or refusal on the part of the peasant to fulfil his duties, or of condemnation for heinous offence; nor could the landlord exchange the fief without giving another equally large and good.

"4. Where there were vineyards, the peasant might retail wines from Michaelmas-day to St. George's; where there were none, to Christmas only.

The peasant might cut wood for building and firing, and gather rushes on his landlord's property, without payment. Soemill, or the obligation to grind at the

HUNGARIAN IN THE NATIONAL COSTUME.

landlord's mill, was forbidden, as likewise all other demands except those specified by this law.

The peasant held this property—for such it really was—subject to the following conditions:—

1. The holder of an entire fief was bound to labour for his landlord, in every year, one hundred and four days, or, if he brought a team of oxen or horses, fifty-two, from sunrise till sunset. This time it was required should be taken in one or two days weekly, as it might be, except during the harvest, when it might be doubled for a certain time, though not increased in the gross amount; and, moreover, one quarter of the labour was to be reckoned in the three winter months.

2. In like manner the holder of half a fief performed half the quantity of service; and the holder of a quarter only a fourth: a mere householder rendered only eighteen days hard labour.

3. Every four holders of entire fiefs were obliged, once yearly, to furnish a man and horse for a two days' journey, the landlord paying the necessary expenses.*

4. Each peasant, for liberty of cutting wood, was obliged to cut and convey to his landlord's dwelling one small cartload of firewood.

5. When the country was infested by beasts of prey (bears, boars, wolves, and foxes), the peasant was to assist in hunting three days, if required, in the course of the year.

6. For his house he paid two shillings yearly.

7. Every fief was bound to pay two hens, two capons, nineteen eggs, and one pound of butter, or eighteen pence; and every thirty fiefs together one calf, or three shillings in money.

8. Should the lord or lady marry, or enter any religious order, the peasant was obliged to make a present similar to the contribution in the former clause; and the same if the lord was taken in battle and forced to ransom himself.

9. For permission to distil, the peasant paid four shillings yearly for each still.

10. Of all the productions of the soil, one-ninth belonged to the landlord, except the produce of the second harvest and the fruits of the garden. Of cattle, lambs, and kids, a ninth was also the lord's due."

In order to enforce prompt obedience to these laws, the seigneur was empowered to inflict summary punishment upon refractory peasants, by means of his officers, to the amount of twenty-five blows; for which, however, he was amenable to the laws, if it were inflicted without due cause.

The *Sedes Dominalis*, or manor court, in which the lord or his representatives appointed the judges, was declared the legal tribunal for the settlement of differences between the peasant and his lord, as well as those that might arise among the peasants themselves. There was a right of appeal to the county court, and

* When there was no post, this was the means used for sending letters.

from that to the *Statthalterei*, in Buda. In civil matters, the jurisdiction extended to all cases under the value of six pounds; in criminal, to the infliction of twenty-five blows.

It will be seen at a glance how many acts of oppression and injustice might still be committed by the lord without infringing any of the above regulations, and how hard, toilsome, and hopeless the peasant's life would still remain even under their protection. But still it was a long step in advance, and fully entitled Maria Theresa to the appellation which the grateful serfs conferred on her—of Mother of her Country. She rightly concluded how much more advantageous it was to have good husbandmen in the fields than good soldiers in the army; and this victory of hers, achieved over prejudice and oppression, in favour of a wronged and wretched caste, will shed lustre on her name when the exploits of her armies and the triumphs of her diplomacy have descended to the same tomb with her beauty, her wit, and her heroism. We cannot dismiss her without referring to an act by which the close of her reign was tarnished. By the Seven Years' War which she carried on with Frederick the Great of Prussia, she was compelled to cede him the whole of Silesia, and we may fairly presume that this loss had something to do with the share she took in the partition of Poland, the most iniquitous outrage ever perpetrated by civilized sovereigns. That unfortunate country was in a state of complete anarchy under the rule of the imbecile Stanislaus Poniatowski, and in 1771 the Austrian minister Kaunitz, forgetful of the extremities to which his own mistress had been reduced thirty years previously, by a similar scheme on the part of France and Bavaria, proposed to the empress of Russia and the king of Prussia to divide it between them. The proposal was eagerly accepted, and Austria was recompensed for the loss of Silesia by the annexation of Gallicia and Lodomeria.

Maria Theresa died in 1780. She had six sons and ten daughters, of whom nine survived her. Amongst the daughters was the unfortunate Marie Antoinette, afterwards queen of France.

CHAPTER XX.

TROUBLES IN THE REIGN OF JOSEPH II. AND LEOPOLD II. AND FRANCIS I.

A.D. 1780—1815.

Maria Theresa was succeeded by her son, Joseph the Second of that name. He was then in the forty-first year of his age; and the highest expectations were formed regarding his skill and ability in the science of government. He had everything in his favour. Though his early training had been confided to two Hungarians, whose prejudiced dulness rendered them anything but well adapted for their office, his great strength of character and natural spirit of inquiry triumphed over the disadvantages of education, and made him one of the most innovating and enterprising sovereigns that had ever sat upon the Austrian throne. In the twenty-fourth year of his age he was called to the imperial crown, but his mother's love of power and long reign prevented him taking any part in the administration of public affairs during his earlier years. He was thus enabled to devote his whole time to the gratification of his ruling passion—the desire of knowledge. He travelled through the length and breadth of the imperial dominions as a private individual, without pomp or attendance, minutely examining all public institutions and establishments, civil and military; arts, manufactures, commerce, and education—all came in for a due share of his study and observation. The condition of the people also did not escape his notice. He entered the huts of the poorest, listened to their stories, and formed plans for the amelioration of their lot, which he afterwards endeavoured to carry out, and which were at least distinguished by honesty of purpose. The consequence of these researches was, that he became speculative in the highest degree, and was afflicted with that contempt for expediency and practicability which speculativeness generally brings with it. When he succeeded to the throne, he found himself in possession of ample materials for carrying his theories into execution. His dominions comprised an area of 180,000 square miles, and contained 24,000,000 of inhabitants, who spoke ten different languages, and were composed of several different nations, with different laws, religion, manners and customs, and holding little communication of any sort with each other. Some were governed by a written code; others by local customs, of which each district had its own; and others by the feudal system, which in most parts flourished in full vigour. The clergy and nobles had all the real power in their hands, and looked upon the citizens with all the dislike and contempt which idleness usually feels towards industry, and the aristocracy of birth and rank towards the more substantial, more useful, but certainly less romantic aristocracy of wealth and enterprise. As for the peasants, they were counted among the beasts of the field, born to minister to the luxury and caprice of the noble, and were, except in the Netherlands, Tyrol, and Austria Proper, in a state of complete vassalage.

Joseph no sooner fond himself in possession of the reins of power, than he formed the stupendous plan of abolishing all these differences and distinctions, and of moulding this vast, disjointed, and heterogeneous mass into one compact and united body, governed by one law, speaking the same language, and living under the same institutions. He accordingly forthwith abolished all the separate jurisdictions in the various provinces, such as the assemblies composed of the nobles and clergy, and a few deputies from the loyal and free towns which shared with the sovereign the right of administering justice and imposing taxes. He divided the whole of the monarchy into thirteen governments, each subdivided into a number of districts or circles. Each of the latter was presided over by a magistrate, who superintended the execution of the laws, and protected the peasantry from the injustice of the nobility. The capital of each government contained a court, one department of which was set apart for the nobility, and the other for the lower classes, and from this there were three degrees of appeal, the final resort being to Vienna. A subordinate officer had the care of the police, but he was under military control, and every department was in absolute and entire subjection to the supreme council or chancery at Vienna; or, in other words, to the arbitrary will of the monarch.

Hungary, of course, was placed under the new regulations, having previously suffered from many violent and arbitrary acts. Upon his mother's death Joseph acknowledged the rights and privileges of the states in a circular letter, but he nevertheless refused to go through the ceremony of coronation, because he was determined to destroy them, and consequently would not confirm them by an oath. Nay, he went farther than this: he wantonly carried off the crown, sceptre, and other regalia, from Presburg, and deposited them at Vienna, thus offering one of the greatest insults in his power to the national prejudices, though he well knew the superstitious veneration paid to these relics by the Magyars, and the importance they attached to their presence within the kingdom. He also abolished the use of the Latin and Hungarian languages, and permitted the German only to be used in all public offices. He destroyed the whole municipal system of the country, upon which the natives, with justice, looked as the great safeguard of their liberties. County meetings were forbidden, as also the election of county officers; the local courts were abolished, and the forms, usages, and times of assembling were so entirely different in those that were established to supply their place, that the whole judicial system was thrown into a state of confusion through which not even the practitioners could find their way, and the proscription of the two languages, in which all the charters and other official documents were framed, naturally inspired the natives with the fear that this was but the prelude to the total abolition of their simplest privileges. With these sweeping innovations were mingled some measures of salutary reform, which had the effect of inducing the Hungarians to bear them for awhile patiently. The convents and monasteries were dissolved, and their vast endowments bestowed upon the schools and colleges; complete toleration was granted to the protestants; a great number of sinecures was abolished; taxation was more equally distributed, and several important privileges were conferred upon the peasantry. The removal of the crown of St. Stephen, however, raised the whole nation into a ferment, and firm remonstrances, the tone and language of which bordered closely on threats, were poured into Vienna. Joseph, nothing daunted, ordered that all resistance to his commands should be put down by force; and strong hints were given, that if the nobility persevered in their opposition, a servile war would be excited, which would overwhelm them and their nationality together. But all was in vain. A diet was loudly called for, and both subsidies and levies were refused. Soldiers were sent to raise both one and the other by force. The crisis was fast approaching, when Joseph surrendered. He had been unsuccessful in a war against the Turks, was encompassed by foreign enemies, harassed by domestic contentions with his own brother, and had seen his best concerted schemes frustrated. He yielded to the demands of the Hungarian nobility, restored their constitution, language, and national dress, sent back the regalia, and promised to have himself crowned in due form speedily. He did not live to fulfil it. He died on the 20th of February, 1790, in the forty-ninth year of his age, and the tenth of his reign. The epitaph which he himself ordered to be inscribed upon his tomb is an excellent commentary upon his career:—"Here lies Joseph, a sovereign, who with the best intentions, never carried a single project into execution." It was well for Hungary that he saw his mistake with regard to her before his decease, and well for his own memory, that, as soon as he saw it he hastened to rectify it.

The crown was received in Hungary with transports of joy. Triumphal arches were erected on the roads along which it had to pass, and before it reached Buda it was attended by an immense crowd. On the night of its arrival, it was placed in the cathedral, and guarded by two magistrates with drawn sabres; every house was illuminated, and the streets resounded with acclamations. Never was the impolicy of irritating a people whom it was so easy to appease, so clearly manifested. Joseph's death, however, and the restoration of the crown and constitution, did not completely put an end to the troubles. He had never been, and accordingly was not, in the eye of the Hungarian law, a legitimate sovereign. The rule of succession was, therefore, said to be abrogated, and the right of election to be revived, and the claims of Leopold, Joseph's brother, to the throne were denied by a large and powerful party. They considered the concessions which had been made by the late emperor previous to his death to have been the result of fear rather than of a desire to do justice. The recent astounding events in France also were not without their influence in increasing the excitement. At the county assemblies dissatisfaction, not only with Joseph's acts, but with Leopold's promises, was openly expressed, and a disposition was clearly evinced not only to adopt the words but to follow the example of the French revolutionary party. An address sent to the emperor from the people of Pesth may furnish a good idea of the state of the public mind at that period:—"The fame, august sovereign, which has preceded you, has declared you a just and generous prince. It says that you forget not that you are a man; that you are sensible the king was made for the people, and not the people for the king. The violent commotions which have agitated our country after so many acts of injustice are thereby somewhat allayed. Scarcely, therefore, could we trust our eyes, when in your first rescript to us of the fourteenth instant, we found not those securities for the safety of our constitution, which our hereditary rights and the inflexible patience of the people under the lawless reign of the late emperor demanded; securities which your majesty has fully granted to the Belgians, an act which will remain as a proof of your sentiments throughout all ages.

"From the rights of nations and of man, and from that social compact whence states arose, it is incontestible that the sovereignty originates from the people. This axiom our parent Nature has impressed on the hearts of all; it is one of those which a just prince (and such, we trust, your majesty ever will be) cannot dispute; it is one of those inalienable imprescriptible rights which the people cannot forfeit by neglect or disuse. Our constitution places the sovereignty jointly in the king and the people, in such manner that the remedies necessary to be applied, according to the ends of social life, for the security of persons and property, are in the power of the people. We are sure, therefore, that at the meeting of the ensuing diet, your majesty will not confine yourself to the objects mentioned in your rescript; but will also restore our freedom to us in like manner as to the Belgians, who have conquered theirs with the sword. It would be an example big with danger to teach the world that a people can only protect or regain their liberties by the sword, and not by obedience."

To this Leopold returned the only answer that was possible, by summoning a general diet for his coronation, an event which had not taken place for fifty years. It was very fully attended by the nobility, who flocked to the meeting full of confidence, and prepared a new inaugural diploma or declaration, which revived all the ancient restrictions which, in former days, had been imposed upon the Hungarian kings. Leopold now found himself in a very critical position. He must either have surrendered every vestige of power, or have it wrested from him, surrounded as he was by enemies, two of whom, Turkey and Prussia, were known to be carrying on intrigues with the malcontents. He, therefore, as a last resource, called in the aid of division, an ally which had many a time previously done good service for his house; and, by stirring up the Sclavonic inhabitants of Hungary against the Magyars, and flattering them with the hope of a separate nationality, he raised a powerful party to support him against the diet. The Magyars, however, nothing daunted, sent deputies to the convention at Reichenbach, which met for the purpose of concluding a peace with Turkey and Prussia, and claimed the right to which we have often alluded, and which was repeatedly secured to them—of taking part in the negotiations on behalf of the Hungarian nation with the same power and authority as the royal plenipotentiaries. This, and many other demands which sought to revive privileges which had long ago fallen into disuse, were embodied in the inaugural declaration which Leopold was called upon to sign. He peremptorily refused to do so after a long discussion, announced his fixed intention of being crowned on no other terms than those accepted by his grandfather Charles and his mother Maria Theresa, and the diet at last gave way. Presburg was, therefore, appointed the place for the ceremonial. The crown and regalia were sent thither, and, on the 10th of November, 1790, the king made his appearance, accompanied by his five sons. His presence, and his revival of the old forms of the constitution seemed to have pacified his enemies, and allayed their discontents. A conciliatory spirit now pervaded the whole assembly. Leopold was received with acclamation; his fourth son, the unfortunate Alexander, was selected from amongst the candidates for the office of palatine, vacant by the death of Esterhazy, the first member of the house of Hapsburg that had ever attained to that dignity. The emperor then thanked them for the warmth of their reception, being so much more cordial than he had ventured to expect, and declared his intention to govern according to the laws; and with great earnestness exhorted his son to fulfil his duty to the nation at all hazards, and without regard to his feelings.

On the 15th of the month, Leopold was solemnly crowned by the new palatine, after having signed a diploma containing the same stipulations as that of Maria Theresa, and he covered himself with popularity by rising up after the usual public dinner of which every new sovereign partook, and announcing his willingness to consent to a law binding every future king to be crowned within six months after his accession to the throne. As this would preclude the possibility of such infringements upon their liberties as had distinguished the reign of Joseph, the declaration was received with shouts of rejoicing; and, in the heat of its enthusiasm, the diet raised the usual honorarium from 100,000 florins to 225,000. Leopold expressed his thanks in an eloquent speech, in which he declared, that the sincerest wish of his heart was to rule them by love, and not by fear.

The diet then proceeded to business, under the presidency of their new palatine; and, after securing and confirming all Leopold's concessions, such as the right of religious toleration, and the priority of the Magyar language in official transactions, they appointed a standing committee, or deputation, of the whole nation, to inquire into the *gravamina*, or grievances of Hungary, with power to review the whole circumstances of the country, and propose a general, efficient, and radical reform. How its labours ended we shall see hereafter. For the present they were suspended by the death of Leopold, in March, 1792, after a short reign of two years.

Leopold was succeeded by his eldest son Francis, then in the twenty-fifth year of his age. No monarch of the house of Austria ever ascended the throne with so many dangers threatening him on every side. The crisis of the French revolution was fast approaching, and the terrible propagandist zeal of the jacobins had spread their doctrines all over Europe, and roused all those bad passions, and delusive hopes by which France was lured on to her doom. Louis XVI. was now in close confinement, and his revolted subjects were deliberating upon his fate. The crowned heads of Europe took the alarm. An agreement had already been entered into at Pilnitz between the king of Prussia and Leopold, in which the two sovereigns bound themselves to march to the aid of the French monarch, and restore him, if not to the possession of absolute power, at least to the possession of his liberty. But this impolitic interference, as all the world now knows, and as any wise man might then have predicted, only aggravated the miseries and dangers of his situation. The leaders of the French people had gone too far to think of receding. Their only hope and only safety lay in advancing, and their objects were never so effectually served as by this threat of foreign intervention. The allied monarchs little knew the terrible force that slumbers in the heart of a great nation, or they would never have threatened to force it to undo its own acts and to eat its words. The revolution rushed on like a flood, and in Hungary it found the seed already sown, and needing but moisture to spring up and bear fruit. The events in Paris were watched at Buda with the keenest interest. Each act in the great drama, on which the eyes of all Europe were fixed, was there discussed with deep earnestness. The debates in the national assembly were eagerly read, and several of the young men entered into correspondence with the chiefs of the Mountain.* A party was soon formed, having for its object the overthrow of the monarchical form of government, headed by Joseph Martinovics, at one time a Franciscan friar, of Rascian origin, subtle, versatile, but possessing little principle. He was the prime organizer of the movement, and commenced his work by distributing revolutionary tracts upon a vast scale—one of the most remarkable of which was the "Citizen's Catechism." They produced their effect, and great numbers of the youth soon joined him in carrying on his enterprise. They were at length, however, betrayed by a servant, who overheard their deliberations, and the principal conspirators were arrested and condemned, some to death, others to imprisonment for life. They met their fate, as might have been expected, with a courage and fortitude that made them martyrs in the eyes of the people. In the same year, 1794, the palatine, the archduke Alexander, was killed by the explosion of some fireworks at a fête in Vienna—some said designedly, in consequence of his being suspected of aspiring to the crown of Hungary.

In the meantime, the Austrian army had been suffering terrible reverses from the French. Army after army was overwhelmed or destroyed by the valour of the republican soldiers and the skill of their generals, and Francis was forced to convoke a diet for the raising of new subsidies and levies. The states voted both

* Jacobinorum Hungaricorum Historia; by Antony Szirmay.

the one and the other, but strongly protested against the continuance of the war, which was in reality at this time a war of aggression, begun for the express purpose of intimidating the French nation, and interfering in the management of its internal affairs. When Napoleon, however, had ascended the imperial throne, and had shown clearly that he was animated by a thirst for universal dominion, there was an instant reaction in the public opinion of the Hungarians against France. Austria had been already invaded. Hungary was threatened, and the diet of 1807 displayed all its ancient horror of foreign occupation. They knew by bitter experience, that the presence of an enemy's troops within its territory is not merely the greatest disaster, but the foulest dishonour that can befal a nation. Austria herself was at this time reduced to the lowest ebb. Her bravest soldiers had been slain or dispersed, and her princes were fugitives from the hereditary dominions of their house. Desperate as had been her situation at Maria Theresa's accession to the throne, it was now still more deplorable. She had still the same resource, but her opponents were very different. The insurrection rose with great enthusiasm, and fought bravely in the ranks of her army. When commencing the campaign of 1808, Napoleon resolved to deprive Austria of this valuable ally by working on the patriotic prejudices of the Hungarians; and consequently, after the capture of Vienna, he issued the following proclamation, which happily the Magyars estimated at its real value. Napoleon's gross duplicity, his innate hatred to liberty, were now becoming too apparent to be glossed over by the brilliancy of his bulletins. He had in like manner promised independence to the Poles, and, having roused their enthusiasm, used them for his own aggrandizement, and then left them to their fate :—

"Hungarians!

"The emperor of Austria, in violation of our treaties, and ungrateful for my generosity towards him, after three consecutive wars, and, above all, after that of 1805, has again attacked my armies. I have repelled this unjustifiable aggression, &c., &c. Hungarians! the moment for recovering your independence has arrived. I offer you peace, the preservation of your territory, of your liberty, and of your constitution. Assemble in your national diet upon the plains of Rakos, according to the custom of your ancestors, and make known to me your determination.

"NAPOLEON."

The proclamation was treated with the contempt it deserved. They had seen enough of French sympathy for the oppressed to make them dread it. Louis XIV. had encouraged Rakotski to take up arms at the end of the seventeenth century, and had promised to support him to the uttermost, but abandoned him long before the conflict was over. And now another French monarch, more false, more ambitious, and more powerful than Louis, was repeating the same offers under the same circumstances. It speaks no less strongly for Magyar prudence, than for Magyar pride and generosity, that they spurned the invader, and remained faithful to the cause of Francis I. Napoleon was not slow in taking vengeance upon them for their refusal. When Vienna was taken, Francis fled to Hungary, as his grandmother had done sixty years before under similar circumstances, and threw himself for protection on the Magyars. The insurrection was instantly levied;

every noble in the kingdom flew to arms; but their chivalrous valour could do little against the trained legions of France. The fiery squadrons of cavalry, which had been so terrible in the old wars against the Turks, were broken and dispersed

BATTLE OF RAAB.

by the veteran troops who had already vanquished the flower of the German and Russian infantry. Presburg was bombarded and fell; the archduke John was totally defeated on the plains of Raab by Eugene Beauharnois; and the countries bordering on the Adriatic were annexed to the French empire.

Francis was now reduced to the last extremity. He lay at the conqueror's mercy, and was compelled to drink the cup of humiliation to the dregs, by bestowing on him the hand of the archduchess Maria Louisa in marriage. Still he did not cease to hope, and with all that desperate tenacity for which his house has ever been distinguished, he continued to plot and labour for deliverance from his vassalage without ceasing. A diet was summoned in 1812, at which the palatine, the archduke Joseph, stated, in his opening address, "that the subject which should now be discussed was, not merely the safety of their own country, but the existence of the whole monarchy." Voluntary subsidies were accordingly voted once more; but an attempt to restore the national credit by the creation of new imposts was indignantly rejected. The reduction of bank notes to a fifth of the original value, a short time after this, justified the mistrust with which the diet looked upon all the financial measures of the Viennese cabinet. The retreat from Russia broke the power of Napoleon; the battle of Leipsic and the campaign of 1814, in which Hungary bore a distinguished part, and, last of all, the crowning disaster at Waterloo, completed his downfal, and placed the Hapsburgs once more in security upon their throne. Hungary had for twenty years taken no thought of her internal condition in her anxiety to save her rulers. We shall now see what return she received for her devotion.

CHAPTER XXI.

CONFLICTS BETWEEN THE DIET AND THE GOVERNMENT.—PROGRESS OF REFORM.

1815—1848.

THE battle of Waterloo, in 1815, put an end to the terrible struggle by which every country in Europe had for twenty years been agitated. The sovereigns of the continent now breathed freely for the first time in twenty-five years; and their first act was to enter into a league against their deliverers, to revoke all their concessions, and break all their promises, and to take every means in their power to restore the principle of legitimacy to the position it had occupied before the French Revolution. There never was a greater proof of human folly. Principles that rest on bases far sounder and more enduring than legitimacy could boast, could not have assumed their old place in men's hearts after such a shock as it had received.

The most audacious of all those who joined in framing the Holy Alliance was the emperor of Austria. The Hungarians reminded him, in 1815, of his repeated promises to redress their grievances, while they were voting him men and money to defend his capital against the assaults of Napoleon. He could not deny the promises, but he emphatically declined to fulfil them. They asked him to convoke the diet, but he had never had any great liking for the diet, and now had less than ever; for it was one of these institutions in which the despots saw most danger to themselves. He, therefore, determined to dispense with it for the future. In 1822, the movements of the Carbonari in Italy gave the cabinet of Vienna great uneasiness. New levies of troops became necessary, and, as a matter of course, new subsidies to clothe, feed, and pay them. As it was resolved not to assemble the diet, the only resource left was, of course, to raise the necessary supplies by a royal ordonnance. But no sooner was this attempted, than the county assemblies met, and offered it the most energetic resistance. Protests, remonstrances, and denunciations were poured into Vienna in rapid succession; and at last the popular ferment reached such a pitch, that the government found it absolutely necessary to yield the point in dispute.

In 1825, Francis I. convoked the diet, and from that moment the old struggle, which the wars with France had suspended, was renewed. The required subsidies were voted, but voted with so many precautionary conditions, that it was evident that the members felt serious alarm for the safety of the constitution. The session was, moreover, rendered for ever memorable by an incident, in itself of trifling importance, but of vast significance when viewed in connexion with subsequent events. It was in it that Count Stephen Szechenyi made his first speech in the Magyar language.

The life of this extraordinary man is more remarkable as an instance of what may be achieved by well-directed energy, labouring in obedience to the dictates of patriotism, than for any brilliant triumphs of eloquence or diplomacy. He was exactly the man for the crisis, and the crisis drew him forth as a magnet draws steel. He took in all the wants of the country at a glance, and immediately set to work to supply them. He was no great orator; so that his influence over the Magyars—an influence such as no private individual has ever acquired over a people, except, perhaps, Kossuth and O'Connell—must be looked upon rather as the triumph of practical good sense and good intentions, than of rhetorical appeals to prejudices or passion. His life, previous to 1825, had admirably fitted him for the great work upon which he was entering. He had passed through vicissitudes enough to sharpen his faculties and increase his self-reliance, without abating his courage or his hopefulness. His knowledge, too, was of a sort which seldom begets pride or self-sufficiency—knowledge of the world and of men, founded on observation and experience. He commenced life as an officer of hussars; and, in the terrible campaigns which preceded the downfal of Napoleon, he had fought in the Austrian service with distinguished courage. Though belonging to one of the oldest and most illustrious families of Hungary,—or rather, perhaps, for that very reason, the system of favouritism and intrigue by which the Austrian army has always been governed, kept him down to the rank of captain during the whole period of his service, seventeen years in all. When peace was restored, his position became intolerable. To a man of active and cultivated mind, the dull routine of garrison life was slavery of the worst kind. He had a seat in the chamber of magnates, to be sure; but as long as he held the emperor's commission, it would, according to military etiquette, have been unbecoming in him to speak his sentiments freely, if they were opposed to the policy of the government.

He accordingly quitted the army, and set out on his travels. His attention was principally fixed upon France and England, but upon the latter in particular. He spent a considerable length of time in this country, occupied in the diligent and careful study of our social and political institutions. He saw that the only hope for any nation in modern times lies in close application to industrial pursuits, and the development of its national resources; and he saw also, that nothing was clearer than that success in such a course was only attainable under a free government. It is not merely the improvement of man's moral and intellectual nature that need liberty of the press and security from the arbitrary violence of power. In the race of industrial enterprise, none must be cumbered with unnecessary weights, nor troubled by vexatious interference on the part of those in power. Hungary was already in possession of free institutions. To preserve and uphold them Szechenyi saw it was necessary that there should be a total change in the habits of her people, that they should learn to rely more on their own efforts, sharpen their intellects by commercial pursuits, and forget their differences of race and language in the common desire to better their material condition.

When he returned home he had formed his plans, and he set about carrying them into effect with a vigour and energy which left little doubt of his success. He had to act in the presence of powerful and ever-watchful enemies; but he determined to baffle them by the moderation of his language, and the legality of his acts; to aim rather at making his principles take deep root in the hearts of the people and work out their own results, than at producing striking effects at the outset.

STEPHEN SZECHENYI.

The first object to which his attention was directed was the restoration of the Magyar language, which, under the Germanizing efforts of Austria, had fallen into almost total disuse amongst the higher classes. He knew how intimately the use of the national language is connected with the feeling of nationality—the mysterious influence which the sound of the tongue in which strong men lisped their earliest prayers at their mother's knee, and in which all the holiest and purest affections of home and childhood found expression—possesses in rousing the feeling of attachment to country and liberty. But the Magyar was now totally neglected by the Magyar gentlemen. Latin was the language of the diet, and of all legal and official documents, and German and French were alone used in good society.

Szechenyi, as the first step in his scheme of reformation, set about rescuing it from the degradation and disuse into which it had fallen; and as the best of all ways to induce others to do a thing is to do it oneself first, he rose in the diet of 1825, and, contrary to previous usage, made a speech in Magyar. His colleagues were surprised; the magnates were shocked; the nation was electrified. None were more delighted than the country gentlemen and yeomanry or small farmers—two classes which, whatever be their faults of ignorance and prejudice, are in every country the foremost supporters of national usages, and the bitterest haters of foreign domination. They, who had always adhered to the language and customs of their forefathers, had seen with regret and apprehension the gradual alienation of the higher nobility from both one and the other, and it was therefore with no small pride that they heard of the adoption of their cause by one of the magnates themselves.

The diet sat for two years, and during the whole of that period Szechenyi continued his use of the native language, in which he strenuously opposed the designs of the court, and was soon considered the leader of the opposition or liberal party, which speedily grew up around him. His efforts were so successful, that before the close of the session, Francis was compelled to acknowledge the illegality of his previous acts, formally to recognise the independence of the country, and promise to convoke the diet at least once in every three years. Szechenyi had nobly testified the sincerity of his purposes, by proposing in the chamber of magnates the establishment of a society for the improvement of the Hungarian language; and upon the objection being raised of want of funds, he instantly offered to subscribe a year's income (£6,000), and his example being followed by count Karolyi György, who gave £4,000, £30,000 were soon raised, and the work was done.*

In the meantime he had been occupied no less busily with his pen than in the diet. Though the number of these amongst the educated classes who made use of Hungarian in speaking was few, the number who made use of it in writing was fewer still. Szechenyi hastened to set the example of adopting it for the latter purpose, by the publication of a work, entitled "Hitel" (*Credit*), in which he inquires into the causes of the want of commercial credit in Hungary, suggests the means of its removal, communicates the result of his observations in England and other countries, mercilessly ridicules the follies and prejudices of his countrymen, rebukes their faults, and sums up all in the advice—"Seek what is practical, depend upon yourselves for your reform, and keep well in mind, that the star of Hungary's glory has yet to shine." The work had at first the effect of irritating

* Paget's Hungary and Transylvania, vol. i p. 209.

and wounding the pride of the gentry, who were indignant at seeing their faults shown up with such homely familiarity, and some of the county assemblies ordered it to be burnt by the hands of the common hangman. But public opinion at last began to do him justice. The nervous energy of his style, the naïveté and clearness of his illustrations, and the air of affectionate advice which he managed to throw round the severest of his rebukes, soon made his works gain ground amongst the people. They were translated into German even, read with avidity, and caused fear and trembling at Vienna.

He soon had the satisfaction of seeing the Hungarian language growing to general use, but he was still vexed to see the total want of unity, co-operation, and communion which prevailed amongst the nobles, owing to the want of a newspaper press, or of any place of re-union where political subjects could be discussed amongst men of the same party with freedom and confidence. This he remedied by the establishment of the casino, at Pesth, upon the plan of the London clubs. He next turned his attention to the establishment of steam navigation on the Danube. It was sad to see that noble river rolling on idly to the sea, when on its broad bosom all the rich products of the country might have been borne to a safe and profitable market, instead of lying idly in the farmers' hands. He accordingly rigged out a boat, sailed down the Danube right to the Black Sea, explored it thoroughly, found it navigable in every part, went over to England, studied the principles of the steam-engine as applied to navigation, brought back English engineers, formed a company, and at last confounded the multitude of sceptics, who scoffed at his efforts, by the sight of a steam-boat on the river in full work. This feat was accomplished in October, 1830. He then stood at the topmost point in popular favour, and all looked to him for guidance in the crisis which had arisen in Hungarian politics by means of the French revolution.

That event produced a profound impression in Hungary, owing to the excitable state in which it found the public mind, and caused the utmost alarm to the government. The *Marseillaise* was sung in the streets of Pesth, and hundreds of the young men of the liberal party started for Paris, to drink in the revolutionary ideas at the fountain head. In the midst of this excitement, the emperor, being in need of new levies, was compelled to call an extraordinary meeting of the diet. The states voted the required subsidies, but sought to impose upon the cabinet a condition binding it to commit the command of Hungarian regiments to Hungarian officers exclusively. This was rejected by the ministry; but so strong was the feeling on the subject, that it required all the efforts of the archduke Joseph, the palatine, who at that time enjoyed great popularity, to get the vote carried without it. The deputies next proceeded to a revision of the constitution, for the first time within a century. The majority in the lower chamber were, of course, liberals; but in the upper chamber, being composed of prelates and wealthy magnates, the conservative party had the preponderance. Of the various demands made by the latter, fourteen were now selected as *preferentalia*, and after a stormy debate, passed both chambers. These may be said to contain every real wrong of which Hungary complained.

"They demand that Dalmatia, Transylvania, Gallicia and Lodomeria should be incorporated with Hungary; that the military frontiers should be placed under the command of the palatine, and governed by Hungarian laws; that the duty on salt should be reduced; that the edicts of government to officers of justice should be discontinued; that the laws respecting the taxes on the clergy should be observed; that the Hungarian chancery should be made really and not nominally independent of the Austrian chancery; that the coinage should bear the arms of Hungary; that the exportation of gold and silver should be prevented;* that paper money should be abolished, and a return made to metallic currency; that the Hungarian language should be used in all official business; that the fiscal estates, such as have fallen to the crown upon the extinction of the families to whom they were granted, should, as the law directed, be given only as the reward of public services, and not sold, as at present, to the highest bidder; and, lastly, that spies should not be employed and trusted by the Austrian government in Hungary."†

These, as may be readily perceived, were all so many demands that the existing laws should be strictly carried into effect—reasonable requests enough, one would imagine; but Austria had no intention whatever of complying with them, and put off giving any answer from day to day, until the session was over. The deputies did not separate, however, without making an eloquent appeal to the cabinet on behalf of the unfortunate Poles, who had risen in insurrection in Warsaw, driven out the grand duke Constantine, and were now awaiting in terrible suspense the attack of the assembled forces of the empire. The fifty-two counties of Hungary offered to raise each 2,000 men, making a total of 104,000, and to arm and support them at their own expense as long as the war should last, and send them to the assistance of the insurgents. But the Viennese cabinet had too much sympathy with the cause of absolutism, and too much mistrust of the liberal party, to give any countenance to the scheme. It accordingly fell to the ground, and the Poles were crushed.

In the interval which followed the dissolution of the diet, Szechenyi still followed up his plan of reform with unwearied diligence, and owing to his exertions, a party was now formed which sought not merely the strict observance of the existing laws, but the reform of them, the abolition of the unjust privileges of the nobles, the emancipation of the peasantry, the establishment of a system of education, the equal distribution of the taxes, the equality of all religious sects, the improvement of the commercial code and of internal communication, and though last, not least, the freedom of the press. These projects were all strenuously debated, but on this occasion without any practical result.

The next meeting was for a long time delayed, upon one pretext or another.

* One of the fallacies of the country gentlemen, but by no means peculiar to those of Hungary.

† Paget, vol. i. p. 160—1.

At last it was convened in 1832, and proved in many respects one of the most important that had ever assembled. The object of the liberal party was to make the revision of the commercial code the first subject for consideration; but the government managed dexterously to postpone this, and bring forward the grievances of the peasantry, thus making itself appear the poor man's friend, and throwing the odium of injustice on the liberal party, in case the necessary concessions were refused through the bigotry of any of the more ignorant members of the nobility.

In the midst of these checks, however, Szechenyi achieved one great triumph. We have already alluded to the singular jealousy with which the nobles looked upon any attempt to impose upon them a fair share of the public burdens. Exemption from all tax or contribution to the public revenue, of whatever kind, they considered one of their dearest privileges. The absurdity, mischief, and injustice of such a claim in a country where the nobles comprised all but the poorest class of the population, happily amongst us, needs no demonstration. Szechenyi saw clearly, that until this monstrous anomaly was removed, there was no hope for the country. It was, however, no easy task; for the abuse was supported, not by self-interest only, but the scarcely less powerful feeling of pride. He therefore attacked the principle of exemption in one of its least details, and thus paved the way for its total downfal. The want of a bridge over the Danube, to connect the two cities of Pesth and Buda, had long been felt. To supply it, however, no one seemed disposed to contribute anything better than talk, until Szechenyi took it in hand. With him, to conceive a project was to carry it into effect. He thought it a national disgrace that the two chief towns of the kingdom, lying on opposite banks of the same river, should, during six months of the year, have no better means of intercommunication than a bridge of boats, and, during the remainder, the ice and a ferry-boat. He accordingly proposed, that a stone or iron bridge should be erected by means of a loan, raised in shares, the interest of which should be paid by a toll levied upon all passengers, whether noble or not, and authorized by an act of the diet. The opposition this met with was immense. The idea of a noble paying any tax, however small, was so new to the Hungarian mind, and withal seemed so monstrous and outrageous, that many of the country gentlemen doubted whether any man in possession of his senses could for a moment entertain it. Every possible objection was raised. It was said the river was too wide, the current too rapid; that in winter the ice would sweep it away. But Szechenyi was not daunted. He supported his scheme in the journals, in the chamber, in the saloons, by argument, entreaty, and ridicule; and at last had the satisfaction of seeing a bill passed authorizing the taxation of the nobles in the shape of a bridge-toll. The principle of exemption had received its death-blow, and the old tories were in despair. Cziraki, the chief justice of the kingdom, imitating the example said to have been set by a noble lord in the House of Peers in England, who, on the passing of the Catholic Emancipation Act, exclaimed, with tears in his eyes, that "the sun of England had set for ever,"—wept bitterly, and declared that "he would never cross this ill-fated bridge, for in its erection he saw the downfal of the Hungarian nobility." Shortsighted old man! Across the bridge lay the path to the salvation and independence of the country, and it is one of the highest proofs of Szechenyi's sagacity that he was the first to discover it.

The next question which came under discussion was the revision of the Urbarial Code, or in other words the laws regulating the condition of the peasantry. The Urbarium of Maria Theresa was a measure of the highest importance, and was looked upon by the peasants as their charter; but there were still many grievances which pressed heavily upon them, one of the greatest being the load of taxation, the whole of which they bore. They could not be removed from their farms, to be sure, without good and substantial reasons; but if they were removed, their liabilities to the state did not cease, and their liabilities to their landlord seldom left them much room for economising. It was, however, clearly the interest of the crown to protect and favour them, for it was to them alone it could look for supplies.

The principle upon which the new Urbarium was based was in itself excellent; "that where it was safe and proper, the rights of the peasant should be increased and his burdens diminished, and in no instance should his privileges, however attained, be curtailed." Acting upon this, the petty tithes, often the means of much vexatious oppression, were abolished; the robot labour due to the landlord as rent, and which, notwithstanding the vast changes in value which property of every kind had undergone since the days of Maria Theresa, still remained fixed at 104 days a year, was reduced to 52; but what was more important than all, was the concession to the peasant of a property in his fief, and, consequently, the right of buying and selling the investitures and improvements. The effect of this measure was, in reality, to attach the taxation to the land and not to a class; for henceforth if a noble became the purchaser of a peasant's fief, he became liable for all the burdens upon it, of whatever kind and to whomsoever due.

The Urbarium of Maria Theresa had left the administration of justice amongst the peasantry in a most unsatisfactory state. The only court to which they could resort in the first instance was the manor court of the estate on which he lived, or, as it was called in Hungarian Latin, the *Sedes Dominalis*, in which the landlord himself presided. In cases of disputes between two peasants, justice no doubt in most cases was fairly and impartially administered; but in that large class of suits which must have arisen out of the peculiar relation in which the peasant and the noble stood to each other, to suppose the latter to be capable of just judgment when he himself was plaintiff or defendant, was to attribute to him an amount of conscientiousness and strength of character certainly not warranted by our experience of human nature. The jurisdiction of this tribunal was, therefore, henceforth limited to suits between peasant and peasant, and all those arising between landlord and tenant were referred to a newly constituted court, composed of five disinterested persons, of whom the magistrate of the district should be one, the right of appeal to the county court remaining in force as before. The noble was also deprived of the power, which he had previously possessed, of inflicting corporeal punishment to the extent of twenty-five blows of a stick upon refractory peasants, and was restricted to a sentence of imprisonment from one to three days, a power which the system of forced labour rendered necessary.

An Englishman may think that, even after these reforms, the condition of the peasantry still remained in a most unsatisfactory state; but when we take into account what it had previously been, and remember the weight of prejudice and self-interest which the promoters of these just and reasonable, though partial, concessions had to contend against, we must acknowledge that modern history presents few cases of a social revolution deserving so much of our attention and admiration.

The question of language was the most delicate which had as yet been touched upon. The preceding chapter will have put the reader in possession of the great diversity of language and race which prevailed amongst the population of Hungary. The main object of the diet now was to obliterate these distinctions, and make the people—as far, at least, as legislation could do it—a united whole. The first step in this direction was clearly the selection of one language out of the many to receive official support and sanction, and thus to pave the way for its adoption amongst all classes. Latin was at that time the language of all official documents and of the courts of law, ever since the reign of Stephen, in the year 1000. He wrote a political testament, in which he declared, singularly enough, that no country could securely exist which spoke but one language, and he promoted the distinction of races by every means in his power. When he resolved upon introducing Christianity into Hungary, he invited priests from Germany to aid him, and they naturally enough made every effort to make Latin—the language of the church and of the learned all over Europe at that period—the official language in their adopted country. They were successful, but the knowledge of it was always confined to the clergy and nobility.* The mass of the common people knew no tongue but their vernacular, and the laws and proceedings of the diet were, of course, sealed books to them. This made no great difference when every poor man was a serf, and when his only business in life was to obey the mandates of his seigneur. But when he was all but emancipated, when serfdom was virtually abolished, when distinctions of caste were about to disappear, and when a voice in the government of the country became a privilege in which the great mass of the population might look forward to share at no distant date, a change became absolutely necessary. To allow the law to continue to speak in an unknown tongue would have been an abuse which no body of legislators could pass over.

The disuse of the Latin, then, was a point upon which all were agreed; but the great difficulty lay in the choice of a substitute. Not that any hesitation was felt as to which of the existing languages had the best right to fill the vacant place;

* See Kossuth's speech at Boston, at the Legislative Banquet.

but it was feared that the choice of any one would exasperate the races who spoke the others; and the event proved that these fears were not without foundation. Still the duty of the diet was not less clear. Every consideration pointed to the Magyar as the only one worthy to become the recognised language of the nation. It was the most vigorous, sonorous, flexible, and highly cultivated of them all. It had been proved equal to every requirement of the poet, orator, and philosopher, and was capable of still greater extension and amelioration. It had, for more than a thousand years, been the tongue of the nobles and gentry, of all the learned, able, brave, and intelligent of the nation. There was no gentleman, of whatever race, who did not know it; there was no peasant who might not acquire it. It was the language which all the youth of the colleges, of the bar, and the county

TOWN-HALL AT PESTH.

assemblies had spontaneously and unanimously adopted it as the vehicle of their thoughts, hopes, vows, and aspirations. Upon none of the others could any man of ordinary sagacity have bestowed a moment's consideration: German was the language of the deadliest enemies of the constitution, and was indissolubly connected, in every Hungarian mind, with the idea of Austrian encroachment and rapacity. The Viennese cabinet had long sought, by propagating it, to denationalise the Magyars. The Sclavonian was liable, if possible, to still greater objections. It was the means by which Russia sought to propagate the doctrine

SERB, CROAT, AND GERMAN.

of "*Panslavism*" amongst the people of eastern Europe, the odious and terrible doctrine which represented the czar as the natural ruler of all who professed his faith and made use of the Sclavonic tongue. As to any of the others spoken in Hungary, it would have been just as absurd to urge their claims to adoption, as to have recommended Welsh or Gaelic to the judges at Westminster for adoption when the Latin and Norman French fell into disuse in the last century.

It was, therefore, proposed and carried, "that from the 1st of January, 1844, the proceedings of all courts in Hungary Proper (thus excluding Croatia and Sclavonia) should be conducted in the Magyar language, and that on and after that date, none should be considered qualified for the degree of advocate, or for any public office, who had not acquired that language." It will thus be seen that a period of eight years was afforded to all young men aspiring to public or professional employment to fit themselves for the change, and it must be remembered that the noble class were not confined to any race in particular. There were amongst the Germans, Wallacks and Sclavacks, great numbers of nobles, and amongst the Magyars, owing to circumstances in the early history of the country, many who had no political rights whatever. Nobility was not confined to any race. It was another name merely for participation in the political rights which in this country every ten pound householder enjoys.

After passing an act obliging the judges to give the reasons for their decisions and publish them, and a resolution praying the king to convene the states at Pesth for the future, instead of at Presburg,* the diet separated in May, 1836.

The man who in future struggles was destined to play so prominent a part, during the whole of these absorbing proceedings, was merely an intent and diligent looker-on. He had watched Szechenyi's efforts, and rejoiced in his successes with a devotion which was in itself an omen of his own still greater triumphs, and in so doing was qualifying himself for the task of carrying on the work, which the former was compelled to abandon when it was but half finished. He was a gentleman of noble origin, of course, but his whole fortune lay in his talents, which at that period were devoted to journalism—a profession which the Hungarians had not yet learnt to estimate at its full value. He was still but thirty years of age, and within the diet he was known as a promising young man, although, amongst the world without, his name—the name of Louis Kossuth, which has since become a household word in two hemispheres—had never yet been heard.

His family were originally from the county of Turocz in Upper Hungary, a district inhabited principally by Sclavacks, and although they were of Sclavonian origin, they were not less Magyar nobles—another proof that the dominant race did not monopolize all political privileges. About the beginning of the present century, his father removed to Bodrog-Szerdahely in the county of Zemplin, where he found it no easy matter to supply all the wants of his increasing family. Louis, his only son, was born on the 27th of April, 1802, and distinguished himself at

* The vicinity of this town to the Austrian frontier always rendered it a favourite place of meeting with the government.

an early age by his precocious talents, and the sweetness and gaiety of his disposition. The elder Kossuth died while his son was still in his childhood, but his widow, a woman of masculine mind and tender heart, managed, out of her impoverished means, to give him such an education as would qualify him for any profession he might choose to enter. At an early age he entered the Calvinist college of Sarospatak, and having completed his studies at the university of Pesth, duly received the diploma of an advocate. He returned to his native place in 1822, and was there appointed honorary attorney in the county court, an office answering to our crown solicitor, at the age of twenty. During this period he appears to have devoted a considerable portion of his attention to field sports, and we do not find that he gave great token of capacity for higher pursuits until the cholera broke out in 1831. While the pestilence was raging, he became the ministering angel of the poor, visiting them in their hovels, administering medicines with his own hands, soothing the agony of the dying, and encouraging the hopes of the survivors. At last the report got abroad amongst them that they were being poisoned by the nobles and the Jews, and they instantly rose in insurrection, and began to commit the most frightful outrages, and it was owing to Kossuth's exertions alone that their delusions were dissipated and still greater mischief prevented. When the crisis passed away, he was a local celebrity, but a celebrity whose claims to notice were founded upon heroism of no common order. When the diet met in 1832, he was selected, according to the custom in such cases, to supply the place of a magnate, who was unable or unwilling to attend. He thus had a seat in the lower chamber, and had a right to speak but not to vote. He found himself placed in the parliamentary arena at a period of unexampled excitement, when vast social, as well as political changes were in contemplation, though to what they might lead none could tell. The political horizon was already clouded, and fear was mingled in the hopes of many, but the deputies little knew that, in the person of a young and unknown lawyer, their guide and prophet was in their midst. His first oratorical effort in the chamber was a failure, either for want of practice or preparation, and he was consequently led to look about for some other means of distinguishing himself as an advocate of liberal principles. He hit upon a happy expedient for serving both the popular cause and his own reputation, and it was all the more valuable from its complete novelty. Whether from the jealousy of the government or the apathy of the Magyars, no printed reports of the parliamentary proceedings had ever yet been published, so that the people remained without any intelligence of the sayings and doings of their representatives, except such as was afforded them by rumour or hearsay. To supply this defect, Kossuth resolved to devote the time, which would otherwise have been wasted in idle listening, to carefully reporting everything that took place, and circulated it all over the country on a small printed sheet. The importance of the proceedings which then occupied the attention of the diet caused it to be read with extraordinary eagerness, and Kossuth rendered it still more attractive by amplifying, and often even embellishing the speeches. The cabinet, however, soon took the alarm, and although the censorship was unknown to the Hungarian law, prohibited the printing and publication of the reports. This was a heavy blow, but Kossuth was not baffled. He instantly gathered round him a great number of young men to act as secretaries, who wrote out a great number of copies of the journal, which were then circulated in manuscript throughout Hungary. The government was completely foiled, and new ardour was infused into the liberal party. When the session was at an end he resolved to follow up his plan by reporting the meetings of the county assemblies, which were then the scenes of fiery debates. The young men thronged to them from every side, as the popular character of the meetings enabled them to infuse more vigour into their denunciations of the government than would have accorded with the dignity and gravity of the chambers of the diet. This he pursued with success. The government stopped his journal in the post-office. He then established a staff of messengers and carriers, who circulated it from village to village. The enthusiasm of the people was fast rising to a flame. A crisis was imminent. It was resolved to arrest Kossuth. Orders were accordingly sent to the archduke palatine to that effect; and although it was a direct violation of the law to deprive a Hungarian noble of his liberty until he had been formally convicted, he was seized, and shut up in the Neuhaus, a prison built at Pesth by Joseph II. He was, however, not brought to trial till 1839, and was then sentenced to four years' imprisonment. The charge brought against him was, that he had circulated false and inaccurate reports; but the real ground of offence was, as every one knew, that he had circulated any reports at all. The government dreaded the strength, union, and combination which the diffusion of accurate intelligence of the proceedings of each assembly would have conferred upon the whole municipal body; for previously the county assemblies had been compelled to act singly and without concert.

But it was from the proceedings against Wesselenyi that the excitement arose which gave Kossuth's journal much of its celebrity and éclat. This nobleman had attended a county assembly in Transylvania, where he possessed some property, and had there strongly urged the electors to instruct their representatives to support the bill for the emancipation of the peasantry, which was then before the diet, pointed out in forcible terms the absolute necessity there now existed for the gradual abolition of unjust and oppressive distinctions, and for making all men equal before the law. He took occasion at the same time to denounce the odious and detestable policy which the government had so long pursued, of stirring up the peasantry against the nobility, and the nobility against the peasantry, and then, taking advantage of these divisions, to spoil and oppress both. He was loudly applauded; no one could deny the truth of what he said, though the vice-ispan, or sheriff, objected to his language as too strong.

Two months afterwards, when the recollection of that particular speech, or at least of the words used, was well nigh lost, and when Wesselenyi had taken his seat in the diet as a Hungarian magnate, the government commenced a prosecution against him for high treason. The baron denied the legality of the proceeding, on the ground that nothing uttered at a public meeting could be made the subject of a process before any other tribunal, unless the president of the meeting, or some member of the assembly, formally objected at the time, and commenced "a verbal process," as it was called, upon the spot. But it never entered the mind of the Austrian cabinet to stand upon strict legality. It had never done so at any period of its connexion with Hungary, and it certainly had no notion of doing so now. His protest was accordingly disregarded by the court, but not by the country. The excitement rose to boiling point. Petitions and remonstrances were poured in from every county. Balogh, a prominent member of the diet, arose in his place, and declared that he adopted Wesselenyi's words as his own. He was forthwith included in the prosecution. His constituents then met, and declared that his language was exactly such as they themselves would have used, that they approved of it, and wished to be answerable for it. The government was now heartily sick of the affair, and caused it to be intimated to Wesselenyi, that if he chose to apply for a pardon, it would be granted him. This he indignantly declined to do, and the proceedings against him were accordingly continued; but although the alleged offence was committed in 1835, the trial dragged its slow length through four years, and it was not till 1839 that sentence was at last pronounced, finding him guilty of mitigated high treason, and sentenced him to three years' imprisonment for having made use of the following words at the county meeting referred to: "The government sucks out the marrow of nine millions of men (the peasantry), but it will not allow us, the nobles, to better their condition by legislative means; but, retaining them in their present state, it only waits its own time to exasperate them against us:—then it will come forward to rescue us. But woe to us! From freemen we shall be degraded to the state of slaves." It was a singular circumstance, that it was owing to the excitement consequent upon these infamous proceedings, that Kossuth owed his first step in political life; that in the very act of striking down one enemy, Austria should have raised up another and a deadlier one.

Most of these rigorous measures were the work of Fidel Palfi, the chancellor of Hungary, a cunning diplomatist of the Talleyrand school, but in all other respects as devoid of talents as he was of patriotism. As a renegade, he was specially marked out for popular execration by the death of his master, Francis I., in 1835, who was thus spared the odium attaching to the prosecution of Kossuth and Wesselenyi, and which fell with full force upon his ministers. Francis was a narrow-minded, bigoted, and suspicious prince, remarkable for nothing save for the obstinate resistance he offered to Napoleon, which, however, was due rather to an animal instinct than any high principle. He hated science and literature, and science and literature seemed to hate him, for they had bestowed on him none of their gifts. He knew no language but his own, and that imperfectly. When he died, numbers were glad, nobody was sorry, and the majority was indifferent. His successor, Ferdinand IV. (of Hungary—VI. of Austria), was afflicted with mental debility when he ascended the throne, and the administration of affairs consequently fell entirely into the hands of the archduke Louis and prince Metternich. Two better exponents of the Austrian system could not have been chosen. Metternich, in particular, had proved himself one of the ablest high priests that had ever ministered at the altar of absolutism. When he first assumed the reins of power in 1832, an amnesty, which set at liberty a great number of political offenders, gave hopes to the liberal party that he was about to adopt the policy of progress and conciliation. They soon saw their error. His ruling passion was a hatred of change; his great mission seemed to be to keep things fixed. He would have stopped the revolution of the earth on its axis if he could, and have placed all the sovereigns and nobility on the side next the sun, and placed a military cordon to keep the people in the darkness. The house of Austria had been remarkable long before his time for its steadfast adherence to the principle of immobility, but it was he who developed it into a policy, and placed it in alliance with legitimacy and divine right. He worshipped facts—he hated opinions. He was constantly occupied in building fortifications between them. But whenever, in obedience to the eternal law of progress—a law which has witnessed the uprise and decay of whole dynasties of despots, and, like truth, will outlive them all—forced him to give ground before the advancing tide of thought and civilisation, he had cunning enough not to struggle against it. He yielded invariably with a good grace, and then set as diligently to work as ever to make intrenchments against another inroad, and, if possible, to make each step the last: building embankments on the sea-shore in a summer calm, and fondly imagining that because the water rippled noiselessly against their base, that there was no fierceness in the winds and no might in the billows!

It is hard to say, however, that this fear of change is not a necessity which the very nature of the Austrian empire forces upon all its ministers. There is no monarchy in the world, except Turkey, made up of such heterogeneous materials. But a very small part of the population is of the same race as its rulers. At the present day the Germans, scattered through the whole of the provinces, amount only to 7,833,157 in all; the Sclaves, scattered in the same manner, 17,760,159; the Magyars form a compact body of 5,470,910; and the Italians a compact body also of 5,506,000.* The *Austrians*, properly so called, number only 3,000,000 in all, and yet they rule over 30,000,000. How this is managed has puzzled many people. There is hardly one department of human knowledge, skill, enterprise, or industry, in which they have ever displayed superior excellence. Their greatest battles have been won by foreign generals in command of foreign troops. Germany owes to them but few, if any, of her intellectual triumphs. Science, art, or literature have received few favours from the house of Hapsburg: maritime supremacy is forbidden it. There is no spring of energy in the Austrian people;

* La Hongrie Historique, p. 199.

no national life, love of liberty and glory, such as have made England and America the dread and envy of the world. A race of stiff, bigoted, and unwarlike monarchs, an effeminate and impoverished noblesse, and a people of slaves,—such has the archduchy of Austria been for centuries; and yet that archduchy—a speck on the map—has grown into a great power, rules over whole nations of foreigners, and has outlived storms before which many prouder and nobler barks have gone down. The explanation of all lies in the policy of division; of setting race against race, and creed against creed; of sowing and perpetuating discord; in working upon national prejudices and antipathies. It is now no longer a secret; since 1848 the world knows it. Let us hope that those whom it most concerns will not forget it, when the hour comes in which most of all there will be need to remember it.

In 1840, the Viennese cabinet first gave evidence of its intention, for a while, at least, to abandon the policy of intimidation, and have recourse to that of conciliation. It saw that it was impossible to arrest the movement which had now commenced in Hungary, and it resolved to make an effort to direct it towards its own ends. The eastern question, which in 1840 was setting the European diplomatists by the ears, caused Austria serious alarm, and induced her to increase her military forces. Levies and subsidies were required from Hungary, and the diet was accordingly summoned. An amnesty had been previously granted, under which Kossuth and Wesselenyi regained their liberty. The former came out broken in health indeed, but a more implacable enemy of the government than ever, and the latter had lost his sight in prison. The address of the chancellor at the opening of the diet was full of promises and blandishments; but the deputies were wise enough to doubt or disbelieve. The old reforms of 1835, which had been but half completed, were again brought on the *tapis*, to receive a finishing touch, and the conservative party strained every nerve not only to put a stop to all further movement in that direction, but to undo all that had been done; but it was signally defeated. The condition of the peasantry received still further amelioration, a commercial code was framed, which gave security and stimulus to industrial enterprise, and revived confidence by the abolition of the mischievous privilege of inviolability, which enabled the noble to bid defiance to his creditors, and also removed some of the civil disabilities under which the Jews were labouring.

In the meantime Transylvania had not been idle. The constitution of this country was based upon a diploma granted by Leopold I., and known as the Diploma Leopoldinum, which was afterwards regarded as the charter of Transylvanian freedom, at least while under Austrian rule, as it was in reality but a confirmation of rights and privileges already in existence. It guaranteed religious toleration, the existence of the Hungarian laws, and the reservation of offices and appointments of state to natives alone, as well as a number of minor immunities. As the imperial power became more firmly established in the country, this charter was gradually infringed upon; and though Maria Theresa acknowledged and accepted it at her accession, the constitution, as well as that of Hungary, fell into total abeyance during the whole of her reign and that of her successor, Joseph.

During the French war, the diet was called together once or twice, as it had been in Hungary, for the purpose of voting supplies, but beyond this the government of the country was as arbitrary as at Vienna. It was said, that of the whole of the articles composing Leopold's diploma, but one had been observed, and that was the one which stipulated that the commander-in-chief of the military force should be a German. The county meetings and municipal institutions of every sort fell into total desuetude, and the whole affairs of the country were administered by the corrupt bureaucracy which in most German states, and of late years in France, has been destroying all that is manly, upright, and independent in the national character.

The famous Three Days of July, in 1830, had as thrilling an effect in Transylvania as elsewhere. The people with one voice demanded the restoration of their institutions; and, as the first step towards the concession of their rights, the government re-established the county meetings. This was an important point, as in the absence of a free press, or, in fact, of any press, it was the only means of agitation. Baron Wesselenyi and some of his friends took advantage of it, by buying land in every county, which gave them a voice in each assembly, and they were thus enabled to pass from one to the other and harangue the freeholders. They denounced in strong terms the arbitrary raising of soldiers and levying of taxes, the increase of the salt tax, and the imposition of duties so high as to be almost prohibitory upon various articles of export or import, and the gross intolerance shewn towards the protestants. The excitement speedily rose to such a pitch, that Baron Wesselenyi announced his intention of allowing no more soldiers to be levied on his estates till a diet was granted, and his example was followed by a great number of counties. The government was now thoroughly alarmed, thought an insurrection was imminent, and troops were sent down to quell it. The court could not understand the possibility of legal agitation without an appeal to arms. But the general in command reported that all was perfectly quiet, and as there was no excuse for resorting to violence, and as it was evident the county assemblies were resolved to persevere, a diet was at last called together in 1834. It was so long since it had been last convened, that few of the deputies knew anything of the forms or usages of parliamentary discussion, familiarity with which forms so important a part of a legislator's qualifications under a constitutional goverment, and a great deal of time was consequently wasted in useless discussions. But still so firm was the attitude assumed by the liberal party, that the cabinet was again forced to take refuge in a dissolution. In 1837, the states were once more assembled, but this time at Hermanstadt, instead of Kolosvar. The inhabitants of the former were nearly all Germans, and it was hoped that the influence of their phlegmatic temperament would moderate the fiery zeal of the Magyars. In this also the government found itself mistaken.

This, as well as the subsequent diet, stood its ground so firmly, that the ministry had at last to yield, and restore the constitution to its normal state.

In the meantime, the political excitement in Hungary had not failed to lend a new impulse to intellectual progress and commercial enterprise. Steamers were launched on the Teyss as well as on the Danube; railways were constructed; the nobles submitted to the ordinary laws of commercial fair dealing, and acknowledged the validity of their own bills. The want of a national bank, however, was the cause of incalculable evils. Landed proprietors, for want of any other way of raising money, were forced to resort to Jews and usurers of all kinds and countries, who fleeced them without mercy. In their distress, they looked to the diet for deliverance. The publishing trade, perhaps, received a greater impetus than any. The national mind seemed to have awakened from its torpor, and girded itself like a strong man after sleep for the coming struggle. Thousands of works in the Magyar language were issued, all bearing the stamp of originality. The theatres were filled nightly by brilliant audiences, who thronged to witness dramas illustrative of the nobler periods of Hungarian history; and the loud plaudits which followed every sentiment which could be possibly twisted into an allusion to the existing state of affairs, gave clear warning of the crisis that was at hand.

Kossuth, after his liberation from prison, had taken up his abode for a short period at a watering place called Parad, for the purpose of recruiting his shattered health, and for a time wholly abstained from taking any part in public affairs. On the 1st of January, 1841, however, a printer in Pesth, named Landerer, obtained permission to publish a journal, entitled *Pesthi Hirlap*, or the Pesth Gazette. He offered the editorship to Kossuth, who accepted it, but only on condition that he should be perfectly untrammelled in the expression of his opinions. At first his articles displayed great moderation, but warming as he went on, his old fervour came upon him once more, and he commenced a series of attacks upon the government as remarkable for their brilliancy and bitterness as for the prudence with which they avoided anything like illegality. The cabinet now, for the first time, saw clearly that they had to deal with an enemy, who might be slain or imprisoned, but who could never be subdued. Szechenyi, the originator of the new movement, began to tremble in the presence of the storm which he himself had raised; but when he ventured to remonstrate, he found he was no longer master of the elements. Kossuth continued his labours, and soon raised the circulation of his paper to 10,000 copies—an immense number in a country where the newspaper press had hitherto hardly had a footing. He made vigorous onslaughts upon the privileges of the noblesse, and pleaded the cause of the middle and lower classes unanswerably. A large body of the aristocracy was irritated, and started a rival journal, which, being supported by the authorities became possessed of great influence, and was mainly instrumental in defeating Kossuth's election, when he was proposed as a candidate for Pesth, in 1843. Nothing disheartened, he continued to denounce abuses, to advocate education and all other social as well as political reforms, till in 1844, owing to a change of ministry which threw the liberals out of office, he lost the editorship of the Gazette; but he had kindled a flame which now blazed fiercely enough of itself.

The only resource to which Austria could appeal in this extremity was to stir up a war of races by calling on the Croats to support her. They were a Sclavonic people, and were desirous of securing the ascendancy of their race and language in all the countries in which Sclaves were to be found. It was obviously the interest of Austria to have discouraged their efforts, instead of promoting them, for the triumph of Sclavism was the triumph of Russia, whose favourite idea from the days of Peter the Great down, has been the extension of Muscovite supremacy over all tribes of Sclavonic origin. The Viennese cabinet, however, spent little thought upon the dangers that loomed in the future; it is one of the characteristics of despotism, that it seldom looks beyond the gratification of the hour. The Sclaves were every day excited against the Magyars by imperial agents, and urged on to resist the establishment of the Magyar as the official language. In spite of all these efforts, the chambers contained an opposition headed by the highest parliamentary talents of the day. In the lower house, Klauzal, Szentkiralyi Szemere, Beothi, Bezeredi; in the upper, Stephen Szechenyi, Louis Batthyanyi, Ladislaus Teleki, and Baron Eotveos. The official language was the principal subject of debate; around this the great battle of the races was to be fought. Austria hounded on the Croats, and her creatures in the diet, aided and supported by the Sclave representatives, offered the most determined opposition at every step of the discussion—an opposition which was not confined to the ordinary tactics of parliamentary warfare, but exhausted all the resources of faction, intrigue, falsehood, and chicanery. An act was, nevertheless, passed, containing the following clause:—"The official language of the diet shall henceforward be the Magyar, exclusively. It shall, nevertheless, be lawful for the deputies of the annexed provinces, who do not speak Magyar, to use the Latin during the six years next ensuing. All public documents emanating from the king, or the tribunals, shall be drawn up in that language. The tribunals and government offices of the annexed provinces shall address themselves to the Hungarian tribunals in Magyar, and the latter shall answer in Latin; the Magyar language shall be taught in all the schools of the dependent provinces, and shall alone be used in those within the frontiers of Hungary Proper." The Croats called this a barbarous and oppressive enactment. It was, in reality, an attempt to vulgarize the Magyar throughout the kingdom, without causing more than the least possible inconvenience to the inhabitants—a measure of which we have already demonstrated the expediency and even the necessity.

Despite of clamour the work of reform went on. The catholic priests had refused to celebrate mixed marriages; the diet declared them valid, if celebrated by a protestant minister. The right of the nobles to the exclusive occupation of public offices and appointments was abolished, and they were thrown open to all

FRANCIS DEAK.	LOUIS KOSSUTH.	LAZARUS MESZAROS.
PRINCE PAUL ESTERHAZY.	COUNT LOUIS BATTHYANYI	BARTHOLOMEW SZEMERE.
BARON JOSEPH EOTVEOS.	COUNT STEPHEN SZECHENYI	GABRIEL KLAUZAL.

without distinction. A bill was brought in, also making it binding on them to contribute in taxes ten millions of florins during the ensuing four years; the conservative party in the upper chamber reduced the sum to four millions. The deputies refused to accept the amendment, and threw out the measure altogether. Many of the nobles, however, unwilling to be subjected to the humiliation of being compelled to take a share in meeting the burdens of the state, voluntarily inscribed their names in a list of those who declared themselves liable to taxation. A motion for the abolition of the feudal privilege, possessed by every noble, of re-purchasing real property at the same price for which it was sold, a long time after its alienation; another intended to abolish all feudal dues for ever, and others relating to the generalization of the jury system, the abolition of capital punishment, and the establishment of a national bank, and of an equitable sale of custom duties between Hungary and Austria, were equally defeated by the pertinacious resistance of the conservative magnates, who adhered firmly to the court.

While this momentous struggle was going on, Kossuth was devoting his attention exclusively to the development of the material resources of the country. An association was formed under his auspices, called the *bedeigyll*, the members of which pledged themselves to abstain from the use of Austrian manufactures until the tariff should be reformed. The effect produced by this was astonishing, and clearly showed how widely the prevailing discontent had spread amongst all classes of the population. The loss to Austrian trade was so great, that large numbers of her manufacturers had to transport their factories into Hungary to save themselves from ruin. During 1846-7 the excitement reached its height. The leaders of the liberal party from all parts of the kingdom met at Pesth during the quarterly fairs of these years, and discussed the various measures of reform in the presence of vast crowds.

In November, 1847, the diet was again summoned. Louis Batthyanyi brought Kossuth forward as a candidate for the country of Pesth. The election was warmly contested by the conservatives, who spared no effort to prevent the return of the redoubtable agitator. Money was lavishly distributed, and the government officials vied in threatening and coaxing the electors to reject him, but in vain. The people fought the battle of their idol in the streets and on the hustings; the ladies of the liberal party, amongst whom were included some of the most fascinating women in Hungary, fought it with more delicate, but more powerful weapons in the drawing-rooms. He was elected by an overwhelming majority. He was now in the diet, with his literary prestige, his impassioned oratory, his popular sympathies, his untiring energy. He was in the front rank of the reformers, and, by unanimous consent, their chief. The lists were open, the champions were ready; the battle that was to decide the fate of the kingdom was about to be fought out before Europe.

The diet was opened with splendour and solemnity. The whole of the imperial family were there—the king, the queen, the heir presumptive, and all his sons.

They answered the addresses presented to them in Magyar, and with great show of cordiality. The Hungarians were delighted, and even the reformers were thrown off their guard. The archduke Joseph had just died. The archduke Stephen, who had been governor of Bohemia, an honest, well-meaning, but timid man, who was completely under the influence of Metternich, was unanimously elected to fill his place. Thus far the court party were triumphant. They had been floating along upon the tide of enthusiasm, which their fine speeches and protestations had raised. The chambers now began to recollect themselves, and look at things calmly. When the motion for an address to the throne came on for discussion, the Croats and conservative members wished to confine themselves to the reiteration of stereotyped compliments; but the liberals, irritated by a recent act of the chancellor displacing the old counts, and substituting administrators in direct dependence on the court, and thus annihilating the municipal independence of the counties, and wishing to repair the reverses of the previous session, drew up an address, in which all their grievances were set forth in firm but respectful language. It passed the lower house; the magnates rejected it. It was placed on the journals of the chamber of deputies, and the royal address remained unnoticed. The first blow was struck; the revolution had begun.

To say that Kossuth was the main cause of this bold step, is almost superfluous. The influence which this extraordinary man now exercised in the chamber was marvellous beyond measure, and certainly has no parallel in parliamentary history. As he surpassed all others in information, research, knowledge of the country, familiarity with details, historical lore, acquaintance with the policy, government, and institutions of foreign nations, and particularly of England, so also he far surpassed them all in command of language. His statements of facts were clear, lucid, and well-arranged; his argumentation was logical and well-linked; and all his appeals to the feelings were utterly irresistible. There was no branch of oratory to which his tongue did not lend an additional charm; there was no chord in the national heart which he did not touch with a master hand. His skill in debate was matchless. The old nobles who deliberated, their sabres at their side, after the manner of their forefathers, and with as few words as if they were in a council of war—and these few in Latin—were astonished at the volubility of the dexterous polemic who reproached, encouraged, refuted, or warned them in a torrent of Magyar, every word seeming to burn as it fell. Nor was he open to the imputation so often cast upon parliamentary men while in opposition—of fertility in objections and accusations, and utter want of the power of originating or executing. He never pointed out an end without pointing out the means as well, and that with a clearness and minuteness which left no doubt of its practicability; he never unveiled a defect without holding up the remedy. The appearance of such a man as this in the diet was a startling event for the conservatives. To combat him in the chamber was useless. It looked foolish to oppose his reforms without stating reasons. There was nothing for it but to appeal to prejudices, to stir up bad passions, to rouse slumbering antipathies; and upon this course they entered; but this led to the battle-field.

There were three parties in the diet—the conservative party, composed of hangers-on of the court, devotedly attached to Austria and to the old order of things; the progressionists, who aimed at moderate reform, the abolition of glaring abuses, and the establishment of a constitutional monarchy upon the model of that of England; the socialist radicals or democrats, very similar to their brethren in France, who desired a total overthrow of everything, and a remodeling of society upon a new basis. Kossuth belonged to the second, perhaps we should rather say to an extreme section of the second, for he was in advance of Szechenyi, and many others whose claims to the character of reformers were undoubted. He wanted their caution, their respect for vested rights even when those rights were, in reality, based upon wrongs. We can hardly condemn them, for precipitation in revolutions is full of danger. This will explain Kossuth's position with regard to the aristocracy. The wealthy magnates hated him as the destroyer of their odious exactions and iniquitous privileges. Are we wrong in concluding that some portion of the antipathy which has blackened his character at the Schoenbrunn and in the salons of Vienna has followed him to England, and continues to slander him in the fashionable coteries of Belgravia? Szechenyi's party filled the colleges and drawing rooms; they were the party of prudence, of compromise—the whig party in short. Kossuth's adherents, on the contrary, were at the plough, in the workshops and factories, in the streets. They were the people who had suffered and toiled for a thousand years, and who were now dreaming of a reign of equal rights, of protected industry, of pure justice. They were the democrats, including under that designation all those whose hopes and sympathies were not bound up in a party or a class, but looked for the welfare and progress of humanity, without distinction of classes, as the goal of their striving. To what political party in England shall we liken these? We dare not say.

The question of the official language was now again introduced, and the old scenes enacted over again. The Croat deputies were strenuous in their opposition. One of them, however, rose in his place, and explained that there were two parties in Croatia—one the constitutional, which was disposed to adhere to Hungary, and carry out her reforms; the other, the party of the government, calling itself "the Illyrian conservative," and declaring that it sought the establishment of an independent Sclave nationality; but its true character was explained by the fact, that it had expelled the Magyar Croats of the former from the election hall at Zagabria, who were thus prevented sending their representatives to Pesth.* However, an act was carried in both chambers,† which ordained the exclusive use of the Magyar language in all branches of the administration, and in

* Journal of the Hungarian Diet of 1847.

† These have been literally transcribed from the "Pesthi Hirlap," of January and February, 1848, by M. Boldenyi, from whose able series of articles, in the "Revue des Deux Mondes," a great deal of information has been derived.

THE DIET VOTING THE SUPPLIES, JULY 11, 1848.

all legal documents, in the schools and colleges, except those for elementary instruction, with regard to which the managing authorities of the district were left to exercise their discretion. Croatia was allowed to continue the use of the Latin in the transaction of her internal affairs; but in all communications with the Hungarian authorities, the Magyar was made indispensable; and the same indulgence was granted to the provinces bordering on the Adriatic—Italian being substituted for Latin. The clause regarding the schools was modified also with regard to the Sclave provinces, instruction only, in Magyar being made requisite. The Magyar was not to be introduced into the Sclave counties in Hungary till six years had elapsed; so that all the officials might be prepared for the change.

The question of equality of taxation was again under consideration, when, on the 4th of March, the news of the Parisian revolution fell among the deputies like a thunder-clap. When it arrived, the lower house was engaged in discussing the state of the monetary system. Owing to the ignorance and extravagance of the imperial financiers, their bank notes were at a discount, and in many parts of Hungary and Bohemia were refused altogether. The greatest confusion prevailed; the business operations of the country were at a stand-still. A motion for inquiry was made by one of the members for Raab. Kossuth rose to speak upon it, amidst profound silence. The diet was powerfully impressed by the news from France; every one felt that a crisis was at hand. He declared his entire concurrence in the motion before the house, but thought that it was trifling to deal with questions of this sort, when interests so much weightier were at stake; it was useless now to inquire into the state of the bank; what they wanted was a separate finance minister and financial administration for Hungary; the total destruction of the bureaucratical system of Vienna; the establishment of the constitution upon a firm basis; a ministry responsible to the people; and, that their own liberties might be safe, he declared it to be their duty to see that the same institutions prevailed in all parts of the Austrian dominions; for it was a folly to suppose that he who was an absolute monarch in Vienna would reign as a constitutional king at Presburg. He concluded by moving an address to the throne, urging upon the government the adoption of certain measures of reform, amongst others: "The emancipation of the country from feudal burdens, the proprietors of the soil to be indemnified by the state; the equalization of taxation; the faithful administration of the revenue to be satisfactorily guaranteed; the further development of the representative system; and the establishment of a government representing the opinions of, and responsible to the people." The speech produced a profound sensation, and the motion was carried unanimously. What Kossuth aimed at was a free confederated empire, a scheme which, had it been carried out, would have given the Hapsburgs a new lease of their throne.

For the present, all went well. The Viennese united in demanding reform. Metternich fled to England; the emperor was terrified. A royal decree granted trial by jury, the freedom of the press, the publicity of the proceedings in the law courts, and promised a representative constitution. When this news reached Presburg, the diet resolved to send a deputation to Vienna to lay their demands before the emperor, and solicit compliance with them. Kossuth was appointed to head it. Ferdinand was in too great danger to hesitate. The archduke Stephen, the palatine, was appointed viceroy of Hungary; he commissioned count Louis Batthyanyi to form a ministry. He framed it as follows:—

Louis Batthyanyi, president of the council; Bartholomew Szemere, minister of the interior; Francis Deak, minister of justice; Prince Paul Esterhazy, minister for foreign affairs; Louis Kossuth, minister of finance; Count Szechenyi, minister of public works; Baron Eotveos, minister of public instruction; Colonel Lazarus Meszaros, minister of war; and Gabriel Klauzal, minister of commerce.

The list was sent to Vienna for the royal confirmation. The emperor hesitated; it seemed too democratic by far. Kossuth's name was in itself a bugbear. But the people were excited. Every throne in Europe was rocking like a child's cradle. This was no time for delay. The confirmation was granted, and the work of reform went on. The task which the diet now took upon itself was one of the noblest that ever engaged the attention of any legislature. Amidst all the crimes, and outrages, and errors, and short-comings which blot the page of history, the acts of this assembly will stand out in high and consoling relief, a finger-post on the road to a holier and brighter future. Lest it should be supposed that we exaggerate the results of their labours, we shall quote the words of one whose testimony in such a case is certainly not open to doubt:—

"By unanimous votes of both houses, the diet not only established perfect equality of civil rights and public burdens amongst all classes, denominations, and races in Hungary and its provinces, and perfect toleration for every form of religious worship, but with a generosity perhaps unparalleled in the history of nations, and which must extort the admiration even of those who may question the wisdom of the measure, the nobles of Hungary abolished their own right to exact either labour or produce in return for the lands held by urbarial tenure, and thus transferred to the peasants the absolute ownership, free and for ever, of nearly half the cultivated land in the kingdom, reserving to the original proprietors of the soil such compensation as the government might award from the public funds of Hungary. More than five hundred thousand peasant families were thus invested with the absolute ownership of from thirty to sixty acres of land each, or about twenty millions of acres amongst them. The elective franchise was extended to every man possessed of capital or property to the value of thirty pounds, or an annual income of ten pounds—to every man who has received a diploma from a university, and to every artisan who employs an apprentice. With the concurrence of both countries, Hungary and Transylvania were united, and their diets, hitherto separate, were incorporated. The number of representatives which Croatia was to send to the diet was increased from three to eighteen, while the internal institutions of that province remained unchanged, and Hungary undertook to compensate the proprietors for the lands surrendered to the peasants to an extent greatly exceeding the proportion of that burden which would fall on the public funds of the province. The complaints of the Croats, that the Magyars desired to impose their own language upon the Sclavonic population, were considered, and every reasonable ground of complaint removed. Corresponding advantages were extended to the other Sclavonic tribes, and the fundamental laws of the kingdom, except in so far as they were modified by these acts, remained unchanged."*

These measures passed the two houses on the 24th of March, and received the royal assent on the 24th of the same month.

The work of reform was accomplished, but the troubles were not yet over. The south and west of Hungary were in arms. When the empire began to totter, all the wronged and outraged races of which it was composed roused themselves, and, in the first delirium of freedom, sought to fling off all control. Lombardy and Venice flew to arms, and dreamed of restoring their ancient glory; Croatia sought to erect a separate nationality, and so did Servia. In the latter, the patriarch of the Greek church, a man wholly under the influence of Russia, convoked an assembly at Carlowitz, which opened up negotiations with Austria as a sovereign state. The Viennese cabinet, through fear of Hungary, at first held aloof; but when Croatia advanced the same pretensions, she hesitated no longer, but stirred the Serbs into open hostilities. The atrocities which followed were frightful. A war of ambuscades, of night attacks, of knives, and merciless butchery of women and children, broke out between the peasantry of the two countries, and turned a large tract of country between the Danube and the Teyss into a howling waste. Houses were burnt, property destroyed, and quarter refused to the unarmed and defenceless, as if savages, and not Christians and neighbours, were at enmity. Scenes of carnage were enacted which have never been described in print, and which never will be described, but which have left terrible memories behind them, and will live for centuries in the traditions of the people.

In Croatia the Austrian agents were hardly less successful. A diet was convoked at Czagabria, by Baron Joseph Jellachich, which refused to accept the new electoral law, and spreading terror over the province, prevented the Croat deputies from attending the Magyar diet. The hordes of the military frontiers assembled in arms, the peasantry rose on every side, and putting themselves under the command of Jellachich, who until then had been a subaltern officer, but on whom the emperor now conferred the title of *ban*, or viceroy, declared their intention of marching to assist Ferdinand against his enemies. Their leader was in close communication with the archduchess Sophia, and thus became the soldier of the camarilla. Instigated by it, he did not hesitate to break off all relations with the diet and commence hostilities.

In July, 1848, the diet resumed its sittings, for the purpose of making prepa-

* Alison.

rations to meet the crisis. They met at Pesth, instead of Presburg, which was too near the Austrian frontier to be a safe place for deliberations. On the 11th Kossuth rose in his place, and addressed the house in reference to the Croat aggression, and the posture of affairs generally. After a passionate appeal to their patriotism, and exhorting them in a strain of the highest eloquence to meet the dangers that threatened them by courage and unanimity, he continued:— "Since the reign of Arpad, Hungary has enjoyed no right which she has not shared fraternally with the Croats; and not content with sharing, more than once

BARON JELLACHICH.

she has accorded them privileges at her own cost. I read in the history of Ireland that England despoiled that country of certain political rights; the Hungarians alone have conceded to a small province more than they themselves possessed. What then is the cause of this revolt? We look for it in vain. Has the last diet wrought any change in our relations? On the contrary, it has opened up a new era for us all. We have won new rights for ourselves and for the Croats also. They enjoy the same liberties as we Magyars. The Hungarian nobility has become responsible for the indemnity due for the abolition of the urbarial dues. Besides all this, the last diet has declared that the Croats have the right of using their own language amongst themselves and in their counties; it has extended their municipal privileges. Is there a nobler privilege than that of regulating the election of representatives to provide in parliament assembled for the liberty and safety of the nation? Well, the last diet has said to our brothers of Croatia, 'Organize your elections, and name your representatives.' By this even the last diet has consolidated the municipal independence of Croatia. There are then no causes for this revolt in the past; certainly there are none in the present. * * * The diet has decreed that the Croats shall be perfectly free to use their own language in the internal administration of the counties, and in their official documents; but let them at least consent to receive all communications emanating henceforth from the ministry and the Hungarian counties in Magyar, and accompanied by a Sclave translation." He then explained the importance attached by the Croats to the dignity of their ban, or governor, and continued:—"Nevertheless, the ministry has not hesitated to invite this insurgent ban to take a seat at the council board to deliberate in concert with the members upon the best means of pacifying Croatia. * * * * We are ready, I repeat, to satisfy all the just demands of the Croats, but we will never put M. Jellachich on a level with the king of Hungary. The king can pardon; it is the duty of Jellachich to obey. We declare, therefore, that the only mean of settling the differences between the Croats and the Hungarian crown is to humbly pray his majesty to act as mediator, by ordering the Croats to convoke their provincial diet. There all opinions can be openly declared, the elections freely conducted; and deputies lawfully chosen will repair to the central Hungarian diet. They will there set forth the wishes of the Croats. If these wants are founded in justice, we pledge ourselves that the nation shall do right in the matter; if not, we pledge ourselves to resign.

"Of their nationality I have already spoken. Concerning its official duties, the cabinet, from the very outset, selected a number of individuals from the provinces, without making any party distinction—nay, for the Croatian affairs it has, in various branches of the administration, formed distinct sections, which are not yet filled up, because the tie between us has been forcibly torn.

"If a people thinks the liberty it possesses too limited, and takes up arms to conquer more, it certainly plays a doubtful game—for a sword has two edges. Still I can understand it. But if a people says, Your liberty is too much for me, I will not have it if you give it me, but I will go and bow under the old yoke of Absolutism—that is a thing which I endeavour in vain to understand."

He then went into details as to the force at the disposal of the government for the defence of the country, declared that a levy of two hundred thousand men was necessary, and for this purpose demanded a vote of 12,000,000 of florins. The chamber, excited by his eloquence, rose up and exclaimed with one voice, "We give it, we give it! LIBERTY OR DEATH!" "You," exclaimed Kossuth, overpowered by this display of patriotic fervour, "you have risen to a man; I bow before the greatness of the nation. If your energy equals your patriotism, I will make bold to say that Hell itself cannot prevail against Hungary!"

The king had issued a manifesto disavowing the acts of the ban, declaring him a rebel, and a traitor and outlaw. Shortly afterwards he was summoned to Vienna, ostensibly to give an account of himself, in reality to take counsel with the camarilla. For several days the rebel, traitor, and outlaw might be seen passing in and out of the royal apartments at Innspruck, where he had several secret interviews with Ferdinand himself, and, to the astonishment and indignation of the Magyars, was sent back to his post with several marks of royal favour. Orders were given that a conference should be held to arrange the differences of the Croats and Magyars, but it was well known that no reconciliation would be effected. Batthyanyi met the ban at court, and during an interview endeavoured to learn from him the precise nature of the grievances of which he and his countrymen complained. But Jellachich refused to treat. "We shall meet again on the banks of the Drave," said the Magyar in parting. "No," was the reply, "I shall seek you on the banks of the Danube."

CHAPTER XXII.

THE WAR OF INDEPENDENCE.

1848-49.

On his return Jellachich took the command of all the imperial forces in Croatia and Sclavonia, amounting in all to fifty-four thousand men, who received supplies

LAKE BALATON.

of arms and ammunition secretly from Vienna. The Serbs and the Sclavonians of the north were also stirred up into insurrection by the emissaries of Austria. The situation was alarming; the deputation demanded a last interview with the emperor, for the purpose of calling his attention to the threatening aspect of affairs, and reminding him that Hungary was as much entitled to his protection as any portion of his dominions, and that his true policy lay not in exciting on race against race, but in endeavouring to reconcile the interests of all, and calling on

BUDA AND PESTH

him to restrain the Croats. They received an evasive answer, left the palace, stuck red feathers in their caps, and abruptly started homewards. The war had begun.

On the 9th of September, Jellachich crossed the Drave at the head of his hordes of marauders, banditti, and half-savage irregulars from the frontiers, and began to commit the most horrible outrages on the line of his march. On the 15th the news reached Pesth, and produced an indescribable sensation. The ministry had resigned, and Count Batthyanyi announced to the assembled diet that the commander of the Hungarian troops, Count Adam Teleki, had surrendered to Jellachich without striking a blow, on the ground, that having sworn fidelity to the same flag, he could not with a good conscience bear arms against him. The weaker spirits in the diet were utterly paralyzed by this accumulation of misfortunes; Kossuth and Batthyanyi were alone cool and collected. The latter was requested to form a new ministry, and difficult as the task was, considering the relations which existed between the diet and the court, he did not decline it. But in the meantime he requested the archduke Stephen, the palatine, to take the command of the forces for the defence of the country against the Croats, and sent another deputation to Vienna, but this time to the Austrian assembly which was sitting in the capital. The Sclavonic element, however, preponderated so largely in that body, that a hearing was refused them by a majority of 186 to 108 votes. Such were the disastrous consequences of the fell dissensions between the various races of the empire.

The archduke, a moderate, conscientious, and highminded man, who in reality had the interest of the country sincerely at heart, at least as much as an Hapsburg could have it, and who saw with horror the terrible danger which was now impending, hastened to obey the instructions of the diet, and set out for the camp accompanied by three civil commissioners. He found the army in the neighbourhood of Lake Balaton, abandoned by its general and face to face with the enemy. The archduke demanded an interview with Jellachich on the lake; but the latter, after some hesitation, refused to grant it. Stephen was terrified when he found hostilities inevitable, and judged that it was time for him to retire from a contest in which his family affection and his political sympathies would be perpetually coming into collision. A mediator he might be, but a partisan never; and when he found himself surrounded by circumstances which he had neither the courage nor the intellect to master, he wisely determined to withdraw from the stage altogether. Resigning the command, therefore, to general Moga, he took refuge on his maternal estates in Germany, where he remained a silent, and, we would hope, not unsympathizing spectator of the misfortunes which afterwards befel Hungary. The diet now resolved to abandon all half measures, and push matters to extremities. To retreat, even had they desired it, was no longer possible; the populace was wrought up to the highest pitch of excitement by the unceremonious dismissal of the Magyar deputation by the Austrian assembly, and by the accounts which were daily coming in of the atrocities perpetrated upon the unoffending peasantry. Louis Batthyanyi laid down the powers with which he had been invested, and a Committee of National Defence was elected on the 25th of September, with Kossuth as its president; and to it was committed the duty of taking the measures necessary for the public safety. On the 22nd, however, the court had thrown aside the mask, and added fresh fuel to the flame of discontent by the issue of two proclamations, one addressed to the people and the other to the troops; in the former the conduct of the liberals was denounced in strong terms, and the latter appointed Count Lamberg commander-in-chief of the army, and called upon Louis Batthyanyi to countersign his appointment.

The proclamations had no sooner appeared than they were torn down and trampled under foot; and when Count Lamberg arrived in Pesth for the purpose of entering on his new office, he was dragged from his carriage when crossing the bridge, and brutally murdered by a mob led on by some students. Batthyanyi, on hearing of this, resigned office, and made a last appeal to the emperor, in the hope of inducing him to withdraw his unconstitutional decrees. His efforts were vain; Jellachich resumed his march; and Batthyanyi resolved to arm his retainers and take the field, but being disabled by a fall, he was prevented from carrying out his intentions, and was thus unhappily reserved for a more ignoble fate. Upon his resignation, the emperor entrusted an old soldier named Adam Recsei, a Hungarian, but a devoted adherent of Austria, with the formation of a new ministry, and at the same time another proclamation appeared, dissolving the diet, and appointing Baron Jellachich commissioner-plenipotentiary in Hungary, with the command of all the forces of the kingdom. This was virtually a declaration of war. Jellachich instantly advanced, and the Magyars rushed to arms from every part of the kingdom, unofficered and unorganised, and armed only with scythes, pitchforks, or bad muskets, but burning with enthusiasm. The two armies met on the 29th, near Sukoro, the Croats numbering about 50,000, and the Magyars, under general Moga, not more than 5,000. The battle was long and bloody, the old antipathies of race and religion combining with the animosity arising out of the recent events to lend new fury to the combatants. After a sharp and determined fire, maintained with equal vigour on both sides, Jellachich's cavalry was driven into the marsh of Velencze, and the remainder of his force gave way before a charge of the whole Hungarian line, and retreated. Moga was foolish or prudent enough to restrain the ardour of his troops, and thus, in all likelihood, lost the opportunity of administering a *coup de grace* to Jellachich's scattered army. The latter requested an armistice of three days, which was granted, but, in direct breach of his agreement, abandoned his position in the night, and fled towards Vienna.

Before he reached it, a revolution had taken place within the walls. The recent events in Hungary had produced a profound sensation amongst the populace, who deeply sympathized with the Magyars in their resistance to the tyranny of the court, under which they too were groaning. Republican principles had been long making way amongst the educated classes, the students, and professional men, and the outbreak in Paris had roused them into action. The citizens rose in arms; the troops gave way; the minister of war, Count Latour, was hanged from a lamp-post; and the emperor fled, leaving the city in the hands of the insurgents. The constituent assembly had declared itself *en permanence*, there were barricades in the streets, and the people were armed, when Jellachich arrived before the gates, with the Hungarians thundering in his rear. An alliance was speedily entered into between the assembly and the diet. Their crime, if it was a crime,

PRINCE WINDISCHGRATZ.

was the same; their strength lay in their resistance to arbitrary power. But never were the terrible effects which despotism produces in paralyzing a people's energies, depriving them of decision of character, and of the power of concentration in the presence of great emergencies, more fully displayed than in the case of these Viennese insurgents. In theorizing, in agitating, in resisting, they were everything that could be desired; but in victory they were divided, wavering, uncertain, as if astounded at their own success. In consequence of never having had any share in the government of the country, they were totally devoid of political education; they had got rid of their tyrants, but could not supply their place—like a mutinous crew who have risen against the cruelties of the captain, but knowing nothing of navigation, find themselves drifting at the mercy of the winds and waves. They deliberated, procrastinated — to-day deciding in one way, to-morrow in another—till the prince Windischgratz, the imperial general, had

EXECUTION OF COUNT ZICHY.

time to collect a large force, and effect a junction with Jellachich under the walls of the city. Bem, an old Polish officer of great skill and courage, who had served with distinction in the armies of Napoleon in 1812 and 1813, and who longed to strike another blow against his ancient enemies ere he died, had made his way into the city, and offered his sword to the assembly. General Klapka, a Hungarian, had followed his example; and under these two officers the fortifications were strengthened, the national guard organized, and everything done that time and circumstances would allow for the defence of the place. In the meantime, the Hungarians were waiting eagerly for the signal from the Viennese to advance to their relief. They feared to cross the frontier upon their own responsibility, lest it should be thought that their object was one of aggression rather than of self-defence. These punctilious scruples proved the ruin of the Austrian insurgents. The latter squabbled; the Hungarians tarried; and when at last Kossuth gave the order to general Moga to advance upon Schvechet, Windischgratz and Jellachich were found combined in overwhelming strength, and raining shot and shell upon the beleaguered city. The Magyar army did not number in all more than twenty thousand men, and most of these were peasants, armed with scythes, who had never seen the face of an enemy in battle array before. Their approach, however, lent new courage to the besieged, who fought under Bem's orders with determined courage. Windischgratz divided his forces; one half kept up the conflict with the Viennese, while the other faced about and attacked the Hungarians. The latter, notwithstanding the vast disparity which existed between them and their assailants in point of numbers as well as of discipline, did not decline the combat. Fortunately, Kossuth was at this time present with the army in person, as general Moga, an old imperialist officer, refused to go into action against his former comrades, and the command was consequently bestowed upon Colonel Goergey. The battle was long and bloody, but the Viennese, having already sustained a siege of twenty days, were forced to surrender, and the full strength of the Austrian artillery having been turned against the Magyars, they, too, gave way and fell back in good order behind the Lajta.

This check, however, was counterbalanced by some successes obtained over a division of Jellachich's army under Roth and Phillippovics, which had been detached for the purpose of invading the southern counties of Hungary. Casimir Batthyanyi and Manuel Perczel were sent off in pursuit of them at the head of a body of the national guard, and owing to the skilful manœuvring of Colonel Arthur Goergey, whose great talents now became fully apparent, the Croats were surrounded and compelled to lay down their arms. The common soldiers were sent back to their homes, and the officers set at liberty on parole. A Hungarian magnate, named Zichy, was found to have been in communication with Jellachich, and to have been one of the principal instigators of this movement. He was arrested, and some of the Ban's proclamations having been found in his possession, he was tried by a court-martial, of which Goergey was president, and condemned to death. He was hanged forthwith.

After the surrender of Vienna, there was a suspension of hostilities for nearly six weeks. The Austrian government was busily engaged in the work of butchering the unhappy rebels, a species of employment for which its army has always shown itself better adapted than for conflict with a foreign foe. The history of its campaigns is but a list of defeats and disgraces; it lays down its arms to an armed enemy, and eagerly takes up the axe and the cord against its fellow-countrymen, or the unfortunate peoples whom the arbitrary decrees of diplomatists have flung, bound and helpless, at its feet. The first victim selected in the Viennese massacres was Robert Blum, the bookseller, the most eloquent, gifted, generous, and enthusiastic of the German democrats. He was followed to the gallows by Jelovizki, one of Bem's aides-de-camp, a Polish officer of great abilities; by Dr. Becher, an eminent writer; by Messenhauser, who had headed the national guard; and by a host of others of less note. The city was abandoned to the rage of the military, who were chagrined at their former defeat and pusillanimous flight; and the inhabitants lived for weeks in a state of terrorism and suspense more horrible than the dangers of actual hostilities. Innocence was no shield, for the courts-martial seldom took the trouble to sift evidence. To be arrested was, in most cases, taken as ample proof of guilt.

The court, however, did not suffer its attention to be distracted from the Hungarians by the horrors which were being enacted around it. The camarilla* was resolved upon the final and complete rupture of the federal relationship existing between Hungary and Austria, and the absorption of the latter into the hereditary dominions of the crown. The archduchess Sophia was, therefore, moving heaven and earth to induce her brother-in-law, the emperor, to rush into extremes, abolish the constitution, and reign by the power of the sword. Ferdinand was an old and silly man; but he was superstitious—we can hardly, in his case, say conscientious—and feared to break the oath he had sworn at his coronation. He demurred, expostulated, and finally flatly refused. The camarilla was baffled, but not defeated. It continued its exertions, and at last wearied out the poor dotard's patience. To escape from his tormentors, he proposed to abdicate the throne in favour of his brother, the archduke Francis Charles. The latter declined the honour, and the crown was then placed on the head of his son, the archduke Francis Joseph, still a mere boy. The preparations for war were now pursued in right earnest. From all parts of the empire contingents were collected for a united and simultaneous attack. Hungary found herself in the midst of enemies. General Schlick threatened her on the north; the revolted Serbs, and Wallacks, and Sclavonians on the south; generals Hammerstein and Puchner, in Transylvania; and prince Windischgratz, at the head of the main body of the Austro-Croat army, advanced on the side of Austria; and the fortresses of Arad and Temesvar were in the hands of the enemy.

The diet, on their side, were not idle, though their position was unquestionably full of peril. The only troops they had at command were a few battalions of volunteers, who had rushed into the field at the commencement of hostilities, without any preparation for active service beyond zeal and enthusiasm. Those in the north were headed by general Meszaros, while Perczel and Batthyanyi acted against the revolted Wallacks and Serbs. The main body of the army, not more than twenty thousand strong, was at Presburg, under the

* A Spanish word, meaning "a little chamber." It is a sort of secret council, composed of the sovereign and the priests and intriguing ladies of the court, which has for a long time been part and parcel of the Austrian government. At the period of which we are writing, the principal members of it were the archduchess Sophia and Cibina.

command of Arthur Goergey, who was doing his utmost to infuse discipline into it by daily drill and manœuvring.

We have mentioned the name of the fatal man of this momentous crisis. He was of noble family, and was still in the prime of life. His military career had been commenced in the Austrian army, but was soon disgusted by the shameless system of favouritism by which promotions were there regulated. When the war of independence broke out, he threw himself into the struggle, more with the desire of avenging the wounds his pride had received from his former masters, than from any feeling of patriotism. He was cold, stern, inflexible, and under a

REFORMED CHURCH AT DEBRECZIN, FROM WHICH THE DECLARATION OF INDEPENDENCE WAS ISSUED.

demeanour of impassible calmness, concealed an ambition that devoured him like a fire. He was the very personification of war in its deadliest aspect—iron-willed, lion-hearted, prompt in decision, unflinching in execution, without elation in victory, without depression in defeat. In a conflict like the present such a man would have been invaluable, had he been in possession of a conscience strong enough to curb the outburst of his bad passions. Goergey might have been a Washington—the only character which a successful soldier could assume in Hungary;—he preferred being a Napoleon, and met with Napoleon's fate—a speedy and unlamented downfal. He first brought his talents into display at the disastrous battle of

Schvechet, by promptness, energy, and dauntless courage, where, as we have already stated, Kossuth made him commander on finding general Moga shrinking from the discharge of his duty. Had he looked upon the great contest, upon which he was now entering, with any other eyes than those of selfishness, fortune would, doubtless, have rewarded his valour, for never was there an instance in which the path of duty was more clearly the road to honour.

The army was in want of arms, ammunition, and, in short, all the *matériel* of war. Kossuth proved himself the soul of the crisis. He travelled all over

CATHEDRAL OF CASSAU.

the country, set foundries to work to cast cannon, obtained supplies of sulphur from copper pyrites, and soon had several powder-mills in full activity; opened contracts for the supply of uniforms and saddlery, planned financial securities to meet the want of money, and organized an efficient commissariat. The catholic clergy, strange to say, on whose behalf the house of Hapsburg had been guilty of so much tyranny and violence in Hungary, this time raised their voices on the side of the right. The bishops met at Pesth, and joined in a solemn and eloquent protest against the attack which was now about to be made upon Hungarian liberty.

On the sixteenth of December the main body of the Austrian army under Windischgratz crossed the Upper Danube; Goergey was defeated in several encounters, and fell back upon Altenburg, and thence upon Buda, and finally crossing the Danube, abandoned all his positions in succession, and retired behind the Teyss, acting upon the system of tactics long established in the Austro-Hungarian wars, which made the latter river a military line in cases of extremity. He had hoped to have effected a junction with Perczel, who was advancing from the Drave with 6,000 men, but the latter was overtaken by the Ban, who signally defeated him.

Another attempt was now made to open up the negociations and avoid further shedding of blood. A deputation, headed by Count Louis Bathyanyi, and composed of moderate men, waited upon Windischgratz in the hope of effecting some arrangement that would put an end to hostilities. Austria now had it in her power, by timely concessions, to secure her territory without the humiliation of calling in foreign aid. But the general, flushed with his recent successes, and in the full assurance that a handful of peasants could never make head against the trained battalions of the empire, sternly refused to treat with rebels, and arrested Bathyanyi. It is the misfortune of military men that they almost invariably over-estimate the resources of their art, and can never be taught to appreciate the tremendous force which lies sleeping in the mighty heart of a nation. Windischgratz, however, seemed to have exhausted his energy in the commission of this inexcusable piece of treachery. Instead of hurrying on towards the Teyss, he lingered at Pesth till the parliament had time to retire to Debreczin, in the centre of the Magyarland, where they held their sittings in the protestant church, and arranged all their measures of defence.

Bem organized an army of 10,000 men in Transylvania, and joining the Szeklers, by rapid manœuvring drove out the Austrian and Russian auxiliaries, and subdued the revolted Wallacks, who aspired to form an independent state under the protectorate of Austria. Windischgratz still continuing the work of hanging in Pesth, Goergey entered into the northern counties, and fell upon the detached corps of the enemy with the rapidity of lightning. Twenty times Schlick and Goetz thought they had him in their grasp, but as often he eluded their pursuit, and appeared when least expected, to attack them in the flank or thunder upon their rear. By a series of manœuvres displaying the highest military ability, he drove them to the foot of the Carpathian mountains, and re-occupied Cassau, the capital of Upper Hungary, where he established his head-quarters.

The Hungarian arms were not so successful in other quarters, however. The fortresses Leopoldburg and Eszek fell into the hands of the enemy, and they laid siege to Comorn and Petervaradin. Windischgratz having by this time wreaked his vengeance upon the inhabitants of Pesth, moved out of the town, with the view of effecting a junction with Schlick, and bringing their united forces to bear upon Debreczin. Dembinski, an old Polish officer of Napoleon's *Grand Armeé*, had at this time been appointed to take the command-in-chief of the Hungarian forces. He sketched out a plan of operations, by which it was arranged that generals Damianics and Klapka should take Szolnok, and, supported by Vetter, should hang upon the enemy's right wing, while Goergey received orders to leave Cassau and second the attack which Dembinski himself was about to make upon their centre at Kapolna. Windischgratz would thus have found himself outflanked, and his army would, in all probability, have been annihilated at one blow, if Goergey's selfish ambition had not disconcerted the whole scheme. He was chagrined beyond measure at finding Dembinski placed over his head, and was too selfish to stifle his resentment and act for the welfare of the country. A general engagement took place at Kapolna, and after a sanguinary encounter of six hours' duration, the Hungarians were defeated, owing to Goergey's positive refusal to obey orders.* Dembinski did not recover his reverse, but fell back hastily upon the Teyss, though Windischgratz showed no sign of advancing. He was superseded in the chief command by General Vetter.

Klapka and Damianics, on the other hand, had executed the movement assigned to them with the most complete success. The Austrian division, under Karger and Othinger, was utterly routed, with the loss of five hundred prisoners and a large quantity of military stores. Bem, as we have already said, was triumphant in Transylvania, having defeated the combined Austrian and Russian forces against overwhelming odds; divisions were breaking out beyond Windischgratz and Jellachich. Sickness, brought on by the marshes, was making havoc in the Austrian ranks. Klapka inflicted another defeat upon them at Tokay. The star of Hungary was in the ascendant. On the fifth of April, it was found that the imperial army was entrenched in full force at Jsaszeg, and the whole of the Hungarian forces were brought up to the attack. It was crowned with success. The impetuous charges of the huzzars swept away eight entire squares, and the Austrians fled, leaving six thousand men dead upon the field, and twelve hundred prisoners, and seven standards in the hands of the Magyars, who lost only two thousand men in killed and wounded. With this battle the demoralization of the Austrian army was complete. The men lost confidence in their officers, were decimated by marsh fever, and harassed in their retreat by the Csikos.† They were soon after driven out of Pesth and Comorn, and suffered a severe defeat at Nagy Sarlo, although General Welden had been sent to supersede poor Windischgratz, whose incapacity, save for the office of striking terror into unarmed

* After the battle Dembinski rode up to Goergey, and asked him what should be the punishment of an officer guilty of disobedience of orders in the presence of the enemy. "Death!" was the stern reply. Dembinski, however, knowing him to be supported by a large body of the army, did not dare to inflict the punishment which the traitor acknowledged that he deserved, and thus weakened his own authority in the eyes of the soldiers generally.

† Shepherds of the plains armed with lassos, bearing leaden balls at the end, with which they struck with unerring aim.

citizens, had been glaring enough since the commencement of the campaign. Jellachich gave up the contest in despair, and on leaving Pesth set out for Croatia at the head of his troops.

It was now clear that Austria was beaten. The triumph of the revolutionary party was complete. A few thousand undisciplined peasants had routed one of the largest and best drilled standing armies in Europe. Those who sneered at the military tactics of the Magyar generals in the earlier part of the war, were now loud in expressing their admiration. Austria was humiliated before Europe; but there was still a lower depth of degradation, and she plunged into it as her

CSIKOS.

only chance of safety. She called in foreign aid. Russia had been looking on at the whole struggle with rage and indignation. In each triumph of the Magyars she saw a blow struck at the absolutist system of which she was the head and front. She longed to interfere, not merely for the purpose of crushing the revolution, but that she might extend her influence over the Sclavonic subjects of Austria, and thus gain a step towards the great point of her ambition, the establishment of a mighty Sclave empire, of which Petersburgh should be the capital and the czar the spiritual as well as temporal head. She knew that if once Hungary were subdued by Russian soldiers, the moral influence of Austria amongst the

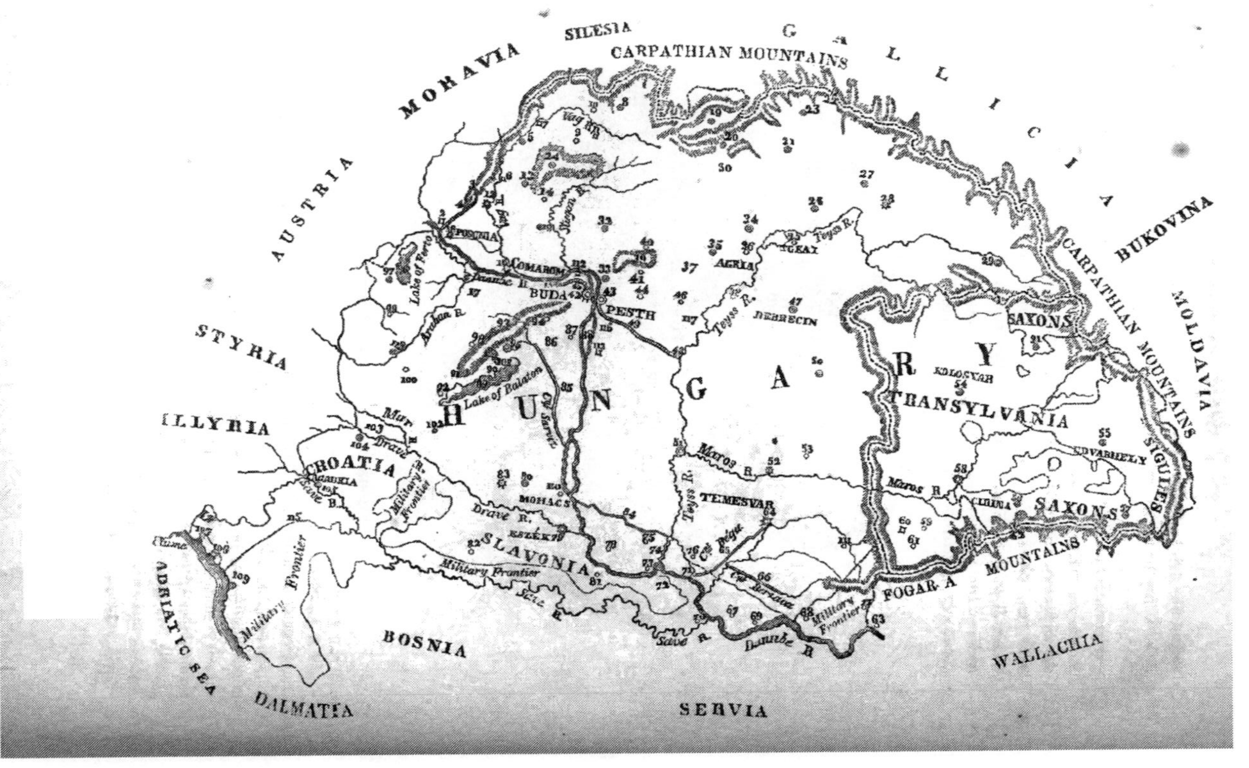

SILESIA
GALLICIA
CARPATHIAN MOUNTAINS
MORAVIA
AUSTRIA
BUKOVINA
MOLDAVIA
STYRIA
ILLYRIA
CROATIA
HUNGARY
TRANSYLVANIA
SAXONS
SIGULES
FOGARA MOUNTAINS
WALLACHIA
SLAVONIA
Military Frontier
BOSNIA
SERVIA
DALMATIA
ADRIATIC SEA
BUDA
PESTH
COMAROM
DEBRECIN
AGRIA
TEMESVAR
MOHACS
KOLOSVAR
Lake of Balaton
Lake of Ferto
Danube R.
Teyss R.
Maros R.
Drave R.
Save R.

Sclave tribes was gone for ever. Nothing can save a government which maintains its authority by the aid of foreign armies.

This was the stage in this struggle for the friends of freedom and representative government to have interfered also. There was nothing abnormal in such a proceeding. Hungary had been long recognized as an independent state by both the great western powers. Negotiations had, at different times, been conducted with her, separately and apart from Austria, by England as well as by France. When Lord John Russell stated, in the House of Commons, that we knew nothing of Hungary, diplomatically, except as a portion of the Austrian empire, he stated what he knew to be untrue (which is impossible), or he was ignorant of what

GENERALS BEM AND DEMBINSKI.

it was his duty to have known. We go to the expense of keeping up large fleets and armies for the purpose of maintaining our influence on the continent, as well as of defending our commerce and possessions; but when the time comes when that influence ought to be exercised for the benefit of humanity, we shrug our shoulders and look calmly on. Hungary was governed by representative institutions; Hungary was disposed to be one of our largest customers, if she had the regulation of her own tariff; she was rising, vigorous, and intelligent. Politically, commercially, morally, she was entitled to support. We refused it; and when we did so, we allowed Russia, our great rival and bugbear, to take a step which she will never retrace—a step nearer to the dominion of eastern Europe from the Baltic to the Grecian Archipelago—a step which will ever reflect disgrace upon France and England, and is fraught with danger and disaster to the best interests of the human race. For France there was some excuse. She was then labouring in the throes of a revolution which paralyzed her energies; but where was our boasted wisdom and foresight, if we could not, for the moment, turn a deaf ear to the teachings of those who can see no greater evil in life than the temporary disturbance of trade, and who would sacrifice the well-being of a hundred unborn generations, to save the living one from the losses and vexations of a single campaign?

Negotiations were accordingly opened up with Russia for the assistance of a large body of troops, the expenses of which were to be defrayed by Austria. She had already furnished a small contingent, which had been routed by Bem in Transylvania. She was now about to send her whole available force across the Carpathians, and Europe was to behold the strange spectacle of two of the greatest military powers in the world ranging themselves in the field against a little nation whose whole male population was not, numerically, greatly superior to their trained armies.

The young emperor, Francis Joseph, had, on ascending the throne, caused himself to be proclaimed king of Hungary, which was clearly illegal until his coronation, as the monarchy was, as we have often stated, essentially elective. Not only this, but he refused to be crowned or to take the requisite oaths, and spoke of Hungary as a rebellious country which he was determined to subdue. This was, in point of fact, a declaration of war, to which there was but one answer—an answer which every Magyar was bound by law to give—an appeal to arms. *No allegiance* was due by any Hungarian to any sovereign, till the diet had proclaimed him, and he had sworn to maintain the constitution. Many months having now elapsed, however, and the country having been driven to extremities by the armed forces of the pretender who called himself its king, the parliament resolved upon publishing a solemn protest against his claims, and upon destroying at a blow all those ties, created by custom or tradition, that might still have subsisted between Hungary and Austria. Accordingly, they issued the Declaration of Independence, on the 14th of April, 1849. The following are some of the principal articles in this celebrated document:—

DECLARATION RELATIVE TO THE SEPARATION OF HUNGARY FROM AUSTRIA.

"We, the legally constituted representatives of the Hungarian nation assembled in Diet, do by these presents solemnly proclaim, in maintenance of the inalienable natural rights of Hungary, with all its dependencies, to occupy the position of an independent European state—that the house of Hapsburg-Lorraine, as perjured in the sight of God and man, has forfeited its right to the Hungarian throne. At the same time, we feel ourselves bound in duty to make known the motives and reasons which have impelled us to this decision, that the civilised world may learn we have taken this step not out of overweening confidence in our own wisdom, or out of revolutionary excitement, but that it is an act of the last necessity, adopted to preserve from utter destruction a nation persecuted to the limit of the most enduring patience.

"Three hundred years have passed since the Hungarian nation, by free election, placed the house of Austria upon its throne, in accordance with stipulations made on both sides, and ratified by treaty. These three hundred years have been, for the country, a period of uninterrupted suffering.

"The Creator has blessed this country with all the elements of wealth and happiness. Its area of 100,000 square miles presents in varied profusion innumerable sources of prosperity. Its population, numbering nearly fifteen millions, feels the glow of youthful strength within its veins, and has shown temper and docility which warrant its proving at once the main organ of civilisation in eastern Europe, and the guardian of that civilisation when attacked. Never was a more grateful task appointed to a reigning dynasty by the dispensation of Providence than that which devolved upon the house of Hapsburg-Lorraine. It would have sufficed to do nothing that could impede the development of the country. Had this been the rule observed, Hungary would now rank amongst the most prosperous nations. It was only necessary that it should not envy the Hungarians the moderate share of constitutional liberty which they timidly maintained during the difficulties of a thousand years with rare fidelity to their sovereigns, and the house of Hapsburg might long have counted this nation amongst the most faithful adherents of the throne.

"This dynasty, however, which can at no epoch point to a ruler who based his power on the freedom of the people, adopted a course towards this nation, from father to son, which deserves the appellation of perjury.

* * * * * * *

"Confiding in the justice of an eternal God, we, in the face of the civilised world, in reliance upon the natural rights of the Hungarian nation, and upon the power it has developed to maintain them, further impelled by that sense of duty which urges every nation to defend its existence, do hereby declare and proclaim, in the name of the nation legally represented by us, the following:—

"1st. Hungary, with Transylvania, as legally united with it and its dependencies, are hereby declared to constitute a free, independent, sovereign state. The territorial unity of this state is declared to be inviolable, and its territory to be indivisible.

"2nd. The House of Hapsburg-Lorraine—having by treachery, perjury, and levying of war against the Hungarian nation, as well as by its outrageous violation of all compacts, in breaking up the integral territory of the kingdom, in the separation of Transylvania, Croatia, Sclavonia, Fiume, and its districts, from Hungary—further, by compassing the destruction of the independence of the country by arms, and by calling in the disciplined army of a foreign power, for the purpose of annihilating its nationality, by violation both of the Pragmatic Sanction and of treaties concluded between Austria and Hungary, on which the alliance between the two countries depended—is, as treacherous and perjured, for ever excluded from the throne of the united states of Hungary and Transylvania, and all their possessions and dependencies, and is hereby deprived of the ttyle and title, as well as of the armorial bearings belonging to the crown of Hungary, and declared to be banished for ever from the united countries and their dependencies and possessions. They are therefore declared to be deposed, degraded, and banished for ever from the Hungarian territory.

"3rd. The Hungarian nation, in the exercise of its rights and sovereign will, being determined to assume the position of a free and independent state amongst the nations of Europe, declares it to be its intention to establish and maintain friendly and neighbourly relations with those states with which it was formerly united under the same sovereign, as well as to contract alliances with all other nations.

"4th. The form of government to be adopted for the future will be fixed by the diet of the nation.

* * * * * * *

GENERALS OF THE HUNGARIAN ARMY IN THE WAR OF INDEPENDENCE.

VETTER. GOERGEY. GUYON.
AULICH. COUNT CASIMIR BATTHYANYI. KLAPKA.

REVOLUTIONARY ARMY IN 1849.

NATIONAL GUARD, INFANTRY. NATIONAL GUARD, CAVALRY. HONVEDS.

"And this resolution of ours we shall proclaim and make known to all the nations of the civilised world, with the conviction that the Hungarian nation will be received by them, amongst the free and independent nations of the world, with the same friendship and free acknowledgment of its rights which the Hungarians proffer to other countries.

"We also hereby proclaim and make known to all the inhabitants of the united states of Hungary and Transylvania, and their dependencies, that all authorities, communes, towns, and the civil officers both in the counties and cities, are completely set free and released from all the obligations under which they stood, by oath or otherwise, to the said house of Hapsburg-Lorraine, and that any individual daring to contravene this decree, and by word or deed in any way to aid or abet any one violating it, shall be treated and punished as guilty of high treason. And by the publication of this decree, we hereby bind and oblige all the inhabitants of these counties to obedience to the government now instituted formally, and endowed with all necessary legal powers.

"DEBRECZIN, APRIL 14, 1849."

Louis Kossuth was in the mean time appointed President-Governor. His first care was to form a cabinet to aid him in the executive administration. Bartholomew Szemere was appointed president of the council; count Casimir Batthyanyi, minister for foreign affairs; Sebastian Vukoritz, minister of justice; and to Goergey was committed the superintendence of the war department. This done, a general consultation was held to decide upon the plan of future operations. The enemy was in full retreat towards his own frontier—broken, disorganized, demoralized; Buda alone was in his hands, and was defended by a strong garrison under general Henzi. Two courses were open to the patriots: the one, to march rapidly on Vienna, crush the flying remnant of the imperial army, and dictate conditions of peace under the walls of the capital; the other, to re-capture Buda, restore the government to its legitimate seat, and, having thus ridded the soil of the presence of foreign troops, leave the subsequent operations of the war to be guided by circumstances. There can be scarcely any doubt that every member of the government saw the superiority of the former at a glance. The Austrian court lay at the mercy of the victors. Vienna was defenceless; the inhabitants were notoriously disaffected; once within its walls, the destinies of the Hapsburgs were in the hands of the diet. By one of those strange pieces of fatuity, however, so trifling in themselves, so important in their results, it was resolved to leave Goergey complete master of his own movements, and allow him to adopt whatever measures to him seemed best. This decision was based upon a principle founded in wisdom, and which has ever proved beneficial in its application—that the general in the field is always the best judge of what ought to be done, and that any interference on the part of the civil authorities is apt to disconcert his best schemes, and involves the total destruction of the vigorous and determined line of action which is necessary in the conduct of a campaign. Had Goergey been an honourable man, their decision had been a safe one; as it was, it was the ruin of the cause.

He was gloating with exultation when he found himself commander-in-chief of the army and minister-at-war. The fondest desire of his heart was gratified; his rivals were humbled, and the fortunes of the nation lay in his keeping. He was not long in making his decision when the alternative was presented to him. He knew the pride and veneration with which the mass of the people and the army looked upon Buda. It was their Mecca, their Moscow, their Jerusalem—the holy city, hoary with age, and crowned with glorious reminiscences. It was considered a heavy blow, a great discouragement, when it was abandoned to the tender mercies of the Austrians in the earlier part of the war, and the peasantry looked with superstitious longing for its rescue. It was not the duty of a general, however, to pander to prejudices of this sort, however amiable. Goergey was popular enough to disregard them, and to look solely to the result of the campaign. But such was his craving after applause, and his anxiety to render himself the hero of the crisis in the eyes of the least reflecting portion of the nation, that he thrust from him an opportunity of closing the campaign by a startling and brilliant *coup de main*, gave the enemy time to recover himself, and lost in a single week all the advantages purchased by five splendid victories and six months of sanguinary warfare. He, accordingly, suffered general Welden to escape, and advanced upon Buda. Pesth, on the opposite side of the river, was in the hands of the Hungarians, under general Aulich, and the inhabitants were animated by the utmost enthusiasm in the national cause.

Goergey summoned Henzi to surrender, but the latter, a brave old veteran, sternly refused, and commenced to bombard Pesth. The eloquence of Kossuth, the perilous position of the nation, the rumours of foreign intervention, had wrought the excitement of the besiegers up to the highest pitch. The night of the sixteenth of May was fixed for the storming of the citadel. The strength of the fortifications was aided by the commanding position which they occupied; a slight breach had been effected, but there was no attempt at a regular siege, and in this one exploit alone Goergey showed in its true light the heartlessness of his ambition and the cool ferocity of his disposition, for he was about to throw away in a useless and sanguinary encounter as much valour and enthusiasm as ever mortal had at his command.

General Aulich was ordered to force the Castle Gate and enter the park, and thence into the fortress; and general Knezich the Vienna Gate and its bastions; the other divisions were directed against the remainder of the assailable points. A pontoon bridge was thrown across the Danube for the purpose of making an attack upon the river side, and the troops advanced to the assault with great enthusiasm.

After a desperate conflict protracted till dawn, the Hungarians were beaten off, and retired to their quarters after suffering heavy loss. Goergey's pride was stung to the quick. What if he failed in this enterprise upon which his heart was so earnestly fixed, and for the achievement of which he had sacrificed so much substantial good! After a short respite, he ordered another onslaught, and this time the honveds ascended the ladders with such fury that the ramparts were carried in a rush, and a terrible hand-to-hand fight ensued in the streets. General Henzi fell in the breach, and was only saved from instant death by

Goergey's interposition ; colonel Allnosh was blown up when attempting to spring a mine under the suspension-bridge. The loss on both sides was tremendous, but Buda was conquered.*

STORMING OF BUDA.

* The following proclamation was issued by Kossuth after the capture of the fortress:—
"Praise to the holy name of God! Praise to the heroes of the national army, who sacrifice their lives to the liberation of our country!

Upon the receipt of the news at Debreczin, the joy was great. The diet voted the thanks of the country to Goergey and his army, and sent him the "Grand

DEATH OF GENERAL HENZI.

"*The fortress of Buda is in our hands!*

"The government has received the following official report of this important event:—

"'BUDA, 21st May, 5 o'clock, A.M.

"'The Hungarian colours are flying from the towers of Buda Castle! The honveds are

Cross of the Hungarian Order of Military Merit." He coldly and almost contemptuously declined it, stating that his principles did not allow him to accept such distinctions; that a passion for them was already arising amongst his officers, which he felt it his duty to repress by his example. The seat of government was once more transferred to Pesth. The enemy had no longer a footing in Hungary, but nevertheless the future was cloudy and ominous.

The ministry had hardly returned to their old quarters, when word came that the Russian intervention was an accomplished fact. The news fell upon all with a shock which at first almost stupified them, but on recovering every preparation was made for a desperate defence. The government solemnly protested against the unjust aggression of the czar, and their agents at the various European courts made strenuous but vain attempts to secure aid against this overwhelming calamity, if only for the sake of preserving the balance of power, as the very existence of the various German states was threatened by the advance of the Russian army. The Hungarian forces found themselves placed in a terrible position. They were evidently about to be enclosed in a wall of steel, and in the face of such odds valour itself seemed useless. On the north, General Prince Paskievitz was advancing at the head of the main body of the Russian army; on the north-west, General Grabbe appeared on the Moravian frontier with several divisions; on the west, the Austrian army, under the ferocious Haynau—his hands still red with the slaughter of the unfortunate inhabitants of Brescia—was

scaling the walls of the fortress on ladders! The enemy's 24-pounders have hoisted the white flag.

"'The first attack, which was commenced at midnight, was directed against the Vienna gate. The castle gate and the breach were attacked at one o'clock in the morning, and continued to the break of day. A murderous fire was directed upon our honveds, from the bastions, towers, and houses. Heavy stones were thrown down upon them; but their devoted courage overcame the resistance of the enemy.

"'The fire of the Austrian troops, though fierce and continuous, has done less execution than might have been expected. But at this moment a street fight is commencing, which is likely to lead to a great sacrifice of life. The enemy retreats from the bastions on the side of the Schwabenberg. One of their detachments holds out in a position near the Wesseinburg gate. Through the breach the honveds pour into the fortress. The fire of artillery and musketry is already silenced in this part of the town, but strong discharges of small fire-arms are heard from the Pesth side of the fortress.

"'6 o'clock 30m. A.M.

"'A powder magazine has exploded. The street fight still continues in the fortress.

"'7 o'clock, A.M.

"'The firing has ceased on all sides. *Buda is conquered!*'

"May the nation gather fresh courage and enthusiasm from the example of this success! May the combat which is still impending be short, and the liberation of the country complete! Peals of bells throughout the country proclaim the victory of Hungarian arms. Pray to God, and thank him for the glory he has vouchsafed to grant the Hungarian army, whose heroic deeds have made it the bulwark of European liberty!

"Debreczin, 22nd May, 1849.

"The Governor of the Commonwealth,

"LOUIS KOSSUTH."

lying at Presburg, waiting to act on the offensive once more, supported by a Russian force under Paniutine; and Transylvania was threatened by two Russian *corps d'armée*, and the remnant of the Austrians who had been defeated by Bem, while the Wallacks were in insurrection, under the conduct of a bishop named Schoguna. They had been persuaded by Austrian agents that it was the intention of the Magyars to abolish the use of their language, and absorb their nationality into that of the dominant race. A war of extermination, similar to that carried on by the Serbs at the commencement of this unhappy struggle, instantly followed. The districts occupied by the Magyars were laid utterly waste; the churches and dwellings were burnt; the growing crops destroyed; the women and children massacred without mercy. Bem once more resumed operations, and the unconquerable old man attacked and routed a second time the force under Malkowski, with all the fire and energy of youth; drove him across the Wallack frontier, and joined Perczel under the walls of Temesvar, which the latter was besieging. Dembinski was encamped at Eperies and Cassau, with 10,000 men, and the troops under Goergey, which stormed Buda, occupied the banks of the Waag and the Upper Danube. Klapka resigned the secretaryship-at-war, and took the command of Comorn. Goergey retained his command after entering on his new office; and by establishing a sort of chancellery at head-quarters, managed to render himself totally independent of the rest of the government, and created a breach between himself and Kossuth which was never effectually healed.

Such was the state of affairs in the early part of the month of June. Prompt, and energetic, and united action was absolutely necessary for the existence of the nation. Klapka and Goergey had agreed upon a plan of defence before the former resigned his post, the main feature of which was the making the strong fortress of Comorn the centre of all operations, the retention of the Upper Danube, and the adherence to a strictly defensive line of operations until the people could be levied and equipped, *en masse*, and sweep the foreigners from the soil. With the small force that was then in a state of fitness for a contest on open ground against the vast hordes of the enemy, it was clearly madness to abandon a strong position and challenge him to a trial of strength. Gunpowder and arms were being manufactured, owing to the indefatigable exertions of Kossuth, with the utmost rapidity; the peasantry were ready to rise to a man. The great point was to gain time without losing ground. Certainly the army that stormed Buda was sufficient to have captured Vienna, but how terribly were circumstances changed since the commission of that fatal and irretrievable error.

To this plan it was clear Goergey had no intention of adhering. To follow his own bent, and account for his actions to no one, and to distinguish himself by brilliancy and daring, without regard to results, was now clearly his object. Accordingly, on the 12th of June, the news having arrived that the Austrian forces, under general Wiss, had reached Csorna, the division, under Kmetty, was detached to attack them when crossing the Raab. The latter came up with the enemy, after a forced march of thirteen hours, and after a murderous conflict, totally defeated them, killing Wiss, though not without very severe loss. The various corps of the invaders were now gradually narrowing the circle within which the Hungarian army lay; even Jellachich was lifting his head, and reappeared in the field at the head of his Croats. To venture out before they disclosed their plan of operations, and before the national army was properly organized and concentrated, was the height of folly, or the deepest of treachery. Whichever it was, Goergey did not shrink from it, and descending into the marshy plains between the Waag and the Danube, engaged a vastly superior force at Zsigard, and was completely defeated. But never was the man's unflinching determination so conspicuous as in the midst of reverses. Collecting his troops, he prepared for another trial of strength almost upon the same ground, notwithstanding an earnest and affecting protest from Klapka, who implored him, as did also the government,

FORTRESS OF BUDA BEFORE ITS CAPTURE BY GENERAL GOERGEY.

at least, to effect a junction with other *corps d'armée* which were held in check in Lower Hungary, and if he would strike, strike on a grand scale. Advice and remonstrances were, however, alike disregarded; and so great was his dislike to Kossuth and jealousy of his popularity, that all instructions coming from him were treated with great indifference, amounting to contempt. On the 20th, while in command of the troops at Aszod, an attack was made on the Austrian army by Colonel Ashboth, before Goergey had arrived on the ground. The cavalry was driven back on Pered, which was occupied by a large force of imperialists with two battalions of field artillery. Ashboth instantly commenced the attack with but two batteries, and was received with a storm of grape-shot, by which the Hungarians were completely broken, and compelled to give ground. Ashboth having assumed the responsibility of the movement, was driven to desperation, and by great exertions succeeded in rallying and leading them back. A fierce hand-to-hand conflict in the streets then took place, and early in the afternoon the Austrians were dislodged and retreated towards Galantha. Just at this juncture Goergey came up, removed Ashboth from his command for breach of his instructions; and although the enemy had been reinforced by 15,000 Russians, and his own troops were exhausted by fatigue and hunger, he determined to renew the attack upon the following morning. After a sanguinary engagement he was driven in succession out of Pered and Kiralyrev, but effected an orderly retreat to Aszod, with the loss of 2,500 men. Another action, at the latter place, ended in a dearly-bought victory for the Hungarians; and the Austro-Russian forces,

GENERAL HAYNAU. PRINCE PASKIEVITZ.

amounting to 40,000, moved forward on Raab, then garrisoned by 6,000 men. Here the patriot army supported its ancient fame by a valiant defence, but was at length defeated with terrible slaughter, in spite of all Goergey's efforts, seconded by Klapka, who had reached the place on the day of the action. This was the crowning point in a series of disasters; it was evident that the Hungarian forces were being cut off in detail, and Klapka hurried to Pesth to take council with the government as to the best course to be pursued under the circumstances. All were of opinion that Goergey had acted recklessly, if not basely, by repeatedly disobeying the orders of the central government, and acting, so far as so proud a man could do, under the advice and instruction of Colonel Bayer, an obstinate and crochetty man, whom he had placed at the head of his chancellery, and unanimously agreed to force upon him the abandonment of the operations on the Upper Danube, and the concentration of the whole of the national forces upon the Teyss. When this was made known to Goergey he promised to obey, but, nevertheless, continued to follow up his own plans as before. There was evidently no alternative but to dismiss him, and this was resolved upon. Accordingly, immediately after Klapka's return to Comorn, a formal decree was issued by Kossuth on the first of July, removing Goergey from the chief command, and appointing Field-Marshal-Lieutenant Lazarus Meszaros to fill his place. But, unfortunately, in the meantime an event had occurred which rendered this measure a nullity.

On the 2nd of July, the combined Austrian and Russian forces made an attempt to force the entrenched camp occupied by 22,000 Hungarians, which lay outside the fortress of Comorn. Instead of concentrating his whole force for the defence of Monostor, an elevation within the entrenchment, which commanded the whole of the neighbouring country, and which a handful of brave men might have held against a host, Goergey's unconquerable love of display induced him to attempt the protection of his whole line against the overwhelming numbers of the assailants. The attack commenced at eight o'clock in the morning, and in the first onset the outworks were carried; but the fortune of the day was restored by Goergey in person, who led the troops into action apparently without the slightest regard for his personal safety, and with a hardihood that astonished even veteran soldiers. In the thickest of the fight, his calm, stern, and inflexible visage awed even cravens into valour, and inspired the bravest with renewed enthusiasm. The enemy were driven back, but their left wing carried the village of Szony; and at six in the evening, after a long and sanguinary combat, Haynau made a vigorous attack upon the Hungarian centre. His cavalry were engaged by the hussars, and a sharp fight followed, in which the infantry gradually joined; and, after three hours of desperate combat, in which Goergey received a wound in the head, the village was recaptured, and the Austrians driven back to their former position. The loss of the Hungarians on this memorable day was upwards of two thousand; that of the Austrians was still greater. But it was a proud day for Goergey. His personal intrepidity and daring had made him doubly popular with the army, and when the despatch arrived which contained the news of his dismissal, he knew that his hold on the troops would enable him to despise it. The soldiers would not so easily suffer their idol to be cast down, and could not readily be brought to believe that he, who was bleeding for the cause of his country, was ruining it by his selfish ambition.

By Klapka's exertions, and at the earnest solicitation of the officers of the army, a compromise was effected between Goergey and the government, by which it was agreed that he should resign the ministry of war, but retain the command of the army of the Upper Danube, Meszaros being still nominally generalissimo. He submitted with ill-disguised rage, but it soon became apparent, by the total want of decision and united action in the cabinet, that he was in reality master of the crisis, and that, by his acts, Hungary must stand or fall, whoever might be nominally at the head of affairs. He became reserved, cold, and distant with his most intimate friends, but scarce sought to conceal his contempt for the orders of the government. Still this did not lessen his influence with the army. He was the idol of the soldiery, the first in fight, the last in retreat, cool, impassible, indomitable; unmoved either by victory or defeat, his followers believed that he had chained fortune to his chariot-wheels, and that even when beaten he was beaten of his own accord, and with some deep-laid design. So hard is it for the most patriotic of men, and the most enthusiastic lovers of liberty, to keep free, amidst the tumults of war, from the dangerous fascination with which military heroes surround themselves.

When the next movements of the troops came under discussion, Goergey was ill of fever. Kossuth advised the junction of Perczel's corps, amounting to ten thousand men, with Visocki's division and Klapka's, and a general concentration of all the forces on the Upper Danube, to be aided by a levy *en masse* of the peasantry. His wishes were complied with, and Klapka commenced his march; but no sooner did Goergey hear of what was taking place than he expressed his dissatisfaction in the strongest possible terms, and Klapka, yielding to his objections, broke up his plan and fell back on Comorn once more. The government fled to Szeguedin; the Austrians occupied Buda, and on the eleventh of July, an action, in which the Hungarians were worsted, was fought under the walls of the fortress of Comorn. Goergey now saw there was no resource but to retreat towards the Teyss, leaving Klapka to defend the fortress. He accordingly commenced his flight—for it was little better—in forced marches, beat off his pursuers at Waitzen, and reached Tokay with the loss of one-fifth of his troops. On the twenty-fifth he wrote to Klapka from Geszthely, speaking with confidence of the security of his position, and hopefully of his future prospects, and urging a strenuous defence of Comorn as "the unconquerable bulwark" of Hungary. The great thing now needed was Kossuth's presence in the camp, to revive the courage of the troops by the magic of his presence and the fire of his words; he was aware of this necessity himself, and attempted to meet it, but the appearance of flying detachments of the enemy compelled him to return to Arad, when on his way to Goergey's head-quarters. The evil influences which then were there at work, were thus allowed to have free course.

Dembinski had in the meantime been ordered to protect Szeguedin, the seat of government, but was attacked and defeated near Szoreg by the Austrians under Haynau, and the Russians under Paniutine. Bem had been compelled to retreat into Transylvania before large masses of the Russians under Grottenhelm and Luders. He was recalled by the government, in the hope that he might be able to infuse new life into the army and retrieve the falling fortunes of the nation. But this hope was blasted by the terrible battle of Temesvar, in which the

Hungarians were utterly routed. Great numbers were slain, and the remnant who escaped were so demoralized that they could not be depended upon to stand another shot from the enemy. The bank, which had hitherto met the expenses of the war, was broken up; the troops were in want of supplies, and had no means of obtaining them except by levying contributions upon the unfortunate peasantry. This was a course to which Kossuth declared he could not consent. Sooner than the army should treat their countrymen as a conquered population, he was ready to sacrifice everything, and first of all to lay down his own power.

All but the shadow of it was already gone. Goergey treated him and the government with indifference, and had of late repeatedly stated that, in order to save the country, the whole authority should be placed in his hands as dictator. As he was the only one of all the generals in the field who had a serviceable force at his command, this was clearly a necessity, and Kossuth prepared to submit to it. He accordingly resigned his powers into Goergey's hands, and his example was followed by the whole cabinet. The following proclamation was then issued, announcing the event to the nation:—

"KOSSUTH TO THE NATION.

"After the unfortunate battles, wherewith God, in these latter days, has visited our people, we have no hope of our successful continuance of the defence against the allied forces of Russia and Austria. Under such circumstances, the salvation of the national existence, and the protection of its fortune, lie in the hands of the leaders of the army. It is my firm conviction that the continuance of the present Government would not only prove useless, but also injurious to the nation. Acting upon this conviction, I proclaim, that—moved by those patriotic feelings which, throughout the course of my life, have impelled me to devote all my thoughts to the country—I, and with me the whole of the cabinet, resign the guidance of the public affairs; and that the supreme civil and military power is herewith conferred on the General Arthur Goergey, until the nation, making use of its right, shall have disposed that power according to its will. I expect of the said General Goergey—and I make him responsible to God, the nation, and to history—that, according to the best of his ability, he will use this supreme power for the salvation of the national and political independence of our poor country and of its future. May he love his country with that disinterested love which I bear it! May his endeavours to re-conquer the independence and happiness of the nation be crowned with greater success than mine were!

"I have it no longer in my power to assist the country by actions. If my death can benefit it, I will gladly sacrifice my life. May the God of justice and of mercy watch over my poor people!

Louis Kossuth, S. Vuckorits,
L. Csanyi, M. Horvath."

This was followed by another from Goergey—

"GOERGEY TO THE NATION.

"Citizens!

"The Provisional Government exists no longer. The Governor and the Ministers have voluntarily resigned their offices. Under these circumstances, a Military Dictatorship is necessary, and it is I who take it, together with the civil power of the state.

"Citizens! whatever in our precarious position can be done for the country, I intend to do, be it by means of arms or by negotiations. I intend to do all in my power to lessen the painful sacrifice of life and treasure, and to put a stop to persecution, cruelty, and murder.

TABLE OF REFERENCES TO THE FIGURES IN THE MAP.

[At places marked thus *, battles were fought in the War of Independence.]

1. Defile of Jablunka (passage of the Russians).
2. Deven.
3. Tyrnavia.
4. Railway from Presburg to Tyrnavia.
5. Trencin.
6. Beczko.
7. Illava.
8. Arva.
9. Kossuth (patrimony of the Kossuth family).
10. Teplitz.
11. Streczen.
12. Leopoldburg.
13. Nitra.
14. *Sarlo.
15. Strigonia.
16. Comorn.
17. Arabon.
18. Posonia (Presburg).
19. Kesmark.
20. Leocsa.
21. Eperies.
22. Defile of Dukla (passage of the Russians).
23. Bartfa.
24. Kremnitz (gold mines).
25. Tokay (vine district).
26. Zemplin.
27. Unghvar (seat of Huns).
28. Mungacs.
29. Szigeth.
30. Mount Tatra.
31. Bisztricz.
32. Gyarmath.
33. Vacz.
34. Miskolcz.
35. Agria.
36. Onod.
37. *Kapolna.
38. Tiszafured.
39. Mount Matra.
40. Parad.
41. Gyongeos.
42. Buda.
43. Pesth.
44. Geodoelloe.
45. Railway from Pesth to Vienna.
46. Jaszbereny.
47. Debreczin.
48. Szolnok.
49. Railway from Pesth to Debreczin.
50. Great Varadin.
51. Szeguedin.
52. Arad.
53. Vilagos.
54. Kolosvar (capital of Transylvania).
55. Udvarhely (chief town of the Szeklers).
56. Cibina (capital of Saxon Land).
57. Corona.
58. Karlburg.
59. *Piska.
60. Deva.
61. Vajda Hunyad.
62. Defile of the Red Tower (passage of the Russians).
63. Orsova (by which Kossuth escaped).
64. Temesvar.
65. Bega Canal.
66. Berzava Canal.
67. Panczova.
68. Fehertemplom (Weiskirchen)
69. Kevi (Kubin).
70. Semlim.
71. Tétel.
72. Petervaradin.
73. Ujvidek.
74. Roman Ruins.
75. St. Thomas.
76. Great Becskerek.
77. Mehadia.
78. Batz.
79. Eszek.
80. Five Churches.
81. Vukovar.
82. Posega.
83. Szigethvar.
84. French Canal.
85. Sarvitz Canal.
86. Alba Regia.
87. *Velentze.
88. Raczkevi Island.
89. Lake Balaton.
90. Tihany.
91. Szigligeth.
92. Keszthely.
93. Bakony Mountains and Forests.
94. Mor.
95. Vesprim.
96. Neusidlesee Lake.
97. Soprony.
98. Papa.
99. Kerszey (Guns).
100. Szala.
102. Kanisa.
103. Isle of Mur.
104. Varadin.
105. Agram, Zagabria (capital of Croatia).
106. Port Royal.
107. Fiume.
108. Fured.
109. Segna.
110. Mohatz.
111. Lugos.
112. Visegrad.
113. Ikervar (birth-place of Count Louis Batthyanyi).
115. River Save.
116. Plain of Rakos.
117. Plain of Hortobagy.

ERRATA.

Page 2, line 32, *for* Tusculam, *read* Tusculum.
,, 90, ,, 30, *for* remains, *read* remain; and in the line following, *for* was, *read* were.
,, 159, ,, 17, *for* or title, *read* and title.
,, 202, ,, 7, from below, *for* them, *read* him.
,, 246, ,, 14, from below, *for* a no less, *read* no less.
,, 344, last line, *for* grand armeé *read* grande armeé.

"Citizens! the events of our time are astounding, and the blows of fate overwhelming! Such a state of things defies all calculation. My only advice and desire is, that you shall quietly return to your homes, and that you eschew assisting in the resistance and the combats, even in case your towns are occupied by the enemy. The safety of your persons and properties you can only obtain by quietly staying at the domestic hearth, and by peacefully following the course of your usual occupations.

"Citizens! it is ours to bear whatever it may please God in His inscrutable wisdom to send us. Let our strength be the strength of men, and let us find comfort in the conviction that Right and Justice *must* weather the storms of all times.

"Citizens! May God be with us!

"ARAD, 11th August, 1849." "ARTHUR GOERGEY."

The directions given to the people to remain at home and pursue their occupations quietly were ominous. One of Kossuth's favourite schemes—and his ideas on this point were shared by most of the other generals—was a general rising on the part of the inhabitants for the purpose of harassing the enemy by a partizan warfare, and cutting of his troops in detail. To this Goergey had testified the strong repugnance which military men generally feel to the employment of irregular forces of any sort and for any purpose. But it was, nevertheless, a movement to which the whole nation was looking as the last sacrifice of despairing valour, the last protest against the destruction of their liberties and the devastation of their country. So that Goergey, by denouncing it in express terms, not only administered a *coup de grace* to the government, but threw cold water on the patriotic zeal of the people, and in some measure prepared them for the catastrophe which was now at hand.

On the very day on which he issued this proclamation, he wrote to the Russian general, Rüdiger, informing him that it was owing to the folly and rashness of the provisional government that this contest had been maintained after his majesty the czar had resolved to interfere; that he, being a man of action, had seen at once that in the face of such overwhelming odds, it was impossible to carry on the war any longer; that he had in consequence called upon the provisional government to make an unconditional resignation of its power into his hands, which it had accordingly done, and that he and his army were now prepared to make an absolute surrender to the Russians, trusting to the czar's clemency to secure the safety of those officers who, having formerly served in the Austrian army, were seriously compromised by the part they had taken in the recent events. He therefore called upon general Rüdiger to surround him, so that he might lay down his arms to him, but declared that he was prepared to annihilate his whole force in a pitched battle sooner than make his submission to the Austrians. A promise had been previously obtained from the officers under him to agree to any arrangement or stipulation he might make, which most of them gave under the impression that he was about to open up negotiations for bringing the war to a happy and honourable termination. The private soldiers—the hussars and honveds* were in like manner cheated into the belief that what was about to take place was a mere matter of form, and that the real object their general had in

* Militia—"Home-defenders."

view was the placing of the grand duke Constantine upon the throne of Hungary in the place of the hated house of Hapsburg.

On the thirteenth of August, Rüdiger appeared at the head of his forces at Vilagos, to receive the surrender of the Hungarian army. The latter, numbering twenty-four thousand tried soldiers, with a large park of artillery, were drawn up along the Szollos road, in two solid columns. Goergey and his staff were magnificently entertained in the Russian camp, and the troops waited in dread suspense for the closing scene in the tragedy. At last the dictator rode out splendidly mounted, cold and calm as ever, and gave the troops order to march, and pile their arms as they passed an appointed spot; announcing at the same time that he no longer felt competent to conduct the war, but if any one else thought himself fit to lead, he would gladly yield him the command. In reply to this cruel mockery, a veteran captain sprang forward and implored him to allow the army to cut its way through the enemy. "Sir," was the stern rejoinder, "this is no time for joking." The terrible truth seemed now for the first time to have burst in all its force upon the soldiers—the war was at an end, and they were in the power of the Russians. The scene which followed baffles description. Any heart less cold than Goergey's would have been appalled at the extent of the calamity that could fling so many gallant men from the height of valorous enthusiasm in one moment to the lowest depths of despair. The honveds—who had tramped side by side through many a stubborn battle, insensible to danger and incapable of fear, who had followed wherever Goergey led, with a devotion unparalleled in all the record of human frailties, follies, and delusions—wept bitterly, and embraced one another, as if for the last time. The hussars dismounted, kissed and hugged their horses, the faithful companions of so much glory and disaster, and sooner than deliver them up to the enemy, drew their pistols and shot them through the head. Some of the officers broke their swords and cast the pieces at Goergey's feet, while others committed suicide on the spot, rather than trust themselves to the tender mercies of a barbarous foe. Everywhere was lamentation and despair. Order was gradually restored, and the troops moved forward towards Sarkad previous to their final dispersion.

While this mournful scene was being enacted at Vilagos, Klapka was playing a hero's part at Comorn. He had received early intelligence of Haynau's departure from Pesth for the purpose of pursuing the government to Szeguedin and attacking Goergey in the south, and with a view of making a diversion in support of the latter, he determined to attack the force that was blockading the fortress. Accordingly, at midnight on the second of August, one division of his forces under colonel Asserman surprised and carried the Austrian position at Almas at the point of the bayonet, and compelled the enemy to fall back upon Gran. Two other columns advanced to Mocsa, where they surrounded an Austrian regiment and compelled them to lay down their arms. Then uniting, they pursued their march upon Csem. The Austrians abandoned it at their approach. The whole army now advanced in battle array. They had the enemy enclosed between them and the Danube. There was but one passage across it at Lovad, and if Asserman gained the heights over that place, and opened his batteries at the time Klapka had calculated, all would have been over. Their retreat would have been cut off and a surrender inevitable. A general movement was accordingly made upon their position. The fire of some heavy field-pieces from their entrenchments at first caused some confusion in the Hungarian ranks. Colonel Schulz was ordered to storm the battery. He led forward the storming columns in a rush, with loud cheering, in the midst of a heavy cannonade and so terrified were the Austrians by this display of courage, that they turned and fled towards Atsh before their assailants reached them. As they ran in one confused mass, the Hungarian artillery rained death amongst them from the heights, while the hussars and honveds pressed close upon them along the plain and cut down the fugitives without mercy. At Atsh they rallied and stood at bay. Once more they were routed, and there was now no resource but to seek safety across the Danube. Luckily for them, they reached the bridge at Lovad before Colonel Asserman had gained the heights which commanded it. They were still crowding across in confusion when his artillery opened upon them and completed the rout. The survivors reached Presburg in disorder, and the Hungarians slept victorious upon the bloody field. Out of an army of 6,000, the Austrians had lost 1,000 killed and 1,000 prisoners, besides 12 field-pieces, 18 carronades, 3,000 muskets, and a large quantity of military stores and provisions. The triumph was complete. Haynau's line of communication with Vienna was now cut off. It was only necessary to raise Upper Hungary, attack him in the rear, and, if Goergey but did his duty, the destruction of the enemy was certain. A courier was sent off to apprise the latter of the joyful news, and promise him the support of an army thirty thousand strong within the ensuing four weeks.

Klapka now marched to Raab—found an immense store of provisions there, as well as ammunition—ordered a levy, *en masse*, in the surrounding counties, which was responded to with enthusiasm. He soon found himself at the head of a large and efficient force, burning to be led against the enemy. He resolved to cross the Austrian frontier, invade Styria, and returning thence with the rifles of the mountaineers, annihilate the Austrian army, under Nugent, at the Platten Lake. On the 11th of August he reviewed the troops, and informed them that he was about to lead them upon a new expedition. The announcement was received with thunders of applause. They were in the highest spirits, flushed with victory, and eager to march once more against the enemy. In the evening he invited the officers of the staff to his quarters to dinner. They, too, were bounding with hope. They were merry, as if they sat at a marriage feast, with no cloud in the future, and no danger near. They drank to the triumph of Hungarian liberty, to the success of Kossuth and Goergey, and to the confusion and overthrow of all despotisms, and that of Austria in particular. They were still in the midst of the festivities when a man in peasant's dress, weary and travel-stained, was led before

THE SURRENDER AT VILAGOS.

the general. It was Paul Almasi, the speaker of the Lower House, who tol in a few words with trembling lips—that all was lost; that Goergey had surrendered, that Kossuth was in Turkey, and that he was a fugitive.

There was no resource but to fall back on Comorn forthwith, and there make the best defence possible, in case the news proved true. This, however, Klapka still doubted. So many lying reports were raised by the Austrian agents, with the view of sowing dissension and breeding want of confidence amongst the patriots, that he felt persuaded that the intelligence in this instance was at least grossly exaggerated. The arrival of great crowds of fugitives, however, belonging to Goergey's army, and the concentration of vast masses of the enemy in the neighbourhood, at last put an end to all doubt. On the nineteenth he was summoned to surrender the fortress, but he declined giving any answer until he was placed in possession of the exact state of affairs in Transylvania and the Lower Danube. Unfortunately the Austrians had, in this instance, no motive for concealment, and

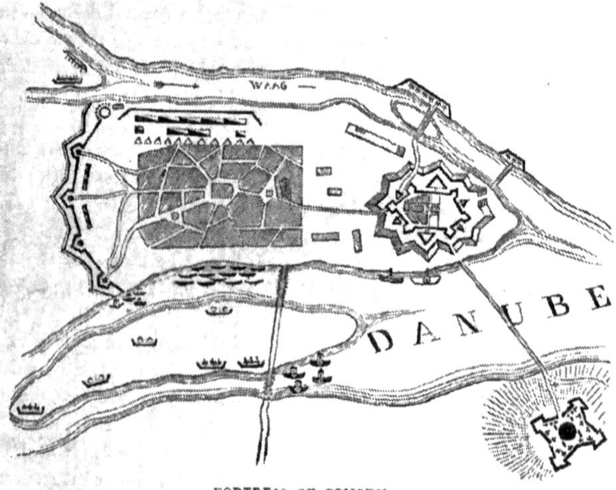

FORTRESS OF COMORN.

they proposed an armistice for a fortnight, during which he might send a deputation to examine into the truth of their statements and satisfy him whether the Hungarian cause was not indeed utterly ruined. To this he agreed, and four commissioners were despatched, two in each direction. The truce was occupied in strengthening the fortifications, increasing the stores, bringing in recruits and drilling them. The officers were animated by the best possible spirit, and declared their determination, one and all, to secure terms of capitulation or perish in the ruins of the fortress. They had learnt that those of their number who had fallen into the enemy's hands at Arad, in spite of the promises of clemency and oblivion which had been showered upon them previous to their surrender, were tried by court-martial, and in some cases executed. The sternest chances of war were preferable to a fate like this. Unfortunately the soldiers did not all partake of the same generous enthusiasm. Klapka's own army were unshaken in their fidelity under all vicissitudes; but the influence exercised upon them by the crowds of fugitives—the scattered remnants of the various other corps, who daily crowded into the fortress during the armistice, was anything but beneficial. They told dismal tales of the misfortunes they had undergone, of the hardships they had endured, and of the utter and final prostration of the national cause. The spirit of discontent thus excited was but too well supported and strengthened by the intrigues of the Austrians, who caused printed bills to be introduced into the fortress, encouraging the soldiers to desert, and to compel their officers to surrender. In one instance an attempt was made to assassinate Klapka by an agent of the Viennese police. The consequences of all this soon became apparent. Desertions became more frequent, and at last the troops began to run off by forties and fifties at a time, and fears arose that a general *debandade* might take place. General Klapka determined to make an example that would strike terror into the waverers. A regiment of the Botskai hussars was decimated, and eight other deserters who had been followed and brought back were shot. This had the desired effect. There was no more talk of mutiny.

On the 2nd of September the deputation returned, confirming the news of Kossuth's flight, of Goergey's surrender, of the delivery of the Hungarian prisoners to the Austrians by the Russians—in every particular. There was still one hope remaining. Comorn was a strong, almost an impregnable fortress; Petervaradin was, if possible, still stronger. They were garrisoned by men who, if driven to extremities, were well known to be capable of anything that courage and obstinacy could achieve. To reduce them both, would cost at best a vast amount of blood and treasure. The Austrians were well aware of this, and were anxious to avoid putting them to the test if possible. Under these circumstances, Klapka thought it possible that, by holding out, they might wring from the conquerors, possibly, a recognition of the constitutional rights of the country, and certainly, the safety of those of his unfortunate comrades who had fallen into the hands of Haynau. Acting on this belief, he sent a message to Haynau with a draft of the conditions on which the garrison of Comorn would surrender, but his hopes were blasted soon after, by the arrival of the news of the unconditional surrender of Petervaradin, and another summons was sent by Haynau, calling upon Comorn to follow its example. In addition to this, the siege of Venice having ended in the capture of that ill-fated city, the Austrians were able to concentrate their whole force around the fortress, amounting in all to 100,000 men, seconded by a train of siege artillery. The armistice terminated on the fourth, and on the fifth hostilities were resumed, and continued with but trifling results till the nineteenth. The position of the garrison was then becoming desperate; they were cut off from all resources; they had no hope of aid from any quarter; their clothes, provisions, and ammunition were failing them; but still sooner than surrender unconditionally, they were prepared to hold out till death. But on that day, for the first time, Haynau signified his willingness to treat, but for a purely military convention,

No allusion to national or political affairs could be admitted. The country, he said, was conquered, and its future was now in the hands of the victors. A council of war was called to decide upon this proposal, and it was resolved to send a petition to the emperor, claiming a restoration of the political institutions of the nation, and treat with Haynau for the surrender of the fortress. In consequence of various attempts made to bribe Klapka to separate his fate from that of his companions in arms, and yield the place for a pension and amnesty, he resolved to take no part personally in the negotiations. A committee of officers was accordingly appointed to meet Haynau, and on the 27th of September the following capitulation was agreed upon at Puszta Herkály, a farm, a short distance from Comorn.

1. The garrison are to be allowed freely to withdraw, without arms; the swords of the officers to remain in their possession.

Foreign passports shall be granted to those officers who have formerly served in the imperial army; to those who do not ask for passports to other countries, a free dismission to their homes—excepting such as voluntarily enter the imperial service.

A free residence at their homes shall be granted to the Houved officers not previously in the imperial service, without restriction as to their future conduct and occupation.

An amnesty is granted to the rank and file of the imperial regiments, and to those individuals who have been in the meantime promoted. They are to remain unmolested, and no legal prosecution shall hereafter be conducted against them.

2. Passports abroad shall be furnished to all who apply for them within thirty days.

3. One month's pay to the officers, and ten days' wages to the rank and file, according to the rates of the Austrian service, shall be paid in Austrian national bank-notes.

4. For the settlement of the various obligations entered into by the garrison, as shown by their orders on the military chest, the sum of 500,000 guilders, *convention's munze* (about £250,000), shall be paid in Austrian bank-notes.

5. The sick and wounded in Comorn, and in the hospitals, shall be properly cared for.

6. Private property, both real and personal, shall be generally retained by the owners.

7. The place, time, and manner of giving up the arms, shall be hereafter determined.

8. All hostilities shall immediately cease on both sides.

9. The fortress shall be given up according to the usages of war after a mutual ratification of the conditions.

On the 1st of October, all that remained of the Hungarian army was paraded in the garrison, to take part in a funeral service in commemoration of the brave men who had fallen in the war of independence. A requiem was solemnly chanted, and then the troops filed past the general, in slow time and in mournful silence. A single heartfelt cheer for fatherland, the utterance of a grief too great for words to convey it, spoke their last farewell. All was over. On the 3rd and two following days, they marched out, laid down their arms, and yielded up their colours, and the Austrians entered the fortress and took possession. The Hungarian nation existed no longer, save in the hopes, and regrets, and undying enthusiasm of a great, but unfortunate race.

CHAPTER XXII.

THE HORRORS OF THE PEACE.

1849—1851.

During the whole of the war of independence, the Austrian press employed itself in heaping execrations upon the wretches whose obstinate resistance to the commands of their legitimate lord the emperor, was desolating the country, and depriving the inhabitants of the benefit of those measures of clemency and favour which his imperial and royal majesty had in store for them. The "restoration of order," and annihilation of the revolution, were to be the commencement of an era of peace and happiness and contentment, in which the people, freed from the cares and anxieties, discords and agitations of the parliamentary system, should dwell in blessed repose under the wing of a paternal government. It was loudly asserted, and even in England the cry found an echo, that the revolutionary party in Hungary were but a branch of the vast body of conspirators against law and order, whose machinations had convulsed society in every part of Europe, and whose main object was the establishment of a community of goods. As a natural consequence of this proposition, the Austro-Russian army was fighting in defence of the sacred rights of property, of the hallowed ties of family, and of all that men valued most on earth.

To the old nobility, enamoured of repose, worshippers of the past—it was no difficult matter to represent change, of whatever kind, as an ogre and monstrosity. Amongst the bourgeoisie of Vienna and Paris, who looked on political rights as they would on silks or calico—good if they brought present profits to the till, rubbish if not—and who could not understand the feeling which prompts men to brave hardship and death for an unseen principle, a charge of communism against the revolutionary leaders was readily received, and the restoration of high funds and a brisk trade was looked upon as an exploit worthy of a hero, and sufficient to entitle him to eternal gratitude. The man who had such a work in hand was, in their eyes, not a man whose word should be lightly doubted. If he said peace would bring clemency and forbearance, even his enemies were to trust him.

But, strange to say, it was not amongst these classes only that this confidence in the Austrian government and its satellites gained ground. Many of the Hungarians, who afterwards atoned for their error by a martyr's death, believed the assurances made to them by the Russians after the surrender at Vilagos, that the emperor but waited the cessation of hostilities to proclaim an amnesty, and bury the past in oblivion. Their delivery into the hands of the Austrians, in defiance of the only stipulation they sought to make when they laid down their arms, and their cruel treatment in the fortresses and military prisons to which they were consigned, did not undeceive them. They were told that it was all in consequence of the obstinacy of Klapka in defending Comorn, and that they could not hope for a relaxation of these severities until resistance was entirely at an end. In full reliance on this statement, many of them wrote letters to that general, imploring him to cease fighting, since fighting had no longer an object, and by an unconditional surrender, restore them to freedom and their homes. Such an appeal as this was hard to resist. It had great weight in inducing Klapka to put an end to the war; for he, too, could not bring himself to believe that the governors of a great empire, and the leaders of victorious armies, would come before Europe as the falsifiers of sworn oaths, and the breakers of plighted faith. Let us see how far his expectations, and those of his unfortunate comrades, were justified by subsequent events.

When the war broke out, great numbers, both of Hungarian soldiers and officers serving in the Austrian army, in Hungary, Italy, and other parts of the empire, feeling that when the nation and the emperor were arrayed against each other, their allegiance was clearly due to the former, deserted *en masse*, and took service under the diet. Every one of these men knew they were fighting all through the contest with a halter round their necks. If taken prisoners, they had no mercy to expect from their old masters. Clearly it was Goergey's duty, before surrendering, to have obtained some guarantee that they should receive an amnesty. To deliver them unarmed and helpless into the hands of the Austrians, was the refinement of cruelty. Nevertheless, this he did. In his letter to general Rüdiger, he feebly expressed a hope, that his majesty the czar would interfere on their behalf. But in a case in which the lives of gallant men are at stake, there should have been no dependence placed on the generosity of potentates or the smooth blandishments of subordinates. If he could not have secured their safety, he should have let them fight it out on open ground, and die a soldier's death, sword in hand. Better be swept down in the flush of generous enthusiasm, than to be strangled by foreign executioners, or perish by inches in the damps of a dungeon.

Immediately after the surrender at Vilagos, the Russians handed over their prisoners without exception to the Austrians, without caution, stipulation, or remonstrance. Goergey alone received a free pardon, and retired to his home. The others were crowded into the gaols and fortresses all over the kingdom, and treated with extreme harshness. Courts-martial were established to try them—composed of men, be it remembered, still reeking from the battle-field, who had a few days previously met their prisoners in mortal combat, and had been over and over again routed by them, with all the bad passions of war still boiling in their hearts. Such a proceeding was probably never heard of in history. It was not royal officers sitting in judgment upon captured rebels, but victorious enemies trying in cold blood men of a different race, different language, and different nationality, who had fought bravely against them in open field, in obedience to the lawfully constituted authorities of their own country. The natural consequences followed. Great numbers were condemned to death, without counsel, without friends, without support or aid of any kind to support them in the presence of bloodthirsty men, and under the terrible weight of adversity which pressed upon them. Greater numbers still were sentenced to lengthened terms of imprisonment in fortresses. The work was proceeding rapidly when it was suddenly remembered that Comorn was still holding out—that these severities might deter the garrison from surrendering, and consequently entail upon the government immense loss in reducing the place by a regular siege. The policy of dissimulation was accordingly again resorted to. The trials were suspended, or conducted with extreme caution. The emperor's own aid-de-camp was sent from Vienna with respites for prisoners under sentence of death. "Let but Comorn surrender," said all the officials, "and the gaols will be thrown open, and the royal clemency displayed in all its glory."

Comorn did surrender on the 4th of October; on the day following, the garrison dispersed towards their homes, after refusing to enter the Austrian service, each provided, according to the terms of the treaty, with a warrant of safety. On the 6th of October, Count Louis Batthyanyi, who had not fought against Austria; who, owing to Austrian treachery, had been in prison the whole winter; whose only offence was his being prime minister, with the emperor's sanction and recognition, before the armed struggle commenced, and having resisted Jellachich, whom the emperor, under his own hand and seal, had declared a rebel and a traitor; a man of ancient family, of immense wealth, of moderate views, of known patriotism, of unblemished honour, revered all over Hungary; who had done all in his power to avert an appeal to arms by mediating between the king and the people—was shot at Pesth. His trial was secret. What occurred at it is not known, and in all probability never will be known, till the victim and his murderers shall stand face to face, where crime shall be blasted and innocence glorified in the presence of pure Justice. He was accused of high treason, simply for acting as has been described in a previous part of this work, and condemned to be hanged. The ignominy of the mode of death appalled him, and he made desperate attempts to cut his throat in prison with a penknife. He failed; but was so mutilated, that the surgeons declared the sentence as it stood could not be executed. It was accordingly commuted to shooting. He took an affectionate leave of his wife and children—marched out to the place of execution, pale from loss of blood, but still dignified, calm, and defiant. A vast crowd had collected to witness the assassination of him whom for years they had looked upon as the foremost man in all the nation. He was blindfolded, cried, "Eljen a haza!"—God bless the country! and fell pierced with balls. His property was confiscated, and his wife and children are desolate in a foreign land. "This blood will be a curse on those who shed it; and men who sully their victory by such crimes have conquered in vain." *

On the same day, at Arad, fourteen general officers who had surrendered to the Russians as prisoners of war, tried in the same way by vindictive enemies whom they had beaten in the field, and to whom they had never yielded, were shot or hanged. Ernest Kiss, Louis Aulich, John Damianich, Nagy Sandor, Ignatz Torok, George Lahner, Charles Count Veczey, Charles Knezich, Ernest Polt Von Poltenberg, Charles Count Leiningen Westerburg, Joseph Schweidel, Aristides Desewffy, William Lazar, Andrew Gaspar. They all met their death with unshrinking fortitude, as proud, as calm, and as victorious in suffering as they had been on the field. Damianich, who was the very type and model of a soldier, accomplished, gifted, studious, courageous, and indefatigable, who had held the fortress of Arad to the very last, defied the whole Austrian army to take it—and surrendered to the Russians, solely on condition that both men and officers should be dismissed in peace and safety to their homes, but who, nevertheless, was delivered up to his enraged enemies,—was carried to the place of execution, being unable to walk in consequence of a fracture in his leg. For four hours he was left sitting there face to face with death, watching the expiring agonies of his friends. He looked on with perfect composure, and when at last his turn came, and he limped to his post, simply remarked, "It is strange that I, who was always first in the attack, should be the last here." Nagy Sandor defied his enemies at the portals of the grave, and warned them as to the future—"*Hodie mihi—cras tibi!*" "To-day it is my turn—to-morrow it will be yours!"

In addition to these, among the statesmen who were judicially assassinated in the same manner, were Ladislaus Csanyi, minister of commerce, one of the most eminent men in Hungary; Baron Sigismond Perenyi, president of the Upper House; Baron Jessenak, lord lieutenant of the county of Nyitria; and Prince Worontiecky. Many of these were venerable for their age, and for an illustrious life spent in the service of the empire, but neither age nor honours were any protection against the atrocities of the courts-martial.

How many more, unknown to fame, were put to death at the same time, without even the poor consolation of feeling that posterity would treasure their names as "household words," will never be known. The executions went on in every county in the kingdom with such rapidity, and such bloodthirsty zeal, that the appalled inhabitants ceased to take count of them, or to allude to them. All those against whom no overt act of hostility could be charged, but whose sympathies were known to be on the side of the patriots, were maltreated, plundered, and persecuted by the military. No sentence was passed without confiscation of property; so that those who were fortunate enough to escape with life and liberty, found themselves beggared outcasts. Count

* Times, October 17th, 1849.

George Krolyi was fined fifteen thousand pounds for having shown "indecent joy" when the Hungarian army entered Pesth. Thousands were immured in dungeons in various parts of the kingdom, for long terms of years, and still lie there, hopeless and forgotten in their living graves. Nor did the cruelties of Haynau—the wretched monster who degraded the soldier's uniform into the livery of an executioner, under whose special direction "this work of pacification," as it was called, proceeded—stop with the men who had conquered him in arms. As a last and crowning disgrace—a stain which all the waters in Christendom cannot wipe out from Austrian colours, and the remembrance of which can never be blotted from men's memories—women were dragged from their homes, and in the presence of "imperial, royal Austrian officers," and in the midst of ranks of armed men, were publicly stripped and flogged for having fulfilled the highest and holiest of woman's duties—succouring and sheltering the fugitive and the outcast. How many instances of this brutality occurred we know not. One case was made sufficiently notorious to fix the character of the rest, and to call forth a shout of execration from all Europe. Madame de Maderspach, the wife of a noble, who had been living in the midst of her tenantry, in the retirement of domestic life, and in the unostentatious discharge of the duties of her station, beloved by all who knew her, whose husband had taken no part in the war, was accused, falsely or not makes no difference, of having afforded an asylum to her own nephew. We shall, however, let her tell her own tale:—

"My heart has been turned to stone;—I can, therefore, with some degree of composure, relate the misfortunes of my house. An army of Hungarians, of 10,000 men, surrendered in our immediate neighbourhood. Two days afterwards some imperialist troops entered Ruskby. It is probable that my enviable family happiness had created enemies at Ruskby, and that they were resolved to destroy it; for I am not aware that any of us committed any fault. I was suddenly, without a previous trial or examination, taken from my husband and children. I was dragged into a square formed by the troops, and, in the place in which I reside, and in the presence of its population, which had been accustomed to honour me, not because I was the lady of the manor, but because the whole tenor of my life deserved it, *I was flogged with rods.* You see I can write without dying of shame; but my husband took his own life. Deprived of all other weapons, he shot himself with a small cannon. A general cry of horror was raised. I was myself taken to Kararsebes."

More than seventy thousand of the Hungarian soldiers who had borne arms in the war, and had surrendered or been dispersed, were torn from their homes, and forcibly enlisted in the Austrian army. This, though cruelty and injustice of the blackest dye, was still not an express breach of faith. But in the case of the garrison of Comorn, the articles of the capitulation were flagrantly and audaciously broken. One of the principal clauses provided for the free withdrawal and personal safety of the soldiers and officers, and on laying down their arms, "warrants of safety" were accordingly furnished them. They had all previously been invited to enlist in the service of his imperial majesty; but to the great disgust of the royalist officers, not one man volunteered. Apparently to avenge this insult, for insult they chose to consider it, notices were served on most of the privates after they reached their homes, peremptorily ordering them to enrol themselves in the Austrian army; and in defiance of the amnesty for which the capitulation stipulated, several of the officers were proclaimed guilty of high treason, and called upon to surrender to be tried by court-martial, and were consequently driven into exile, with its attendant poverty and suffering. Of the thirty-three generals who led the Hungarian armies through this eventful struggle, twelve were shot or hanged; three were sentenced to lengthened terms of imprisonment in fortresses—a lot infinitely worse than death itself; some have since fallen victims to disease; and others are wandering the wide world over, living on the memory of their wrongs and the hope of revenge. Of seventy-seven colonels belonging to the three arms of the service, two only were executed; eighteen received sentence of imprisonment for eighteen years; eleven, for sixteen years; eight, for twelve or ten years; some are dead; others were saved by forming part of the garrison of Comorn; and the rest, says general Klapka, are "fugitives somewhere."

Kossuth, with 5,000 men, amongst whom were generals Bem and Dembinski, Guyon, and others, escaped across the frontier into Turkey, and threw themselves upon the protection of the sultan. They reached Orsova on the 18th of August, and received a welcome from the pasha of Widdin; but owing, it is suspected, to the operation of Russian gold or Russian threats, they were afterwards made to undergo great privation, though the sultan had made a liberal allowance for their maintenance, and pestilential disease at last breaking out amongst them, they were carried off by hundreds. Soon after a formal demand for their extradition was made upon the Porte, both by Austria and Russia, in clear violation of international law, and the demand was accompanied by a threat of invasion in case of refusal. The situation of the sultan now became perplexing. Such a request was in itself an insult, but how to repel it with the feeble resources at his command, was a question more easily asked than answered. He applied both to France and England to learn what course they would take in case he asserted his undoubted right to protect and succour all who sought shelter in his dominions, but was unable to obtain an assurance of aught beyond a moral support. To meet the difficulties of the case Redschid Pasha suggested that the refugees should embrace the Moslem faith, in which case compliance with the demands of the allied powers would be impossible, as their allegiance would, according to the Mahometan law, have become irrevocably transferred to the Porte. When the proposal was made, Kossuth rejected it without hesitation, but Bem, Guyon,* and others—men of action rather than of thought, in whom hatred of absolutism had become a veritable religion—accepted it at once. To calm the fears of the powers,

* Bem is since dead: Guyon is Pasha of Damascus.

with respect to the remainder of the fugitives, they were removed from the frontier and shut up in prison at Kutayah, but not before the sultan had expressly declared his determination to stake the existence of his empire upon their safety. The United States government having come to the determination to send a frigate for the purpose of bringing them to America, or any other country in which they chose to settle, Turkey consented to yield them up; and accordingly, on the 7th of September, 1851, Kossuth and his suite, and a considerable number of his companions, embarked on board the "Missisipi." The ex-governor left the vessel at Gibraltar for the purpose of paying a visit to England, and arrived at Southampton on the 23rd of October. In England he received an enthusiastic welcome, and after a somewhat lengthened visit to America, he returned to London, where he has taken up his abode until circumstances shall enable him to re-enter his native country.

Since the surrender of Comorn, the state of Hungary has been a sealed book to the rest of Europe. Extraordinary precautions have been taken by the Austrian authorities to prevent the entrance of any person coming from countries in possession of a constitutional government, or in which liberal views are known to prevail. One traveller,* an American gentleman, managed to overcome the scruples of the police, and make his way into the interior; but although extremely guarded in his conversation and inquiries, he soon drew down on him the suspicion of the authorities, was arrested, tried secretly by court-martial, browbeaten and bullied by coarse and brutal soldiers, and at last thrown into a dungeon, where he might have remained for an indefinite length of time, if he had not found means of making known his position to the American consul, whose energetic remonstrances speedily procured his release, accompanied, however, by expulsion from the Austrian territories. He bore testimony to the utter prostration of the people under the grinding tyranny of military despotism, the extinction of literature, the daily and nightly terror caused by the spies who infested every corner of the land,—the streets, the cafés, the salons, the hotels, and even the family circle, watching and treasuring each word as it fell, and labouring with devilish ingenuity to twist innocent expressions into seditious or treasonable allusions,—the ferocious insolence of the police, the unchecked brutality of the soldiery, the crowded state of the dungeons—crammed with wretches who had lingered in agony for months and years, untried, and in ignorance, not only of their accusers, but of the offences with which they were charged; the terrible cruelties practised in the fortresses, the torturings, the beatings with sticks, the daily fusillades on the glacis, and all the other horrors and enormities by which tyranny heaps outrage on humanity, and blasphemes God. But he bore testimony, too, to the reverence with which Kossuth's name and memory are treasured in the hearts of the people; to the pride with which they look back to that surpassing struggle in which the valour of their sons and brothers

* Mr. C. L. Brace.

so long baffled the rage of despots, and fertilized the soil of every county with their blood; to their hatred of their oppressors, and their firm belief in the speedy advent of a day of terrible retribution.

Since him, no traveller from the west of Europe has been equally fortunate. The only information we have received regarding the state of affairs in Hungary, has been derived from the scanty, imperfect, and often inaccurate intelligence furnished by newspaper correspondents resident in Vienna. Even the passing glimpses thus afforded, however, are amply sufficient to give an idea of the miseries of the population. We hear that so many were arrested on such a day for some mysterious conspiracy; that on another so many were shot or hanged by sentence of court-martial, that discontent is prevalent, revolutionary agents never idle, the police ever vigilant. That martial law has supplied the place of the ancient laws and government of the country, and that of that proud and great constitution which survived the shocks and storms of a thousand years, not a trace remains save in the people's memories, are facts which none seek to deny, and from them each of us may draw his own conclusion. Regarding the causes which led to this terrible state of things, there has been a great deal of angry discussion, even in England; but no one who is sincerely desirous of arriving at the truth, who has no interests to serve but those of freedom and humanity, can have any opinion on the subject but the one—that the destruction of Hungarian liberty was a great crime, and that the Hapsburg family were the perpetrators of it. The assertion that Kossuth was in any way instrumental in bringing about the catastrophe, is false; the oftener it is reiterated the greater falsehood it becomes, for it is reiterated in the face of repeated refutation. He sought to bring about changes in the constitution certainly, but no changes that were not reforms, and no reforms that were not constitutional. Instead of injuring, he wished to strengthen it, to protect, restore, and build bulwarks round it. These measures were hateful to the Hapsburgs; they sought to baffle them by stirring up a war of races. They dissimulated till they had matured their plans, and then joined their forces with those of rebels in arms against the Hungarian parliament, and made the rebel cause the cause of royalty and tyranny. When Hungary resisted, she resisted in defence of laws which her sovereign had sworn to maintain. When she was crushed, she was crushed by a man to whom she owed no allegiance, who had not sought to conceal his hatred of her people, and his determination to subdue her.

Those in England who believe that liberty of speech, and thought, and action, are essential to the development both of man's intellectual and moral nature, will profoundly regret her fall. For we know well that true progress consists not merely in the accumulation of wealth, or the diffusion of luxury, but in the constant and earnest endeavour to infuse into national thoughts and aspirations more and more of those "weightier matters of the law," Truth, and Justice, and Mercy; in keeping a lofty standard of excellence, a great and pure ideal ever before us—not, indeed, in the hope that we may reach it, but that we may daily approximate to it. But, without political freedom, this is impossible. In England and America there are thousands who profess to have the welfare of the human race at heart, to desire earnestly its growth in every virtue that can ennoble and dignify it. Their missionaries are to be found in every clime, labouring earnestly to spread the knowledge of Him who brought liberty to the captive and light to the blind. But, strange to say, these men look upon the political condition of the continent as a thing which, as citizens of a free state, they certainly must lament, but with which, as Christians, they have nothing to do. This is a deplorable fallacy. Hordes of savages dancing before the images of their gods, form a less solemn and awful spectacle than great nations, amongst whom art, and science, and the elegances and luxuries of civilization have attained a high state of development, with their intellect paralyzed, their tongues tied, all liberty of action, save in the common and petty affairs of life, utterly denied them—their very thoughts forbidden to flow, save in smooth and narrow channels; every generous emotion repressed, and the base one of fear cultivated into an unnatural exuberance; all honourable incentives to energy and activity removed. The one is a wild forest, with its points of grandeur, sublimity, and beauty, which labour and diligence may make to blossom as the rose, but the other is a fruitful field overrun with hateful weeds, and showing the industry of generations of husbandmen wasted and gone for nought. The continental nations should be our allies in diffusing the blessings of Christianity and peace throughout the world. But how can they be so, when countries like Hungary and Italy are prostrate at the feet of brutal soldiery, barbarians of the nineteenth century, as ferocious and unscrupulous as those of Attila or Genseric, as careless of truth and justice as if they worshipped Thor or Mars, instead of Him who first cancelled the law of might, and made love and justice our law for evermore? If peoples, governed as these are, were fertile in the qualities which make nations great—in public spirit, moderation, enterprize, humanity, and high principle, they would be as wonderful prodigies as the thorn at Glastonbury which blossomed in the midst of winter. These virtues are the products of liberty, of a free press, of equal law, and of self-government.

This, then, is continued a question which concerns all who look for and labour to hasten the advent of a better, holier, and happier state for all mankind. As such, it is especially a question for those who call themselves Christians *par excellence.* We cannot separate Christianity from politics. Rightly considered, the latter is subordinate to, ought to be founded upon, and regulated by the other. If men are not governed upon Christian principles, they are governed upon the devil's principles. There is no medium. "But," in the words of the Persian fatalist in Herodotus, "the saddest of all griefs is to see clearly and yet be able to do nothing." It is useless, if not cruel, to point out evils, if there be no remedy. In pointing out a political evil, however, to an Englishman or an American, it is seldom necessary to point out each step in the course he should follow with regard to it. One of the proudest characteristics of the Anglo-Saxon race is the indomitable energy it has always displayed in finding the means of righting wrongs when they are once set fully before it. What we want in this case is the creation of a higher standard of national duty, the infusion of a better tone into our diplomacy, an enlarged sympathy with our neighbours—not a sympathy which shall prompt us to meddle in their internal arrangements, and to seek to hinder them managing their own affairs in their own way, but one that shall repress the aggression of the strong, cause the rights of the weak to be respected, and support justice at all hazards. To do all this it is not necessary to fight against principles, to say that we will repress the growth of this or that theory by force of arms, or shed blood for the promotion of class interests. This was one of the follies of a past generation, the penalty of which we are now paying. We need also, an abler class of diplomatists—men trained to their work, familiar with the state of public opinion, learned, indefatigable, lovers of liberty, with a man's respect for simple manhood. We have had enough of fiddlers, courtiers, and gay idlers.

These are some of the objects to the attainment of which our attention should first be directed. If our greatness consist merely in our wealth, the sooner we cease boasting of it the better. If it consist also in immense moral influence backed up by immense physical strength, unless we use them for high and noble purposes, it were better we had never acquired them. An individual in possession of such advantages would find no difficulty in determining the course he ought to follow. A nation should find none either. As rigid an account will be required of the latter regarding the use made of its talents as of the former.

CHAPTER XXIV.

THE HUNGARIAN CONSTITUTION—VARIETY OF RACES.

In the primitive organization of the Magyars the public expenditure was devoted almost exclusively to one object—the defence of the country. The civil administration, founded upon municipal institutions, was so simple and inexpensive as to require almost no taxation whatever. The king and high dignitaries of the realm received their salaries chiefly in revenues derived from large landed estates, specially devoted to that purpose, in addition to a proportionate share of the proceeds of the salt mines, &c. Therefore, the chief expenditure being strictly of a military character, it cannot be said that at this period the nobility was exempt from taxation; but the reverse. It had to bear the burden of providing for the maintenance of the commonwealth; for it had, at its own expense, to bear arms in its defence. It thus became a fundamental principle, that those who had to fight and provide for their own subsistence during the war, were not required to pay other taxes; but all who were not liable to the performance of military duty were liable to taxation.

The system of national defence was organized in the following manner:—From fifty-two to sixty-six strongholds, or fortresses, were selected as rallying points, and to each of them was assigned a piece of territory whence it drew its supplies. This was the origin of the counties, which became the basis of the political organization also. They are called very expressively *varmegye*, from *var* a fortress, and *megye* a district, or territory. Over each county was placed a supreme count, fö-ispan, the commander of its forces in war, and its chief magistrate in peace. The nobility had to assemble under his banner, and it was his duty to levy a certain amount of taxation upon the non-fighting portion of the population, one-third of which he sent to the king, who, in his turn, was obliged, out of this and the revenues of the royal domains, to raise and support the royal banderia.* The service expected from the nobles was, however, in proportion to their ability. The poorer of them, who had not a horse, served in the infantry—those who had, in the cavalry. Any who had tenants (*jobbágy*) led a certain proportion of them into the field—for instance, one mounted horseman for every twenty tenants—hence the famous hussars.† Those who had estates sufficiently large, whether their own property, or held in virtue of some office or dignity, to muster

* Royal army—from the Italian *banderia*, a banner.

† From *husz*, twenty, and *ar*, price—the price or value of twenty.

men enough for one banner,—from 800 to 1000, brought their own banner into the field, one or more according to their ability. In the "banner-holders" was the origin of the magnates, or peers, of the Hungarian constitution.

The military defence of the country was then provided for in the following order:—First, it devolved upon the king to take the field with his own banner. If this were not sufficient, the private banner-holders were called out; and then the poorer noblemen, that is, those who had not men enough for one banner, under the banner of their country. The last resource, in cases of extreme danger, was a levy, *en masse*, of the whole population.

From this it will be seen what an important part the banner-holders, or magnates, had to perform, being next in duty and in importance to the king.

This duty, then, to fight in defence of the country, constituted not only the chief, but the only source of political rights. No right could exist without this corresponding duty—and the duty was never imposed without granting the corresponding right. And it was natural that those who were bound to fight should have a voice in deciding the question of peace or war; and, consequently, they all had a voice in the councils of the nation, but none else; so that when, in consequence of the frequency of hostile inroads, it was found necessary to have, besides the fortresses, fortified towns to serve as places of refuge for the inhabitants of the adjoining country, these, however small they might be,—many of them like our rotten boroughs, were invested with political rights, and represented in the parliament; while other large and populous, but open and unfortified cities, were not so represented, because they bore no part in the national defence.

Upon this principle, those who contributed the largest share to the protecting force of the country, received most authority and consideration in the great council; and this is the origin of the high standing of the magnates in that body.

Originally, all the nobility, or in other words, all the fighting men, were required to attend the national assembly in person. They were, in fact, mass meetings. But this was soon felt by the poorer nobles to be an intolerable burden; and they therefore assembled at home in their counties, passed resolutions, and framed instructions for deputies whom they sent to the central diet to represent the county nobility—that is, those who did not go into the battle-field with their own banner, but under the banner of the county. This was the origin of the lower chamber, or house of representatives, answering to our Commons.

The banner-holders, on the contrary, had too expensive and heavy a share in the national defence to absent themselves from the assembly, as they could not fail to be largely affected by its decisions; and they accordingly came to form the *Table of Magnates*, or House of Lords: so that in process of time, the diet became split into two bodies; one composed of those who went into battle with their own banner; the other, of the representatives of absent nobles who fought under the county banner.

It often happened, that a magnate was prevented attending in his place in parliament through age or sickness, or absence on public duty, or the dignity was enjoyed by a widow; and in this case he or she was permitted to send a deputy instead, something similar to the custom amongst our peers of voting by proxy. These deputies, representing at least one banner, had both a voice and a vote, and continued to enjoy both privileges so long as there was any truth or reality in their representation—that is, so long as there was a duty corresponding to the right.

But by and by times changed, and the institutions changed with them. The forms remained, but the spirit departed. The duties ceased to exist, and the corresponding rights became merely nominal. This revolution was wrought by the introduction of standing armies. This mode of defending the kingdom was a favourite with the kings, because it furnished them with an instrument for establishing absolute power; and it was a favourite with the aristocracy, because it relieved them of the troublesome duty of serving in person. The whole burden of maintaining the state was thus thrown upon the people, who furnished soldiers for the army, and were taxed for its support. The nobles declared, that if the country were attacked, and the regular army proved insufficient for its defence, they would rise *en masse*. To this word the term *insurrection* was applied, a word which in Hungary never conveyed the idea of armed resistance to authority. Under this futile pretext, the nobility kept all the political rights to themselves, and threw all the duties upon the people. This unnatural and unjust state of things continued until 1848, when Kossuth took the lead in a movement having for its object the reform of the constitution, based upon the principle of "equal rights, equal duties."

In the meantime, however, facts and reality were making vigorous attacks on forms and fictions. The country nobility were yearly increasing in number, and they were strengthened by union with that large body, composed of the educated portion of the people—such as clergymen, professors, schoolmasters, lawyers, physicians, chemists, engineers, artists—who, under the title of "honourable classes," were admitted to a full share in their rights and privileges. Between the poor members of nobility also, and the people, a perfect identity of interests had grown up. Thousands of the former lived as the people and amongst them, followed the same avocations, and shared the same toils and hardships. The relation between them, in fact, very much resembled that existing between our electors and non-electors. The country nobility then, aided by the municipal institutions, and managing the affairs of their counties in public assemblies with perfect freedom of speech, and increasing in energy and spirit every year, gradually acquired a greater preponderance in parliament through their representatives. The magnates, on the contrary, having fallen from the proud position occupied by the ancient banner-holders, to that of empty title-holders, and representing no particular interest in the nation, lost their influence day by day. They had nothing to recommend them to notice but titles, which no one valued, because they were sold openly by the bankrupt Austrian court. They still continued to send deputies in their absence, however; but these deputies, though permitted to speak, lost the privilege of voting. So that the upper chamber, being mainly filled by courtiers or bigoted tories, became a dead weight upon the constitution, and was firmly opposed to all reform. Such was the state of affairs in 1848.

VARIETY OF RACES.—It was the misfortune of the barbarians who fixed their seats in eastern Europe, in the regions bordering on the Danube, after the fall of the Roman empire, that, owing to whatever cause, they could never amalgamate with their neighbours. In all the tempests of war, invasion and revolution, which

ANCIENT DACIANS.

have since rolled over them, they have remained almost as distinct in the great features of language, manners, and dress, as when they struck their tents on the plains of Asia. They have for many a century been paying the penalty of their conservative spirit by undergoing all the evils of foreign conquest and domination. No country has suffered more from this cause than Hungary, for in none has the state of things consequent upon the original invasion been so faithfully preserved down to the present day.

The different races now inhabiting Hungary and Transylvania are the Magyars, Szeklers, Saxons, Sclaves, Sclavacks, and Wallacks, Czigany, or Gipsies, each of which speaks a different language, and, as a general rule, occupies a separate district. Of the Magyars we have already spoken at sufficient length. We shall refer to the others in the order in which they are supposed to have entered the country.

The WALLACKS are said to be the descendants of the ancient Dacians, who inhabited the province of Dacia when it was conquered by Trajan in the second century of the Christian era. They were a people originally, no doubt, from Thrace, belonging to the great Hellenie family; and, as they are referred to under that name by Herodotus, we may safely conclude that they were the first inhabitants of the country. The name Dacia was applied by the ancients to a great extent of territory, comprising all that lay between the Teyss, the Danube, and the Dneister, or, in other words, the eastern part of Hungary, Transylvania, Wallachia, and Moldavia. The inhabitants of the country, in the period immediately preceding the birth of Christ, appear to have acquired some of the arts of civilized life, and to have more than once proved themselves a match for the armies of the empire. The valour and misfortunes of their last king, Decebalus, have cast a lustre round his name little short of that which has attended the exploits of our own Caracalla. His genius and daring had made him the terror of Rome, when Trajan ascended the throne of the Cæsars, and resolved at once upon his destruction, and the restoration of the empire to its ancient glory. He accordingly led an army against him in the early part of the second century, and totally subdued him.

Dacia appears to have remained in the possession of the Romans until the reign of Aurelian, when the imperial troops were at length compelled to retire and abandon it to the Goths, after occupying it for one hundred and seventy years. For a long period afterwards, the inhabitants experienced little rest. They were overrun by all the barbarians, who were making their way into Europe from the north-east—the Goths, Gepidae, Huns, Bulgarians, Avars, Sclaves, &c.; all of whom left behind a greater or less number of stragglers, who became mingled with the rest of the population. The original inhabitants being brought under the domination now of one, now of another, sank into a state of hopeless servitude, and lost all marks of their ancient freedom and glory, though they still affected to despise the latest arrivals, and to pride themselves upon their Roman descent, a distinction to which they could, however, lay no claim, except such as could be founded upon the trifling infusion of foreign blood which must have taken place by intermarriage with Trajan's colonists. At the time the Magyars arrived in the country, they appear to have partially recovered their independence, and to have been governed by a native prince, bearing the title of *knaz* or *ban*. The secretary of Bela I. of Hungary, an able writer, though his name has not come down to us, makes mention of a Wallack prince, named Gelu, whose rule appears to have extended over all the territory included in modern Transylvania, as well as of some of his successors. Their sovereignty was, however, short-lived. They speedily fell under the yoke of the Magyars, and they have ever since been the conquered race, the villains of Hungary. Those to whom our observations here principally apply, appear to have been cut off from the cradle of their race, and are now chiefly found in the south and north-west of Hungary, and the south-west of Transylvania. While Transylvania was under the government of her native princes in the period between 1527 and 1713, when the country finally fell under the yoke of Austria, a number of them were enfranchised upon condition of doing military service, and have ever since possessed all the rights of the Magyar nobles, and they have been for a long time past gradually raising themselves to a footing of equality in Hungary. In 1791, two Greek bishops transmitted a petition to the emperor, praying him to assign to the Wallacks their legal and rightful position in Transylvania. This document was sent down to the diet, who passed a resolution, declaring that in accordance with article six of the law of 1744, the Wallacks did not form a separate and distinct people, but were part and parcel of the nation amongst whom they dwelt,—that the Wallack noble was in every respect equal to the Magyar noble, and the Wallack peasant to the Magyar or Saxon peasant. In 1843, the bishops of Bulasfalad and Szeben again called the attention of the diet to the treatment experienced by the Wallacks, in those districts in which the Saxons were in the majority. They declared that although the Magyars were making praiseworthy and noble efforts to obliterate all marks of the conquest, the Saxons were doing all in their power to keep alive the old distinctions, and were treating the Wallacks in every respect as an inferior and servile race. Relying on the vote of 1791, in which the Saxon deputies had concurred, the bishops demanded that the Wallacks should be placed on a footing of perfect equality; should be admitted to the corporations; and should have an equal share in the land attached to the villages. Their petition was supported by some of the most eloquent men in the diet, but it was not till 1848 that the last traces of serfdom, inequality, and conquest, were entirely wiped out. Unhappily the concession came too late; the Wallacks could not, or at least did not, appreciate it, and by their neutrality or hostility in 1849, they hastened the catastrophe which placed the Magyars at the mercy of their tyrants.

The whole of the Wallack or Roumain race amounts at the present day to about 6,400,000, divided in the following manner:—Moldavia contains 1,500,000, Wallachia 2,000,000, Bulgaria 100,000, Brabia 1,000,000, Bucovina 300,000, Hungary and Transylvania 2,500,000. The Hungarian and Transylvanian Wallacks, as might be expected, have all the vices and defects of slaves.

THE SCLAVACKS.—The great Sclave family, which at one period appears to have occupied nearly the whole east of Europe, from the Baltic and Adriatic to the banks of the Volga, and which still predominates in Russia, Poland, and along the Danube, is now divided into several members, two of which, the Sclavacks and Sclavonians, are found in great numbers in Hungary. They appear at one time to have peopled the greater part, if not the whole, of the country, and to have been driven into their present mountainous seats by the invasion of the Magyars, just as in England the Celtic portion of the population was compelled to retire to the mountains of Wales, and the remote fastnesses of Cornwall, before the advance of the Saxons. The Sclavacks in Hungary are now confined to the mountainous district lying between the Danube, the Teyss, and the most northern range of the Carpathians, where they still retain their primitive language and customs. The former differs from the Polish and Bohemian, but in no greater degree than the Welsh from the Erse and Gaelic. Other branches of the same family, amongst whom are the Serbs, or colonists from Servia, and Rusniacks from Russia, are also found in other parts of Hungary; but all these are few in number and have settled in the country at a more recent period.

SCLAVACK VAGABONDS—DROTOSTAT.

The Sclavacks mostly belong to the Roman Catholic church, except a few, who are Lutherans, and are supposed to be the descendants of Bohemian Hussites who fled from the persecutions in their native country in the fifteenth century. They generally bear the usual marks of conquest and subjection—laziness, dislike to work, vacant expression of the countenance—seldom lighted up except by cunning, deceit, treachery, dirt and discomfort, patient endurance of insult and injury, and insatiable rapacity, love of begging, and proneness to intoxication. Both men and women indulge to excess in the use of ardent spirits. Their houses are much like those of the Wallacks, built generally of unhewn stems of pine, and carelessly thatched with straw, and shared by their pigs and cattle. They are totally wanting in the proud self-respect and love of personal comfort which distinguish the Magyars; and the more secluded they are from intercourse with their conquerors, the coarser and more brutal they are in their manners. They are in general about middle height, strongly built, of light complexion, with coarse features, generally shaded by long flaxen hair. The most degraded are, unquestionably, those known as the *Drotostat*, a vagabond race, who earn a livelihood by tinkering.

The CROATS are another great branch of the Sclave family, and though not in reality belonging to Hungary Proper, yet have appeared so prominently at many

CZIGANY, OR GIPSIES.

periods in Hungary, being politically a part of the kingdom, that it would be impossible to pass them over without notice. Their original name was *Horvates*, so called after Horváth, the name either of a great property or of a Hungarian noble; but it was soon changed in consequence of their continued and frequent relations with the conquering race, and the subsequent annexation of their territory to Hungary under some of her early kings. Croatia contains an area of about 172,000 square miles, and a population of 492,267. It is divided into three small counties, a part of which belonged, before the battle of Mohatz, to Upper Sclavonia; but it was enlarged by Ferdinand I., in return for the services rendered to the Hapsburg family by the inhabitants.

The Croats are at present the least advanced in civilization of all the tribes that people Hungary. In fact, it would be hard to point to many traits of character or manners that raise them above the savage. They are to a man tall, active, and robust, capable of enduring any amount of fatigue, hardship, or privation; and it is a point of honour amongst the women to equal the men in courage and fortitude. Those on the frontiers, to whom for many hundred years has been committed the defence of the boundaries of the empire against the Turks, are remarkable for their warlike disposition. They take this duty in turns, a certain portion of the male population being constantly in arms; and then, after serving a stipulated period, returning to their farms and making way for their fellows. In time of war, when the force called the *insurrection*, or general levy of the whole of the inhabitants, every man takes arms and repairs to a particular post. Jellachich was in this way enabled to raise a vast force in 1848, and to act with potent effect both in Italy and during the Hungarian war of independence. During that eventful period, Croatia had it in her power to have utterly overwhelmed the house of Hapsburg.

The Croat possesses all the Russian imperturbable stedfastness under a heavy fire. There is but little impetuosity in his courage, but at close quarters nothing can surpass his ferocious intrepidity. The Croat infantry has long formed one of the most valuable forces in the Austrian services; and during the wars of the succession under Maria Theresa, and in those of the Republic and Empire against France, they played a prominent part, and made their name terrible all over Europe. They do not possess a very large force of cavalry; it is composed of hulans, seressans, and the ban, or viceroy's, frontier guard. The uniform of them all is very rich, and presents a striking and pleasing contrast to the coarse and heavy monotony of the appearance presented by the Austrian troops. The costume of the inhabitants in the districts bordering on Hungary differs but little from that of the Magyars.

The Croats construct their own houses, if houses they can be called, as they are seldom anything better than miserable huts, divided into two compartments, one for the family, the other for the cattle and pigs. The life led by the inmates is coarse and brutal. Both men and women indulge to excess in the use of ardent spirits; and the consequence is, that though the unmarried women are remarkable for their chastity, conjugal fidelity is almost unknown. Their religious creed is that of Roman Catholicism, or rather, a very clumsy imitation of it in the shape of a wild mixture of Christian doctrines with the grossest and most debasing superstitions; and this, combined with their strong attachment to their native soil, renders them exclusive to a degree bordering on fanaticism. Of a literature, they have not even that indispensable element—a good language.

The Serbs, another tribe of the Sclavonic family, dwell to the south of Hungary. Servia was originally a Turkish province, and it was about the year 1690, in the reign of Leopold I., that a crowd of fugitives came from the right bank of the Danube, and demanded an asylum amongst their neighbours. The request was granted, and, as a return for their services against the Turks, they were invested with civil rights. But they very soon gave signs of their intention to abuse the hospitality of the Magyars, by endeavouring to form a province, independent of the rest of the kingdom. As Austria was ever on the watch to take advantage of discord such as this, in order to rivet her own yoke more firmly, she pretended to recognise Servia as an independent state, and established at Vienna a Serb chancery. The remonstrances of the Hungarian diet, however, induced her to forego her design.

The country known as Servia at the present day comprises the countries of Batz, Verocza, Temes, Torontal, Posega, and the military frontiers, containing 385,742 Magyars, 357,198 Wallacks, 1,985 Greeks, 14,549 Jews, and 5,691 French—altogether 1,116,427 inhabitants, besides 1,295,093 Serbs, and 500,000 Croats or Sclavonians.

The Serbs are in general tall, robust, and capable of enduring great fatigue and privations. All the children are bathed in the rivers in winter as well as in summer, and run upon the snow and ice with naked feet, and without any other garment than a shirt.

Their costume differs but little from that of the Magyars. In some districts, however, it very much resembles Turkish, many of whose customs they still retain, such as that of sitting cross-legged, and allowing their beards to grow. They are very hospitable, and always manifest the liveliest joy upon the arrival of a stranger. Food is immediately prepared and set before him, and before he goes to bed the mistress of the house washes his feet. Their food is principally vegetables and milk during the summer, and meat during winter, usually pork; but their favourite dish is sauer kraut. They make also a sort of pudding from flour mixed with milk and lard. They are generally very ignorant, and remarked for their cunning and mendacity. Literature, except poetry, they have none, and their only musical instrument is a sort of hurdy-gurdy.

THE SAXONS are German colonists who settled in Hungary and Transylvania in the reign of Geyza II. In the former they no longer form a compact and distinct settlement. They are scattered in the north in the county of Scepuse, and towards the south in the neighbourhood and even in the midst of the Serbs. In Transylvania they have preserved their manners and physiognomy. They are distinguished by their industry in agricultural labours, and numerous other handicrafts—a circumstance which fully justified the observation of Joseph II., when giving Maria Theresa the result of his observations upon the people of the country through which he had travelled. "I have seen one industrious Saxon, and one hundred idle Wallacks." The Germans are ever greedy of gain, and spare no pains or fatigue to heap up riches. Although they have preserved their distinctive characteristics in Transylvania, it is well known that there is none easier of fusion with other peoples, as is proved by the case of the ancient Franks, who became absorbed into the Gauls, and by that of the modern Alsatians, who have become entirely French since the annexation of their province. The Hungarian kings assigned them a separate territory, with permission to regulate their internal affairs in whatever manner pleased them. This they took advantage of to frame a set of exclusive and intolerant laws. Whilst every German could claim the right of citizenship wherever he fixed his residence, no Hungarian was allowed under any circumstances to purchase a house in a German town, and the Wallacks were excluded with still greater rigour. Then came the reformation to widen the breach still further. Whilst the Transylvanians became Calvinists, or still remained in the Roman Catholic church, the Saxons, following the example of the German states, embraced Lutheranism.

The CZIGANY, or GIPSIES.—The gipsies are found in great numbers in Hungary, under the names of *Czigany*, or Bohemians. According to the old Magyar historian, Pray, they were driven out of Asia by Tamerlane, and wandered into Hungary through Thrace and Macedonia. They, as is well known, practise the art of divination, and assert that they came originally from Egypt. Like their confrères in various other countries, they persist, notwithstanding all the efforts made to reclaim them, in following a nomade life; but, receiving no education, having no home, no fortune, and no friends, they are generally half-starved, wretched, and degraded. The czigany delights in festivities of any kind. On ordinary days, whenever he does not leave his encampment on the borders of the steppe, or near the river, or at the edge of the wood, he may be seen lounging about amongst his fellows, his breast bare, exposed to the heat of the sun in summer, and the rigours of cold in winter, his only clothing being a sort of dirty, ragged shirt, which is never washed from the day on which it is made to that on which it falls to pieces on the shoulders of the wearer. But on Sundays he cuts a very different figure. He will not appear in the towns and villages, to join in the sports and revels of the people, and tell their fortunes, without putting on a very different costume. He then dresses as a Magyar, and assumes the bearing of a magnate. He does not pay much attention as to whether the details harmonize. Something brilliant he must have—perhaps the embroidered coat of a noble placed over a pair of tattered pantaloons.

Some of the gipsy bands are said to be able to discourse very fine music. One of their favourite tunes is "Rakotski's March," the Hungarian national anthem.

THE END.